The Informed Writer

Charles Bazerman

Baruch College
City University of New York

Houghton Mifflin Company   Boston
Dallas   Geneva, Illinois
Hopewell, New Jersey   Palo Alto   London

To Shirley Geok-lin Lim

Printed in the U.S.A.

Library of Congress Catalog Card Number: 80-68140

ISBN: 0-395-29715-X

Contents

To the Teacher

When we say that we want students to be literate, we are asking for much more than the bare mechanics of reading and writing. We want the ideas that students discover in their reading to mean something significant to them and to be absorbed into their thinking. We want their writing to reveal that they are conversant with and have informed opinions about their reading.

The literate writer is an informed writer. The writers that we want our students to become will know how to do more than cite a few statistics or string together quotations. The informed writer is able to grasp the meaning, purpose, and style of a range of books and periodicals on a given topic and to deal with the disagreements among the various sources. The informed writer works to synthesize the available knowledge and eventually is able to transform all the information discovered in the sources into an original paper reflecting his or her own perspective.

It is well to remind ourselves that reading and writing are inextricably linked. Students can express command of their reading through restatements of a text's meaning and through thoughtful comments about its larger significance. Students can find ideas for their original writing in response to all they hear, see, and read — with ideas from reading gaining importance as they become more educated. Intelligent, persuasive writing requires the student to be in control of and responsive to all these sources of thought. The informed writer must learn to restate, build upon, and react to reading — must acknowledge intellectual debt while asserting intellectual independence.

The student's ability to fuse reading and writing is the foundation of the research paper. Failure to use ideas from reading leads to a paper of unsupported, undeveloped opinions. Inability to use and acknowledge sources properly leads to plagiarism. And the inability of students to assimilate their reading into their writing leads to an undigested mash of borrowed material — without evaluation or synthesis. Only when the student has made the necessary link between reading and writing can the research paper incorporate a wide selection of sources yet reflect the student's own voice and ideas.

This text teaches the skills that allow a writer to transform a stack of loosely related sources into an original, well-supported, thoughtful, coherent argument. In addition to preparing students for the research paper, these skills are prerequisite to all their future writing, whether in academic disciplines, professions, business, or public affairs.

Each chapter develops specific skills, illustrates them with sample writing, and provides the student with practice writing assignments. In Part I, students learn to confront a single text. Starting with brief passages, Chapters 1 and 2 draw the students' attention to a text's meaning and structure through paraphrase and summary. Besides increasing comprehension, the task of reformulating a text in their own terms provides students with flexible means for referring to another writer's thoughts within their original papers. To encourage an active response to their reading, students are asked, in Chapter 3, to make marginal annotations, to keep reading journals, and to write informal essays. The intention of Chapter 4 is to call the student's attention to a writer's underlying purpose — and the techniques the writer employs to achieve that purpose. Through analyses of purpose and techniques, students gain a deeper insight into their reading by learning, for example, to recognize manipulative writing. In Chapter 5, the culmination of Part I, students must combine all the skills acquired thus far — of understanding, response, and analysis — in order to write an evaluative book review.

In Part II, the student is asked to compare, evaluate, and synthesize ideas from several sources. As the main task of Chapter 6, students compare the ideas they discover in books with their own personal experiences, observations, and experiments. In Chapter 7, students juxtapose and analyze several texts to identify areas of agreement and disagreement, to evaluate disagreements, and to synthesize the information found in various sources. Finally, when prepared for the task, students are led, step by step, through the preparation of a long research paper, which demonstrates how to work out an original argument. The keystone Chapter 8, on the research paper, integrates all the skills presented thus far. The *review of the literature* and the *proposal* are intermediate assignments in Chapter 8 to help students determine what the sources have to offer and what their own statement will eventually be. The student is shown that the writer of a research paper can and should use sources creatively.

In conclusion, Part III (Chapters 9 and 10) presents an overview of writing skills and of proper methods of documentation. Mastery of these skills grows as students tackle increasingly difficult writing tasks and as they enter more fully into a literate conversation with their reading. These two chapters are most helpful if referred to in conjunction with the main writing assignments introduced earlier in the book.

Two additional features are noteworthy. First, the selections in each chapter tend to focus on a single subject so that students will be able to read and write with increasing precision and subtlety on the subject. Second, the writing class becomes its own writing community. Wherever possible, students serve as one another's audience and share in the processes of understanding reading, writing, and editing. They also learn to address the same questions together and thus become a small research community. Writing becomes a more meaningful activity when it is meant for a specific audience and when it encourages social interaction. The teacher is part of that interaction, participating fully and guiding it to greater precision, control, and literacy.

My debts are many. First I must thank my students, whose desire to learn motivated me. Then I must thank those teachers who have had a lasting effect on me, although not always in ways that would meet their approval: Allan Bloom, J. V. Cunningham, Anthony Gabriele, and Robert Merton. I am also grateful to those many friends and colleagues whose ideas and suggestions helped me shape this book, among them Fred Baumann of Kenyon College, Nancy Cotton of Wake Forest University, John Dore of Baruch College, David Hoddeson of Rutgers State University, Lim Teck Kah of Drexel University, Martin Pearlman, the late Mina Shaughnessy, Carole Slade of Columbia University, Norman Storer of Baruch College, and Harvey Wiener of LaGuardia Community College. I wish to thank Rita Sturm of the University of Albuquerque, Kenneth W. Davis of the University of Kentucky, Harry H. Crosby of Boston University, and Joseph F. Trimmer of Ball State University for their helpful reviews of the manuscript. Thanks are also due to the staff at Houghton Mifflin who helped realize this project.

I appreciated a year's sabbatical from Bernard M. Baruch College, the City University of New York, to work on this book.

Most important, I am deeply grateful to my wife, Shirley Geok-lin Lim, who tolerated my writer's moods and who kept me from slipping into premature satisfaction.

Charles Bazerman

Introduction: The Written Conversation

Preview

Although writing may seem a solitary occupation —
you alone at your desk — writing involves other
people. You respond to and build on other people's
writing; then you write for other people to read. As
a writer, your relationship both to writers whose
ideas you are responding to and to your readers,
those you have in mind as you write, can be compared to an extended conversation. As in spoken
conversation, the more you know of the ideas and
concerns of the other participants, the more successfully you can communicate your own thoughts.
When compared to the immediacy of spoken conversation, the reflectiveness of written conversation
gives you greater opportunity to think out, develop,
and polish your statement.

Tuning in the Conversation

Imagine this: your political science professor asks you to write your opinion of a disagreement between Congress and the president over a proposed new energy law. If you know the facts and have a strong opinion — you don't want energy to be squandered as in the past or you don't want oil drilling that will threaten wild life — you sit down at the typewriter and pound out the required number of words. You sit back in relief and look at your work with some pride. There it is, an original paper written entirely from your own mind. Or is it entirely from your own mind?

Of course, you had to learn the basic facts on the subject from somewhere — perhaps from newspapers or television. Persuasive editorials may have influenced you or made you react strongly against the proposed law. A bit more deeply in the background are ideas you have read or have heard about this particular president and his relations with Congress. Even further back are the high school teachers and textbooks explaining the structure and history of our government. You relied on all these resources even before you began writing. Then as you wrote, you couldn't forget the course material and new approach presented by your professor through lectures and assigned readings. After all, you are writing for that particular professor.

When you write, your statements are your own; you are responsible for organizing your thoughts and words. But those thoughts obviously started elsewhere — with things you have read, heard, and experienced. A social scientist might say that your words are "socially imbedded," that is, your words are surrounded and conditioned by the acts, words, and attitudes of the many people who form your social context.

Think of a conversation. In a spoken conversation it is essential to pay attention to what has just been said and to the person one is addressing. Even when arguing for your original ideas, you are attempting to convince people directly in front of you. To make other people feel you are talking *with* them and not *at* them, you must listen to the facts, ideas, and emotions that they express in order to know what kinds of answers they will understand and accept.

As you react to others in spoken conversation, so you do in written conversation. The more you understand and assimilate what others have stated previously, the more you understand the context of the conversation in which you are participating. If you have a sense of the people to whom you are writing, you can then discover why you are writing and what you should write.

As you gain more control of the relationship between reading and writing, you will become more skilled in written conversation. Just by going to school and by completing writing assignments, you have figured out some ways to turn the material you have read into papers and into essays required on exams. However, you may sense that you have not transformed this material very much and that you are sticking very close to the ideas of your textbooks — with little of your own opinion. When you do express your own written opinion, you may write from the top of your head without paying sufficient attention to all you have read and have learned. This book will help you gain more of a command over the material you read, so that you can make full use of the material without being a slave to it. The skills presented in this text will help you integrate knowledge gained from sources outside yourself and your own ideas so that you may express your own informed viewpoint.

This book discusses (1) the techniques of precise reading, (2) the comparison and critical evaluation of ideas, (3) the effective use of source materials, and (4) the means to develop and support your own viewpoint. Each chapter is built around written assignments to enable you to practice the skills discussed in the chapter. All the chapters and assignments aim at giving you a method by which you may enter into the informed conversation of any field or area of interest — whether personal, business, professional, or academic. Although the conversation of each field has distinctive qualities, this book examines what they all share in common. You can build upon the general approach described here as you become involved in the conversations of the fields you personally find important.

Written Versus Spoken Conversation

To envision all the people that form the context of a written conversation is a difficult task of imagination. Although the participants in a spoken conversation are limited to those in hearing distance, the participants in a written conversation include all those whose words you have read or heard on the subject and those who are likely to pick up and read what you have written. Fortunately, the immediate conversational context for most writing is limited to a few persons. A student writing an assigned paper in a philosophy course may only be responding to a few authors she has read as part of the course and to the lectures of the professor; her readers will be that same professor and perhaps a classmate or roommate. A biochemist, although ultimately relying on all those teachers and writers of scientific works that contributed to her training, may base her immediate work on the findings of only a few colleagues, and she may address her highly technical conclusions to only a few specialists. The biochemist may feel the need to address a wider audience only if she discovered something that had broad social implications, like an insight into the growth of cancer cells. And she would need to reconsider the basic literature of biochemistry only if her findings called into question fundamental principles she had learned earlier.

Or consider again that philosophy student, whose case is typical of most students in most disciplines: the range of sources she would have to ponder for much of her education would be limited to the books assigned or recommended by her teachers. A research paper or personal curiosity may lead her to look at other sources, but only near the end of her academic work would she regularly work with less generally familiar material. And only at that late point would the audience for her work move beyond the classroom. Thus the academic context — in which most readers of this book find themselves — readily defines the participants of most written conversations. We can recognize the writers to whom we are responding through the *canon,* that is, the recognized major works of any discipline, and we can recognize our readers through the academic procedures of who reads student papers — the professor, graduate assistants, or seminar members.

In addition to the difference in participants, there are further differences between written and spoken conversation. In writing, the words alone must carry the entire message; writing does not have voice pitch, pauses, facial expressions, or gestures to pick up where words leave off. Nor can you keep an eye on your audience to see if a baffled face, wandering attention, or an angry look suggests you change what you are saying. The reader cannot stop you, ask you questions, raise objections, or demand clarifications. Writing must stand intelligible, complete, and convincing in itself.

Because your audience is not there to interrupt you as you write, you can think through your ideas fully, and you can find the best way to state them. When speaking, you must reply on the spot with whatever thoughts come immediately to mind. In talking, in fact, you may be more concerned with keeping the conversation going in a pleasant way than with logic, consistency, or truth; one topic leads to another with only the loosest connection, and a topic rarely remains stable for long. Because speech goes by so fast, you may get away with many careless, unconsidered, and even irrelevant comments. You may not always speak to the point — nor do you always even care if you are making a substantive point. In the process of writing, you have time to consider, develop, and sharpen every statement. When stuck, you can take a long pause, go out for coffee, and then pick up where you left off. If words wander, you can later edit out the digression. When revising, you can satisfy yourself that the argument is coherent and fully developed, and you can polish the words before any reader sees them. When the reader finally does get your writing, that reader can go through it slowly — evaluating everything that is there — or is not there. The conversation committed to paper slows down, grows thoughtful, and becomes more careful.

Who Participates?

The best way to get a feel for any conversation — oral or written — is to listen in for a while before you make your own comments. In that way you come to know the participants, the issues, the level of the conversation, the typical ways of speaking, and the rules of proof and evidence being used. The more you listen, the more likely you are to have ideas you want to contribute, and the more likely you are to phrase the ideas in ways that will fit the conversation. The following selections describe how two famous social scientists learned more about the written conversations in which they were participating.

Jung's Listeners

The first selection describes how letters from a television audience impressed the psychologist Carl Jung. By reading those letters Jung understood better the strong reactions of the audience. The interest of ordinary people moved Jung to expand his writings beyond a limited discussion with professionals. Communicating with nonspecialists changed the focus of Jung's writing from theoretical scientific considerations to practical knowledge helpful in everyday life.

[The television interview] brought Jung a great many letters from all sorts of people, many of them ordinary folk with no medical or psychological training, who had been captivated by the commanding presence, the humor, and the modest charm of this very great man, and who had glimpsed in his view of life and human personality something that could be helpful to them. And Jung was very pleased, not simply at getting letters (his mail was enormous at all times) but at getting them from people who would normally have no contact with him.

It was at this moment that he dreamed a dream of the greatest importance to him. . . . He dreamed that, instead of sitting in his study and talking to the great doctors and psychiatrists who used to call on him from all over the world, he was standing in a public place and address- ing a multitude of people who were listening to him with rapt attention and *understanding what he said. . . .*

When, a week or two later, [a publisher] renewed his request that Jung should undertake a new book designed, not for the clinic or the philosopher's study, but for the people in the market place, Jung al- lowed himself to be persuaded.[1]

The letters Carl Jung received made him more aware of a larger group of people interested in hearing his ideas. He then acted to broaden the number of participants in his written conversation.

Mead's Audience

The anthropologist Margaret Mead also has advanced knowl- edge among the specialists in her field and has made that knowledge accessible to the general public. Here she tells how the interchange between herself and the readers of her magazine column motivated her to continue the discussion. The contact with the lives and concerns of real people gave life to her own writing. The following comments appeared in the preface to a collection of columns she originally wrote for *Redbook,* a popular magazine.

Going to the field, anthropologists expect to — hope to — struggle with new questions of how to make sense of an unfamiliar mode of living. Past experience provides a framework for thinking about what is strange; but the new experience also sheds a different light on what is already familiar.

Thinking about American culture as I meet with different audiences also has this kind of challenge for me. With every new question pro- posed to me by a particular audience, my memory takes me back to some experience in field work — to an early morning in Samoa forty years ago, to the market in a Balinese village twenty-five years ago, to Peri Village, in the Admiralty Islands, in 1928, when it seemed to me that only misery lay ahead for the proud Manus people, and to my visits to Peri in the past ten years, when Manus leaders have sat talking with me about their children's modern careers and the future of all the peoples of New Guinea.

These are the experiences on which I draw, and each new audience, concerned with a different problem, refocuses my thinking about the

---

[1]John Freeman, "Introduction," in Carl G. Jung, *Man and His Symbols* (Garden City, N.Y.: Double- day, 1964), p. 10.

past and the present. But the vividness of field experience also enters into my awareness of an audience. I remember very vividly my first radio broadcast. It was in Australia. As I tried to focus words flung out into a void, I suddenly visualized mothers all over the country bathing and feeding their children, hustling them into their night clothes and tucking them into bed, while they half-listened to my talk. In order to speak to them, I found that I had to take into account all the other things the listening mothers must be doing at that hour.

I could see these mothers in my imagination, but I could not know how they responded to what I said. Today all this is changed. I can sit in New York and, using my own telephone, give a telelecture to students on seven different college campuses. At the end, each group of students can ask questions, so that we are all drawn together in our give and take. Or a lecture may be put on video tape. Then I can sit with the listening audience and participate in their responses. Over the years the audience has become far more a part of what is being said. The lecture and the monologue have become dialogues.

In much the same way these essays are a product of initiation and response. Readers send in questions, argue points, agree or explode in furious disagreements, and from all this we learn. There are also the occasions on which we have talked with a few of them as a group. Once on the anniversary of Hiroshima a group of young wives and mothers came together to discuss what they are doing and what they were telling their children about war and peace. On another occasion a group met with us to talk about their marriages and their hopes for their children's future. And as I go about the country giving lectures, there are very often young people in the audiences who identify themselves as readers by their comments on one or another of the *Redbook* columns. Later, when the next column is in the making, I remember what they have said. All this is what makes the material come alive for me.[2]

Carl Jung and Margaret Mead both shared their professional knowledge with nonprofessional audiences so that the general reader might benefit from expert advice. Yet Jung and Mead relate to their audiences differently. Jung appears almost as a prophet, lecturing on profound ideas to an audience waiting for his words. Mead, on the other hand, wants to interact closely with her readers to find out what is on their minds and what their problems are. Jung wants to present general truths for many people to use; Mead seems to want to help separate individuals. Despite the differences, however, both Mead and Jung understand and try to improve their relationships with their readers. Just as couples must work

[2]Excerpt from pp. xii–xiii "Going to the field . . . makes the material come alive for me." in *A Way of Seeing* by Margaret Mead and Rhoda Metraux.

Copyright © 1970 by Margaret Mead and Rhoda Metraux. By permission of William Morrow & Company.

at romantic relationships to make the relationships successful, writers must work at the relationships they establish with their readers.

Your Audience

The writing relationship you probably know best is the one between you and your teachers. The teacher selects material to discuss with you, gives you books to read, and assigns writing for you to do. You in turn write papers for the teacher to read; the teacher returns those papers with corrections, comments, and grades. The comments may then lead you to write differently in the future.

As you learned more and advanced to higher grades, you were able to write more developed papers on more complex subjects. At the same time the attitudes and expectations of the teachers became more demanding. Remember those first times you had to write by yourself in school, perhaps about a class trip to the zoo or your pet turtle. The teacher probably discussed the topic with you beforehand and then read and praised that youthful literary effort. A sympathetic teacher was encouraging you to express yourself, and proud parents were looking for early signs of ability. Almost any faltering attempt would satisfy that group of readers and lead you into the next stage of the written conversation — more complicated papers.

Now consider the last essay you wrote for one of your college teachers. How much guidance and encouragement were you given beforehand? What level of knowledge and skills was necessary to prepare the assignment? And with what predisposition do you think the teacher read the essay — with willingness to accept any attempt or with a demand for a high level of performance? Although both the second-grade and the college essays are in the context of the teacher-student relationship, there is a whole education of difference between the two.

As your education and interests become more specialized, your writing will increasingly depend on your being informed by the knowledge of your specialized field. Your teachers and fellow students — and later your coworkers and employers — will come to expect that you are basing your statements and judgments on your ever-increasing body of knowledge, on things you have read and learned. In your future career you may be frequently called upon to write papers and reports summarizing your contribution to a project, based on background information, economic considerations, your company's needs, and so forth. Many professionals — scientists, engineers, professors — prepare journal articles reporting on their research and conclusions. Responsible involvement in community affairs requires that you first become informed.

Throughout your life, you will be participating in increasingly informed conversations, and you will be called upon in many ways to express your informed opinion.

Writing Assignment

Write a short essay of perhaps three hundred words, discussing either (1) your changing relationship with the readers of your school writing as you moved from first grade to college *or* (2) one particular relationship with a reader of your writing, either in school or out. In either case you should consider who the reader or readers were, what you knew about them, how you knew this information, and what you tried to do in your writing as a result of knowing your reader. You may also consider whether the readers had any favorable attitudes toward your work, what kinds of reactions the readers had toward your writing, and whether you changed your approach to writing in response.

Try to support your generalizations with as many specific details as possible. Before writing the essay, try to remember details such as individual assignments and pieces of writing, and choose those details that you think will be of interest to the reader. If possible, include comments made on your earlier papers by teachers.

Consider this essay as part of a written response to this chapter. The audience will be your classmates, who have been considering the same issues, but from their own experiences and perspectives.

I
Read Well to
Write Well

1

Paraphrase: The Author's Thoughts in Your Words

Preview

By writing a careful paraphrase, you will clarify for yourself the full meaning of another writer's statements. In the process of writing a paraphrase, you must pay close attention to the meaning of the original passage in order to reproduce that meaning in your own words. Substituting synonyms for individual words and rearranging the sentence structure will help you find a new way to express the original meaning. Paraphrasing not only will help you increase your own understanding of a particular passage but also will allow you to communicate the meaning of that passage to others. In your own writing, you will frequently include a paraphrase, particularly when you need to refer to another writer's work in the course of making your own original statements. The paraphrase is a skill useful for both reading accurately, when you want to take precise notes on what you have read, and for writing, when you want to reproduce other writers' ideas.

Hear What's Said;
Read What's Written

An everyday situation illustrates the difficulties of communication. A man is an hour late; a woman who is waiting for him grows more irritated with each passing minute. Her irritation is now turning into words that she will shower on him when he finally arrives. As he is running to meet her, he is rehearsing his own string of legitimate excuses. When they finally meet, each has built such a wall of words that a hard collision is guaranteed. Neither wants to hear what the other has to say.

The problem that this couple faces so dramatically is the same problem that we all experience in smaller ways every day. We protect our fixed point of view by well-established arguments. We resist hearing any new or different explanations of anything we think we know about already. All day, every day, we sit inside ourselves trying to make sense of the world around us. If anyone comes along and tries to tell us something new — or adds up experience and knowledge to get a different total — we don't easily give up our own viewpoint to adopt a new one. Nor do we want to work at fitting new ideas into our old scheme.

Curiosity and desire for knowledge are strong human drives, but we also have opposite instincts to protect the viewpoints we have already come to believe in. These conserving instincts, in their most admirable form, stand behind our sense of integrity (as in *integer,* maintaining wholeness). But they also work to protect our thoughts from the effort of dealing with too many challenges. If we know or care little about a subject, hearing something new about it will not disturb us; but if we have made up our minds and hearts, new ideas are a serious threat to our peace of mind. C. Northcote Parkinson, the economist and observer of bureaucracies, noticed that the less important a decision is, the more time is devoted to discussing it.[1] Two hours will be spent on the new color scheme of the executive conference room, but only five minutes on the opening of the new factory. On the important issues, everybody either has a fixed opinion or doesn't want to face the effort and the responsibility of a serious decision.

Overcoming Resistance

To make sense of what other people write, we must first overcome the more lethargic part of our own minds that would just as

[1]C. Northcote Parkinson, *Parkinson's Law and Other Studies in Administration* (Boston: Houghton Mifflin, 1957), p. 32.

soon not know. That part of the mind, unfortunately, uses many tricks and bad habits to protect itself from assaults. The first and most obvious method of resisting the challenge of another writer's thoughts is to never pick up the book that might give us a hard time. Assuming we do get as far as looking at the words, there are many additional ways of carrying on the self-deception — of appearing to read while not really reading.

Reading with an assumption that the book doesn't contain anything worthwhile allows the reader to focus on those parts that most support such a preconception and to ignore those things that the book actually does well. If a reader is looking for a weakness, the reader will find it.

Almost all books do have limitations that a predisposed reader can detect. A historian who refuses to consider any argument that is not supported by documented statistical evidence keeps herself from a broad spectrum of materials — such as personal diaries or cultural artifacts — that might better convey the spirit of the times. She thus limits herself to those few areas of history that yield statistics, primarily population figures and economic studies of record-keeping civilizations. Such a historian will reject everything else as too speculative or too lacking in proof. Even without the application of such limiting principles, most books do have their weaknesses. To avoid judging a book too hastily, we should give it a fair reading, offering the book the full benefit of the doubt to see what sense it might possibly make. The time for evaluation is after we have obtained as much as we can from the work.

Similarly, if we argue against the book before we have absorbed its total sweep and all the evidence offered, we are apt to misjudge. Disturbing books are likely to make us react negatively at many points along the way. If we react too fast at each point, we may never understand the main idea.

Misassumptions

If we aren't quarreling with a challenging book, we may be assuming it says what we want it to say — and not what it actually does say. We may latch on to phrases that sound similar to ideas we believe, and then we may skim across those parts that sound unfamiliar or too complex. Just because we interpret a few words as similar to our own thoughts doesn't mean that the writer had anything like our thoughts in mind. We may even ignore a few key qualifying words such as "not generally" or "rarely" to make the book read the way we want it to read. Even if we avoid such extreme distortion, we still may smooth over more subtle differences. Given the variety of human thought, we cannot assume that any writer shares our exact thinking on all points.

Right Word, Wrong Meaning

We may even read a word, know the meaning of it, and still misunderstand the meaning the author intended. Words, particularly abstractions, can mean many different things to different people. To a debater a *point of view* is an opinion, to an art critic it is the angle from which we view a piece of sculpture, and to a novelist it is the character through whose eyes we see the story. Certain loosely defined words like *fact, objectivity,* and *determinism* have been under dispute for centuries, and each user is likely to have a particular meaning in mind. If we want to understand a particular writer, we have to understand the word according to that writer's definition.

Other words gain such popularity so rapidly that they get used to describe many different ideas before any one meaning gets set: the kind of analysis called *structuralism* — currently such a vogue word — differs substantially in the fields of anthropology, sociology, religion, literature, history, and philosophy.

Even if a word is used with its most common meaning, we still might misunderstand it unless we remain sensitive to the *context*. Everyone knows what the animal called a *horse* is; but that animal means very different things to a jockey, a bettor, and a ten-year-old child. In order to understand how and why any writer is using any word, we have to recognize the writer's way of thinking and his or her special interests. In reading an author interested in the present-day uses of military force in international politics, we must be receptive to an entirely different kind of reasoning than we would find in a writer interested in the social structure of a militarized country. Each of the two works might shed light on the other, but they are operating in two separate spheres.

Review for an Overview

Once a reader is receptive to the language and the spirit of a written work, the reader still has to be willing to see how the parts fit together into a coherent whole. Every book does not fit together well: the argument may ramble, or the later chapters may contradict the earlier. Sometimes a book is coherent on one level, clearly presenting the chronological narrative of, say, Thomas Jefferson's life, but lacks coherence on another — not explaining the development of his character. Until we have made a serious attempt to draw the parts together in our own minds, we will have no basis for evaluating a book's coherence — and no sense of its overall significance. Fortunately, most books are more than collections of loosely connected statements, and we must look for the significant connections. If we avoid the temptation of reading without really reading seriously, and if we then come to a reasonably accurate understanding of just what the writer meant, we will have a solid foundation for reacting, evaluating, and accepting — or rejecting — what we have read. To absorb the text in all its fullness — and to avoid any wrong assumptions or misreadings — we must first concentrate on what is on the author's page.

The remainder of this chapter is devoted to paraphrase, a task that requires a close reading of a given passage and a careful rewriting of the author's meaning. By recasting another writer's thoughts into our own words, we are forced to pay close attention to the content of statements and the precise meanings of words. Insofar as we all sometimes use any of the tricks of non-reading discussed above, the task of paraphrase will keep forcing our attention back to the page. In later chapters, after having determined what the printed page says, we will return to expressing personal thoughts and reactions — and to contributing to the conversation.

Rethink; Restate

Every school day at almost every level, many students are asked to restate in their own words information received from books, lectures, and films. Teachers assign this kind of loose paraphrase to see whether students have remembered and understood the course material. For such purposes, a student only needs to reproduce a few key concepts without making gross errors of meaning. True paraphrase, however, is part of a larger process of understanding and responding to a specific written passage. Before you can use or argue with anyone's ideas, you must understand these ideas accurately. Careful paraphrase requires close attention to every nuance of meaning so that, when you later come to refer to these ideas or argue against them, you will know exactly what you are working with. Paraphrase can serve as a form of note taking, allowing you to preserve the writer's exact meaning in those terms you understand best. Even more important, paraphrase can serve as a way of referring to other writers' thoughts in your own original papers so that

> **Paraphrase can serve as a way of referring to other writers' thoughts in your own original papers so that you can build on and answer their ideas even while you are advancing your own ideas.**

you can build on and answer their ideas even while you are advancing your own ideas.

A *paraphrase* is a precise restatement of a passage in your own words and phrasing in order to clarify the meaning. The task at first does not appear difficult. However, words that are similar are not always interchangeable, and the meanings of words shift subtly with their context and their use. Further, sentences put words into exact relationships. Thus an accurate paraphrase forces you to consider both the exact use of words and the sense of the entire statement. In considering the word-by-word meaning of a text and in searching for possible substitutions, the paraphraser must literally come to terms with what has been written. The looseness of understanding that often remains hidden in the privacy of your silent reading is challenged by the necessity of turning that understanding into written language.

In writing paraphrases you must attend to two things: the meaning of words as they are used in context and the relationship between words. In both you must reach for more than loose approximation. You must include all that was in the original, without adding anything new and without misjudging the original content.

In Other Words

Two techniques will help you gain a precise understanding of the original: substituting synonyms and rearranging the sentence structure. To paraphrase the opening sentence of the Gettysburg Address, for example, you might first replace the original words with other words of the same meaning. The original, as you know, reads

Four score and seven years ago, our fathers brought forth on this continent a new nation, conceived in liberty and dedicated to the proposition that all men are created equal.

First, replacing synonyms may lead to this first draft of the paraphrase:

> Eighty-seven years before now, our ancestors began in North America a new country, thought of in freedom and based on the principle that all people are born with the same rights.

Then restructuring the sentence might lead to a more total paraphrase:

> Our ancestors thought of freedom when they began a new country in North America eighty-seven years ago. They based their thinking on the principle that all people are born with the same rights.

But the Same Meaning

After substituting words and rearranging the sentence, you must then ask yourself whether the paraphrase means the same as the original. For example, the phrase *created equal* might be paraphrased *made the same,* but *made the same* suggests that people look and act exactly alike — not Lincoln's meaning. The context of the phrase is political, and Lincoln refers to political equality; therefore, *born with the same rights* is a more accurate paraphrase.

Any paraphrase that does not consider the total meaning of the original can easily become as absurd as the distortions made by a student and a teacher who were discussing the meaning of a famous line from Shakespeare's *The Merchant of Venice.* The line is "the quality of mercy is not strained," which may be accurately paraphrased as "compassionate forgiveness is given freely and easily." But the student tried substituting words without considering context; she wanted to know whether *strained* in the passage meant "strained as in rubber band or strained as in soup." The teacher, looking only at the sentence structure, answered, "Well, since it's *not* strained anyway, I don't see that it matters."

Substituting words and moving sentence parts around do not guarantee accurate paraphrase; the meaning of the paraphrase must always be checked against the meaning of the original.

Paraphrase: Selection 1

The best way to see how paraphrase can lead to more precise understanding is to do a few and to explore the problems that arise. You will get the most from the following examples of paraphrase if you write your own paraphrases of the sample passages before reading my versions. When comparing your paraphrases to the sample paraphrases, remember that there is no absolute right and wrong — only variations on how close the paraphrase comes to the original meaning.

THE STRANGE WORLD OF THE MOON [1959][2]

The moon is a small world and the diameter of 2,160 miles gives her a volume equal to 1/49 of the Earth's. Yet whether we explore her vicariously through a telescope or at some future date directly, it is her surface rather than her volume that will concern us first and foremost. This equals about 1/14 of our planet's total superficial area or approximately 10 million square miles. Moreover, most of the terrestrial globe is under water, only 57,500,000 square miles being dry land, while the moon has no seas. Thus she has over 1/6 of the total combined area of our continents, counting Antarctica, to offer to the explorers who first make a successful landing among her rather forbidding mountain landscape.

This straightforward account of scientific measurements of the moon has the appearance of a simple collection of numbers and facts. But each number is put in relationship with other numbers, and the meaning of each statistic requires an understanding of basic concepts of geometry, geography, and astronomy. A historical factor also enters into our understanding of the passage: it was obviously written before the first moon landing. The following paragraph is a paraphrase of Selection 1.

Sample Paraphrase

The moon's size is less than that of most heavenly bodies. The earth is forty-nine times the volume of the moon, which measures 2,160 miles across. But when we observe the moon either at our current distance through a telescope or in the future when we land on it, what we notice first — and are primarily interested in — is the exterior, not the interior. The surface of the earth is only fourteen times the roughly 10 million square mile surface of the moon. Because less than half — only 57,500,000 square miles — of the earth's surface is not covered by seas and oceans, which do not exist on the moon, the dry surface area of the earth, even including Antarctica, is less than six times the dry surface of the moon. The first humans to land on the rugged terrain will find a large area to explore.

[2]V. A. Firsoff, *Strange World of the Moon* (New York: Basic Books, 1959), p. 26.

Thought Process: Comments on the Paraphrase

Although words are changed and clauses rearranged, none of the original meaning is left out and nothing is added, except to explain an idea implicit in the original. One such implicit idea surfaced when I tried to find an equivalent for the phrase *small world*. Smallness is, of course, relative and can be either a physical or a psychological concept. Similarly, *world* can describe a variety of things from all of physical creation to a social circuit to a psychological framework. But the statistical comparison that immediately follows the phrase clearly fixes the scale and context: the worlds are the spheres in our galaxy, measured in a geometrical way.

Other mathematical relationships are given in the ratios and in the references to diameter, surface area, and volume. In restating these concepts, particularly the proper choice of substitutes for terms of size, one must be careful to avoid any distortion of meaning. In fact, by working through these mathematical relationships as they develop sentence by sentence, one grasps the underlying comparison of the passage: though apparently small, the moon has much land surface and no oceans.

In a close reading of the original, two minor phrases stick out: "at some future date" and "who first make a successful landing." That this piece was written before the first human landing on the moon affects both the attitude and knowledge of the author. The astronauts' direct observation of the moon would not, in fact, have changed any of the statistics of size presented here, but the description of the landscape might have been less forbidding.

Paraphrase: Selection 2

The lunar landscape, seen for the first time in 1969 by astronauts Aldrin and Armstrong, is the subject of the next excerpt for paraphrase. You may find this passage more difficult to paraphrase than the previous one, even though it does not require as much technical knowledge. In order to be able to picture Norman Mailer's description well enough to paraphrase it, you will have to call on many kinds of experience.

OF A FIRE ON THE MOON [1970][3]

They were looking at a terrain which lived in a clarity of focus unlike anything they had ever seen on earth. There was no air, of course, and so no wind, nor clouds, nor dust, nor even the finest scattering of light from the smallest dispersal of microscopic particles on a clear day on earth, no, nothing visible or invisible moved in the vacuum before them. All light was pure. No haze was present, not even the invisible haze of the finest day — therefore objects did not go out of focus as they receded into the distance. If one's eyes were good enough, an object at a hundred yards was as distinct as a rock at a few feet. And their eyes were good enough. Just as one could not determine one's altitude above the moon, not from fifty miles up nor five, so now along the ground before them no distance was real, for all distances had the faculty to appear equally near if one peered at them through blinders and could not see the intervening details. Again the sense of being on a stage or on the lighted floor of a room so large one could not see where the dark ceiling began must have come upon them, for there were no hints of gathering evanescence in ridge beyond ridge; rather each outline was as severe as the one in front of it, and since the ground was filled with small craters of every size, from antholes to potholes to empty pools, and the horizon was near, four times nearer than on earth and sharp as the line drawn by a pencil, the moon ground seemed to slope and drop in all directions.

In addition to describing the individual objects seen by the astronauts, Norman Mailer captures the strangeness of a new way of seeing. In coming to terms with this passage, we must gain a clear mental picture of those familiar visual experiences to which Mailer compares the unfamiliar scene. Even though some words present problems of interpretation, the greater problems are to comprehend the entire canvas being painted and to understand a new way of perceiving objects where there is no atmosphere. As the passage progresses, the perceptual analogies become increasingly more difficult, building on the perceptions already established in the earlier parts.

Sample Paraphrase

Astronauts Armstrong and Aldrin were seeing during that moment a region of ground in front of them with unearthly sharpness and definition. Although the visual sharpness was new to the astronauts,

[3]From *Of a Fire on the Moon* by Norman Mailer, p. 402, by permission of Little, Brown and Co. Copyright © 1969, 1970 by Norman Mailer.

the conditions that caused it were permanent features of the moon's world. No atmosphere, no movement of air, no atmospheric collections of water vapor, nor even particles too small to see, would reflect or refract light. Light as it passed through the emptiness remained unchanged, unmodified. The clearest day on the earth still had the slight obscuring of unnoticeable mist, but objects on the moon appeared equally distinct no matter how far away they were. The astronauts' sharp vision perceived something a hundred yards distant as clearly as a nearby rock. Just as the astronauts could not tell by sight whether they were five or fifty miles above ground while landing (as explained by Mailer earlier in the book), in the same way they had no sense of distance on the surface. Since all objects looked equally clear and since the construction of their helmets yielded only a narrow field of vision, obscuring objects between the astronauts and the thing they were looking at, they had nothing to go by in determining distance. The astronauts must have had another sense (also mentioned earlier by Mailer): the sense of standing in a room that is very tall and lighted only toward the bottom — as is a theater stage. In such a space one loses the sense of distance, for one cannot tell in the darkness exactly where the dark space ends and where the ceiling begins. In this case the astronauts would have had such a view in front of them instead of overhead: they saw no fading out of the mountains one beyond the other (as they would fade out in the mist on earth). The silhouette of each mountain was as distinct and craggy as the silhouette of the one before it. The loss of the sense of distance, the large number of nearby ridges of craters (measuring a few inches to many yards in width), and the relative nearness of the crisply defined horizon (only a quarter of the distance it would be on earth) all added up to the sensation that the surface of the moon fell away, curving downward in all directions from where the astronauts stood.

Thought Process: Comments on the Paraphrase

Mailer makes use of geometry, meteorology, geography, theater design, architecture, and even mountain gazing to recreate an unusual sense of space. Each sentence builds on the previous one, and concepts accumulate; therefore, I found I had to repeat earlier information in the later sentences to make all the relationships explicit, such as the phrase added in parentheses "as they would fade out in the mist on earth." Mailer also puts together many complex ideas very compactly; for clarity's sake I added fuller explanations, such as the "blinders" effect of the helmets. And I broke down the longer, complicated sentences into various parts: Mailer's long last sentence becomes five shorter ones in the paraphrase. Although the paraphrase is not as skillful, efficient, or graceful as the original, it does identify each of the concepts Mailer employs.

One early example of the need for expansion to bring out the full meaning of the original prose is the entire second sentence of the paraphrase to explain Mailer's phrase "which lived." Similarly, in the first sentence of the paraphrase I added the phrase "during that moment" to make explicit the concept of duration implied in the continuous form of the verb "were looking," used in the original. In the paraphrase, I substituted *see* for *look;* although there is at times a distinction between the words — *seeing* implying greater intensity and recognition than *looking* — the rest of the passage makes clear that such a distinction is not being made here. All the looking is quite observant.

I found sentences four through seven most difficult to paraphrase and consequently learned the most from them. Here two phenomena — the clarity from lack of atmosphere and the narrowing of vision caused by the helmets — combined to eliminate a sense of distance. At this point I had to imagine the effect of each phenomenon clearly so that the statement of their combined effect would make sense. In the discussion of a single idea, a certain amount of fuzziness may slip by; but when two ideas are combined, the lines of definition must be sharp. On top of these two factors Mailer later adds three more factors, each needing a precise definition: the ceiling analogy, the intervening craters, and the nearness of the horizon. Unless all the parts add up intelligibly, the final picture of the ground sloping away would not make sense.

You probably paraphrased the Mailer and Firsoff passages differently, pointing out other aspects of the originals. In some instances your paraphrases may have come closer to the meanings of the passages than the sample paraphrases here. By comparing paraphrases and finding explanations for the differences, you will better understand the shades of meaning conveyed by different word choices. Some choices may more accurately reflect the original, but in other cases the word choices may emphasize different aspects of the original.

When to Paraphrase

If you were to paraphrase all your reading, you would get to read very little, although you would know that little reading very well. Obviously paraphrasing for your own purposes should be saved only for extremely difficult passages that must be worked through word by word to wring out all the meaning.

Paraphrasing can also serve you in your own writing: you can use the paraphrase to restate a passage in terms your reader will understand more clearly. You can also use paraphrase to interpret difficult concepts and to make explicit facts and ideas that are implicit in the original. You will need to paraphrase when you want to take precise notes of your reading and when you wish to mention another writer's exact ideas in your own research papers.

To Explain Simply

When someone who is not as knowledgeable as you is having difficulty understanding some assigned reading, the best way you can help is through paraphrase. If, for example, a younger member of your family is having problems with the reading for her ninth-grade class in social studies, she may ask your help in explaining the preamble to the Constitution:

> We the People of the United States, in Order to form a more perfect Union, establish Justice, insure domestic Tranquility, provide for the common defence, promote the general Welfare, and secure the Blessings of Liberty to ourselves and our Posterity, do ordain and establish this Constitution for the United States of America.

You might help out by paraphrasing the original something like this:

> All the citizens of the United States are setting up and agreeing to this set of basic rules for our government. We are doing this for several reasons. We desire a better government with fewer problems than we had before. We want to guarantee everyone is treated fairly. We want to make sure that we have peace within the country and that we can protect ourselves from outside attack. We want to help all of us live better. And we want to enjoy freedom not just for ourselves but for all the people who come after us.

Notice how the paraphrase makes the passage easier to understand. A long, complex sentence is broken down into several shorter ones, and the parts are rearranged so that only one idea is discussed at a time. The unfamiliar terms, such as *domestic tranquility,* are replaced by more common words, such as *peace within the country*. Finally, abstractions such as *general welfare* are made more concrete, as in *all of us live better*.

In many technical and scientific areas, the paraphrase of basic principles is an important way of explaining the complexities of a subject to the reader. Textbooks and popularizations of science often rely heavily on simplifying paraphrases of more complex writing.

To Interpret the Text

In addition to helping the student, the paraphrase can aid professionals in coming to agreement over the meaning of important pieces of writing. In literature, philosophy, and religion, experts often disagree on their interpretations of significant books. Only by paraphrase can they make their readings explicit enough to enable them to compare and discuss their individual interpretations.

Another area where it is essential for professionals to develop a shared understanding of important texts is the law. Many legal books attempt to clarify exactly what particular laws say and, consequently, how they should be applied in particular circumstances. If there were not some agreement over the meaning of laws, our system of government would collapse.

However, laws in their original phrasing frequently have ambiguous or unspecific meanings, which leave unclear how they should be applied to a particular case. In all legal arguments, the courts must interpret the exact meaning of laws; thus many parts of legal decisions are a kind of extended paraphrase, clarifying the meaning and function of the laws. Legal texts, in turn, make use of these decisions and other legal precedents in order to restate the laws according to current legal practice.

Consider, for example, the Eighth Amendment to the Constitution. This part of the Bill of Rights outlaws "cruel and unusual punishments." You can see that the exact meaning of the phrase *cruel and unusual punishments* is open to various interpretations. What makes one punishment cruel and another acceptable? If it weren't unpleasant, it wouldn't be a punishment. The only way to clarify the meaning is to include much legal background in the paraphrase, as Corwin and Peltason do in *Understanding the Constitution:*

> The historic punishments banned are burning at the stake, crucifixion, breaking on the wheel, the race and thumbscrew, and in some circumstances, solitary confinement. Capital punishment inflicted by hanging, electrocution, lethal gas, or a firing squad are permissible. And the Supreme Court has ruled that there was no constitutional inhibition against electrocuting a prisoner after a first attempt failed because of a power breakdown.

Punishment may be cruel and unusual if it is out of all proportion to the offense as, for example, capital punishment for a petty crime.
The Supreme Court declared unconstitutional a California statute that
made the mere act of being addicted to drugs a crime because it
inflicted punishment simply for being ill. Chief Justice Warren, speaking for the Court in an opinion supported by only three other justices,
ruled that Congress violated the Eighth Amendment when it attempted
to make loss of citizenship part of the punishment for members of the
armed forces who had been convicted and dishonorably discharged for
desertion during time of war.[4]

This author is writing for a nonprofessional audience; legal points are, of
course, explored in much greater detail in books for practicing lawyers.

To Restate the Case

Works like the United States Constitution and the Bible express laws and ideas on which people build their lives. Thus paraphrases
that expand on their full meaning are valuable in themselves. More often,
paraphrases of specific passages are used by writers as passing references
or as background material. If a philosopher is arguing with the ideas of a
previous thinker, the philosopher must first restate the point he is arguing against. If a historian of science wants to show how one idea grew out
of another, she must give a clear restatement of both ideas before she can
demonstrate the connection. If a lawyer wants to cite an earlier judicial
interpretation that strengthens his case, he must restate the important
points of that judicial interpretation. In each of these cases, a precise
paraphrase is often the method used to restate a passage. The other
methods of restating a text passage are by quoting directly or by summarizing the major points. Each method has its advantages for different
situations. The comparative advantages and appropriateness of each are
discussed in detail on pages 331 to 334.

The paraphrase allows as much completeness as a quotation, but it is
more flexible in allowing you to fit the original material in with the flow
of your argument. Through the paraphrase you can bring out your interpretation, and you can emphasize those points most essential for your
argument. Moreover, you can write the paraphrased sentences so that
they fit in smoothly with the surrounding material of your argument.
Your argument does not have to stop short as another voice takes over;
with paraphrase the voice always remains your own.

[4]Edward S. Corwin and Jack W. Peltason, *Understanding the Constitution*, 4th ed. (New York: Holt,
Rinehart and Winston, 1967), p. 131.

The paraphrase allows as much completeness as a quotation, but it is more flexible in allowing you to fit the material in with the flow of your argument.

You must always clearly identify the source of the ideas you paraphrase — usually by mentioning the author's name in the text and by footnoting the reference. This documentation allows the reader to distinguish between your own ideas and the ideas from your source. (See Chapter 10 for a full description of documentation.)

James Madison, for example, paraphrased parts of the Constitution effectively in *Federalist Paper Number 62.* Before the Constitution was approved, Alexander Hamilton, James Madison, and John Jay wrote a series of newspaper articles in support of the proposed government. In one of these articles, Madison discussed the proposed composition of the Senate. In order to argue in behalf of various provisions of Article I, Section 3 of the Constitution, he first provided paraphrases of those provisions. However, because he is paraphrasing instead of quoting, he can also bring in material from an earlier section of the Constitution, which describes the composition of the House of Representatives. Thus paraphrase gives Madison the flexibility to compare the provisions of two sections within a single sentence. Once he has set up his comparisons through paraphrase, he can then argue in favor of the provisions.

> The qualifications proposed for senators, as distinguished from those of representatives, consist in a more advanced age and a longer period of citizenship. A senator must be thirty years of age at least; as a representative must be twenty-five. And the former must have been a citizen nine years; as seven years are required for the latter. The propriety of these distinctions is explained by the nature of the senatorial trust, which, requiring greater extent of information and stability of character, requires at the same time that the senator should have reached a period of life most likely to supply these advantages; and which, participating immediately in transactions with foreign nations, ought to be exercised by none who are not thoroughly weaned from the prepossessions and habits incident to foreign birth and education. The term of nine years appears to be a prudent mediocrity between a total exclusion of adopted citizens, whose merits and talents may claim a share in the public confidence, and an indiscriminate and hasty admission of them, which might create a channel for foreign influence on the national councils.

In conclusion, the paraphrase can serve many purposes beyond a teacher's desire to see whether students have read and understood the textbook. When carefully written, a paraphrase aids your own understanding of a key or complex passage; it allows you to share that understanding with those less knowledgeable than you are and with your professional peers; and it allows you to discuss other writers' viewpoints while you still keep control over the flow of your own original argument. Recasting other writers' thoughts into your own language is an essential tool of conversation, written or spoken.

Writing Assignments

1. Paraphrase each of the following passages about the moon and our knowledge of it. The first passage discusses a lunar map maker; the second presents problems in the lunar calendar that eventually led to the beginning of astronomy; and the third explores the relationship between the external appearance and the internal structure of the moon. Since all the paraphrases are for your own understanding as a reader, consider the audience to be yourself in your most demanding mood.

a. From *New Guide to the Moon* by Patrick Moore:

> The first known map of the Moon was drawn around the year 1600. It was the work of William Gilbert, physician to Queen Elizabeth I, who is best remembered today as the pioneer investigator of magnetic phenomena. Gilbert's map was not actually published until 1651, but it must have been completed before the end of 1603, for the excellent reason that this was the year in which Gilbert died. The main dark regions are shown in fairly recognizable form; for instance, the patch which he calls the "Regio Magna Orientalis" is identifiable with the vast plain known to us as the Mare Imbrium.
>
> There are two points of special interest about Gilbert's map, quite apart from its being the first. He regarded the dark areas as land and the bright regions as seas — the reverse of the general view at that time. More importantly, Gilbert drew his chart with the naked eye. Telescopes did not come upon the astronomical [scene] until the end of the first decade of the seventeenth century.[5]

[5]Patrick Moore, *New Guide to the Moon* (New York: W. W. Norton, 1976), p. 74.

b. From *The Copernican Revolution* by Thomas S. Kuhn:

Because they are easily visible and conveniently spaced, the moon's phases provided the oldest of all calendar units. Primitive forms of both the week and the month appear in a Babylonian calendar from the third millennium B.C., a calendar in which each month began with the first appearance of the crescent moon and was subdivided at the 7th, 14th, and 21st days by the recurrent "quarters" of the moon's cycle. At the dawn of civilization men must have counted new moons and quarters to measure time intervals, and as civilization progressed they repeatedly attempted to organize these fundamental units into a coherent long-term calendar — one that would permit the compilation of historical records and the preparation of contracts to be honored at a specified future date.

But at this point the simple obvious lunar unit proved intractable. Successive new moons may be separated by intervals of either 29 or 30 days, and only a complex mathematical theory, demanding generations of systematic observation and study, can determine the length of a specified future month. Other difficulties derive from the incommensurable lengths of the average lunar and solar cycles. Most societies (but not all, for pure lunar calendars are still used in parts of the Middle East) must adjust their calendars to the sun-governed annual climatic variation, and for this purpose some systematic method for inserting an occasional thirteenth month into a basic year of 12 lunar months (354 days) must be devised. These seem to have been the first difficult technical problems encountered by ancient astronomy. More than any others, they are responsible for the birth of quantitative planetary observation and theory. The Babylonian astronomers who finally solved these difficulties between the eighth and third centuries B.C., a period during most of which Greek science was still in its infancy, accumulated much of the fundamental data subsequently incorporated into the developed structure of the two-sphere universe.[6]

c. From *The Old Moon and the New* by V. A. Firsoff:

The Moon is full of holes, big and small, like Swiss cheese, and . . . this frivolous analogy may come nearer the truth than learned verbiage laden with long Greek and Latin words, for the subsurface layers of the lunar globe seem indeed to resemble Swiss cheese in structure. On the surface, however, the holes are 'sealed' and appear as comparatively shallow depressions, round, polygonal and at times more or less irregular, walled or unwalled on the outside. The last-mentioned are usually small and referred to as crater-pits, but in the larger examples an upraised rim is invariably present, becoming more and more complicated with increasing size, until the term "crater" no longer conveys the essence of the structure that would be more accurately described as a "mountain ring." Nevertheless, these walled depressions are generally known as craters.[7]

2. Paraphrase the opening lines of the Declaration of Independence to restate the meaning to a ninth-grade student.

When in the Course of human events, it becomes necessary for one people to dissolve the political bands, which have connected them with another, and to assume among the powers of the earth, the separate and equal station to which the Laws of Nature and of Nature's God entitle them, a decent respect to the opinions of mankind requires that they should declare the causes which impel them to the separation. — We hold these truths to be self-evident, that all men are created equal, that they are endowed by their Creator with certain unalienable Rights, that among these are Life, Liberty and the pursuit of Happiness. — That to secure these rights, Governments are instituted among Men, deriving their just powers from the consent of the governed, — That whenever any Form of Government becomes destructive of these ends, it is the Right of the People to alter or to abolish it, and to institute new Government, laying its foundation on such principles and organizing its powers in such form, as to them shall seem most likely to effect their Safety and Happiness.

3. Paraphrase Sir Isaac Newton's discussion of his three *laws of motion* as presented in *Principia* (1726). The paraphrase is for a college class in the history of science; you will be asked to compare your interpretation with those of other students.

Law I. *Every body perseveres in its state of rest, or of uniform motion in a right line, unless it is compelled to change that state by force impressed thereon.*

Projectiles persevere in their motions, so far as they are not retarded by the resistance of the air, or impelled downwards by the force of gravity. A top, whose parts by their cohesion are perpetually drawn aside from rectilinear motions, does not cease its rotation, otherwise than as it is retarded by the air. The greater bodies of the planets and comets, meeting with less resistance in more free spaces, preserve their motions both progressive and circular for a much longer time.

Law II. *The alteration of motion is ever proportional to the motive force impressed; and is made in the direction of the right line in which that force is impressed.*

[7]V. A. Firsoff, *The Old Moon and the New* (New York: A. S. Barnes, 1969), p. 104.

If any force generates a motion, a double force will generate double the motion, a triple force triple the motion, whether that force be impressed altogether and at once, or gradually and successively. And this motion (being always directed the same way with the generating force), if the body moved before, is added to or subducted from the former motion, according as they directly conspire with or are directly contrary to each other; or obliquely joined, when they are oblique, so as to produce a new motion compounded from the determination of both.

Law III. *To every action there is always opposed an equal reaction; or the mutual actions of two bodies upon each other are always equal, and directed to contrary parts.*

Whatever draws or presses another is as much drawn or pressed by that other. If you press a stone with your finger, the finger is also pressed by the stone. If a horse draws a stone tied to a rope, the horse (if I may so say) will be equally drawn back towards the stone; for the distended rope, by the same endeavor to relax or unbend itself, will draw the horse as much towards the stone, as it does the stone towards the horse, and will obstruct the progress of the one as much as it advances that of the other. If a body impinge upon another, and by its force change the motion of the other, that body also (because of the equality of the mutual pressure) will undergo an equal change, in its own motion, towards the contrary part. The changes made by these actions are equal, not in the velocities but in the motions of bodies; that is to say, if the bodies are not hindered by any other impediments. For, because the motions are equally changed, the changes of the velocities made towards contrary parts are reciprocally proportional to the bodies.[8]

4. Paraphrase the opening of *Philosophy in a New Key* by Susanne Langer. The paraphrase is to show your interpretation of the full meaning of the passage to your instructor. Here you are demonstrating your understanding of a philosopher's insights.

Every age in the history of philosophy has its own preoccupation. Its problems are peculiar to it, not for obvious practical reasons — political or social — but for deeper reasons of intellectual growth. If we look back on the slow formation and accumulation of doctrines which mark that history, we may see certain *groupings* of ideas within it, not by subject-matter, but by a subtler common factor which may be called their "technique." It is the mode of handling problems, rather than what they are about, that assigns them to an age. Their subject-matter may be fortuitous, and depend on conquests, discoveries, plagues, or governments; their treatment derives from a steadier source.

[8]Isaac Newton, *Principia,* trans. Andrew Motte (Berkeley: University of California Press, 1962), pp. 13–14.

The "technique," or treatment, of a problem begins with its first expression as a question. The way a question is asked limits and disposes the ways in which any answer to it — right or wrong — may be given. If we are asked: "Who made the world?" we may answer: "God made it," "Chance made it," "Love and hate made it," or what you will. We may be right or we may be wrong. But if we reply: "Nobody made it," we will be accused of trying to be cryptic, smart, or "unsympathetic." For in this last instance, we have only seemingly given an answer; in reality we have *rejected the question.* The questioner feels called upon to repeat his problem. "Then how did the world become as it is?" If now we answer: "It has not 'become' at all," he will be really disturbed. This "answer" clearly repudiates the very framework of his thinking, the orientation of his mind, the basic assumptions he has always entertained as common-sense notions about things in general. Everything has become what it is; everything has a cause; every change must be to some end; the world is a thing, and must have been made by some agency, out of some original stuff, for some reason. These are natural ways of thinking. Such implicit "ways" are not avowed by the average man, but simply followed. He is not conscious of assuming any basic principles. They are what a German would call his "Weltanschauung," his attitude of mind, rather than specific articles of faith. They constitute his outlook; they are deeper than facts he may note or propositions he may moot.[9]

5. Write a short letter to your parents. Try to convince them to make a certain purchase, change a particular attitude, or do something that they have until now refused to do. In the course of this letter, paraphrase statements that your parents have repeatedly given as advice, but paraphrase them in such a way that the ideas argue for your side. Don't twist the meaning of your parents' favorite statements around entirely, but through rephrasing, show how their statements are applicable to the point you are making.

[9]Susanne Langer, *Philosophy in a New Key* (Cambridge, Mass.: Harvard University Press, 1951), p. 15. Copyright © 1942, 1951, 1957 by the President and Fellows of Harvard College; © 1970, 1979 by Susanne K. Langer. Reprinted by permission.

2
Summary: The Author's Main Ideas

Preview

Summary, like paraphrase, allows you to reproduce another writer's thoughts — but in shortened form. In writing a summary, you focus on the most important statements of the original passage and eliminate less important material. This short restatement can take one of three forms — *summary, abstract,* or *précis;* each one corresponds to a different method of shortening — deletion, selection, or miniaturization. As you become adept at summarizing, you will use all three methods. Like paraphrase, summary can be used for many purposes: to understand the main points and structure of an author's argument; to convey that understanding to others; to present background information quickly; and to refer to another writer's ideas in the course of your own original statement.

The Essence of the Matter

The word-by-word attention required for a good paraphrase will lead you across all the contours of another writer's thought. You will follow the main trail of meaning, the ridges of fine distinctions, the cutbacks of qualifications, and the waysides of association. As the weary hiker on such a slow trek, you must mentally pull together all the major events of the journey in order to feel some sense of the total experience. Writing a summary allows you to review the entire journey as a whole.

To establish the essentials of another writer's idea — rather than to provide a complete and detailed restatement — is the purpose of summary writing. A summary will help you understand the major direction, the main points, and the overall shape of the more detailed original. A summary restates the essence of the original in as few words as possible — *but not necessarily different words*. Of course, you must give adequate credit to the original, by techniques described fully in Chapter 10. Unlike the paraphrase writer, who must discover new ways of restating the meaning, the summarizer must only look for the most compact and quickest restatement.

Three Techniques

Three terms are often used to describe the rewriting of a longer piece in short form: *summary, abstract*, and *précis*. Once you become familiar with the three methods, you will most likely develop your own hybrid technique, depending on your preferences and the type of material you are summarizing. But for simplicity's sake, each method will be treated separately.

I. Summary

One meaning of the word *summary* is "done without delay or formalities," as in a *summary* trial. *Summary* is also related to the mathematical term *sum*, what a series of numbers adds up to. Thus the summary writer quickly moves to the main points, excluding all the less important information and the formalities, but including those points necessary for understanding the main argument.

> **A summary will help you understand the major direction, the main points, and the overall shape of the more detailed original text. A summary restates the essence of the original in as few words as possible.**

Principle I.

Use only the most important information in the original, leaving out everything that does not represent a direct, major step in the argument.

Method I. Deletion

First, read through the passage for a general understanding of its meaning. Then cross out all unnecessary words, all repetitions, all digressions, and all minor supporting detail. Leave only the main points, the most prominent examples, and the most important supporting details. Then rewrite the remaining material in concise, coherent sentences (see pages 309 to 315).

This method works best where clearly stated major points are each developed with extensive detail or example. This type of prose, as in the selection below, generally has clearly identifiable topic sentences at each new stage of the argument; and generalizations are related to specifics in obvious ways.

The following example illustrates the method of summary: first, the passage is given in its original form; then the method of deleting all superfluous material is shown. Finally, one possible rewrite of the summary is given. You will gain more from the discussion if you first try to write your own summary of the passage.

SLEEP: OUR UNKNOWN LIFE[1]

Unlike human subjects, animal subjects in the sleep laboratory obviously cannot be awakened and asked what they were dreaming. So until relatively recently it was impossible to state with absolute certainty that any animal actually dreamed. Then, by a happy accident, experimenters obtained pretty solid evidence that at least one animal has dreams.

[1]Reprinted by permission of Elsevier/Nelson Books from the book *Sleep: Our Unknown Life*, pp. 104–105. Copyright © 1972 by Richard Deming.

A team of researchers at the University of Pittsburgh was attempting to find out if sleep loss would cause hallucinations (or microsleep dreams, if Dr. Ralph Berger's theory is correct) in monkeys, as it did in human beings. The initial procedure was to strap each monkey to a chair inside what had originally been a telephone booth. A projection screen was placed directly in front of the monkey, and colored slides were periodically shown on it. Each time a slide was projected, the monkey received an electric shock unless it repeatedly pressed a bar in front of it.

All the monkeys used in the experiment quickly learned to avoid the shock by pressing the bar. They pressed it on an average of fifty times a minute whenever an image appeared on the screen.

After a monkey had learned its lessons and had been thoroughly deprived of sleep, the researchers fitted it with contact lenses that dimmed its vision without completely blinding it. They left the screen in place, but projected no more slides onto it. Then they waited for the monkey to develop hallucinations and start pressing the bar.

Unfortunately for the purposes of the experiment, all the animals simply went to sleep. Each time they put a different monkey into the converted telephone booth, the same thing happened. Finally, as the experimenters ruefully watched one of the monkeys through the viewing window, it passed into deep sleep, then back up into REM sleep — and suddenly, in its sleep, it began furiously pressing the lever.

Obviously the monkey was seeing images in its sleep, which could only mean that it was dreaming. Therefore, while the experiment failed in its initial purpose, it did prove something equally important — that at least one animal, the monkey, has dreams during sleep.

Same Passage: All Minor Information Deleted

~~Unlike human subjects, animal subjects in the sleep laboratory obviously cannot be awakened and asked what they were dreaming. So until relatively~~ recently ~~it was impossible to state with absolute certainty that any animal actually dreamed. Then, by a happy accident, experimenters obtained pretty~~ solid evidence that ~~at least~~ one animal has dreams.

~~A team of~~ researchers ~~at the University of Pittsburgh was attempting~~ to find out if sleep loss would cause hallucinations ~~(or microsleep dreams, if Dr. Ralph Berger's theory is correct)~~ in monkeys, ~~as it did in human beings. The initial procedure was to strap each monkey to a chair inside what had originally been a telephone booth. A projection screen was placed directly in front of~~ the monkey, ~~and colored~~ slides ~~were~~ periodically shown ~~on it.~~ Each time a slide was projected, the monkey received an electric shock unless it repeatedly pressed a bar in front of it.

~~All the~~ monkeys ~~used in the experiment quickly~~ learned to avoid the shock ~~by pressing the bar. They pressed it on an average of fifty times a minute whenever an image appeared on the screen~~.

~~After a monkey had learned its lessons and had been thoroughly~~ deprived of sleep, ~~the researchers fitted it with contact lenses that~~ dimmed its vision ~~without completely blinding it. They left the screen in place, but~~ projected no more slides ~~onto it. Then they waited for the monkey to develop hallucinations and start pressing the bar~~.

~~Unfortunately for the purposes of the experiment, all the~~ animals ~~simply~~ went to sleep. ~~Each time they put a different monkey into the converted telephone booth, the same thing happened. Finally, as the experimenters ruefully watched one of the monkeys through the viewing window, it passed into deep sleep, then back up~~ into REM sleep — and ~~suddenly, in its sleep, it~~ began ~~furiously~~ pressing the lever.

~~Obviously~~ the monkey was seeing images in its sleep, ~~which could only~~ mean ~~that it was~~ dreaming. ~~Therefore, while the experiment failed in its initial purpose, it did prove something equally important — that at least one animal, the monkey, has dreams during sleep~~.

Sample Summary

Definite evidence of dreams in any animal is only recent. In an experiment on hallucinations caused by sleep loss, monkeys had to press a bar to avoid shock when slides, shown periodically, appeared. Trained in this manner, the monkeys were deprived of sleep, had their vision dimmed, and were placed before the screen, but no slides were projected. Although falling into REM sleep, one monkey repeatedly pressed the bar, apparently seeing images and, therefore, dreaming.

Thought Process for Summary

Much of the original repeats basic information or provides secondary details of the experiment, extraneous judgments (such as "unfortunately"), the researcher's interests, and background material. These, as indicated by the deletion marks, were eliminated. Most of the major information can be found in one sentence in each paragraph; we can trace a strong pattern of topic sentences amplified by secondary details.

In addition to eliminating secondary material, I was able to achieve substantial shortening by the use of more complex sentence patterns, which established the relationships between the parts of the argument. In the original, the writer uses simpler, shorter sentences and puts the parts of the argument together slowly; in a summary, the writer can add up the parts more compactly.

II.   Abstract

The term *abstract* comes from the Latin *abstraho,* meaning —
among other things — *to drag away* or *to draw away from.* These meanings
suggest two things: first, we drag out certain parts of the original; that is,
we pull out the essence, leaving the rest behind. Second, as we draw away
from the original, we get more of an overview of the entire piece. We
come to see how a given piece of writing is built on a structure of
underlying ideas.

Principle II.

*By pulling out the central ideas, show the framework on which the writing is
built.*

Method II.   Selection

Read through the passage for a general understanding of the ideas discussed. Then underline only the key words, those that express substantial
information or major statements. Ask yourself: "What is central here?
What is the author's specific point? What statements draw the whole
piece together?" Where an underlying idea is only expressed indirectly,
write a direct statement. Then restate the material you have abstracted in
concise, coherent sentences.

This method is most appropriate where topic statements are not obviously stated at every stage or are stated in such extended, complex ways
that the central point of the passage is not self-evident. Often such situations arise when there is a lack of balance between generalization and
details, either because the piece contains too many generalities or because
details are recounted with little indication of what they mean when considered as a whole. In the following example, the heavily detailed, chronological narrative tends to obscure the major ideas. You will benefit from
trying your own abstract of the passage before reading the sample
abstract and discussion that follows.

THE CASE OF RANDY GARDNER[2]

In 1965, the Stanford group was involved in a sleep deprivation
experiment that seriously undermined the notion that unduly prolonged

---

[2]Selection is reprinted from *Some Must Watch While Some Must Sleep* by William C. Dement, pp.
8–12, with permission of W. W. Norton & Company, Inc. Copyright © 1972, 1974, 1976 by William C.
Dement. Originally published as part of The Portable Stanford series, Stanford Alumni Association,
Stanford, California.

wakefulness could lead to impairment, and particularly that psychosis would be the inevitable result. In January of that year, I chanced to read in the newspapers that a San Diego youth, Randy Gardner, had successfully completed about eighty hours of a planned 264-hour vigil in a high school science fair project aimed at establishing the world's record for prolonged wakefulness. At that time the Guinness Book of World Records listed the record as 260 hours, although real documentation was lacking.

Seeing an opportunity to study prolonged sleep deprivation again, I recruited my colleague, Dr. George Gulevich, now head of the Psychiatric Inpatient Service at Stanford, to accompany me to San Diego with a portable electroencephalograph. The boy's parents welcomed our professional assistance because they were anxious about the consequences of the experiment. Until that time the experiment had been conducted by Randy himself with two of his schoolmates. Although his friends admitted it was not easy to keep him awake in the middle of the night, they testified that he had absolutely not been allowed to sleep. Our main concerns were to verify the lack of sleep and to supplement the inexperienced monitoring of the schoolboys.

Randy, who was seventeen, was a slim boy in excellent physical condition. He was cooperative and friendly throughout, although in the middle of the night when he grew drowsy and wanted to rest his eyes, he would object strenuously because we would not allow him to close his lids for any prolonged period of time. As the vigil wore on and impressive durations accumulated, the nation's press and TV became more and more involved until the whole affair began to resemble a circus. This was certainly very stimulating to the young lad and probably aided him in his ability to remain awake. In general, the daytime was relatively easy, but at night we were driven to increasingly heroic measures to help Randy resist sleepiness and to bolster his flagging motivation.

I have two very vivid memories from this study. The first is of spending several hours after 3 a.m. on the last night in a penny arcade where Randy and I competed in about one hundred games on a baseball machine. Randy won every game — which attests to his lack of physical or psychomotor impairment. The second is that, having sacrificed a good deal of sleep myself, I carelessly turned the car into a one-way street the wrong way, and immediately attracted the attention of a policeman. Because of the unusual circumstances, I forgot about the ticket until six months later when a warrant was issued for my arrest. It cost me $86 to redeem myself.

At the end of the long vigil, before going to bed, Randy held a press conference in which the three major TV networks and reporters from papers all over the United States participated. Randy conducted himself in an absolutely impeccable fashion. Asked how he was able to stay awake for eleven days, he answered lightly, "It's just mind over matter."

Dr. Laverne Johnson, a Stanford alumnus, had read about this experiment and had volunteered his laboratory at the San Diego Naval Hospital. There, at 6:12 a.m., precisely 264 hours and 12 minutes after his alarm clock had awakened him eleven days earlier, Randy Gardner went to sleep. I must admit that I didn't have the faintest idea about how long he would stay asleep, and I certainly didn't know what to tell the hordes of reporters who buzzed about demanding predictions. Randy slept for only fourteen hours and forty minutes, and when he awoke he was essentially recovered. He was actually up and out at 10 p.m. and stayed awake without difficulty until the next night, which was about twenty-four hours. His second sleep after the long vigil was eight hours and seemed quite normal. He has since been followed by Dr. Johnson, for whom he worked in the ensuing years, and appears to be completely healthy and unaffected by the experience — except for whatever effect being a transient national celebrity may have had on his psyche. Except for a few illusions — one or two minor hallucinatory experiences — Randy demonstrated no psychotic behavior during the entire vigil, no paranoid behavior, no serious emotional change.

The crucial factor in surmounting the effects of prolonged sleep loss is probably physical fitness. There is almost no degree of sleepiness that cannot be overcome if the subject engages in vigorous exercise. As the vigil wears on, almost continuous muscular activity is necessary to forestall overwhelming sleepiness. Many individuals simply would not be able to maintain this amount of activity, and would therefore appear to succumb to the debilitating effects of sleep loss. Although the elderly are said to require less sleep, deprivation studies have not been done in such individuals for obvious reasons. However, some years ago, Wilse Webb of the University of Florida showed that elderly rats could not tolerate prolonged wakefulness.

At any rate, if the subject is highly motivated and in top physical condition, as was Randy Gardner, we have begun to suspect that the vigil could go on indefinitely.

Same Passage: Key Words Underlined

In 1965, the Stanford group was involved in a <u>sleep deprivation experiment</u> that seriously <u>undermined</u> the notion that unduly <u>prolonged wakefulness could lead to impairment</u>, and particularly that <u>psychosis</u> would be the inevitable result. In January of that year, I chanced to read in the newspapers that a San Diego <u>youth, Randy Gardner</u>, had successfully completed about eighty hours of a planned <u>264-hour vigil</u> in a high school science fair project aimed at establishing the world's record for prolonged wakefulness. At that time the Guinness Book of World Records listed the record as 260 hours, although real documentation was lacking.

Seeing an opportunity to study prolonged sleep deprivation again, I recruited my colleague, Dr. George Gulevich, now head of the Psychiatric Inpatient Service at Stanford, to accompany me to San Diego with a portable electroencephalograph. The boy's parents welcomed our professional assistance because they were anxious about the consequences of the experiment. Until that time the experiment had been conducted by Randy himself with two of his schoolmates. Although his friends admitted it was not easy to keep him awake in the middle of the night, they testified that he had absolutely not been allowed to sleep. Our main concerns were to verify the lack of sleep and to supplement the inexperienced monitoring of the schoolboys.

Randy, who was seventeen, was a slim boy in excellent physical condition. He was cooperative and friendly throughout, although in the middle of the night when he grew drowsy and wanted to rest his eyes, he would object strenuously because we would not allow him to close his lids for any prolonged period of time. As the vigil wore on and impressive durations accumulated, the nation's press and TV became more and more involved until the whole affair began to resemble a circus. This was certainly very stimulating to the young lad and probably aided him in his ability to remain awake. In general, the daytime was relatively easy, but at night we were driven to increasingly heroic measures to help Randy resist sleepiness and to bolster his flagging motivation.

I have two very vivid memories from this study. The first is of spending several hours after 3 a.m. on the last night in a penny arcade where Randy and I competed in about one hundred games on a baseball machine. Randy won every game — which attests to his lack of physical or psychomotor impairment. The second is that, having sacrificed a good deal of sleep myself, I carelessly turned the car into a one-way street the wrong way, and immediately attracted the attention of a policeman. Because of the unusual circumstances, I forgot about the ticket until six months later when a warrant was issued for my arrest. It cost me $86 to redeem myself.

At the end of the long vigil, before going to bed, Randy held a press conference in which the three major TV networks and reporters from papers all over the United States participated. Randy conducted himself in an absolutely impeccable fashion. Asked how he was able to stay awake for eleven days, he answered lightly, "It's just mind over matter."

Dr. Laverne Johnson, a Stanford alumnus, had read about this experiment and had volunteered his laboratory at the San Diego Naval Hospital. There, at 6:12 a.m., precisely 264 hours and 12 minutes after his alarm clock had awakened him eleven days earlier, Randy Gardner went to sleep. I must admit that I didn't have the faintest idea about how long he would stay asleep, and I certainly didn't know what to tell the hordes of reporters who buzzed about demanding predictions. Randy slept for only fourteen hours and forty minutes, and when he awoke he was <u>essentially recovered</u>. He was actually up and out at 10 p.m. and stayed <u>awake</u> without difficulty until the next night, which was about <u>twenty-four hours</u>. His <u>second sleep</u> after the long vigil was <u>eight hours</u> and seemed quite <u>normal</u>. He has since been followed by Dr. Johnson, for whom he worked in the ensuing years, and appears to be completely <u>healthy and unaffected by the experience</u> — except for whatever effect being a transient national celebrity may have had on his psyche. <u>Except for a few illusions</u> — one or two minor hallucinatory experiences — Randy demonstrated <u>no psychotic behavior</u> during the entire vigil, no paranoid behavior, no serious emotional change.

The <u>crucial factor</u> in surmounting the effects of prolonged sleep loss is probably <u>physical fitness</u>. There is almost no degree of sleepiness that cannot be overcome if the subject engages in vigorous exercise. As the vigil wears on, <u>almost continuous muscular activity</u> is <u>necessary to forestall overwhelming sleepiness</u>. Many individuals simply would not be able to maintain this amount of activity, and would therefore appear to succumb to the debilitating effects of sleep loss. Although the elderly are said to require less sleep, deprivation studies have not been done in such individuals for obvious reasons. However, some years ago, Wilse Webb of the University of Florida showed that <u>elderly rats could not tolerate prolonged wakefulness</u>.

At any rate, if the subject is highly motivated and in top physical condition, as was Randy Gardner, we have begun to suspect that the vigil could go on indefinitely.

Sample Abstract

Observations of Randy Gardner, a high school student who stayed awake for 264 hours, contradicted the belief that prolonged wakefulness leads to impairment and psychosis. Two researchers, after hearing of his ongoing attempt to stay awake, observed Randy to verify and monitor his lack of sleep. The cooperative and friendly seventeen-year-old boy, in excellent physical condition and stimulated by media attention, stayed awake during the day with relative ease but needed much support at night. Randy's lack of physical and psychomotor impairment was made clear by his numerous consecutive victories at a penny arcade game on the last night and by his presence of mind at a final news conference. Although awake for eleven days, Randy recovered after a sleep of only fourteen hours and forty minutes. After another twenty-four hours of wakefulness, he returned to a normal eight-hour sleep. Followup studies indicate that he is healthy and unaffected by the experience; during the long vigil, he had exhibited no psychotic behavior other than a few illusions. Physical fitness was apparently the crucial factor, for almost continuous muscular activity was necessary to overcome the overwhelming sleepiness; this finding was supported by another experiment that showed elderly rats incapable of tolerating prolonged wakefulness.

Thought Process for Abstract

The important ideas of the original are buried in the chronological account of human actions, the many details reinforcing the scientific validity of the experiment (such as professional titles, laboratories, statistics), and amusing sidelights. The important material, which I underlined, is almost randomly spaced and quite disconnected — a few words here and a few words there. The rewritten sentences draw together information from scattered statements in the original. The last sentence of the rewrite, for example, brings together almost equal components from the beginning, middle, and end of the original paragraph. Though many of the original words remain, several sentences are restructured around the scientifically important material instead of human activities. The shift in style from the concrete dramatic mode to the abstract scientific mode makes less exciting reading but brings out the underlying ideas more prominently and more efficiently.

III.   Précis

Précis is the French word for "precise" or "exact." The shortened version must still give a precise picture of the original, as though it were an exact miniature. The proportions, order, and relationships of the parts must remain the same. Think of a large photograph reduced to wallet size: in a relative sense all the parts remain the same with only the scale changed.

Principle III.

Retain the order, relative proportions, and relationships of parts of the original. The logic, development, and argument — although all shortened — must retain their essential shapes.

Method III.   Miniaturization

Read the passage several times for full understanding. Then restate each paragraph in one or two sentences. If the paragraphs are not roughly the same length, combine short paragraphs. Pay particular attention to the transitions and connections between sentences so that your statements will be in the same relationship as the original. Keeping the same order of statements, group the rewritten sentences in paragraphs to combine several related paragraphs of the original.

Where the arrangement, logical development, and balance of parts of the argument are important, the précis will most accurately reflect the shape of the original. Generally this method is most appropriate for more complex and subtly argued originals. Again you will benefit most if you attempt a précis of the passage below before reading the sample précis and the discussion that follow.

THE PSYCHOLOGY OF TIREDNESS[3]

We have already discussed sleep deprivation, and this has taught us something about the functions of sleep; but sleep deprivation is an artificial, stressful condition, occurring in a complex social-experimental setting. In many human sleep-deprivation situations the subject has a desire to perform well; especially if he is in a group, there is an ésprit de corps that can produce good performance in spite of sleep deprivation. This is particularly true in laboratory sleep-deprivation experiments, where the subject is challenged, mobilizes his defenses, and has a "set" to perform well. When sleep deprivation is used in a different setting, for instance as part of a "marathon" group dynamics session, the set is rather to regress and to become more "open"; here very different results are found. All behavioral sleep-deprivation results are thus heavily influenced by the setting and expectations.

I will now turn to a related situation which is closer to our everyday experience — simple tiredness. By tiredness I do not mean the fatigue after exercise, from which one recovers merely by lying down without sleeping, but the tiredness at the end of a day, apparently reversible only by sleep. One approach to the functions of sleep is to examine carefully the state of tiredness and to determine what characteristics or structures of the mind appear to wear out during the day and to need restoration by sleep. A study of what happens during a day as one becomes increasingly tired suffers from none of the above problems connected with experimental sleep deprivation; on the other hand, tiredness might be expected to produce less marked or obvious changes than prolonged sleep deprivation.

It is surprising how little has been written that can be useful to us here. Although a number of books and articles exist apparently dealing with tiredness or fatigue, they usually consider the muscular aspects and say almost nothing about the psychology of tiredness. Nonethe-

[3]From Ernest L. Hartmann, *The Functions of Sleep,* pp. 123–127. Copyright © 1973 by Yale University Press. Used by permission.

less, it is perfectly obvious both from our own subjective experience and from observation of other persons, especially children, that considerable changes in psychological functioning are produced by tiredness, and these are what we shall examine here.

This chapter necessarily will be clinical and somewhat impressionistic, and findings will be conceptualized in psychiatric and psychoanalytic terms. What I will discuss here is based on experience with patients in psychotherapy and psychoanalysis, several hundred interviews with normal and abnormal sleepers in various sleep studies, observation of children, and introspection. The chief problem lies in attempting to extricate constant themes from the changing, variegated clinical material, for the effects of tiredness clearly depend to a great extent on the background mental characteristics of the person, as well as on his social and physical environment.

Nonetheless, it appears to me that two patterns or "syndromes" of tiredness can be identified. They are seldom present in pure form, and not everyone reports both types, but a large number of individuals, when they stop to think about it, can pick out these two very different characteristic sorts of tiredness in themselves. One is the tiredness that comes after a day of purely physical activity, such as a day of skiing or physical work. This could be called physical tiredness or simple tiredness and is associated usually with a relaxed feeling in the musculature, including the facial and head muscles, and very seldom with any tightness or headaches. It is usually described affectively as either pleasant or neutral and is not associated with any characteristic psychic changes: people find it difficult to say that their mental functioning was altered in this kind of tiredness. In children my impression is that this physical tiredness is associated with relaxation and with rapid sleep onset without fuss or bother.

The second kind of tiredness, which we might call mental tiredness, is reported more frequently after a long day of intellectual or emotional and intellectual work. This tiredness, with which most of us are all too familiar, is often accompanied by tension or tightness of the muscles, especially muscles of the face and head; and it is usually described with a negative tone — it is unpleasant or at best neutral. It sometimes has the paradoxical effect of making it hard to fall asleep. Associated with this sort of tiredness is an obvious lack of energy or unwillingness to try anything new; irritability and anger are also prominent. One feels uncomfortable and on edge in social interactions and wants to be left alone in an undemanding situation. One tends to read easy material and to lapse into wish-fulfilling daydreams.

The following are some of the words and phrases people have used in describing themselves, their friends, or their children at times when I believe they are discussing this second kind of tiredness: "cranky, impatient, selfish, dissatisfied, feel cuddly, want support, think loosely, sensuous, crying, stubborn, loss of energy, quick to anger, depressed, unaccepting, less sense of power, less self-confidence, more babyish, hate to be disturbed, don't want to think, can't think in a concentrated fashion, want to read easy material, I want what I want when I want it, want to be patted, less superego, less idealistic, more grabby, more selfish, very aggressive, hard to control, perseverates, repeats the same phrases or actions, temper tantrums, refuses to get to sleep although very tired, unwilling to act, less feeling of freedom, poor social functioning, poor adaptation, more denial of painful reality, distractible, hard to keep attention centered, hard to stick to one subject for long, unable to change mind, a little paranoid, less need to achieve, less control, less integration."

The above are very general effects of this sort of tiredness. The exact effects obviously vary with the individual's personality structure. In some persons with a tendency toward depression, increasing depression is characteristic of tiredness, and they may even go to sleep to avoid depression. For others (especially certain patients with sleep-onset insomnia) the great problem in becoming tired is the feeling of losing control, losing one's normal ways of dealing with sexual and especially aggressive impulses.

Sample Précis

The effects of artificial sleep deprivation change with the social setting and the motivation of the subjects; therefore, the general applicability of laboratory experiments is limited. However, effects of the more familiar end-of-the-day tiredness can be studied in a more everyday setting, although the effects will probably not be so pronounced. Despite the obvious psychological changes produced by tiredness, little has been published on the subject.

The following account of tiredness, generalized from clinical experience and interviews, is necessarily impressionistic and relies upon psychological concepts. Two patterns of tiredness emerge from individual reports, although rarely in pure form: The first, physical tiredness, produced by purely physical activity, is associated with a pleasant relaxation of musculature — without tightness, headache, or psychic changes; in children it easily leads to sleep. The second, mental tiredness, occurring usually after long intellectual and possibly emotional work, is associated with unpleasant tightness of muscles (especially of the head and face), difficulty in falling asleep, irritability, lack of energy, desire to withdraw, and daydreaming. People describe themselves and others with this second kind of tiredness in terms of antisocial feelings, psychological discomfort, and loss of mental will and ability. These general effects of mental tiredness do, however, vary with the structure of individual personalities.

Thought Process for Précis

Each paragraph of the original qualifies the previous one and leads in a new direction, and an accurate précis must reflect all these turnings of thought. At the beginning of the passage, the limits of deprivation experiments point to the need for more naturalistic tiredness studies, but then the lack of these studies is decried. The opening three paragraphs preface the author's own observations and are, therefore, rewritten into one paragraph in the précis. The second paragraph of the précis develops the author's scheme of two types of tiredness, but only after he has made an opening apology. The comparison between the two types of tiredness presented in two paragraphs of parallel structure in the original is reflected in two sentences of parallel structure in the précis. The author's clearly greater interest in psychological tiredness leads to two further paragraphs in the original. His emphasis is reflected in the précis by additional sentences on the second type of tiredness.

The many turnings of the original require a reliance on transitional words in the précis to tie the different sentences into proper relationship (such as *however, though*). Because each sentence of the précis must often capture the argument of an entire paragraph, much subordination, qualification, modification, and parallelism occur within sentences. An argument as qualified and well developed as the one in this passage needs the *completeness* offered by miniaturization (précis) rather than the essential points left by deletion (summary) or the bare framework unearthed by selection (abstract).

Developing Skills

The sample summaries in this chapter are about one-quarter the length of the full versions; however, the relative length of any summary is not a fixed proportion. The compactness of the style of the original, the compactness of the summary writer's style, and the purpose of the summary all help determine how short the summary will be.

If the original is densely written (that is, much information is presented in few words), then making the summary too short may destroy the integrity of the ideas communicated. If the original contains subtle relationships, complex sentences, difficult concepts, and relatively few details and examples, then it is very hard to eliminate many words and still maintain the sense of the original. On the other hand, if an author introduces only one idea to a page, repeats that idea in different ways, gives many similar examples, and relies on simple sentences that present only one or two bits of information, then the summary can eliminate much without distortion or oversimplification.

The second factor, the tightness of language in the summary, is a matter of skill and practice. Certain techniques of combining sentences, choosing words, and tightening phrases, described in Chapter 9, help increase the amount and subtlety of information you can present in a limited space while still preserving the clarity of the original. Of course, if you combine too much without keeping the lines of meaning and sentence structure absolutely clear, you may wind up with word salad instead of intelligible prose. Particularly abstract and conceptual language may become confusing in too densely written passages, even if your writing is precise and without ambiguity. Compactness in writing must, therefore, be practiced in moderation, keeping the balance between density of meaning and ease of reading. Often a clear, simple statement is the most compact.

Summaries Serve Different Purposes

How you will eventually use the summary will then determine what is important and what is unimportant to include. The relative distinction between major and minor pieces of information depends very much on the interests of the anticipated readers of your summary.

If the purpose of the summary is to give only a general idea of what is in the original — so that the reader can decide whether or not to read the full version — then the summary can be quite spare, even less than one percent of the original. Some professional journals are simply collections of short abstracts of work published in other specialized journals. Journals such as *Research in Education, Biological Abstracts,* and *Economic Abstracts* help keep professionals aware of new work in their fields; however, to obtain substantive information, the researcher must turn to the original. A typical professional abstract might contain bibliographical information, the major thesis or findings, and a suggestion of the method or the argument, as in the following example from *Psychological Abstracts.*

7244. **Webb, W. B. & Agnew, H. W.** (U Florida) **Are we chronically sleep deprived?** *Bulletin of the Psychonomic Society,* 1975 (Jul), Vol 6(1), 47–48. — Studied the sleep of 16 healthy males (mean

> **How you will eventually use the summary will then determine what is important and what is unimportant to include. The relative distinction between major and minor pieces of information depends very much on the interests of the anticipated readers of your summary.**

age 21.7 yrs) for 4 consecutive nights in the laboratory using all night EEG. For the 1st 3 nights, Ss retired for sleep at 11:00 PM and were aroused in the morning at 7:00 AM. On the 4th night, Ss retired at 11:00 PM and were allowed to sleep in the morning until they awakened spontaneously. The ad lib sleep night resulted in 126 min more sleep than was found on the 3rd night of controlled sleep. Results suggest the hypothesis that living in contemporary society produces a state of chronic sleep deprivation in humans.[4]

The other extreme is the summary that is so detailed the reader can get all necessary information without reference to the original. In government and business, higher level officials who have too many responsibilities and too little time may make important decisions on the basis of summaries of reports and background documents. Subordinates who sift through the volumes of original material to prepare such summaries must select all the information that a manager might find useful in making the decision. The informative summary is, in fact, a set part of official reports so that readers can get to the essential findings without having to wade through all the evidence.

On the more popular level, such condensations of best sellers as those published by *Reader's Digest* provide readers without the patience to read full books a semblance of the originals — although subtlety, style, characterization, and other literary qualities frequently suffer.

In the middle length are those summaries for various references purposes. A book tracing the development of economic thought might give a few pages to the summary of Adam Smith's *Wealth of Nations* to introduce the reader to that economist's ideas. Books like *Masterplots,* which summarizes the plots of famous plays and novels, serve to refresh readers' memories about books read long ago as well as to help new readers through the more difficult original. The various kinds of study

---

[4]*Psychological Abstracts,* 59 (1975) 7244, p. 755.

> When you are incorporating a summary into your own
> writing, remember that you should only summarize as
> much of the original text as is necessary to advance your
> own argument; do not let the summary overwhelm the
> direction of your own writing.

guides and pamphlets you may be familiar with also serve this last function: they are only useful to help you through the original but cannot
stand in place of the full work.

When to Summarize

The most frequent and most important use of summary is to
refer to another writer's work in the course of a new and original essay.
Summary has the advantage over paraphrase in allowing the writer to
pick out and focus on only those aspects of the original that are most
relevant to the new points being made. The flexibility of wording in a
summary also allows the writer to fit it in smoothly with his or her
original, ongoing statements.

When you are incorporating a summary into your own statement, it is
important to remember that you should only summarize as much of the
original text as is necessary to advance your own argument; do not let the
summary overwhelm the direction of your own writing. A fuller discussion of the relative merits and appropriateness of each form of reference
— summary, paraphrase, quotation, and name — can be found on pages
331 to 334.

Freud's Use of Summary

The quotation below from Sigmund Freud's *The Interpretation
of Dreams* presents one of the prominent summaries of the past century. It
demonstrates how a summary can be used to advance a new idea and
how, at the same time, the summary is shaped by the new writer's
specific interests. In the chapter "The Material and Sources of Dreams,"
Freud explores the conflicts that give rise to typical dreams. In discussing
dreams about the death of a much-loved relative, Freud considers how
infantile attraction to the parent of the opposite sex leads to competition

with the same-sex parent and a desire to replace that same-sex parent.
The tension created by the attraction and competition, if not resolved,
may lead to adult neurosis and may become the material of dreams.
Finding these same tensions expressed in the Greek myth of Oedipus,
Freud then summarizes the story as it appears in Sophocles' play, *Oedipus
Rex*.

> Oedipus, son of Laïus, King of Thebes, and of Jocasta, was
> exposed as an infant because an oracle had warned Laïus that the still
> unborn child would be his father's murderer. The child was rescued,
> and grew up as a prince in an alien court, until, in doubts as to his
> origin, he too questioned the oracle and was warned to avoid his home
> since he was destined to murder his father and take his mother in
> marriage. On the road leading away from what he believed was his
> home, he met King Laïus and slew him in a sudden quarrel. He came
> next to Thebes and solved the riddle set him by the Sphinx who barred
> his way. Out of gratitude the Thebans made him their king and gave him
> Jocasta's hand in marriage. He reigned long in peace and honour, and
> she who, unknown to him, was his mother bore him two sons and two
> daughters. Then at last a plague broke out and the Thebans made
> enquiry once more of the oracle. It is at this point that Sophocles'
> tragedy opens. The messengers bring back the reply that the plague will
> cease when the murderer of Laïus has been driven from the land.
>
> But he, where is he? Where shall now be read
> The fading record of this ancient guilt?
>
> The action of the play consists in nothing other than the process of
> revealing, with cunning delays and ever-mounting excitement — a proc-
> ess that can be likened to the work of a psycho-analysis — that
> Oedipus himself is the murderer of Laïus, but further that he is the son
> of the murdered man and of Jocasta. Appalled at the abomination
> which he has unwittingly perpetrated, Oedipus blinds himself and for-
> sakes his home. The oracle has been fulfilled.[5]

The summary is followed by a detailed analysis of the themes of the
play, as Freud sees them, and leads to the first formulation of the now
famous *Oedipus complex*. Although the story he summarized eventually
gave its name to a major concept, the summary was originally just a tool,
a way of providing an example to be analyzed, buried in among other·
examples and other ideas.

---

[5]From *The Interpretation of Dreams* by Sigmund Freud, translated from the German and edited by
James Strachey, pp. 294–295. Published in the United States by Basic Books, Inc., Publishers, New York,
by arrangement with George Allen & Unwin Ltd., and the Hogarth Press, London. Published elsewhere
by George Allen & Unwin, Ltd.

Freud's summary of the play does cover all the major actions and adds nothing; however, the psychologist's interests — as defined by the surrounding chapter — cause him to concentrate on certain aspects of the play: "ancient guilt," parentage, good intentions, unavoidable destiny, and the sense of abomination. Other critical commentators, moved by different concerns, claim Freud distorted the play and emphasize other aspects — such as the role of kingship, Oedipus's pride in thinking he could avoid fate, or Sophocles' detective-style unraveling of the plot. These dimensions are also in the play but are considered more significant by those interested in character, political philosophy, Greek ethics, and dramatic craftsmanship. Freud's actual purpose was to present underlying causes for dream stories, and that is why he summarized the story as he did.

Notice that in introducing the quotation from Freud, I used a brief summary of his surrounding chapter to give background material and to explain how Freud integrates *his* summary into his discussion. My summary of Freud's chapter was, of course, shaped by the point I was making about the use of summary.

Writing Assignments

1. Using the deletion method, summarize this passage, titled "Snoring," again taken from *Sleep: Our Unknown Life* by Richard Deming.[6]

In 1950 Cyrus H. Johnston of Richmond, Missouri, received a patent on a device to prevent snoring. It was a metal yoke that strapped around the neck and prevented the mouth from opening during sleep, thereby forcing the sleeper to breathe through his nose.

Mr. Johnston's patent was the 2,528,370th granted by the United States Patent Office since the present system of issuing patents was started in 1836. It was the 275th issued for a device to stop snoring.

Since then the number of patented inventions to stop snoring has climbed past 300. They include everything from Mr. Johnston's yoke to a pajama top with a rubber ball sewn into the middle of the back, making it uncomfortable to sleep on the back. The premise is that snoring is most common in that position. A less cruel device designed to accomplish the same thing is a tiny record player that fits in the pajama-top pocket. If the sleeper rolls onto his back, it automatically

[6]Reprinted by permission of Elsevier/Nelson Books from the book *Sleep: Our Unknown Life*, pp. 116–119. Copyright © 1972 by Richard Deming.

turns on and murmurs in the recorded voice of the snorer's spouse, "Roll over, darling."

A St. Louis woman whose husband tried out the device wrote about it to Abigail Van Buren, whose daily column of advice, *Dear Abby,* appears in hundreds of newspapers across the country. The contraption worked, she reported, but not exactly the way it was intended to. The recording never made her husband roll over, but it did awaken her, whereupon she would yell, "Dammit, shut up!" and he would.

Experimenters estimate that about one out of four adults snores at least occasionally, and that one out of eight is a regular snorer. More men than women snore, but the habit is by no means strictly a male eccentricity. In the newspaper comics, of course, only husbands snore, but in many real-life marriages either both parties snore, or the wife is the only offender.

The usual cause of snoring is simply that either the soft palate or that little tonguelike appendage at the rear of the throat called the uvula is too close to the lining of the throat, or perhaps both are. Every time the mouth gapes open, the throat passage narrows, and air, passing over these tissues during breathing, causes them to vibrate. The effect is similar to that of blowing air through the mouthpiece of a reed instrument. No presently accepted surgery can correct this condition. In such cases the only way to stop snoring is to wear some device to keep the mouth closed. The usual one prescribed by doctors, even since Mr. Cyrus Johnston's invention, is the Thomas collar. This padded collar stretches the neck and keeps it unmobile while a patient is recovering from a neck injury. Because it pushes up against the chin, it tends to keep the mouth closed while the wearer is sleeping.

The Thomas collar is hardly a comfortable thing to sleep in, though. There are two more practical and comfortable ways to solve the snoring problem. The first, applicable when only one partner in a marriage is a snorer, is to stagger bedtimes slightly so that the nonsnorer is already asleep when the snorer climbs into bed. The second, for couples who both snore, is to wear earplugs.

2. Using the selection method, write an abstract of this second passage from *Some Must Watch While Some Must Sleep* by William C. Dement.[7]

The creative and problem-solving functions of dreams have been almost totally ignored by scientific investigators. The subject was approached as early as 1892 by Child, who attempted to gather some

[7]Selection is reprinted from *Some Must Watch While Some Must Sleep* by William C. Dement, pp. 98–99, with permission of W. W. Norton & Company, Inc. Copyright © 1972, 1974, 1976 by William C. Dement. Originally published as part of The Portable Stanford series, Stanford Alumni Association, Stanford, California.

statistics. In a questionnaire distributed to 151 male and forty-nine female college students, he asked: "During sleep have you ever pursued a logically connected train of thought upon some topic or problem in which you have reached some conclusion, and the steps and conclusion of which you remembered upon awakening?" Of 186 students who responded to this question, sixty-two or 33.3 percent answered in the affirmative. Some of the examples given were a chess game played in a dream, an algebra problem solved, a bookkeeping error found, and a translation of Virgil accomplished.

At Stanford we explored the phenomenon of problem solving in dreams through a series of problem-solving experiments involving 500 undergraduate students in three consecutive class meetings. Each student was given a copy of a problem and an accompanying questionnaire and instructed not to look at the problem until fifteen minutes before he went to bed that night. Before going to bed the student was to spend exactly fifteen minutes in an attempt to solve the problem. In the morning he was supposed to write on the questionnaire any dream recalled from the previous night. If the problem had not been solved, the student was supposed to work on it for another fifteen minutes in the morning. The student's solution to the problem was entered on the questionnaire, which was then returned to the instructor to be scored by several volunteers who were looking for solutions that could be attributed to dreams. The students were instructed not to discuss the problem among themselves until the next class meeting. Here are the three problems and their solutions:

Problem 1: The letters O, T, T, F, F . . . form the beginning of an infinite sequence. Find a simple rule for determining any or all successive letters. According to your rule, what would be the next two letters of the sequence?
Solution 1: The next two letters in the sequence are S, S. The letters represent the first letters used in spelling out the numerical sequence, "One, Two, Three, Four, Five, Six, Seven, etc."
Problem 2: Consider the letters H, I, J, K, L, M, N, O. The solution to this problem is one word. What is this word?
Solution 2: The solution is the word "water" derived from the chemical formula H_2O or H-to-O as given in the problem.
Problem 3: The numbers 8, 5, 4, 9, 1, 7, 6, 3, 2 form a sequence. How are these numbers ordered?
Solution 3: The numbers, if spelled out, are ordered alphabetically.

The total response represented 1,148 attempts at problem solving. Using a rather intricate scoring system, we judged that eighty-seven dreams were related to the problem, fifty-three directly and thirty-four indirectly. If a solution was presented in the dream, the judges scored it as correct or incorrect, whether or not the subject recognized it as such. The correct solution appeared only nine times — all in the first experiment. On two of these occasions, however, the solution that appeared in the dream had already been obtained by the subject during the fifteen minutes before bed. Of the 1,148 attempts, therefore, the problem was solved in a dream on only seven occasions.

The following dream report contained one of these solutions:

"I was standing in an art gallery looking at the paintings on the wall. As I walked down the hall, I began to count the paintings — one, two, three, four, five. But as I came to the sixth and seventh, the paintings had been ripped from their frames! I stared at the empty frames with a peculiar feeling that some mystery was about to be solved. Suddenly I realized that the sixth and seventh spaces were the solution to the problem!"

3. Using the miniaturization method, write a précis of this second passage from *The Functions of Sleep* by Ernest L. Hartmann.[8]

In the studies described in chapter 5 we have demonstrated psychological differences between long and short sleepers, and we have at least associated different personalities with different lengths of sleep; however, it must be kept in mind that we have recorded an *association,* but have not so far established a causal relationship. It may be that a certain personality or life-style requires more sleep; or, on the other hand, it may be that obtaining more sleep produces certain personality or life-style characteristics; or both could be completely independent effects of some third cause. A study of variable sleepers can help to differentiate between these possibilities, since we can examine behavioral-psychological changes and sleep changes in their natural time course.

We have completed two formal studies on variable sleepers and, in addition, I have interviewed a large number of variable sleepers more informally. The two studies each involved sending a questionnaire to a population of 1,000 to 2,000 persons. In the first study the population was equally distributed between faculty, staff, and students at a large urban university. The second sample was chosen from voter registration lists in the three urban and suburban communities.

After some preliminary questions about age, habitual sleep time, and so on, each subject was first asked to describe in his own words any period when his sleep requirement was greater or less than usual; then some specific periods or events were listed, and he was asked whether such periods or events had any effect on his sleep requirement. About one-third of the subjects who completed the questionnaires were

---

[8]From Ernest L. Hartmann, *The Functions of Sleep*, pp. 71–75. Copyright © 1973 by Yale University Press. Used by permission.

further interviewed in person or by telephone so that we could clarify their answers and also gain further insight into the kinds of periods they were talking about. The problem that required most clarification involved a differentiation, when the subject indicated less sleep need under certain conditions, as to whether he really meant that he got along normally on a reduced amount of sleep, or whether he had misunderstood the question and was actually saying that he had difficulty sleeping — insomnia — at these times. In most cases we were able to make this differentiation quite accurately, and we kept only the answers of the subjects who clearly felt that their *sleep requirement* was decreased. (If the subject's answers, or the answers plus the interviews, made it clear that at certain times he slept less but that this was a matter of insomnia — inability to get the sleep he wanted — he was of course not considered to have a decreased requirement for sleep at such times, since his sleep requirement could not be estimated). In the case of a report of *increased* sleep need, we had to exclude subjects who were merely saying they "got away from things" by spending a lot of time in bed (not necessarily sleeping). This line of demarcation was occasionally a thin one.

Between the two studies, a total of 501 usable responses were obtained. . . . On any given question a large proportion of normal individuals do not notice in themselves a clear difference in sleep requirement. However, 70% of the respondents noticed a change in sleep requirement under at least one of the conditions we specified. It is clear from the data that for most of those who did notice changes, sleep requirement increased at times associated with stress, depression, or change in occupation and at times characterized by increased mental, physical, or emotional work. Decreased sleep need was associated with "times when everything is going well" or involvement in work that the subject found pleasant. The changes in the direction of increased sleep with stress, change, or depression usually were found at times when there was a focus *inward,* on the self. An outward focus, on work, for instance, was often associated with decreased sleep need. Thus increased mental activity was usually related to increased sleep need, but a few persons clearly described *decreased* need at such times; it turned out they were speaking of pleasant and intensely involving work, such as "writing an interesting thesis."

4. Write short abstracts (roughly twenty-five words each) of three papers you have written for previous courses. The abstracts are to inform other members of the class of the kinds of interests and ideas you have.

5. Imagine that one of your teachers has announced a quiz on a five-page section from the textbook for the next day. That evening you receive a phone call from a close friend and classmate who is out of town playing with a rock band. You tell your friend about the test, but he has left the textbook home and will not be returning until fifteen minutes before the next class. As a good friend, you offer to meet him before class with a summary. Using a five-page section of any textbook from your current courses, prepare such a summary.

6. For an appropriate college course, rewrite the children's story "The Three Little Pigs" in summary form so that the summary might serve as an example of one of the following themes:

a. In times of need, one should rely on family members to provide shelter and help.

b. An obsessive desire for security is an appropriate response to a threatening world.

c. The destructive alienation of the villain-type of personality only leads to further isolation, frustration, and hatred for the world.

3

Reacting to Your Reading: Marginal Notes, the Reading Journal, and the Informal Essay

Preview

When you react to your reading, you start to make a link between the ideas suggested by the page and what happens in your mind — your responses. This link is essential for any kind of intellectual work. Because reactions pass so quickly, turning your responses into words will help you hold on to them. Both writing notes in the margins of your books and keeping a reading journal will help you remember and develop your thoughts about reading. The *informal essay of response* allows you to explore at length your most intriguing reactions.

The Reader's Active Role

When Freud compares the process of dramatic disclosures in *Oedipus Rex* "to the process of psychotherapy," he makes a link between his experience with patients and his reading. The psychiatrist's mind links his daily experience of psychotherapy with the script of a Greek play written twenty-five hundred years earlier to produce a new thought. This act of intellectual assimilation — reading as part of thinking — is the place where minds meet and intellectual exchange begins. Unless the ideas of writers stimulate the thoughts of their readers, communication of ideas would have little point. Ideas, nonetheless, can be and are shared through reading.

We need not, however, accept a thought easily, just because somebody once wrote it and convinced a publisher to print it in a book. For one thing, books on the same subject may disagree, as discussed in Chapter 7; sometimes books simply contradict reality, as shown in Chapter 6; and some books are out to manipulate the reader, as described in Chapter 4. Even if books were always right, always in agreement, and always respectful of the reader's independent judgment, reading still should not be swallowed whole and undigested, for then we would only be accepting sentences — collections of words and punctuation — and not evaluating the writer's thoughts, which might be of personal significance to us. Unless we begin to see how the printed words fit in with everything else we think and know, our superficial reading leads only to limited interest and quick forgetting.

Personal Meaning

The only way that your reading will have bite — that is, will affect and stay with you — is for you to react. By responding actively, you can start to see what you actually think about the ideas you read and how these ideas relate to the questions that you find personally important. The previous chapters of this book have cautioned you to hold such reaction in check until you understand what is written, but once you know the meaning of the printed word, you have to ask yourself in many forms: "What do I think about this idea? Is this writer right or wrong? Do I agree or disagree? How does this idea relate to my ideas and experience?"

At times the personal importance of particular books moves us with unquestionable force. We know immediately when those books speak to our condition: while in prison, Malcolm X began to read history books and started to grasp the process of racial oppression at work. As he writes in his *Autobiography*, these volumes provided what he was looking for: "Ten guards and the warden couldn't have torn me out of those books." Information directly applicable to our personal situation can excite our minds in ways that may have the strength of a religious conversion.

More frequently, we must make efforts to grasp the book before it will excite us, as Malcolm X was excited. The initial impetus that leads us to read a particular book may be unformed and tentative; glimmers of thoughts may be forgotten as our eyes move on to the next sentence, to the next paragraph, to the next chapter. A nagging desire to get up for another cup of coffee or anxiety about an upcoming exam may prevent us from reacting fully to the words in front of us. Without conscious effort to record, sort out, and develop full responses to reading, the ideas quickly fade to the back of the mind; memories of the book soon settle into the vague categories of interesting or dull.

Not paying attention to your personal reactions may lead you to feel disconnected from the communication going on — as though some other people were arguing about something that you had no interest in. Words parade past the eyes and boredom settles in the mind. You have a case of pseudo-boredom. Genuine boredom occurs when you are reading material you already know only too well; nothing new appears to occupy the mind. Pseudo-boredom comes when you feel you just cannot be bothered to figure out what all the new information and ideas mean; the mind backs away from a real and demanding occupation. The cure for real boredom is to find a more advanced book on the subject; the only cure for pseudo-boredom is to become fully and personally involved in the book already in front of you. By recording and developing your reactions and thoughts, you can talk back at the book and consider yourself engaged in conversation with the author. Although the consecutively numbered pages of the book keep coming past you in a straight line, you can turn the thoughts expressed on them in your own direction. Once you are involved, the boredom will vanish.

First Reactions into Words

The way to begin sorting your first reactions to your reading is to put them in words — either by talking or by writing. The problem is to find someone you can trust with these tangled, contradictory, half-formed thoughts. Struggling to find words to express your dim intuitions, you may not be convinced of the correctness of whatever is crossing your mind. To whom can you speak or write without committing yourself permanently to your unconnected fragments of reactions and your rambling journeys to nowhere? Sometimes a friend will let you talk out your ideas without making you defend every tentative assumption, which you yourself might reject the next moment, but a friend with sufficient patience to hear out all the most trivial ramblings that occur during reading is a rare find.

Mark Twain's letters to the novelist William Dean Howells reveal such a friendship. Twain trusted Howells enough to change his opinions from one sentence to the next in the most informal manner. In the following passage, Twain sorts out his opinion about a new book by Bret Harte, explaining how he shifted his opinion of Harte's work on a second reading.

Dear Howells —

. . . Chatto[1] sent me Harte's[2] new book of Sketches, the other day, ("An Heiress of Red Dog," etc). I have read it twice — the first time through tears of rage over the fellow's inborn hypocrisy & snobbishness, his apprentice-art, his artificialities, his mannerisms, his pet phrases, (such as the frequent "I regret to say,") — his laboriously acquired ignorance, & his jejune anxiety to display it. O, my God! He rings in *Strasse*[3] when street would answer every purpose, and *Bahnhof*[4] when it carries no sharper significance to the reader than "station" would; he peppers in his seven little French words (you can find them in all his sketches, for he learned them in California 14 years ago,) . . . The struggle after the pathetic is more pathetic than the pathos itself; if he were to write about an Orphan Princess who lost a Peanut he would feel obliged to try to make somebody snuffle over it.

The second time I read the book I saw a most decided brightness on every page of it — & here & there evidences of genius. I saw enough to make me think, "Well, if this slovenly shoemaker-work is able to command the applause of three or four nations, what *mightn't* this ass accomplish if he would do his work honestly & with pains?" If I ever get my tedious book finished, I mean to weed out some of my prejudices & write an article on "Bret Harte as an Artist" — & print it if it will not be unfair to print it without signature.[5]

By the end of the passage, Twain has reversed his opinion about Harte: Twain admits grudgingly that Harte does show some "evidences

[1]Chatto — Chatto & Windus, a London publishing company
[2]Harte — Bret Harte (1836–1902) wrote about the American West
[3]*Strasse* — German for *street*
[4]*Bahnhof* — German for *station*
[5]From Samuel Clemens, *Selected Mark Twain — Howells Letters* (Cambridge, Mass.: Harvard University Press, 1967), pp. 130–131. Copyright © 1960, 1967 by the Mark Twain Company. Reprinted by permission.

of genius." Twain, however, would only make such an admission to his close friend Howells, for he still considers Harte too craftless to deserve even his grudging public endorsement. If he ever does publish his ideas on Harte, Twain does not want to sign his name to the article.

Marginal Annotations: A Running Account of Your Thoughts

Even the best of friends will not be by your elbow every time you read. A more realistic practice is to write down your thoughts, reactions, and questions as they occur to you in the margin of your book — next to the passage that triggered the response. Once you overcome your inhibitions about writing in books that you may have learned from parents defending themselves against your scribbling period, marginal comments flow almost naturally from the desire to answer the writer back. The conversation starts to come alive. In grade school and high school, your teachers also warned you against writing in the textbooks that the school had loaned you. Even now, when using library books and other borrowed material, you should indulge the urge to comment only in a separate notebook or on a handy paper napkin. If you own the book, show that it is really yours by leaving your thoughts in it. When you reread the book at a later date, you will know what you liked and what you didn't, what reminded you of a personal experience, and which ideas stimulated your interest and curiosity. Or if you weren't sure just what you thought back then, you can sort out the many directions of your earlier thoughts when you return for a second look.

Lord Macaulay, the historian, writing during the middle of the nineteenth century, was in the habit of annotating his books, as the more recent historian George Trevelyan describes:

> His favorite volumes are illustrated and enlivened by innumerable entries, of which none are prolix, pointless, or dull; while interest and admiration are expressed by lines drawn down sides of the text, — and even by double lines, for whole pages together . . .[6]

In a typical example, Macaulay annotated a general comment by Cicero, in his essay *On Duty:* "Exquisitely written, graceful, calm, luminous and full of interest; but the Epicurean theory of morals is hardly deserving of refutation." Macaulay continues with acid comments, like the following,

---

[6]Lord Macaulay, *Marginal Notes*, ed. George Trevelyan (London: Longmans, Green, 1907), p. 9.

throughout the margins: "trashy Sophistry, admirably explained" and "beautifully lucid, though the system is excessively absurd." At one point Macaulay cites a very personal example: "Does not a man feel grief when he sends his favorite son to India?"[7] Macaulay mixed personal and philosophic comments throughout the margins of many of his books.

Annotate to Clarify

With pencil in hand, ready to comment on your reading, you may find you want to make two different kinds of remarks: some to help you understand the meaning of the text more fully and others to express your own reactions, evaluations, and associations. Although annotation works best with no rules — the whole trick is to feel free to jot down whatever comes to mind — it helps to keep the two kinds of comments separated. My own practice is to put comments on the meaning in the narrower margin near the book's spine and to leave all the other margins — the wider side, top, and bottom — for reactions.

You may already use annotations for meaning as a study technique. Underlining key statements, numbering supporting arguments, defining unusual words, and paraphrasing difficult passages help you approach the surface meaning of a text. But annotations can go more deeply to establish the connections and logic of the entire selection. In the margin you can explicitly state underlying assumptions of the text, that is, ideas only indirectly suggested by the original. Marginal comments can provide an overview of where the argument has come from and where it is going to; they can bring out the structure of the original as well as restate the obvious meaning of the words. Where the meaning of words or structure is unclear, a well-placed question mark — even better, a purposeful question — will remind you of what is puzzling.

Annotate to Evaluate

On the second level of annotation, your thoughts interact with the ideas suggested by the text. Feel free to express the most outrageous of opinions in the most informal way. Since for the most part no one but you will see these comments, allow yourself freedom: wander from the point, contradict yourself, speculate without substantive support, be irreverent, and express extreme opinions. All these are acceptable

[7]Macaulay, p. 40.

> **Since for the most part no one but you will see these marginal comments, allow yourself freedom: wander from the point, contradict yourself, speculate without substantive support, be irreverent, and express extreme opinions.**

indulgences in marginal notes. Any type of phrase, mark, smudge, or sign that conveys your attitude is legitimate. With this freedom — with this pleasurable irresponsibility — you will eventually find your own topics, your own things to say. To get you started, however, here are some typical kinds of comments:

ongoing phrases and marks of approval and disapproval — √, *, ???? NO!, not bad, exactly, yeccch, nonsense, right

disagreements — I can't agree because . . . , no, the actual facts are . . .

exceptions — doesn't hold for the case of . . .

counterexamples — isn't case x just the opposite?

supporting examples — exactly what happens in case y

extensions — this could even apply to . . .

discoveries — this explains why . . .

possible implications — Would this mean that . . . ?

personal associations — My uncle acts just like that *or* In student government . . .

reading associations — Z in his book argues the same thing *or* This fits in with what A wrote.

distinctions — But then again it's not like Z's argument because . . .

   It doesn't take long to get in the spirit of annotation; once you are attuned to it, you can throw out all these suggestions and develop comments most appropriate to the way you think. In the Writing Assignments at the end of this chapter, a passage by Cicero has been provided for you to annotate. The passage is about friendship — a subject with which everyone has had direct experience. Probably you will find much that you like and much that you do not like in it. The important thing is to react and put your reactions in writing.

Scholarly Annotation

The annotations discussed so far in this chapter have been for personal use; personal annotations are a way to assert oneself during the reading process. Scholarly annotations, that is, published rather than personal notes, can serve a wider audience by presenting a perspective — interpretive, evaluative, or informational — on a major literary work or on a primary legal or Biblical text. By the use of formal annotation, a second writer can discuss the work of the first, with the words of both appearing on the same page. In the Hebraic tradition, for example, marginal commentary is the main method of theological debate, with as many as eight or ten different sets of marginal annotations by different writers filling up the large margins around a few short lines of the original sacred text. Each commentator presents a consistent interpretation of the holy text, but is often at odds with the other commentators printed on the same page.

In such learned marginal commentary, we can see the seed of the footnote — another device for adding additional information, interpretation, and perspective to the original passage. Well-conceived and carefully written footnotes can be quite informative, lending whole new dimensions to the basic text; they are the place for a second voice to speak, often adding more recent findings and interpretations to the original. In Chapter 10, the theory and practice of the footnote will receive full treatment. At this point, an example of scholarly annotation will show how the annotator lends his wisdom to the original text, even if that text is only a few lines of a children's rhyme. The following, from *The Annotated Mother Goose*, illustrates how the second opinion of footnotes adds to the original.[8]

Sing a Song of Sixpence,[6]
A bag full of Rye,[7]
Four and twenty[8]
Naughty boys,[9]
Bak'd in a Pye.[10]

6. Scholars have seen supposed references to this nursery rhyme in *Twelfth Night — Come on, there is sixpence for you; let's have a song;* and in Beaumont and Fletcher's *Bonduca* (1614) — *Whoa, here's a stir now! Sing a song of sixpence!*
7. *A pocket full of rye* in most later versions. It is possible that "a pocket

[8]Taken from *The Annotated Mother Goose* by William S. & Ceil Baring-Gould, pp. 26–28. Copyright © 1962 by William S. & Ceil Baring-Gould. Used by permission of Clarkson N. Potter, Inc.

full" was once a specific measurement in recipes, as "a tablespoonful of sugar."

8. We shall find that "four and twenty" is one of the numbers most frequently met with in "Mother Goose" rhymes. It is, of course, a "double dozen" and the number 12 is rich in associations, traditions, and superstitions.

9. Later *Four and twenty blackbirds.* Theories about this rhyme abound: the "blackbirds" are the twenty-four hours in a day, "the king" is the sun, and "the queen" is the moon, for example. On the other hand, Katherine Elwes Thomas identified the king as Henry VIII, the queen as Katherine, and the maid as Anne Boleyn; the "blackbirds" were four and twenty manorial deeds baked in a pie — as in "Little Jack Horner" (Rhyme 50). Still another theory holds that this song celebrates the printing of the first English Bible — the "blackbirds" being the letters of the alphabet set in pica type ("baked in a pie").

10. According to Iona and Peter Opie, the editors of *The Oxford Dictionary of Nursery Rhymes,* an Italian cookbook of 1549, translated into English in 1598, actually contains a recipe "to make pies so that birds may be alive in them and flie out when it is cut up." They continue: "This dish is further referred to (1723) by John Nott, cook to the Duke of Bolton, as a practice of former days, the purpose of the birds being to put out the candles and so cause a 'diverting Hurley-Burley amongst the Guests in the Dark.'"

When taken to the extreme, the personality and viewpoint of the commentary writer can become so strong that they overwhelm the meaning of the primary text; Vladimir Nabokov parodies this heavy-handed use of scholarly notes in the novel *Pale Fire.* The novel is in the form of a scholar's footnotes to the poem of his next door neighbor; the demented scholar — who imagines himself the exiled King of Zembla — is so wrapped up in his own fate that the footnotes keep wandering away from the poem to an imagined murder plot against the scholar. But if the marginal commentator takes sufficient care to avoid an obsessive overuse of footnotes, annotation remains one of the most direct ways for readers to develop some perspective and background on a text.

The Reading Journal

At some points your comments may outgrow the limits of the margin. A desire to pursue one thought at length, a need to enlarge on your perception of the reading as a whole, or a need to sort out a number of confusing issues will lead you from an inch of margin to a blank sheet

> **The reading journal works best when it is a regular habit.
> If you waited for the spirit to move you before you pulled
> out the journal, you would not use the notebook very
> often.**

of paper. The reading journal provides the space for more extended ideas
— and particularly for ideas not tied to any one particular passage of
the original.

A reading journal is a diary of your thought processes. After each
session of reading, you simply start writing about your most dominant
or curious impressions, just as in a diary you might review and comment
on the day's most noteworthy events. By its nature a journal will ramble,
for you may have no idea what you are going to say when you begin each
entry. The act of getting words and ideas on the page will help you
discover what it is you want to write about. Since the journal is only for
your own use, you need not worry about shifting the topic, contradicting
yourself, making sense, or being convincing — those weaknesses in your
writing that teachers are always bringing up. Correctness of language
and problems with spelling should not even cross your mind. All that is
important is to put down your first reactions and to continue to explore
them, until you have worked them out fully.

The Reader's Habit

The journal works best when it is a regular habit. If you
waited for the spirit to move you before you pulled out the journal, you
wouldn't use the notebook very often. Set aside fifteen minutes after
every reading assignment (you may wish to limit yourself to one course
or subject at the beginning) for a chance to establish the habit. Some days
you may not get very far with any one idea, but on other days your
thoughts will gain a momentum of their own. When you look back on
what you have just written, you may be surprised to see all you had to
say. To enable you to look back in the journals at a later time, you should
keep all the entries together in a notebook or file folder. You should also
date the entries and identify the book and page numbers to which you are
responding.

Since both journals and marginal annotations are messages written to
yourself, you will get much more out of them if you do read them over

within a day — and again several months later. As a short-term benefit, you will be able to find topics and ideas for assigned essays — as well as the specific supporting evidence. Notice whether you kept returning to one particularly interesting idea or whether you can spot a pattern to your agreements or disagreements with a piece of reading. If you discussed one particular passage of the original at length, that discussion might be the seed of something more extended — a research project. Over a longer period, you will start noticing how the process of your thinking has developed. You will probably be quite surprised by the differences between your first and your most recent entries. Over a long span of time, a reading journal can become an intellectual diary — a record of the development of your ideas.

As with marginal comments, what you write in the journal is up to you; with time you will find the most appropriate ways to express your own interests. No matter what topics or modes of expression you are drawn to, it is important to pursue your line of reasoning to its natural conclusion. Although you may shift away from an uncompleted thought, try to return to it. Take your ideas seriously enough to see where they lead. In the course of developing your ideas, a viewpoint and an attitude will emerge that are yours alone. Tentative ideas will grow in strength to become ideas that you will want to express to others in your essays.

Self-Discovery

Until you become comfortable with the journal, you may be at a loss about how to begin. One warm-up technique is to restate those parts of the reading that most impressed you and then to explain why they made that impression. One student, just learning to use her journal early in the semester, responded to some memorable parts of her reading — Joyce Maynard's "My Secret Life with the Rolling Stones" — to lead into some personal comparisons.[9]

This essay struck a soft spot in me. I was really glad to see that I wasn't the only person who imagined Bob Dylan at 60. I also used to wonder what Jagger would look like sitting in a rocking chair with Bianca singing "I ain't got no satisfaction — no satisfaction . . ." It also reminded me of the first time I had seen "Sticky Fingers." The zipper on the cover grossed me out.

As Joyce Maynard said, the Stones did and do represent the bad guys. Since they look "counterculture," parents associate them with hippies, drugs and other unacceptable things. After re-reading the es-

[9]*New York Times,* 22 June 1975.

say I find that a major difference between my idolization of rock musicians & hers is that while she adored them at 12–13 yrs old, I knew them as a 15–16 yr old. My idealization was post-teenybopper. I really didn't listen to music much before then & I only appreciate music after it has been out for many years, while it is old stuff to most people; I don't have to get re-acquainted with it since I only heard it for the first time. But I suppose it could be nostalgic for someone like Maynard who is older and knew the music as a teenybopper. Maybe that whole feeling of nostalgia made her write this essay. To her the Rolling Stones must be a nostalgic group and when the tour came around she took a moment to remember who she was and where she has gone since that period.

Response to Virginia Woolf

Later in the semester, the same student commented in her journal on Virginia Woolf's essay "Professions of Women."[10] Notice how she moved much more directly into a comparison with a movie she had seen recently.

This has been my favorite essay concerning working & jobs. I quickly compared the dilemma faced by the writer to the confusion encountered by Lillian Hellman in *Julia.* Both were haunted by their inner emotions, which hampered their writing. Women have to overcome years of socialization that stereotype them in their writing, that tell them what are "nice" subjects and what's a "nice" way to write. The idea of purity left them guilty and confused, and they had to overcome this.

Eric Hoffer's Journal

Eric Hoffer, a blue-collar worker turned social theorist, kept a journal of his readings, thoughts, and activities during one year while he was working as a longshoreman and writing another book. He later published the journal under the title *Working and Thinking on the Waterfront: June 1958–May 1959.* In it, the reader can see patterns of thoughts emerging from almost random observations — just as in the student's journal. However, the writing here has been reworked, polished, and edited for publication. In one early entry, Hoffer wanders through many items before he finally finds a topic he wants to pursue.

[10]Virginia Woolf, *The Death of the Moth and Other Essays* (New York: Harcourt Brace Jovanovich, 1942).

JUNE 23[11]

The kink in my back is gone. Yesterday's work did it. The world looks clean and fresh after last night's rain. I have a long list of chores to do, and I am just getting ready to clean my room. Before starting I read the last few pages of *Byzantium.* I cannot tell as yet what I got out of the book. It corrected my view of the Byzantine Empire as a stagnant body. It needs vigor to last a thousand years.

5 P.M. . . . turned to a new travel book by Lord Kinross. This is a continuation of his book on the interior of Asia Minor.

7 P.M. The second Kinross book, so far as I read, is inferior to the first. Since I am in the mood to make it easy for myself I switched to another book — a delightful one. It is a book of letters written by an American woman who lived in Jerusalem 1953–54. It is a warm, sensitive, honest book. My first reaction is: What delightful people Americans are. I ought perhaps to say fine people. And saying this I reflect that I certainly am not an American. Under similar circumstances I would have been neither delightful nor fine. Here she is among total strangers and she does not carp or criticize, or betray the least trace of bad temper. The American's capacity for fraternization is a noble feature, a true foretaste of the brotherhood of man. The book is *Letters from Jerusalem* by Mary Clawson. I shall probably sit up all night reading it.

Note how Hoffer, like our student, interprets his own mood, "I am in the mood to make it easy for myself," and then presents his reactions to a "delightful" new book.

In a number of places, reading leads Hoffer to think about the interpretation of political events. Here the description of certain actions taken by Nikita Krushchev, then the leader of the Soviet Union, leads Hoffer to wonder about the personalities of revolutionaries.

MARCH 4

Five and a half hours on the *Matsonia* at Pier 35. Kolin's gang. Little to do, and a cheerful bunch.

As I was reading about Khrushchev's juvenile shenanigans this morning it struck me that there has been a process of juvenilization going on all over the world for decades. Almost all the leaders of the new or renovated countries have an element of juvenility or even juvenile delinquency in their make-up: Khrushchev, Castro, Sukarno, Nkrumah, Nasser, Sékou Touré — you name them. Arthur Koestler maintains that revolutionaries are perpetual juveniles — that there is

[11]Specified excerpts with deletions from *Working and Thinking on the Waterfront* by Eric Hoffer, pp. 14, 52–53, 133–134, 139, 156. Copyright © 1969 by Eric Hoffer. Reprinted by permission of Harper & Row, Publishers, Inc.

something in them that keeps them from growing up. Now it is possible to see some family likeness between the adolescent who steps out of the warmth of the family into a cold world and knows not how to come to terms with it, and the revolutionary who cannot come to terms with the status quo. Then you look around you and you realize that the American go-getter who has no quarrel with the status quo is as much a juvenile as any revolutionary. Finally there is the juvenile character of most artists and writers. What quality can these diverse human types have in common? The answer that suggests itself is that all of them have a vivid awareness of the possibility of a new beginning; of a sudden, drastic, miraculous change. To a mature person drastic change is not only something unpleasant, but he denies its reality. He sees drastic change as a falling down on the face: when we get up we are back where we started plus bruises and dishevelment. The change that endures is that of growth — a change that proceeds quietly, and by degrees hardly to be perceived. To the juvenile mentality continuity and gradualness are synonymous with stagnation, while drastic change is a mark of dynamism, vigor, and freedom. To be fully alive is to feel that everything is possible.

On another day, Hoffer's mood leads him to think about the spirit of an author he is reading:

OCTOBER 26

I woke up with the idea that it was Monday. It cheered me somewhat to realize that it was not yet. I spent several hours downtown eating breakfast and strolling about.

I wonder how much of the feeling of well-being that I have had now and then during the past two days comes from the book I am reading — Van der Post's *The Lost World of the Kalahari*. Nothing this man ever writes could be without the excitement of life. And even as he brings to life the landscape, the plants, the animals, and the human beings he also manages to put the quality of himself in every word. You wonder what would happen if he became the absolute ruler of a primitive African state, and how little it would require to change him into an ancient lawgiver, a magician, a healer. His prose though unlabored is genuine poetry. You begin to realize that the chief function of poetry is to use words as charms to evoke life and colors and smells — a sense of joy, of awe, of compassion, and so on.

Yet all the time you know that it is the man and not his words that count. Wherever he puts his foot the earth becomes portentous. It is as if his presence has diverted the elements and forces from their routine pursuits. The whole world is addressing him, and concerning itself with his tastes and intentions.

At times, seemingly out of nowhere, large thoughts come upon him, and he draws together large portions of his reading in theoretical speculation.

APRIL 6

10 P.M. What puzzles me is the enormous dovetailing between the participants in the historic process. Take for instance the lustful dovetailing between the manipulators and the manipulated. The absolute despot lusts to dehumanize — to turn people into things — while the weak, weary of the strain of human uniqueness, long to drop the burden of free choice. All the metaphysical double-talk about the *Zeitgeist,* world spirit, historic necessity, superindividual tendencies and the like cluster around this puzzle. I would love to spend the rest of my life playing with this puzzle.

There is such a thing as fashion in thinking. There was something in the air that both Darwin and Marx and others picked up when they elaborated their theories. The integration of man with nunhuman nature which preoccupied scientists, philosophers and writers in the nineteenth century — the romantics and the realists, the idealists and the cynics — had perhaps a common origin, and I have to find it. To say that the onset of the industrial revolution created a demand for a new type of man, malleable and mechanized, does not explain anything. Darwin and Freud had nothing to do with the industrial revolution, and the romantics were violently against it. The industrialists wanted money, the politicians power, the scientists searched for regularities. Each one of the actors wanted something different, yet they all labored at the same task.

From this expansion of thoughts, it is only one step further for Hoffer to consider the writing he is involved in — the process, the difficulties, the satisfactions, and the dissatisfactions.

MAY 11

The article on man and nature which I am writing for the *Saturday Evening Post* is coming along fine. Almost every idea in the train of thought has been worked out long ago. What I have to do is dovetail them more or less smoothly. There are a few gaps to be filled. One is the idea that man's creativeness originates in the characteristics which distinguish man from other forms of life. In other words, human creativeness is basically unlike any creative process that may be found in the rest of creation. I also must have a pithy section on the role of magic (words) in human affairs. The title of the article will be "The Unnaturalness of Human Nature." I ought to have it finished and typed before the end of this month.

The fact that I can put together a good article by fitting ideas into a mosaic bothers me a little. It would have done me a world of good to be able to pour forth a stream of writing, to have new ideas gush from my mind onto paper. My sort of writing lacks the quality of catharsis. Yet only writing — any sort of writing — can justify my existence.

Journal Entry: A Research Paper

Our student, writing in her journal later in the semester — after it had become a habit — considered the problems of a research paper that she was in the process of writing. The journal then gave her the opportunity to consider both sides of the written conversation — to consider both her reading and her writing.

I am going through the final stages of organizing my paper. The topic gets more involved as I continue & I have difficulty trying to limit it. I stumbled into the constitutional issue pretty late, and it really might change my mind if I knew enough about it. But to really cover it would take a doctoral thesis, so I'm going to limit myself just to the political reasons for the gun control law being passed in '68, and I'm going to drop consideration of the merits of the law. What I'm learning about the political process there reminds me of things that keep happening every day. One group makes a lot of noise about an issue and people submit to their cries. Most will not stand up for their beliefs and will buckle in under pressure, in this case from the National Rifle Association. The NRA's pressure was partly responsible for the weakening of the bill. But that constitutional issue still bothers me because the NRA might have been right on that basis.

The hardest part is coming with the organization of the mass of materials. I feel like the facts are going to take over the paper and I won't be able to bring in my ideas clearly enough.

Writing the Informal Essay of Response

Except for those friends who borrow your books, few people will see the first suggestions of thoughts in your marginal comments and your reading journals. This privacy allows you the freedom to explore new possibilities of ideas. Although many of your ideas about your reading will remain private, these private opinions will mingle with your opinions about other reading in the back of your mind. All these opinions will contribute to the bases of your thinking.

At times, however, you will need to express a direct and fully developed response to some reading selection. On such occasions you must select, focus, and narrow the various and wandering comments of your journals and annotations. A simple catalogue of your top-of-the-head opinions — as expressed in those first written reactions — will not form a coherent, well-developed response. Your thinking must go through several stages of development before it can lead to a full, coherent *informal essay of response*.

Finding the Subject

First, on rereading and rethinking your comments, you might want to reject many offhand reactions. After writing down your comments, you may have seen their limitations and may have been able to take your thinking a step further. Your first thought, for example, that an author seemed too technical, may have lead you to see that the close attention to the process of automobile manufacture was necessary in this case — to explain why certain design changes would be more costly than they would first appear.

Second, as you start to gather your thoughts, you may find that they do not fall into a single clear pattern, either because your comments were contradictory or because they were too wide-ranging. In both cases you must limit your subject, either by finding some *pattern* of consistency in your seemingly unconnected thoughts or by narrowing your focus to the single issue that you will be able to handle best. This dilemma of divergent and possibly contradictory thoughts is exactly the one expressed by our student in her journal, quoted earlier. She sensed that if she pursued the constitutional issues of the right to bear arms she might gain a perspective that would contradict the conclusions of her political analysis of gun legislation. Since she felt she lacked the time and knowledge to resolve the constitutional issue, she decided to put it aside and limit herself to the more manageable political question. Therefore she focused on those political forces that contributed to the law's final form.

Third, once you limit your subject, you must see toward what conclusions your various reactions are heading. You must decide upon a main conclusion or *thesis* that will guide the overall direction of the paper. An *informal essay of response* provides the reader with a single journey into your thoughts; if you take the reader to too many places, the impression will be weakened and diffused. The essay should provide a single strong reaction stemming from any issue suggested by the original text. That issue need not be the most dominant or the most obvious point of the original; it needs to be only an issue that interests you most. Nor do you need to provide an overall evaluation of the material upon which you are commenting; that type of overall evaluation will be the topic for more narrowly defined essays discussed later in this book.

Any comment that was appropriate in the journal or the marginal annotations may be expanded into the theme of your essay of response. Often a side issue or a passing comment in the original may suggest more thoughts to you than the author's primary idea. You might even take up an issue the original leaves open, such as exploring the long-term consequences of some idea in the original or insisting upon the importance of some point given short shrift. Personal parallels — that is, comparisons drawn between the original and your own experiences and beliefs — are often a good strategy by which to explore your response to the original.

Fourth, once you have decided on the approach you will take in the essay, you should reread the original text and your first comments to consider two things. First, by rereading the original, you should make sure that your reaction is still substantial and clearly justified. Sometimes the original will say something different from your memory of it. If the idea still seems promising, rereading will help develop the idea further and help identify key passages, details, and examples that you might not have been looking for on earlier readings. Focusing on a topic will sharpen your eye for relevant details that you can incorporate into your essay.

Fifth, after you have gathered, sorted out, and developed your ideas, you need to plan how this material will fit together. You must organize your thoughts, but they may not be easily expressed by the usual formal organizational schemes, such as by a main statement backed up by several supporting arguments or by a series of comparisons or contrasts. If your thoughts do happen to fit into such patterns, one of them may serve you well; for example, if you actually do object to the original's conclusion on four main grounds, you may follow the conventional scheme. More likely no strict pattern will accurately reflect your thoughts, and you will have to invent some new organization to fit your ideas. Basic principles still are important — still be aware of beginning, middle, and end and still maintain a sense of continuity and coherence — but in this type of informal essay the stages by which your idea develops are up to you. Later in this chapter, examples of informal essays by George Orwell will show some of the ways unusual organizations can reflect the idiosyncratic shape of one person's ideas.

Finding a Pattern

Whether you apply a ready-made pattern or develop an organization specifically tailored to suit the shape of your idea, the opening sentences of the essay should indicate: (1) the book that evoked the response; (2) the particular item that caught your attention; and (3) where the response is headed. Your response — developed in the manner you find most appropriate — becomes the main body of the essay. You should never lose contact with this response, or the issues of the original reading that prompted the response. Develop each part of your response fully, and clearly show how each idea grows out of the previous idea. No matter how creative the organization and ideas of your essay are, the reader must be able to understand the organization and ideas fully. Carefully chosen examples will help the reader see your complete idea. Careful transitions between ideas and the constant tying of each point back to the main idea will help the reader see how your whole essay fits together. The ending should provide a sense of completion — perhaps by a final direct restatement of the original stimulus.

These organizational suggestions leave room for individual creativity — and a great variety of individual differences. Unlike essay questions on an exam where the question suggests an organization ("Discuss three causes . . .") and where the assigned readings and lectures limit the material for your reply, the informal response essay is bound only by the thoughts you have to communicate: it has the flexibility and individuality of the informal essay first developed in the sixteenth century by Montaigne and Bacon. George Orwell, British political commentator and novelist who wrote *1984* and *Animal Farm,* is a more recent master of the informal essay.

George Orwell's Response

During the 1940s, Orwell's weekly newspaper column frequently took its theme from his recent reading. One of these short responses, given below, begins by mentioning what Orwell considers an unusual subject for a novel — the life of a slave. He shows surprise that a theme so common in actual history should be so rare in print — that the life of slavery should remain obscure. One idea leads to another, but Orwell does not wander from the subject of *The Gladiators* and slave rebellion.

I have just been reading Arthur Koestler's novel *The Gladiators,* which describes the slave rebellion under Spartacus, about 70 BC. It is not one of his best books, and, in any case, any novel describing a slave rebellion in antiquity suffers by having to stand comparison with *Salammbô*, Flaubert's great novel about the revolt of the Carthaginian mercenaries. But it reminded me of how tiny is the number of slaves of whom anything whatever is known. I myself know the names of just three slaves — Spartacus himself, the fabulous Aesop, who is supposed to have been a slave, and the philosopher Epictetus, who was one of those learned slaves whom the Roman plutocrats liked to have among their retinue. All the others are not even names. We don't, for instance — or at least I don't — know the name of a single one of the myriads of human beings who built the Pyramids. Spartacus, I suppose, is much the most widely known slave there ever was. For five thousand years or more civilisation rested upon slavery. Yet when even so much as the name of a slave survives, it is because he did not obey the injunction "resist not evil," but raised violent rebellion. I think there is a moral in this for pacifists.[12]

Since this piece is not an evaluative review, Orwell does not concern himself much with making a complete evaluation of the book and its ideas; he never in fact discusses anything beyond the unusual choice of subject matter. Yet he has left the reader with a thought worth thinking about.

In the next selection Orwell focuses on just one part of the events recounted in a novel, but that part — the executions — reminds him of other literary examples of the same grisly event. All the examples he thinks of lead him to a general observation on the complexity of human reactions to executions and on the distortions of journalistic propaganda. Although this essay seems to take up many issues, its argument is a coherent reaction to the original passage from Anatole France's novel: the emotional immediacy and truth of execution stories often lead to memorable writing.

> As I glanced through an old favourite, Anatole France's *Les Dieux Ont Soif* (it is a novel about the Reign of Terror during the French Revolution), the thought occurred to me: what a remarkable anthology one could make of pieces of writing describing executions! There must be hundreds of them scattered through literature, and — for a reason I think I can guess — they must be far better written on average than battle pieces.
>
> Among the examples I remember at the moment are Thackeray's description of the hanging of Courvoisier, the crucifixion of the gladiators in *Salammbô*, the final scene of *A Tale of Two Cities*, a piece from a

[12]Excerpted from *The Collected Essays, Journalism and Letters of George Orwell*, Volume III, p. 198; copyright © 1968 by Sonia Brownell Orwell. Reprinted by permission of Harcourt Brace Jovanovich, Inc. and by permission of Mrs. Sonia Brownell Orwell and Martin Secker & Warburg.

letter or diary of Byron's, describing a guillotining, and the beheading of two Scottish noblemen after the 1745 rebellion, described by, I think, Horace Walpole. There is a very fine chapter describing a guillotining in Arnold Bennett's *Old Wives' Tale,* and a horrible one in one of Zola's novels (the one about the Sacré Coeur). Then there is Jack London's short story, "The Chinago," Plato's account of the death of Socrates — but one could extend the list indefinitely. There must also be a great number of specimens in verse, for instance the old hanging ballads, to which Kipling's "Danny Deever" probably owes something.

The thing that I think very striking is that no one, or no one I can remember, ever writes of an execution *with approval.* The dominant note is always horror. Society, apparently, cannot get along without capital punishment — for there are some people whom it is simply not safe to leave alive — and yet there is no one, when the pinch comes, who feels it right to kill another human being in cold blood. I watched a man hanged once. There was no question that everybody concerned knew this to be a dreadful, unnatural action. I believe it is always the same — the whole jail, warders and prisoners alike, is upset when there is an execution. It is probably the fact that capital punishment is accepted as necessary, and yet instinctively felt to be wrong, that gives so many descriptions of executions their tragic atmosphere. They are mostly written by people who have actually watched an execution and feel it to be a terrible and only partly comprehensible experience which they want to record; whereas battle literature is largely written by people who have never heard a gun go off and think of a battle as a sort of football match in which nobody gets hurt.

Perhaps it was a bit previous to say that no one writes of an execution with approval, when one thinks of the way our newspapers have been smacking their chops over the bumping-off of wretched quislings in France and elsewhere. I recall, in one paper, a whole series of photos showing the execution of Caruso, the ex-chief of the Rome police. You saw the huge, fat body being straddled across a chair with his back to the firing squad, then the cloud of smoke issuing from the rifle barrels and the body slumping sideways. The editor who saw fit to publish this thought it a pleasant titbit, I suppose, but then he had not had to watch the actual deed. I think I can imagine the feelings of the man who took the photographs, and of the firing squad.[13]

Although his purpose is not to evaluate France's book, Orwell makes a more general judgment about all writers — that only writers who have not witnessed executions can be blinded by nationalism into approving of this gruesome event.

[13]Orwell, pp. 267–268.

In a final example, Orwell responds in a more conventional way: he disagrees with a statement made in an Introduction to a Dickens novel. But even here he does not tackle the major argument of Chesterton's Introduction; in fact, we never learn what that Introduction is about. Instead Orwell focuses on a passing comment, "there is nothing new under the sun," that reveals one of Chesterton's beliefs — a belief with which Orwell distinctly disagrees. By arguing with that passing comment, Orwell is able to define major differences between them and to raise issues of great sweep. As Orwell moves from Chesterton's specific statement to the larger philosophical and political issues behind it, he reveals how opposed their two world views are. His own thinking on the same subject emerges; in response to Chesterton, Orwell winds up defining his own position.

Looking through Chesterton's Introduction to *Hard Times* in the Everyman Edition (incidentally, Chesterton's Introductions to Dickens are about the best thing he ever wrote), I note the typically sweeping statement: "There are no new ideas." Chesterton is here claiming that the ideas which animated the French Revolution were not new ones but simply a revival of doctrines which had flourished earlier and then been abandoned. But the claim that "there is nothing new under the sun" is one of the stock arguments of intelligent reactionaries. Catholic apologists, in particular, use it almost automatically. Everything that you can say or think has been said or thought before. Every political theory from Liberalism to Trotskyism can be shown to be a development of some heresy in the early Church. Every system of philosophy springs ultimately from the Greeks. Every scientific theory (if we are to believe the popular Catholic press) was anticipated by Roger Bacon and others in the thirteenth century. Some Hindu thinkers go even further and claim that not merely the scientific theories, but the products of applied science as well, aeroplanes, radio and the whole bag of tricks, were known to the ancient Hindus, who afterwards dropped them as being unworthy of their attention.

It is not very difficult to see that this idea is rooted in the fear of progress. If there is nothing new under the sun, if the past in some shape or another always returns, then the future when it comes will be something familiar. At any rate what will never come — since it has never come before — is that hated, dreaded thing, a world of free and equal human beings. Particularly comforting to reactionary thinkers is the idea of a cyclical universe, in which the same chain of events happens over and over again. In such a universe every seeming advance towards democracy simply means that the coming age of tyranny and privilege is a bit nearer. This belief, obviously superstitious though it is, is widely held nowadays, and is common among Fascists and near-Fascists.

In fact, there *are* new ideas. The idea that an advanced civilisation need not rest on slavery is a relatively new idea, for instance: it is a good deal younger than the Christian religion. But even if Chesterton's dictum were true, it would only be true in the sense that a statue is contained in every block of stone. Ideas may not change, but emphasis shifts constantly. It could be claimed, for example, that the most important part of Marx's theory is contained in the saying: "Where your treasure is, there will your heart be also." But before Marx developed it, what force had that saying had? Who had paid any attention to it? Who had inferred from it — what it certainly implies — that laws, religions and moral codes are all a superstructure built over existing property relations? It was Christ, according to the Gospel, who uttered the text, but it was Marx who brought it to life. And ever since he did so the motives of politicians, priests, judges, moralists and millionaires have been under the deepest suspicion — which, of course, is why they hate him so much.[14]

Much reading has, of course, gone into Orwell's thinking expressed here. The essay is informed by the Bible and Marx's works, as well as a general knowledge of the history of Europe and Asia. The issue of whether or not there are any new ideas may have occurred to Orwell earlier — perhaps in response to another statement similar to Chesterton's. The more you read, the more knowledge and insight you bring to bear in responding to the author's point. In this case, Chesterton's comments did act as a catalyst to bring together Orwell's complex thoughts on the subject — all that was stored in his mind to help him make sense of the written page.

All three of Orwell's responses quoted here were developed by the *associations* he made between his own ideas and another writer's. Though he wanders through many levels of ideas to explore the issue, he never loses contact with the starting point — the original issue that aroused his response.

In the last paragraph of the last example, Orwell rejects Chesterton's idea and returns to the fundamental issue of conservatives versus progressives — those who favor the old ways and the old privileges versus those who see change as adding to life's possibilities. The last sentence, though it seems to raise entirely new issues, is only a return to the fundamental argument of the essay.

Although you might not agree with Orwell's politics or with the conclusions he draws, you can find much in the associative process he uses to express his own attitudes in response to the attitudes of others. Your thoughts will not always unfold simply, according to predeter-

[14]Orwell, pp. 97–98.

mined patterns. Where a simple pattern fits, use it, but your thoughts may develop their own unusual or distinct shape as they move from marginal note to journal comments to full statement.

Writing Assignments

1. Write a letter to a friend who attends another college. Give your candid reactions to some of the courses you are taking this semester and to the books you have to read for those courses.

2. Annotate the following passage from Cicero's *On Friendship*. [15]

In the first place, how can there be a "life worth living," as Ennius puts it, unless it rest upon the mutual love of friends? What could be finer than to have someone to whom you may speak as freely as to yourself? How could you derive true joy from good fortune, if you did not have someone who would rejoice in your happiness as much as you yourself? And it would be very hard to bear misfortune in the absence of anyone who would take your sufferings even harder than you. Finally, the other things on which we set our hearts have each of them a strictly limited utility: money, that we may spend it; power, that we may acquire a following; honors, that we may gain praise; pleasure, that we may enjoy it; health, that we may be free of pain and make full use of our physical endowments; friendship, on the other hand, brings with it many advantages. Wherever you turn, it is at your side; there is no place not open to it; it is never untimely, never in the way. In short, not even water and fire, as the saying goes, are as universally essential to us as friendship. And I am not now speaking of the friendships of everyday folk, or of ordinary people — although even these are a source of pleasure and profit — but of true and perfect friendship, the kind that was possessed by those few men who have gained names for themselves as friends. For when fortune smiles on us, friendship adds a luster to that smile; when she frowns, friendship absorbs her part and share of that frown, and thus makes it easier to bear.

Now friendship possesses many splendid advantages, but of course the finest thing of all about it is that it sends a ray of good hope into the future, and keeps our hearts from faltering or falling by the wayside. For the man who keeps his eye on a true friend, keeps it, so to speak, on a model of himself. For this reason, friends are together when they are separated, they are rich when they are poor, strong when they are weak, and — a thing even harder to explain — they live on after they have died,

[15]From Cicero, *On Old Age and On Friendship* (trans. Frank O. Copley), pp. 55–56. Copyright © 1967 by The University of Michigan Press. Used by permission.

so great is the honor that follows them, so vivid the memory, so poign-
ant the sorrow. That is why friends who have died are accounted
happy, and those who survive them are deemed worthy of praise. Why,
if the mutual love of friends were to be removed from the world, there is
no single house, no single state that would go on existing; even agriculture would cease to be. If this seems a bit difficult to understand, we
can readily see how great is the power of friendship and love by observing their opposites, enmity and ill will. For what house is so firmly
established, what constitution is so unshakable, that it could not be
utterly destroyed by hatred and internal division? From this we may
judge how much good there is in friendship.

3. Start a journal for your readings in this course; include entries on
assignments in this text and on any other book you may use for this
course. Make entries as well about research material you find in preparation for a major research paper for this or another course. Also comment
on the problems and the progress of your own writing assignments.
Keep the journal going throughout the semester. For the last entry, read
through the entire journal and comment on the journal as a whole:
whether you gained from it, whether you noticed changes in your
thinking, and whether any particular interests emerge.

4. Write an *informal essay of response* either on Cicero's comments on
friendship (see Question 2) or on a very different view of the same
subject from Dale Carnegie's book *How to Win Friends and Influence
People*. In either case, the audience for the essay will be your classmates.

DO THIS AND YOU'LL BE WELCOME ANYWHERE[16]

Why read this book to find out how to win friends? Why not
study the technique of the greatest winner of friends the world has ever
known? Who is he? You may meet him tomorrow coming down the
street. When you get within ten feet of him, he will begin to wag his tail.
If you stop and pat him, he will almost jump out of his skin to show you
how much he likes you. And you know that behind this show of affection on his part, there are no ulterior motives: he doesn't want to sell
you any real estate, and he doesn't want to marry you.

Did you ever stop to think that a dog is the only animal that doesn't
have to work for a living? A hen has to lay eggs; a cow has to give milk;
and a canary has to sing. But a dog makes his living by giving you
nothing but love.

When I was five years old, my father bought a little yellow-haired pup
for fifty cents. He was the light and joy of my childhood. Every afternoon

about four-thirty, he would sit in the front yard with his beautiful eyes staring steadfastly at the path, and as soon as he heard my voice or saw me swinging my dinner pail through the buck brush, he was off like a shot, racing breathlessly up the hill to greet me with leaps of joy and barks of sheer ecstasy.

Tippy was my constant companion for five years. Then one tragic night — I shall never forget it — he was killed within ten feet of my head, killed by lightning. Tippy's death was the tragedy of my boyhood.

You never read a book on psychology, Tippy. You didn't need to. You knew by some divine instinct that one can make more friends in two months by becoming genuinely interested in other people than one can in two years by trying to get other people interested in him. Let me repeat that. *You can make more friends in two months by becoming interested in other people than you can in two years by trying to get other people interested in you.*

Yet I know and you know people who blunder through life trying to wigwag other people into becoming interested in them.

On course, it doesn't work. People are not interested in you. They are not interested in me. They are interested in themselves — morning, noon, and after dinner.

The New York Telephone Company made a detailed study of telephone conversations to find out which word is the most frequently used. You have guessed it: it is the personal pronoun "I." "I." "I." It was used 3,990 times in 500 telephone conversations. "I." "I." "I." "I." "I."

When you see a group photograph that you are in, whose picture do you look for first?

If you think people are interested in you, answer this question: If you died tonight, how many people would come to your funeral?

If we merely try to impress people and get people interested in us, we will never have many true, sincere friends. Friends, real friends, are not made that way.

Napoleon tried it, and in his last meeting with Josephine he said: "Josephine, I have been as fortunate as any man ever was on this earth; and yet, at this hour, you are the only person in the world on whom I can rely." And historians doubt whether he could rely even on her.

The late Alfred Adler, the famous Viennese psychologist, wrote a book entitled *What Life Should Mean to You*. In that book he says: "It is the individual who is not interested in his fellow men who has the greatest difficulties in life and provides the greatest injury to others. It is from among such individuals that all human failures spring."

5. Write an informal essay of response based on the following column written by George Orwell in October, 1945 — only a few months after World War II was ended by the first atomic bombs dropped on Japan. Your response, of course, will be affected by the thirty-five years that have elapsed since the advent of nuclear weapons. Orwell, on the other hand, was trying to predict the effect of something utterly new. One question you may respond to is how true Orwell's predictions turned out to be. Consider the audience for your paper politically aware adults concerned about the future, and write as though your essay will appear in a general-circulation political magazine.

YOU AND THE ATOM BOMB [1945][17]

Considering how likely we all are to be blown to pieces by it within the next five years, the atomic bomb has not roused so much discussion as might have been expected. The newspapers have published numerous diagrams, not very helpful to the average man, of protons and neutrons doing their stuff, and there has been much reiteration of the useless statement that the bomb "ought to be put under international control." But curiously little has been said, at any rate in print, about the question that is of most urgent interest to all of us, namely: "How difficult are these things to manufacture?"

Such information as we — that is, the big public — possess on this subject has come to us in a rather indirect way, apropos of President Truman's decision not to hand over certain secrets to the USSR. Some months ago, when the bomb was still only a rumour, there was a widespread belief that splitting the atom was merely a problem for the physicists, and that when they had solved it a new and devastating weapon would be within reach of almost everybody. (At any moment, so the rumour went, some lonely lunatic in a laboratory might blow civilisation to smithereens, as easily as touching off a firework.)

Had that been true, the whole trend of history would have been abruptly altered. The distinction between great states and small states would have been wiped out, and the power of the State over the individual would have been greatly weakened. However, it appears from President Truman's remarks, and various comments that have been made on them, that the bomb is fantastically expensive and that its manufacture demands an enormous industrial effort, such as only three or four countries in the world are capable of making. This point is of cardinal importance, because it may mean that the discovery of the atomic bomb, so far from reversing history, will simply intensify the trends which have been apparent for a dozen years past.

It is a commonplace that the history of civilisation is largely the history of weapons. In particular, the connection between the discovery of gunpowder and the overthrow of feudalism by the bourgeoisie has been pointed out over and over again. And though I have no doubt exceptions can be brought forward, I think the following rule would be

[17]From *The Collected Essays, Journalism and Letters of George Orwell*, Volume IV, pp. 6–10, copyright © 1968 by Sonia Brownell Orwell. Reprinted by permission of Harcourt Brace Jovanovich, Inc. and by permission of Mrs. Sonia Brownell Orwell and Martin Secker & Warburg.

found generally true: that ages in which the dominant weapon is expensive or difficult to make will tend to be ages of despotism, whereas when the dominant weapon is cheap and simple, the common people have a chance. Thus, for example, tanks, battleships and bombing planes are inherently tyrannical weapons, while rifles, muskets, longbows and hand-grenades are inherently democratic weapons. A complex weapon makes the strong stronger, while a simple weapon — so long as there is no answer to it — gives claws to the weak.

The great age of democracy and of national self-determination was the age of the musket and the rifle. After the invention of the flintlock, and before the invention of the percussion cap, the musket was a fairly efficient weapon, and at the same time so simple that it could be produced almost anywhere. Its combination of qualities made possible the success of the American and French revolutions, and made a popular insurrection a more serious business than it could be in our own day. After the musket came the breech-loading rifle. This was a comparatively complex thing, but it could still be produced in scores of countries, and it was cheap, easily smuggled and economical of ammunition. Even the most backward nation could always get hold of rifles from one source or another, so that Boers, Bulgars, Abyssinians, Moroccans — even Tibetans — could put up a fight for their independence, sometimes with success. But thereafter every development in military technique has favoured the State as against the individual, and the industrialised country as against the backward one. There are fewer and fewer foci of power. Already, in 1939, there were only five states capable of waging war on the grand scale, and now there are only three — ultimately, perhaps, only two. This trend has been obvious for years, and was pointed out by a few observers even before 1914. The one thing that might reverse it is the discovery of a weapon — or, to put it more broadly, of a method of fighting — not dependent on huge concentrations of industrial plant.

From various symptoms one can infer that the Russians do not yet possess the secret of making the atomic bomb; on the other hand, the consensus of opinion seems to be that they will possess it within a few years. So we have before us the prospect of two or three monstrous super-states, each possessed of a weapon by which millions of people can be wiped out in a few seconds, dividing the world between them. It has been rather hastily assumed that this means bigger and bloodier wars, and perhaps an actual end to the machine civilisation. But suppose — and really this is the likeliest development — that the surviving great nations make a tacit agreement never to use the atomic bomb against one another? Suppose they only use it, or the threat of it, against people who are unable to retaliate? In that case we are back where we were before, the only difference being that power is concentrated in still fewer hands and that the outlook for subject peoples and oppressed classes is still more hopeless.

When James Burnham wrote *The Managerial Revolution* it seemed probable to many Americans that the Germans would win the European end of the war, and it was therefore natural to assume that Germany and not Russia would dominate the Eurasian land mass, while Japan would remain master of East Asia. This was a miscalculation, but it does not affect the main argument. For Burnham's geographical picture of the new world has turned out to be correct. More and more obviously the surface of the earth is being parcelled off into three great empires, each self-contained and cut off from contact with the outer world, and each ruled, under one disguise or another, by a self-elected oligarchy. The haggling as to where the frontiers are to be drawn is still going on, and will continue for some years, and the third of the three super-states — East Asia, dominated by China — is still potential rather than actual. But the general drift is unmistakable, and every scientific discovery of recent years has accelerated it.

We were once told that the aeroplane had "abolished frontiers"; actually it is only since the aeroplane became a serious weapon that frontiers have become definitely impassable. The radio was once expected to promote international understanding and co-operation; it has turned out to be a means of insulating one nation from another. The atomic bomb may complete the process by robbing the exploited classes and peoples of all power to revolt, and at the same time putting the possessors of the bomb on a basis of military equality. Unable to conquer one another, they are likely to continue ruling the world between them, and it is difficult to see how the balance can be upset except by slow and unpredictable demographic changes.

For forty or fifty years past, Mr H. G. Wells and others have been warning us that man is in danger of destroying himself with his own weapons, leaving the ants or some other gregarious species to take over. Anyone who has seen the ruined cities of Germany will find this notion at least thinkable. Nevertheless, looking at the world as a whole, the drift for many decades has been not towards anarchy but towards the reimposition of slavery. We may be heading not for general breakdown but for an epoch as horribly stable as the slave empires of antiquity. James Burnham's theory has been much discussed, but few people have yet considered its ideological implications — that is, the kind of world-view, the kind of beliefs, and the social structure that would probably prevail in a state which was at once *unconquerable* and in a permanent state of "cold war" with its neighbours.

Had the atomic bomb turned out to be something as cheap and easily manufactured as a bicycle or an alarm clock, it might well have plunged us back into barbarism, but it might, on the other hand, have meant the end of national sovereignty and of the highly-centralised police state. If, as seems to be the case, it is a rare and costly object as difficult to produce as a battleship, it is likelier to put an end to large-scale wars at the cost of prolonging indefinitely a "peace that is no peace."

4

Analyzing the Author's Purpose and Technique

Preview

In this chapter we will analyze how the overall purpose motivating the writer will determine the techniques he or she uses. The writer's purpose — the reasons for writing a particular article or book — may be manipulative, as in propaganda and advertising, or may be more straightforward, as in informative writing. In either case, understanding the writer's underlying purpose will help you interpret the context of the writing and will also help you see why writers make the decisions they do — from the largest decisions of what information to present to the smallest details of what word to use. The chapter concludes with instructions on how to write an *analysis of purpose and technique;* mastery of this kind of analysis will help you bring critical awareness to your reading and research.

The Writer's Purpose

The *purpose* behind an action determines the kinds of actions an individual will take to realize that purpose. Sinister purposes — such as those of villainous gold diggers in old movies who plot against the fortunes of naive heiresses — may be manipulative and deceitful. More frequently, purposes are straightforward and honest, such as an architect's desire to create an attractive and functional student center for a college campus. In both cases the techniques employed are derived from the larger purposes. The suave gentleman compliments the rich young lady to make her fall passionately in love with him so that she will sign over the gold-mining stocks. In designing the student center, the architect places the recreation lounges far from the study areas to allow students to carry on different activities without disturbing one another. The overall purpose in one's mind leads to the specific, technical details worked out on paper and in reality.

Everything that you read has an underlying purpose that has helped the writer decide what words should go on the blank piece of paper. The more the writer is aware of what purposes lie behind his or her writing and the more control the writer has of the details of writing, the more clearly and fully an *overall design* will emerge. Therein lies the skill of the writer. And the skill of the reader is in becoming aware of that overall design and in seeing how the writer uses details in writing to achieve a larger purpose. With that awareness, the reader can then judge whether the writer has succeeded in doing what he or she has set out to do. The active reader reads more than the words and more than even the ideas: the active reader reconstructs the larger design.

In this chapter, we will first consider the various purposes a writer may have and the ways the reader can determine that purpose. Next, we will discuss the writer's handling of techniques and then present a case study exploring several examples of how technique is related to purpose. The chapter ends with specific instructions on how to write an *analysis of design,* in which you will explore both a writer's purpose and technique.

Disguised Manipulations

Living as we do in a merchandising culture, we are all sensitive to the designs of advertising. We know the purpose of most advertisements is to make us open up our wallets. We are also aware of most of the techniques, even though we may not be immune to them. Adver-

> **The active reader reads more than the words and more than even the ideas: the active reader reconstructs the writer's larger design.**

tisers use charged language, appealing art, and attractive models to play upon our fantasies — whom we would like to be and whom we would like to love us — and make use of our fears of rejection. Even the techniques of amusement — if we laugh at the advertisement, we may remember and buy the product — lead us away from thinking about the value purchased by our money.

Federal regulations now outlaw claims that are outright deceptions, and occasional advertisements are simply informative, just letting us know that a product with specific features is available on the market. Nonetheless, even the plainest advertisements emphasize certain of the consumer's needs and attitudes at the expense of others. Most advertisements try to distract us from a simple rational consideration of what we need and what we actually receive in return for our money.

Similarly, the purpose of propaganda is to make us forget reason so that we will support irrational political positions. Propaganda may serve to further political ambitions, to gather support for questionable governmental policies, or to confuse political discussions by deflecting attention away from the real issues.

McCarthyism

In the early 1950s, Senator Joseph McCarthy relied heavily on propaganda to advance his own career and to create extreme anticommunist fear and hysteria. The following is an excerpt of a speech McCarthy delivered in the Senate on July 6, 1950, shortly after President Truman announced that the United States would provide troops to carry out a United Nations action in Korea. Notice how McCarthy turns his apparent support of the president's decision into an attack on members of the president's administration and on other Americans.

> Mr. President, at this very moment GI's are consecrating the hills and the valleys of Korea with American blood. But all that blood is not staining the Korean hills and valleys. Some of it is deeply and permanently staining the hands of Washington politicians.

Some men of little minds and less morals are today using the Korean war as a profitable political diversion, a vehicle by which to build up battered reputations because of incompetence and worse.

The American people have long condemned war profiteers who promptly crowd the landscape the moment their Nation is at war. Today, Mr. President, war profiteers of a new and infinitely more debased type are cluttering the landscape in Washington. They are political war profiteers. Today they are going all-out in an effort to sell the American people the idea that in order to successfully fight communism abroad, we must give Communists and traitors at home complete unmolested freedom of action. They are hiding behind the word "unity," using it without meaning, but as a mere catch phrase to center the attention of the American people solely on the fighting front. They argue that if we expose Communists, fellow travelers, and traitors in our Government, that somehow this will injure our war effort. Actually, anyone who can add two and two must realize that if our war effort is to be successful, we must redouble our efforts to get rid of those who, either because of incompetence or because of loyalty to the Communist philosophy, have laid the groundwork and paved the way for disaster.

The pattern will become clearer as the casualty lists mount. Anyone who criticizes the murderous incompetence of those who are responsible for this disaster, anyone who places the finger upon dupes and traitors in Washington, because of whose acts young men are already dying, will be guilty of creating disunity.

Already this cry has reached fantastic pinnacles of moronic thinking. Take, for example the local *Daily Worker,* that is, the *Washington Post.* The other day this newspaper ran an editorial in effect accusing the University of California of injuring the war effort by discharging 137 teachers and other employees who refused to certify that they were not members of the Communist International conspiracy. This, Mr. President, would be laughable if it came merely from the Communist Party's mouthpiece, the *New York Daily Worker,* and its mockingbirds like the *Washington Post.* Unfortunately, a few of the Nation's respectable but misguided writers are being sold this same bill of goods, namely, that to have unity in our military effort the truth about Communists at home must be suppressed.[1]

McCarthy begins by *flag waving,* that is, by playing on strong national feeling. By praising American soldiers, he makes himself appear patriotic with only the interests of his country at heart. He also arouses in his listeners patriotic feeling in support of the self-sacrificing GI's. But in the second sentence, he turns this patriotic feeling against Washington politicians. McCarthy starts *name calling,* which he continues throughout the

[1]*Cong. Rec.,* 6 July 1950, p. 9715.

speech. With no detailed evidence or other support, he labels certain unidentified members of the government as incompetents, communists, dupes, and traitors. He repeats these labels throughout his attack, but he never becomes specific about who these traitors are, what their exact crimes are, and what his evidence is. Thus he makes only *blanket accusations* that cannot be pinpointed and therefore cannot be proved or disproved.

Guilt by Association

As part of his labeling, McCarthy employs *guilt by association:* he associates members of the government with war profiteers who had been the object of public hatred for many years. Similarly, he associates the *Washington Post*, a respected independent newspaper, with the *Daily Worker,* the official newspaper of the Communist party.

Finally, the whole excerpt relies on *scapegoating,* putting the blame on those who are not truly responsible. If American soldiers are dying and if casualty lists are mounting, McCarthy wants to make it appear that the fault belongs to our government officials and newspapers — especially those that McCarthy does not like. Rather than saying it is the North Korean army killing our soldiers, McCarthy puts bloodstains on "the hands of Washington politicians."

Unfortunately, propaganda is sometimes very effective, particularly at times of crisis when emotions run high. Playing on the Korean War and Russian expansion in Eastern Europe, McCarthy temporarily gained substantial power and created a climate of terror in this country, a climate that took many years to dispel.

Doublespeak

Another kind of manipulation is achieved through *doublespeak,* named after techniques described in George Orwell's novel *1984.* In that novel a totalitarian government uses confusing language to obscure important issues and ideas. By using such slogans as *War Is Peace, Freedom Is Slavery,* and *Ignorance Is Strength,* the government in *1984* keeps its citizens from understanding what is happening to them.

Today we also experience such dissociation of events from their meaning when bureaucratic language is used — when *death* is called *negative termination of illness* and *embezzlement* is called *temporary readjustment of asset localization.* The purpose of such language is to make us not think about what is actually happening.

Straightforward Purposes

When advertisers or propagandists try to manipulate our opinions and actions, we may become suspicious of the details of their statements. Fortunately, only a small fraction of writing is deliberately manipulative in purpose. More often the writer's purposes are more honest, and the techniques used are not aimed at distorting our judgment. A novelist may simply wish to amuse us. A reporter may wish to inform us as objectively as possible. A political commentator may want us to think seriously about a matter of public concern. Still, we should know their larger designs, not to guard ourselves — as we do against propaganda and misleading advertising — but to understand the legitimate uses we can make of their statements.

If you are not aware of the larger design of a book, you may be misled about the meaning. Perhaps when you stop by the local bookstore, you pick up a paperback and start reading in the middle:

> Mario stood in the doorway, a strange light flashing from his eyes. His lips barely moved, "Carmen, I am here."
> "But Mario, I thought, . . ." her voice quivered.
> "No. There was one thing I had to do first." His deliberate steps matched the pounding of her heart. His eyes, flashing fire, fixed on her. He stopped in front of her, his lips slightly opened as if he had something to say, but couldn't say it. He reached for her.

True passion? You love romances and are about to buy it. But wait. You turn to the cover. *Compelled to Murder.* You do not enjoy thrillers so you put it back on the rack. The overall design of the work helps define the purpose and technique of each small part: the same words that bring expectation and a melting heart in a romantic fantasy bring fear and dread in a murder plot.

The message that words convey depends on the purpose of the words within the context of a larger communication. For example, when the following words appear in a dictionary, they simply provide a definition, one piece of information among many other similar pieces of information.

affective: adj. 1. *Psychology.* Pertaining to or resulting from emotions or feelings rather than from thought.[2]

[2] © 1978 Houghton Mifflin Co. Reprinted by permission from *The American Heritage Dictionary of the English Language.*

The dictionary tells you that *affective* is one word in the English language with a specific spelling and meaning, used particularly in the field of psychology. If, however, that same definition appears with a dozen other terms on a ditto sheet handed out by your psychology professor on the first day of class, the message is that you had better learn that word, for it is part of the basic vocabulary for the course. If your English professor writes the definition in the margin of your paper — after circling the word you wrote and changing the *a* to an *e* — the message is that you confused *affective* with the more common word *effective*. In each of these cases, a knowledge of the larger context helps us see the purpose of the words and receive the message intended.

A Catalogue: The Purposes of Writing

Written language is of such flexibility and scope that it is turned to an almost infinite variety of purposes. Any catalogue of writing purposes can only suggest broad categories. The following catalogue is only a first step to help you begin thinking about any book or article. As you think about actual pieces of writing, you may need to add new categories or to define more subcategories. You may also find that one piece of writing may serve several purposes.

Scholarly Inquiry

To present new findings, recent information, the results of experiments

To present new interpretations, speculations, thoughts

To gather together all that is currently known on a subject, to see how it fits together, and to reach some conclusions

To show the relationship of two areas of study and to show the light one sheds on the other

To determine the truth of some matter and to prove that truth to other researchers

Transmission of Knowledge to a Wider Audience

To satisfy curiosity

To provide practical information for everyday use

To provide an introduction into an area of knowledge

To instruct rigorously, passing on the most recent knowledge, skill, or technique

The Conduct of Business and Government

To promulgate laws, regulations, guidelines

To report information needed for making new decisions, laws, policies

To argue for certain lines of action

To request funds or propose an activity to be funded

To keep track of funds, projects, activities; to report on accomplishments and failures; to evaluate activities

To sell, advertise

The Support of a Community of Common Beliefs

To state one's beliefs; to take a stand

To repeat the accepted beliefs of a group; to encourage and reinforce these beliefs

To share recent developments and events that are of mutual concern

To gain tolerance for one's beliefs in the wider community

To persuade others of the correctness of certain views; to gain approval

To recruit active support; to proselytize

Instigation of Public Thought and Action

To raise questions

To criticize the actions of others; to reprimand

To weaken the support of opponents

To persuade to act, vote, donate, etc.

To inform of issues of concern

Entertainment

To amuse and to delight

To arouse emotions and sympathies

To appeal to fantasy and imagination

Clues to the Author's Purpose

We cannot read the minds of authors to tell what their true purposes were, but we can tell much about their purposes by many externally available clues.

Overt Statements

Pieces of writing that begin or end with commands like "vote for Paulsen" or "donate to this worthy cause today" make no secret of their intentions. Obviously, titles can clearly indicate purpose, such as *How to Be a Big Winner on the Stock Market, The Encyclopedia of Sports, A Report on the Status of Mine Inspection Procedures, The Case for National Health Insurance,* and *Spanish Self-Taught.* Often in scholarly or professional books and sometimes in more popular works, the introduction or preface specifically states the purpose and outlines the issues that gave rise to the book. In the following passage from his preface to *The General Theory of Employment,* John Maynard Keynes lets the reader know exactly what he proposes to do and to whom his book is directed; the author clearly spells out his overall purpose, both in terms of the current state of economics and in terms of his own development.[3]

This book is chiefly addressed to my fellow economists. I hope that it will be intelligible to others. But its main purpose is to deal with difficult questions of theory, and only in the second place with the applications of this theory to practice. For if orthodox economics is at fault, the error is to be found not in the superstructure, which has been erected with great care for logical consistency, but in a lack of clearness and of generality in the premises. Thus I cannot achieve my object of persuading economists to re-examine critically certain of their basic assumptions except by a highly abstract argument and also by much controversy. I wish there could have been less of the latter. But I have thought it important, not only to explain my own point of view, but also to show in what respects it departs from the prevailing theory. Those, who are strongly wedded to what I shall call "the classical theory", will fluctuate, I expect, between a belief that I am quite wrong and a belief that I am saying nothing new. It is for others to determine if either of these or the third alternative is right. My controversial passages are aimed at providing some material for an answer; and I must ask forgiveness if, in the pursuit of sharp distinctions, my controversy is itself too keen. I myself held with conviction for many years the theories which I now attack, and I am not, I think, ignorant of their strong points.

The matters at issue are of an importance which cannot be exaggerated. But, if my explanations are right, it is my fellow economists, not the general public, whom I must first convince. At this stage of the argument the general public, though welcome at the debate, are only eavesdroppers at an attempt by an economist to bring to an issue the

[3]From John Maynard Keynes' Preface to his *General Theory of Employment, Interest, and Money*, pp. xxi–xxiii (Royal Economic Society Edition of Keynes' Writings, Vol. V, Macmillan; in the United States and Canada, Cambridge University Press; paperbound edition in the United States, Harcourt Brace Jovanovich, Inc.). Used by permission.

deep divergences of opinion between fellow economists which have for the time being almost destroyed the practical influence of economic theory, and will, until they are resolved, continue to do so.

The relation between this book and my *Treatise on Money,* which I published five years ago, is probably clearer to myself than it will be to others; and what in my own mind is a natural evolution in a line of thought which I have been pursuing for several years, may sometimes strike the reader as a confusing change of view. This difficulty is not made less by certain changes in terminology which I have felt compelled to make. These changes of language I have pointed out in the course of the following pages; but the general relationship between the two books can be expressed briefly as follows. When I began to write my *Treatise on Money* I was still moving along the traditional lines of regarding the influence of money as something so to speak separate from the general theory of supply and demand. When I finished it, I had made some progress towards pushing monetary theory back to becoming a theory of output as a whole. But my lack of emancipation from preconceived ideas showed itself in what now seems to me to be the outstanding fault of the theoretical parts of that work (namely, Books III and IV), that I failed to deal thoroughly with the effects of *changes* in the level of output. My so-called "fundamental equations" were an instantaneous picture taken on the assumption of a given output. They attempted to show how, assuming the given output, forces could develop which involved a profit-disequilibrium, and thus required a change in the level of output. But the dynamic development, as distinct from the instantaneous picture, was left incomplete and extremely confused. This book, on the other hand, has evolved into what is primarily a study of the forces which determine changes in the scale of output and employment as a whole; and, whilst it is found that money enters into the economic scheme in an essential and peculiar manner, technical monetary detail falls into the background. A monetary economy, we shall find, is essentially one in which changing views about the future are capable of influencing the quantity of employment and not merely its direction. But our method of analysing the economic behaviour of the present under the influence of changing ideas about the future is one which depends on the interaction of supply and demand, and is in this way linked up with our fundamental theory of value. We are thus led to a more general theory, which includes the classical theory with which we are familiar, as a special case.

Knowledge About Publication

Even if the author does not state the purpose of a piece of writing directly, where an article appears reveals much. An article appearing in a professional journal like *Journal of the History of Ideas, Harvard Theological Review,* or *Journal of Geology* would most likely present new information or research and evaluate current knowledge with a scholarly intent. An article in a general circulation magazine devoted to one field, like *Scientific American, Psychology Today,* or *High Fidelity,* would more likely present existing knowledge in a way understandable and useful to the nonspecialist, rather than presenting scholarly research. An article in a magazine brought out by a corporation or some other special-interest group, such as *Ford World, Teamster International,* or *Gun and Rifle,* would tend to convey a favorable impression of the organization's interests. Thus the stated and unstated editorial policy of the magazine helps define the purposes of all articles that appear in it.

With books, attention to the publisher, the place of publication, and the date will give first approximations of purpose. A book from a reputable academic press, such as University of Pennsylvania Press or Stanford University Press, will usually have a scholarly purpose aimed at the advancement of knowledge. Commercial publishers range from well-established houses — such as Norton, Houghton Mifflin, and Random House, which, among other material, publish nonfiction books of some seriousness of purpose for a general market — to sensationalist houses more concerned with playing on prejudices or exploiting current popular topics than with providing substantive knowledge. In addition, special-interest publishers press the causes or beliefs of specific groups: many religious publishing houses, for example, the Newman Press, are currently thriving. The more you know about the publisher, the more you will know about the purposes of its books.

The date and place of publication also may be a clue to understanding the purpose of the book. A book about Vietnam published in the United States in 1967 will probably be either highly critical or strongly supportive of American participation in the Vietnam War, and a reader would be wise to look out for partisanship; a book published a dozen years later by the same publisher on the same topic may be inquiring into what happened or how Americans now view the morality of that war. Books on the same topics published in both years by the Foreign Languages Press in Beijing, China, will have obviously different purposes. Everything you know about the history of the issues will help you place the purpose of each book involved. If you become engaged in research touching on some controversy, you will become particularly aware of such factors.

Knowledge About the Author

In much the same way, knowledge of a particular author will give you some sense of the purposes of his or her books, but beware of oversimplification, for the same person may write different types of books. However, if an author is known primarily as a supporter of some

Check List of Technique

Overall Structure

What holds the writing together as a whole?

How does one paragraph, one chapter, one part lead to the next?

Is the progress by a chronological narration? By a grouping of related topics? Through the steps of a logical argument? By comparison? Association? Repetition? By accumulation of detail? By analysis? By the breaking down of the subject into parts?

Content Choices

What parts of the subject are discussed in great detail? What parts are summarized?

What statements does the writer assume as given (and therefore does not back up by proof)?

What relevant topics are ignored?

What topics could have been discussed but were not?

Expansion of Topics

In what ways are individual topics developed? Are arguments given? Are anecdotes told?

Is the reader asked to believe certain ideas or to take certain actions? Is the reader asked to imagine consequences?

Does the expansion of statements prove the statements? Help the reader understand? Keep the reader interested or amused? Obscure the issues? Develop implications?

Choice of Evidence

What types of information are used to support main statements: statistics, anecdotes, quotations, original observations, scientific theories, legal or philosophical principles, definitions, appeals to emotion, to the imagination, to common sense?

Uses of Reference

How extensively does the writer rely on other sources? (Are there frequent mentions of other books or articles?) Do you notice any indirect reference to the work of others?

What methods are used to refer to other works: reference by name only, paraphrase, summary, or direct quotation?

How complete is the documentation? Bibliography?

What kinds of material does the writer cite: contemporary newspaper accounts, private diaries, government documents, specialized scholarly studies, theoretical works, best-selling nonfiction books, statistical reports, literary works?

What purpose does the reference serve in the writing: Does the reference provide specific evidence? Provide the actual words of a person being discussed? Provide an assertion by an authority? Present an example for analysis? Explain a point? Present the background of a new idea? Distinguish between conflicting ideas? Place current work in the context of previous work? Present an idea to be argued against?

Level of Precision

Is the subject simplified or presented in all its complexity?

Are all important distinctions brought out?

Are many supporting details given or are only broad principles stated?

Are potential difficulties in the argument discussed?

Sentence Structure

Are the sentences short or long? Simple or complex?

Are the sentences declarative statements? Do they set up a complex condition (*if . . . then . . .*)?

Do the sentences have qualifiers (even though . . .)?

Do the sentences describe actions (*Sandra runs;* or *Gear c transmits the power to drive wheel d.*)? Describe physical qualities (*Sandra has a pulse at rest of 63;* or *Gear b and gear c are in a reduction ratio of 12 : 1.*)? Relate actual events to abstract ideas (*The disagreement of the leaders over the terms of the treaty marked the beginning of new tensions between the two countries.*)? Discuss only abstractions (*International organizations are formed in part to resolve disputes between countries without resort to war.*)?

Word Choice

Are the words short or long? Common or unusual? General or technical? Emotionally charged or scientifically objective?

Relationship Between the Writer and the Reader

Does the writer address the reader as an expert speaking to other experts? Or to the general reader?

Does the writer make sure that the reader follows the discussion?

Does the writer interest the reader through humor, drama, or unusual examples?

Is the writer hesitant or assertive?

How much knowledge does the writer assume the reader has?

Evaluating the Effectiveness of Technique

After observing a writer's technique, you will be able to determine if that technique is appropriate and successful for the writer's purpose — whether stated or implied. You will begin to notice how the successful comic writer makes you laugh by piling up absurd details. You will notice how carefully a historian has gathered together materials, has weighed alternatives, and has moved to a well-argued conclusion. You will notice how the philosopher uses a precise vocabulary in an attempt to minimize confusion about abstract meaning.

In certain instances you may notice a definite split between the stated purpose of a book or article and what is actually achieved on paper. A book that claims to present new findings may, on closer inspection, rely heavily on previously discovered evidence put together in a familiar pattern. The comic writer may not pace his jokes correctly or may be too predictable. A detective story may read so tediously that no one would want to spend leisure hours reading it. An author's evidence might prove only part of his or her thesis. Writers may fail in their purposes in an infinity of ways, and even the best of books have weaknesses. However, weakness is relative: a book that does not live up to a grand purpose might still tell you more than one that achieves an extremely small goal. Misjudgment, lack of skill, or an attempt to do too much may explain these unintentional differences between a writer's intended purpose and actual accomplishment.

Since we are aware that some writing sets out to mislead, we must understand the deception to understand the true design. Beneath a pile of evidence may lie a prejudiced assumption: when a report advises against building a community college in a poor neighborhood because that community has not previously produced many college graduates, the writer's prejudices may have translated the lack of opportunity into an

---

In certain instances you may notice a definite split between the stated purpose of a book or article and what is actually achieved on paper.

---

assumption that the people of that community cannot succeed. Thus the reporter's recommendation to deny opportunity may be made to sound respectable and even-handed while still delivering its unjust message.

The outright lie, the partial lie, and the partial truth will continue to appear in print. Deception can be achieved in many ways, and it helps to be aware not just of the deception but also of the motive behind the author's deception.

The Camel on the Pack: A Case Study

An analysis of some of the voluminous writing on the tobacco industry will give you a specific sense of how a writer's purpose is realized through every detail of the writer's technique. Although you might first imagine — as I did before I looked carefully at these articles — that most recent writing on tobacco would center on the health issue and would therefore have persuasive, or polemical, purposes, the writers, in fact, have very varied purposes in writing about the industry. These varied purposes result in substantial differences among their writings — even though these authors are, on the surface, dealing with very similar topics.

The Company Camel

The first item I pulled off the library shelf was a pamphlet entitled *Our 100th Anniversary,* put out by R. J. Reynolds Industries, Inc., one of the major cigarette manufacturers. Handsome, multicolored photographs of cigarettes, packs of cigarettes, machinery, factories, advertisements, and members of the corporate family were arranged in an eye-appealing layout; the photographs reinforce the impression that the company's main purposes were self-celebration and a good public image.

The author, sympathetic to the corporate position, writes a chronological narrative of growth — from Joshua Reynolds's one-man peddling business into a large and diversified multinational corporation. Since the purpose of the pamphlet is to develop a good public image, we obviously do not hear of corporate wheeling and dealing or tedious details of corporate statistics and financing. Most of the history is made up of amusing anecdotes to personify Reynolds Industries as humane and good-natured, not a cold, calculating industrial giant. Business manipulations are only presented in the attractive form of the clever hero getting past a stupidly obstinate opponent; competition is only mentioned when it has been thoroughly defeated. Success comes to the corporation management because they are so humanly charming; nostalgia makes corporate history warm and touching. The following description of the appearance of the new Camel brand typifies this anecdotal, nostalgic technique. Business, production, and even tobacco get short shrift as most of the text is devoted to the familiar symbol on the pack.

> In Richmond the lithographers prepared two labels, "Kamel" and "Camel" with the latter winning out. A great deal of attention was paid to the wording, especially to the famous inscription advising purchasers: "Don't look for premiums or coupons, as the cost of the tobaccos blended in Camel Cigarettes prohibits the use of them." The label's background of temples, minarets, an oasis, and pyramids was much like it is today, but the camel in the foreground was a pathetic, one-humped beast with short, pointed ears, two-pronged hoofs and a drooping neck.
>
> Is this a camel? the Reynolds people asked each other. Consulting the "Encyclopedia Britannica," they learned that a one-humped dromedary could indeed be called a camel, although no one was too pleased with the creature's looks. Luckily, Barnum & Bailey came to town, Monday, September 29, 1913, and Roy C. Haberkern, Reynolds' young secretary, went to investigate. With a photographer, he visited the circus menagerie and found not only a dromedary, but a two-humped camel as well. When the animal boss refused permission to photograph them, Haberkern pointed out that Reynolds had always closed offices and factories for the circus, a practice that could easily be discontinued. The trainer relented, but demanded a written release from the company.
>
> Haberkern raced back to the closed office building, climbed through a window, wrote the agreement, and signed Reynolds' name to it. Back at the fairgrounds the circus man conceded and brought out the two animals. The camel posed willingly, but Old Joe, the dromedary, wouldn't hold still. The trainer gave him a slap on the nose. Old Joe raised his tail, threw back his ears and closed his eyes as the shutter

snapped. From that photograph an improved label was designed and Old Joe became the most famous dromedary in the world.[4]

The language is simple and direct; the author uses a familiar vocabulary and avoids complicated sentence patterns. This easily understood section forms a little self-contained narrative with a problem, some complications, a crisis, a clever solution by the young hero, and a happy ending. The details create an image of company employees as friendly and humanly fallible: with good intentions, they first illustrate a pathetic animal; but they are eager to improve and willing to laugh at themselves. They succeed by willingness to negotiate, by well-timed bending of the rules in a good cause, and by general good will. The author hopes that this amusing circus story and the pleasant image of the company will make us feel more kindly toward the corporate giant.

Camel Reconsidered

The immortalized camel reappears — but in a different way — in Susan Wagner's book *Cigarette Country: Tobacco in American History and Politics*. At first glance, the book appears to be a popular commercial venture intended for a general audience: about two-hundred-fifty pages, medium-size print, catchy chapter titles — and no footnotes, bibliography, or index. No immediate indication links the author with either antismoking forces or the cigarette companies; in the preface she states her motivation to be purely curiosity.

This is not a book with a cause. It is not an antismoking tract nor a how-to-stop-smoking book. I found myself drawn into the subject quite by chance. My interest developed out of another project, my book *The Federal Trade Commission,* published by Praeger earlier this year. As I researched a chapter on cigarette advertising for that book, the entire subject of tobacco began to interest me as a sociopolitical phenomenon. Smoking *is* a strange habit to have become so much a part of American life and mythology.

The more I delved into the history of tobacco the more it intrigued me. It is a history filled with a freaky variety of anecdotes and ironies, beginning with an irony — namely, that, without realizing it, Columbus, when he discovered tobacco, discovered a source of far greater riches than all the gold carried away from the New World by the Spanish

[4]From Jerome Beatty, Jr., *Our 100th Anniversary 1875–1975.* Copyright © 1975 R. J. Reynolds Industries, Inc. Used by permission.

conquistadors. I was fascinated, too, to learn that from the earliest times tobacco had been simultaneously hailed as a cure-for-whatever-ails-you and as a foul habit harmful to health.[5]

She is a professional writer, unearthing a story that she hopes book buyers will find as intriguing as she does. For her, an interesting part of the "sociopolitical phenomenon" of smoking is the increasing role of advertising in the cigarette industry. As part of the discussion of advertising, she brings in Old Joe, the dromedary.

At first, Reynolds didn't realize what he had in Camels and continued to push his Reyno brand, as well as Osman, a new blend of flue-cured and Turkish. The first real sales campaign for Camels was launched in Cleveland, Ohio, where pictures and coupons and other sales gimmicks were dispensed with as an excuse to price Camels at the low rate of 10 cents for a pack of twenty cigarettes. When the trials proved successful, Reynolds decided to concentrate on one brand and push it hard. It was easier for Reynolds than the other firms that already had heavy investments in their established cigarette brands to do such a thing. All the Reynolds brands were new. In its national campaign of 1914, Reynolds adopted "teaser" advertisements, such as "Camels! Tomorrow there will be more Camels in this town than in all Asia and Africa combined!" Then came the picture on the package, clearly a concession to the early taste for Turkish leaf. Its brand image and package design were inspired by "Old Joe," a Barnum & Bailey dromedary. Reynolds spent nearly $1.5 million on advertising Camels during the brand's springboard year, and sales began to climb steadily.[6]

Susan Wagner mentions the dromedary as an advertising theme of exotic character — one detail among many about the extent and type of advertising for the brand. Her candid judgment about the lack of coupons, the reasons for Reynolds's flexibility (that it had no established brand) and the businesslike attitude toward advertising are parts of a truth that the author of the company pamphlet had no interest in bringing out. This passage describes a shrewd business process rather than a humorous, narrative episode. Like the company pamphlet, the style is simple, direct, and aimed at a general audience; however, the narrative provides more factual, general information and fewer personal incidents, vivid actions, and character confrontations. Wagner's verbs, for example, indicate general actions in a nondramatic fashion — *realize, was, proved,*

[5]From *Cigarette Country: Tobacco in American History and Politics* by Susan Wagner, p. vi–vii. Copyright © 1971 by Praeger Publishers, Inc. Reprinted by permission of Holt, Rinehart and Winston, Publishers.
[6]Wagner, p. 50.

decided, came, spent, began — rather than the vivid, energized verbs in the company anecdote — *raced, climbed, refused, pointed out, relented, demanded, conceded, threw, snapped.*

The Fighting Camel

Old Joe takes yet another bow in *Trust in Tobacco: The Anglo-American Struggle for Power* by Maurice Corina. This book is a bit thicker than the previous one, with smaller print and much scholarly apparatus (footnotes, bibliography, index, statistical charts, and several extensive statistical appendices). Although this writer deals with the same historical material as the other two, his interests are narrower and more serious: he intends to examine the growth, struggles, and structure of the giant tobacco corporations. In his introduction, the author states that he hopes the narrative "will contribute to public understanding and knowledge at a time when interest in the great corporations has never been so strong and before the big tobacco companies, now fast diversifying their interests, submerge into other industries." The author clearly believes that knowledge of the tobacco companies is important so that they can be watched and controlled if necessary.

Old Joe lumbers into view in a chapter entitled "Unlawful Conspiracy and Realignment." In this chapter, the author discusses competition among the large companies after the Federal Trade Commission had broken the monopolistic American Tobacco, owned by Buck Duke.

That new and fiercely competitive forces had been unleashed in the United States market in the period between dissolution of Duke's Trust and his death was very evident to every American smoker. The Reynolds, Liggett & Myers, Lorillard, and American Tobacco enterprises were locked in a marketing battle of national dimensions, a struggle which finally established cigarettes as the first choice of American smokers. Holding good his promise to "give Buck Duke hell," Richard Joshua Reynolds had launched several cigarette brands, such as Reyno and Osman. They included one offered in 1913 in the Cleveland sales territory featuring the motif of Old Joe, a dromedary owned by the Barnum and Bailey circus. The brand, a blend of fine cured Bright, sweet Burley and some Turkish leaf, was called Camel, priced at 10 cents for twenty. Soon the nation's tobacco stores were queueing for stocks as smokers saw local advertisements heralding the new brand: *"Camels! Tomorrow there will be more Camels in this town than in all Asia and Africa combined."*

Duke had outlived Reynolds by seven years. But that was time enough for him to see the dramatic change in cigarette marketing which flowed from Reynolds' Camel brand. It gave Reynolds no less than 40 per cent of the nation's cigarette comsumption by the end of the Great War. Camels were firm, well-blended machine-made cigarettes. They were well named, for smokers seemed to prefer exotic names, even if some Turkish cigarettes were sham, oval-shaped blends selling alongside the genuine mixtures of Oriental and Turkish leaf. There was such a proliferation of names — at least fifty brands — that Camels, easy to say and remember, enjoyed an immediate acceptance. Reynolds had set out to establish Camels as a national favourite, taking on American Tobacco's Omar, Lorillard's Zubelda, and Liggett & Myers' pioneering paper cup-packeted Fatimas. Camels stood out amid the Deities, Moguls, Murads, Helmars, Meccas and Hassans. The Cairo, Zira, Oasis, Muriel and Condax brands were others to feel the competitive challenge. Turkish-type cigarettes had continued to sell well in spite of such bright Virginian brands as Sweet Caporals, Piedmont, Home Run and Picayune, among others.[7]

This passage is an analysis of competitive forces. In almost every sentence, Reynolds Tobacco is compared to other companies and fit into the larger pattern of market trends. Within individual sentences, the competition between companies is established: four companies are "locked in a marketing battle"; a personal rivalry exists between Reynolds and Duke; Duke watches the changes wrought by Reynolds; and the Camels win out over many other brand names. The word choice reinforces the competitive fervor: *fiercely competitive, unleashed, locked in, battles, give hell, outlived, dramatic, taking on.* Such vocabulary, not always supported by evidence, may make us wonder if the author is trying to make the case seem stronger than it actually is through verbal exaggeration. Despite the scholarly appearance of the book, detailed analysis shows limits to its scholarly objectivity. Nonetheless, the interpretation of events comes across sharply. Within such a context Old Joe seems part of the calvary, and the slogan about the invasion of camels becomes a corporate battle cry.

The Camel Vanishes

Another book on the industry, *Tobacco: The Ants and the Elephants,* doesn't contain a single camel or dromedary — and for good reason: this book is concerned with the economics of tobacco growing, the plight of the farmers, and proposals for government support. The

---

[7]From Maurice Corina, *Trust in Tobacco: The Anglo-American Struggle for Power,* pp. 144–145. Copyright © 1975 by St. Martin's Press, Inc. Used by permission.

author, Charles Mann, received his doctorate in economics from Harvard and is on the staff of the Rockefeller Foundation. Like Corina's, the book is fully documented — packed with charts, statistics, and equations. But because Mann's purpose is to show the human meaning of economic facts and government policy, he also includes the personal testimony of many farmers and their individual stories. He argues that, unless government policy changes, many farmers will be hurt; only by personal stories can he make that hurt visible. Since his concern is current and future policy, the past serves only as background for the current difficulties. He discusses the early years of this century — when Old Joe was posing for pictures — in only one paragraph, in a chapter entitled "The Geography and Politics of Tobacco."

> The twin influences of surging tobacco demand and falling cotton demand had major impact on tobacco production. By 1920 there were more than six hundred thousand acres under tobacco in North Carolina, about half of it in the coastal plain or new belt. In the North and South Carolina border belt as well, tobacco replaced cotton, with South Carolina's tobacco acreage rising from 25,000 acres in 1910 to 98,000 in 1920. Georgia, producer of particularly high-quality cotton, shifted to tobacco only when the cotton crop was decimated by the boll weevil. Georgia's tobacco acreage rose abruptly from 7,100 acres in 1918 to 25,000 in 1919. As cigarette demand climbed during the 1920s, flue-cured production grew more rapidly in the new areas than in the old, reflecting the newer's greater comparative advantage.[8]

The writer organizes this entire paragraph around the principle that production follows demand. The claim of the opening sentence is proved in the sentences that follow by three sets of comparative, before-and-after statistics. Each case is more striking in the rapidness of change than the previous one. The final sentence extends the comparison in general terms into a later period and comments on even more rapid expansion into newer areas. Thus the opening general statement of ratio is repeated four times, each time with different statistics. Always the focus is on production of tobacco and its spread, for Mann is here concerned only with the economics of tobacco.

Interestingly, none of the material we have just looked at touches on the health controversy. Although the relationship of smoking and disease is an important issue, the writers of these pieces had other purposes in

[8]From Charles Kellog Mann, *Tobacco: The Ants and the Elephants*, p. 30. Copyright © 1975 by Olympus Publishing Co. Used by permission.

mind. The issues raised in each, the overall organization, the development of issues, the kind of evidence, the word choice, and even the sentence patterns are determined by the particular purpose of each writer.

The Essay Analyzing Purpose and Technique

Perhaps in literature classes you have already written a literary analysis, discussing how certain aspects of a story, such as character development or the use of irony, contribute to the overall meaning of the story. The task of literary analysis is similar to an *analysis of purpose and technique,* except that your subject is a piece of nonfiction prose rather than a poem or short story. In this type of analysis, you show how the details of technique contribute to the larger purposes of the writer. Purpose and technique, considered together, make up the writer's overall design.

The first problem in developing this type of essay is selecting a text to analyze. First, if you choose a selection in an area about which you have some knowledge, you will already have a sense of the typical purposes and techniques of writing in that area. If, for example, you have followed a presidential campaign closely and are familiar with the issues, you already have the background against which you can consider any single campaign speech. Second, if you pick a selection related to a larger project that you are engaged in, such as a term paper, you may have additional motivation for doing the analysis. The sample essay at the end of this chapter, for example, was written in the course of research for a paper on the 1968 gun control law, mentioned earlier in our student's reading journal. This short analysis helped the student clarify something of the emotional and political climate leading up to the passage of the law. Finally, you should choose a short passage with striking features of purpose and technique, so that you can focus your paper easily and can cover all the details in a relatively short paper. As you become more adept at this type of analysis, you may wish to tackle more subtle or more extensive texts; however, at first, simple short passages will be difficult enough.

Your next task is a thorough reading and understanding of the selection. In order to analyze a text, you must know the text in detail, paying attention to every word.

Once you have understood both the complete meaning and organizational structure of the text, you should focus on identifying the details of technique. Marginal annotation is especially useful here — to help you remember details you spot as you are reading. In the margin, you can number the steps of an argument and comment on the relationship of one point to the next. You can comment on the type of evidence, on the sentence structure, on unusual word choices — or on any hunches you have about the writer's purpose. These initial marginal reactions may lead you to further thoughts and observations. Particularly useful is questioning anything that seems unusual: "Doesn't this example contradict an earlier example?" or "Why does the author linger on this point?" One clue may start you noticing a recurrent element or a general pattern.

After noting the various techniques of the selection, you should sit back and think what overall purpose the author may have had in mind — what purpose all the details serve. A journal may help you work out the connections among the separate elements you have noticed.

You should begin to think about writing your essay only when you have some consistent idea about how the selection achieves its purpose. Then you must decide on a main *analytical statement,* that is, a central idea controlling the essay, much like a thesis statement. You must decide whether you will limit yourself to one element of the overall design or will consider all the related elements in one selection; then you must select what your supporting statements and major evidence will be. Again use journal entries and random jottings to sort out your thoughts.

Before you begin the actual writing of the essay, reread the selection one more time with the following tasks in mind:

• Check to see if your analytical statement fits all the evidence of the selection or explains only a small part.
• Figure out how you will assemble all your own ideas and evidence to be an accurate representation of the original's design; let the design of your own paper crystallize by a final survey of the selection to be analyzed.
• Fill in details of evidence you missed in previous readings or which have become more important in light of your analytical statement.

Only with your thoughts beginning to take shape and your evidence assembled are you ready to write. If you skip over any of the steps just described, you may run into problems. Without accurate understanding of the text, your analysis will be misguided. Without calling attention to specific details of technique, your discussion will slide back into summary or generalizations. Without thought about the order in which the parts of your analysis fit together, the essay will be a disorganized jumble. Finally, without verifying your analysis against the text, you may miss important evidence or may make misleading claims. Writing a complex essay, such as an analysis of a writer's purpose, requires you to do many different kinds of preparatory tasks in order to develop your ideas fully.

Only when you have completed all the preliminary tasks are you ready to communicate your findings to your readers.

The Development of Your Analytical Essay

The main purpose of your analytical essay is to present a major insight into the overall design of a selected passage of writing. That insight is the *analytical statement* of the essay, described above as similar to a thesis statement or topic sentence. To flesh out the analytical statement, you must explain what you think was the writer's purpose and must give specific examples of writing techniques employed in the original text. In other words, your task is to show your readers the *pattern* of purpose and technique that you have discovered in a given selection.

Because this analytical task is such a specific one, you must take care that you do not gradually slide into a different task, such as a summary or a personal response. If your essay begins to sound like a paraphrased or summarized repetition of the original selection, you should stop and rethink what you are doing. In the course of your analysis, you may need to summarize or paraphrase a small part of the original as evidence for some claim you make, but such repetition of the original must be limited and only in service of the point you are making. Similarly, if you find yourself responding more to the content of the piece than to its design, you need to stop and think. Any personal reaction or response that you discuss should be directly related to the overall design. In this kind of essay, you do develop your own thoughts and opinions, but these thoughts and opinions must be directed toward explaining the writer's purpose and technique.

The introduction of your analytic essay should first identify the passage you are analyzing by stating the title of the book or article and the author. Include a copy if possible; otherwise give exact page and line references. Next, the analytical statement should clearly identify the major purpose and the major techniques of the original. This analytical statement will control all that follows in the paper.

The body of your essay should elaborate upon the separate elements that make up the larger design. Here you enumerate all the techniques you have discovered, supported by specific examples — using quotation, paraphrase, summary, or description. You must relate each technique to the overall analytical statement, so that the reader sees how each detail is tied in to the larger design. Transitional statements at the beginning of each paragraph (such as "Once again the author misleads the reader when

> **Transitional statements at the beginning of each paragraph help to tie the parts of the paper together.**

he implies . . ." or "The emotional anecdote discussed at length prepares the reader for the direct appeal for sympathy in the last paragraph") help to tie the parts of the paper together.

Also useful are extended discussions of the relationship of each technique to the overall purpose, as in the following example: "This particular use of statistics focuses the reader's attention on the issue of economic growth, while it excludes consideration of the effect on individual lives, which the author earlier stated was not accurately measurable. By admitting only statistical evidence and limiting the way it may be interpreted, the author can offer clear-cut — but one-sided — evidence for continuation of the current policy." The connections you make between the details of technique and the analytical statement are what will give your essay its direction and strength.

Each individual paragraph of the body of your essay may either be organized around one specific technique used throughout the passage or may focus on the variety of techniques appearing in a small part of the passage. In the first method your cumulative paragraphs will establish all the relevant techniques — one after the other. You should plan carefully the order in which you present the examples of techniques. In one analysis, for example, an early examination of a writer's attempts to slander through word choice may establish the ideas necessary to expose the disguised strategies of organization. In another analysis, the smaller details of technique may fall in place only after the larger organization is first examined.

The second method, of covering all the techniques in each small section at one time, results in going through the original selection in chronological order. This method is particularly useful if the text goes through several distinct stages. The chronological method explores how the writer builds one stage on the previous ones by adding new elements, by shifting gears, or by establishing emotional momentum. This second method is used in the sample essay that follows.

The danger of the chronological method, however, is that you may slip into summary by just repeating the arguments in the original order. Beware of transitions like "the next point the author makes is . . . backed by the next point that . . ." Such transitions indicate that you are forgetting your analysis and are slipping into a repetition of the original argument. A way to avoid this problem is to show how the character of the writer's argument shifts and develops by stages. Always keep your eye on *purposes* and *technique*. Thus the weak transition cited above might be improved in the following way: "At this point the author initiates a new stage of her argument: whereas up to here she has been arguing smaller separate points, here she brings them all together as part of a broader conclusion." Make sure you are not carried away by your example. Tell only enough to support your statement; otherwise, the ever-present temptation to summarize may overcome you. If you find the temptations to slip into summary too strong, you should avoid chronology altogether; organize your paper around specific techniques, for the first method forces you to rearrange and rethink the material.

In the conclusion of your analysis, you should do more than simply repeat your main points. You should drive home your analytical statement in a striking way that grows out of all you have said previously. After having shown the reader all your ideas and specific evidence, you should be able to come to a more penetrating observation than you could at the beginning — before you laid out the evidence. If you have additional moral, ethical, or intellectual reactions to the selection, the conclusion is the place to express such reactions. Since there is no single, all-purpose way of concluding, you should feel free to experiment. The only important point to remember is that the conclusion should grow out of and reinforce the analysis.

The following is a student sample essay analyzing the article reprinted on pages 117–119.

Sample Student Essay

Analysis of Purpose and Technique
in "Guns: Like Buying Cigarettes"

The unsigned article "Guns: Like Buying Cigarettes," appearing in <u>Newsweek</u> on June 17, 1978, turns an apparent report of events into an outraged call for action by a number of techniques aimed at crystallizing the reader's anger. Although this article appeared in the news section of the magazine, known primarily for reporting events, this piece goes beyond reporting to attempt to create support for gun legislation.

Even before the reader gets to the article, a mood is prepared by a ten-page story on the recent assassination of Senator Robert F. Kennedy. The story includes a dramatic picture of the senator being lifted from a pool of blood. Distress at these events becomes anger when the reader turns to the article on guns and sees the accompanying photograph captioned, "The Gun That Killed Robert Kennedy." The emotionally aroused reader will then have his or her emotions confirmed and focused by this article. Anger against the assassin is turned to anger against guns.

The title of the essay makes a link to another killer, cigarettes. The comparison emphasizes that objects like guns and cigarettes are to blame rather than people. The comparison creates further emotion by what it leaves unstated, that guns are obviously more threatening. The reader feels, "How can such terrible things as guns be sold over the counter, virtually unregulated? If a youngster can get a pack of cigarettes, can he also get a gun as easily?"

In the opening paragraph, the author re-emphasizes the gun as the villain, by linking guns to their victims and leaving out the murderers who pulled the triggers. The long catalogue of weapons sounds like a frightening arsenal. The language reflects that threatening atmosphere and reminds one of a gangster movie: <u>cut down</u>, <u>felled</u>, <u>snub-nosed</u>, <u>snuffed out the life</u>.

The next paragraph defines the problem in larger terms, providing statistics on the effects of guns. The writer

moves from the dramatic specificity of the first paragraph
to the staggeringly large numbers of the second paragraph
and again points the finger at guns rather than people as
the villain. The characterization of the general problem as
a "national tragedy" also involves an interesting shift.
Usually the term "national tragedy" refers to some specific
event like a single assassination, a war, an earthquake,
but this author wants to link such events with a more
general condition. Notice that the topic is not even the
<u>use</u> of guns; the author is talking about the <u>availability</u>
of guns. The link between all the guns available and the
particular guns described so vividly in the first paragraph
is brought out by the term "fantastic arsenal." The comparison to war deaths also makes the link between guns
and real deaths.

   The writer continues to stir up our emotions in later
paragraphs by using such words as <u>grim statistics</u>,
<u>outrage</u>, <u>overwhelmingly approved</u>, <u>extraordinary achieve-
ment</u>, and <u>glaringly weak</u>. Readers are never in doubt about
which side of the legislative struggle they should support.
When the opposing view is introduced, the views of the
National Rifle Association (NRA) are given only four lines
after the whole article has been stirring up feelings in
the opposite direction. The NRA's position is immediately
buried under all the laws of other nations.

   The writer buttresses the case against guns with surveys,
a presidential address, and more statistics. After readers
are overwhelmed with the gravity of the situation and are
thoroughly enraged by the easy availability of guns, the

emotions are turned to sadness as the writer remembers Robert Kennedy's speech on his proposed gun law. The reader is left feeling that the law should be passed, if only in Kennedy's memory.

Throughout the article, emotional language plays upon the vulnerable feelings of Americans who have just experienced a string of shocking assassinations. The writer whips up the emotions, turns them against the object of guns, and finally offers a way to get rid of the menace through legislation. This article and others like it must have been to some degree successful in capitalizing on the nation's mood for legislative action, because a major gun law was passed later that year.

GUNS: LIKE BUYING CIGARETTES[9]

By now the weapons have become inexorably linked with the victims. It was a 6.5-mm. Mannlicher-Carcano carbine that cut down John F. Kennedy. It was a .30-'06 Enfield rifle that killed Medgar Evers. It was a .30-'06 Remington pump rifle that felled Martin Luther King. And it was a snub-nosed .22-caliber Iver Johnson revolver that snuffed out the life of Robert F. Kennedy. Though the guns vary in size, shape and ballistic characteristics, all of them share one thing in common — they are, as President Johnson angrily pointed out last week, as easy to get as "baskets of fruit or cartons of cigarettes."

Indeed, the very availability of firearms in the United States amounts in one breath to a national tradition and a national tragedy. No one knows exactly how many guns are in private hands in the country; estimates range from a conservative 50 million up to an astounding 200 million. What this fantastic arsenal produces, however, is eminently measurable. In 1966, for instance, guns of one kind or another accounted for 6,500 murders in the U.S., 10,000 suicides and 2,600 accidental deaths. Since the turn of the century, three quarters of a million Americans have been killed by privately owned guns in the United

---

[9]From *Newsweek*, 17 June 1968, p. 46. Copyright 1968, by Newsweek, Inc. All rights reserved. Reprinted by permission.

States — more Americans than have died in battle in all the wars fought by the U.S.

Passage: Last week, the weight of these grim statistics combined with the outrage at the assassination of Robert Kennedy and the recent emphasis on fighting crime in the streets to push the first piece of gun-control legislation through Congress in more than 30 years. The gun-control provisions, part of an omnibus anticrime bill overwhelmingly approved by the House of Representatives and sent on to the President, makes it illegal for a person to purchase a handgun in a state other than his own, either by mail order or directly over the counter. In addition, it prohibits felons, mental incompetents and veterans who received less than honorable discharges from possessing any kind of firearms at all.

Some members of Congress were quick to claim that the gun-control legislation was an extraordinary achievement. "This bill is far, far tougher than anyone realizes," said Sen. Thomas Dodd of Connecticut, who has been fighting for gun control for years. Considering that the bill was passed over the objections of one of the most formidable lobbies in Washington, the 900,000-member National Rifle Association, which has argued long and hard that there is no connection between the availability of firearms and the spiraling crime rate, Dodd's optimism was at least understandable. Judged against the strict gun-control standards in most other civilized countries of the world, however, the legislation — and, for that matter, the NRA's argument about availability — seemed glaringly weak.

Loophole: The public apparently shares this view. The day Senator Kennedy was shot, a nationwide Gallup survey showed that most people in the U.S. favored the registration of all firearms in the country. The President also had reservations about the legislation. No sooner had the gun-control measure cleared the House last week than Mr. Johnson made a nationwide television address. The President said that strict curbs on who can own guns had had a profound effect on crime in other countries. "Each year in this country, guns are involved in more than 6,500 murders," he said. "This compares with 30 in England, 99 in Canada, 68 in West Germany and 37 in Japan." Growing more emotion, Mr. Johnson denounced the bill before him as a "halfway measure. It covers adequately only transactions involving handguns. It leaves the deadly commerce in lethal shotguns and rifles without effective control." Later, Mr. Johnson indicated that he would try to plug what he described as "the brutal loophole" in the law by trying to extend the bill's provisions to the interstate sale of rifles and shotguns as well as handguns.

Responsibility: But similar amendments proposed by Sen. Edward Kennedy last month were defeated, and it seemed likely that the President's proposals would find the going just as rough. Still, there was little doubt that for the moment, at least, Congress would have to look hard to discover a more appropriate memorial to Robert Kennedy. It was just two years ago that Bobby told his colleagues: "We have a responsibility to the victims of crime and violence. For too long, we have dealt with deadly weapons as if they were harmless toys. Yet their very presence, the ease of their acquisition and the familiarity of their appearance have led to thousands of deaths each year and countless other crimes of violence as well. It is time that we wipe this stain of violence from our land."

Writing Assignments

1. Analyze the overall design of a short article you have come across as part of your research for a major research project. The audience for your analysis will be someone who shares your research interest.

2. In an essay of five-hundred words, analyze the design of a chapter in an elementary textbook on a subject you know well. Consider how effectively the chapter introduces the subject to a beginning student. The reader of your analysis will be a teacher who must decide whether to use the textbook in a course next semester.

3. In an essay of five-hundred words, analyze the purpose and technique of *one* of the following passages on friendship. The readers of your analysis will be your classmates; compare the different designs of the three selections as analyzed by different members of the class.

a. From Cicero's philosophic essay "On Friendship" on pages 81–82 of this text.

b. From Dale Carnegie's self-help book *How to Win Friends and Influence People* on pages 82–83.

c. From Harry Stack Sullivan's chapter on preadolescence in *The Interpersonal Theory of Psychiatry*:

NEED FOR INTERPERSONAL INTIMACY[10]

Just as the juvenile era was marked by a significant change — the development of the need for compeers, for playmates rather like oneself — the beginning of preadolescence is equally spectacularly marked, in my scheme of development, by the appearance of a new type of interest in another person. These changes are the result of maturation and development, or experience. This new interest in the preadolescent era is not as general as the use of language toward others was

[10]Selection is reprinted from *The Interpersonal Theory of Psychiatry* by Harry Stack Sullivan, M.D., pp. 245–246, by permission of W. W. Norton & Company, Inc. Copyright 1953 by the William Alanson White Psychiatric Foundation.

in childhood, or the need of similar people as playmates was in the juvenile era. Instead, it is a specific new type of interest in a *particular* member of the same sex who becomes a chum or a close friend. This change represents the beginning of something very like full-blown, psychiatrically defined *love*. In other words, the other fellow takes on a perfectly novel relationship with the person concerned: he becomes of practically equal importance in all fields of value. Nothing remotely like that has ever appeared before. All of you who have children are sure that your children love you; when you say that, you are expressing a pleasant illusion. But if you will look very closely at one of your children when he finally finds a chum — somewhere between eight-and-a-half and ten — you will discover something very different in the relationship — namely, that your child begins to develop a real sensitivity to what matters to another person. And this is not in the sense of "what should I do to get what I want," but instead "what should I do to contribute to the happiness or to support the prestige and feeling of worth-whileness of my chum." So far as I have ever been able to discover, nothing remotely like this appears before the age of, say, eight-and-a-half, and sometimes it appears decidedly later.

Thus the developmental epoch of preadolescence is marked by the coming of the integrating tendencies which, when they are completely developed, we call love, or, to say it another way, by the manifestation of the need for interpersonal intimacy. Now even at this late stage in my formulation of these ideas, I still find that some people imagine that intimacy is only a matter of approximating genitals one to another. And so I trust that you will finally and forever grasp that interpersonal intimacy can really consist of a great many things without genital contact; that intimacy in this sense means, just as it always has meant, closeness, without specifying that which is close other than the persons. Intimacy is that type of situation involving two people which permits validation of all components of personal worth. Validation of personal worth requires a type of relationship which I call collaboration, by which I mean clearly formulated adjustments of one's behavior to the expressed needs of the other person in the pursuit of increasingly identical — that is, more and more nearly mutual — satisfactions, and in the maintenance of increasingly similar security operations. Now this preadolescent collaboration is distinctly different from the acquisition, in the juvenile era, of habits of competition, cooperation, and compromise. In preadolescence not only do people occupy themselves in moving toward a common, more-or-less impersonal objective, such as the success of "our team," or the discomfiture of "our teacher," as they might have done in the juvenile era, but they also, specifically and increasingly, move toward supplying each other with satisfactions and taking on each other's successes in the maintenance of prestige, status, and all the things which represent freedom from anxiety, or the diminution of anxiety.

5

Evaluating the Book as a Whole: The Book Review

Preview

A book review tells not just what is in a book but also what a book attempts to achieve and how it can be used. To discuss the uses of a book, you must explore your own reactions, for these reactions reveal how you have responded to the book. Thus, in writing a review, you combine the skills of describing what is on the page, analyzing how the book tries to achieve its purpose, and expressing your own reactions. The nature and length of the review depend on the book, the purpose of the review, and the anticipated audience. The shorter the review, the more succinctly you must present your judgments. By writing reviews, you will develop your critical skills as a reader and researcher, and you will be mastering a form of writing that is sometimes assigned in college courses in the humanities and social sciences.

The Use of Tools

Every month *Popular Mechanics* reviews tools, informing its readers about the uses of new gadgets on the market. Here is one example, a review of a thumb wheel ratchet.

THUMB WHEEL RATCHET[1]

I found S-K Tools' new quarter-inch thumb wheel ratchet terrific for reaching into cramped spaces. It gives good leverage and maneuvers in the tightest places you'll encounter under your hood. Thumb wheel set comes in an 8-piece pouch — six sockets plus the ratchet and a short extension. All are compatible with your present quarter-inch tools. We have seen S-K Set No. 4908-78 in auto parts stores for $12. Or order from S-K Tool Group, Dresser Industries, 3201 North Wolf Rd., Franklin Park, Ill. 60131. — *M.L.*

No matter how beautiful, ingenious, or well made the tool is, no one will spend any money for it unless it works. The new tool must help the user accomplish a task more easily than before. Thus a review of a tool must take into account not just what a tool is but also what the needs and experiences of the user may be. If the writer of the above review never was frustrated in working a full-sized ratchet into a tight place, he would not have been so happy to discover a thumb wheel ratchet and would not have endorsed it so highly. From the recommendation of leverage and maneuverability, the reader knows that M. L. has spent happy moments under the hood of his own car with this wonderful new invention.

A review of tools may even — strangely enough — report on the emotional response of the dirt-under-the-fingernails reviewer; as any reader of *Popular Mechanics* would know, there is a sensual pleasure and a personal relationship between the working person and tools. The following review of a synthetic chamois tells us as much about the emotions of the reviewer B. H. as about the product: the frustration over confusing labeling, the grudging admission of the product's quality, and the supreme romanticism in praising the smell and feel of the natural product.

SYNTHETIC CHAMOIS[2]

"Okay, what's in the tube?" ask friends who see the product container labeled "Fireman's Friend." There's no way to know that it's a

---

[1]Reprinted from *Popular Mechanics*, June 1978, p. 62. Copyright © 1978 by the Hearst Corporation. Used by permission.
[2]Reprinted from *Popular Mechanics*, June 1978, p. 62. Copyright © 1978 by the Hearst Corporation. Used by permission.

> **A book is a tool for communication between two minds; how a reviewer reacts helps you know how well the writer communicated.**

synthetic chamois. It got its name because its first users were firemen, say the distributors. (Well, you've never seen a dirty fire engine, have you?) This high-quality plastic-sponge "skin" or "total towel" as it's variously called by its makers, is 17 by 27 inches and costs $9 — cheaper than a real chamois skin. Yes, it works almost as well, is tough and durable, doesn't dry out in time like an animal skin, doesn't rot, is grease resistant and is conveniently stored wet in its own case. But, no, it doesn't feel and smell like the real thing and I'm enough of a sensualist to stick with chamois. Fireman's Friend, Inc., Box 64, Elmhurst, Ill. 60126. — *B.H.*

Books as Tools

If reviewers of ratchets and plastic cloths find it necessary to mingle personal experience and pleasures with concrete descriptions of the products, then how much more does a book reviewer need to mingle personal thoughts and strong reactions with a description of the content in order to give readers a fair estimate of a book? A book is a tool for communication between two minds; how a reviewer reacts helps you know how well the writer communicated.

This text has thus far kept methods of developing your subjective responses separate from methods of gaining objective knowledge of a text. Marginal annotations, journals, and the response essay have encouraged you to look into yourself for personal reactions, which you have then developed. On the other hand, paraphrase, summary, and analysis of purpose have sharpened your vision for what exactly appears on the page — outside of yourself. In actuality, the division of labors isn't that simple. The more deeply you understand what is on the page, the more you will react. Since it is natural to respond intensely to an intensely received message, the more engaged you are in a subject, the more you will want to understand what others have written. An animated conversation is a two-way affair.

In the evaluative book review, these two streams — an accurate reading and a strong response — come together, for the reviewer should indicate what is in the book and what the contents might mean to a reader. The reviewer's own reaction reveals to the potential book buyer what may be gained from reading the book. If the reviewer does not go beyond a summary of the original, this dull restatement gives the reader no clear direction to follow. If, however, the reviewer indicates the kind of communication that passed between two minds via the printed page, the reader can decide whether the book offers the kind of mental interaction he or she wants.

Because writing a review makes you consider not just what a book says and how it is put together but also what thoughts it evokes in you and what personal use you can put it to, writing a book review forces you to come to terms with a book. You evaluate the entire transaction between the author and yourself.

New York Times Review

Consider the following review by Anatole Broyard of the *New York Times*. Broyard succinctly presents the contents of the book *Death As a Fact of Life* — the task of summary — and also paraphrases some of the more impressive moments of the book. As he might reveal in a journal or in marginal notes, Broyard indicates at length how the book affects him as an individual and discusses the personally important questions the book raises. In essence, he reveals the sum of his own thoughts on the subject — as in an informal essay of response. We see Broyard, excited and concerned, speculating about what he has read and engaging author David Hendin in conversation. Even the analysis of Hendin's technique is closely related to the reviewer's reactions as a reader.

THE OBSTETRICS OF THE SOUL[3]

"I don't understand what I'm supposed to do," Tolstoy said on his deathbed — and neither do most of us. The conspiracy of silence with which we surround the subject of dying led Geoffrey Gorer, the British anthropologist, to coin the phrase "the pornography of death." But a "good death" is an indispensable end to a good life — so crucial, in fact, that a German writer called it the "obstetrics of the soul." To die with dignity is important not only to the dying person, but also to his or her survivors, who will always be able to remember the one they loved in this light.

According to David Hendin in his *Death as a Fact of Life,* dying today is often rendered obscene by technology. Many patients are kept alive

---

[3]From *Aroused by Books,* by Anatole Broyard, pp. 34–36. Copyright © 1974 by Anatole Broyard. Reprinted by permission of Random House, Inc.

when they are no longer human beings, but simple circulatory systems, breathing but otherwise unresponsive tissue. Under these circumstances, life may sometimes be more terrifying than death. The dying person's relatives and friends are elbowed away from him by machines. And since these machines interfere with the natural course of decline, no one knows exactly when death will come and the patient often expires with only technology for company. In this connection, the author quotes Theodore Fox's famous remark: "We shall have to learn to refrain from doing things merely because we know how to do them."

Mr. Hendin quotes surveys to show that most dying people would prefer to talk about it, and are greatly relieved when the silence is broken. I know that as I read his book, I felt my own anxieties about death first articulated, then partially assuaged. It *is* therapeutic to bring that immemorial enemy of ours out into the light. As the author points out, for some of us the threat of death can have an integrative rather than a disruptive function. It can make us see our life as a coherent whole and give us an opportunity to sum it up emotionally and intellectually — to deny the fashionable charge of "meaninglessness or absurdity."

Accepting death is not necessarily a form of resignation, of giving up: it may be a positive reorientation. We can look *back* over our life as well as forward to its end. We can congratulate ourselves on what we have done and reverse the old saw that "you can't take it with you." By renouncing the terrible duty of pretending, Mr. Hendin says, we can take the bandages off our fears and our feelings and die with love instead of lies as the last thing we hear.

The author has done a brilliant and highly sensitive job of bringing together the literature of death — from the need for revising our legal, medical and psychological criteria to the fact that the dead are forcing the living into an ever-decreasing space. He discusses the science of cryonics, or freezing the body in the hope of future resuscitation (cost, $20,000); the case for and against euthanasia; the need to train doctors to *face* death as well as to fight it; the "hospices" being built for dying people, so that they can spend their last days in as homelike an atmosphere as their medical needs permit; the advantages of cremation and its relative unpopularity in the United States, and much more.

I found the chapter "Children and Death" especially moving. Mr. Hendin knows how to evoke a feeling as well as most novelists and he is never, as far as I can remember, guilty of mere sentimentality in dealing with the most highly charged subject in our emotional repertory. Warning us against feeding inane euphemisms to children, he cites the case of a little boy who was told that his dead mother "went up into the sky." Shortly afterwards, the boy was taken on a visit by airplane and was very sad and disappointed because he had looked on every cloud but had not seen his mother. Informed that his infant brother had been picked up by God and taken to heaven, another child kept his windows locked, refused to cross open spaces and played only in the shade of trees for fear the same thing would happen to him.

Unacknowledged death haunts us far more effectively than the ghosts of our childhood. The author feels that the more fully it is faced, the sooner we are likely to recover from the shock of someone's death. If we do not make peace with them and separate ourselves from the dead through appropriate periods of mourning and grief, we may find it difficult to attach ourselves to anyone who might help replace them afterwards.

Though there is not a superfluous page in *Death as a Fact of Life,* I found myself — emotionally, not morbidly — drawn to those passages dealing with the dying person. When Mr. Hendin speaks of the indignity of deterioration, I remember the humiliation I saw in my own father's face when he was a Rube Goldberg tangle of tubes and life-coercing machines. His difficulties were increased by his "still upper lip" philosophy that locked both of us in the anguish of all that we wanted to, and could not say. A terrible loneliness lurked in his eyes, but it was too late for him to learn or to change.

What the author does not say because it may be beyond the scope of his intent is that our entire life is a preparation for our death, and we may expect to die well or badly depending on how we have lived. Freud told a story of visiting William James at a time when the American psychologist and philosopher had a brush with death in the form of a heart attack. He could not refrain from asking James afterward how he had felt about the prospect. James replied that he had lived his life and done his work. Death held no terrors for him. Edmund Bergler, the psychiatrist, remarks in one of his many books that, after a satisfying sexual experience with someone we love, it is natural to feel sleepy. I mention these two remarks because I feel that, somewhere between them, we may find the answer to one of life's most intimidating questions.

Broyard's personal reflections are always in contact with Hendin's themes and questions. We gain a clear impression of the main theme of the book — that the dying and surviving do better to face death — and the various subtopics explored under that theme, ranging from present-day attitudes to the possibilities of cryonics. We also observe how each of these topics affects the reviewer and inspires his personal meditations. When the reviewer contemplates his own understanding of death and his attempts to come to terms with it, he is doing precisely what the book has urged him to do: he is facing death as a fact of life. The more deeply he reads the book, the more deeply he goes into himself. This personal journey lets readers of Broyard's review know what it might be like to read the book themselves, to consider the same questions, to face similar memories, and to experience troublesome feelings.

Fortunately for the sake of our good spirits, not all books ask us to look so deeply into ourselves. Most of the books we read do, however, remind us of our previous experiences, knowledge, thoughts, or emotions. The reviewer, though not always soul-searching, does need to seek out that part of the self touched by the book. Just as the reviewer of the thumb-screw ratchet describes his triumph in getting at difficult corners and the reviewer of an artificial chamois considers its sensual pleasures, so must the book reviewer find the appropriate kinds of response for each book.

Specialized Periodical Review

A specialized interest may be shared by only a limited group of people, but writers appealing to that interest try to provide what these individuals are looking for. Flower growing, for example, is not a hobby shared by everyone, but to those who do share it the experience and knowledge involved are quite real and concrete. The review below from *Horticulture,* a magazine on gardening, reveals what information the book contains and how that information may appeal to the interested reader. Through the experience and feelings of the reviewer, we see the realms of practical action, background knowledge, nostalgia, and aesthetic pleasure.

THE COMPLETE BOOK OF BULBS[4]
by F. F. Rockwell and Esther Grayson. Revised by
Marjorie J. Dietz.
New York: J. B. Lippincott. $10.00.
Reviewed by Jean S. Kennedy

The gift of a dozen Red Emperor tulip bulbs and no idea of how to plant them led me to the purchase of my first book on gardening. This was many years ago and the book was one of the first editions of Rockwell and Grayson's *Complete Book of Bulbs.* It remains, for me at least, one of the best books on the subject for the amateur.

Now there is a new edition, carefully revised by Marjorie Dietz. The list of pesticides has been brought up to date along with a discussion of federal and state controls, controls which didn't exist at the time of the book's first publication. Hopefully it may never be necessary to use any of the treatments but the references are there if needed. Excellent planting guides inside the front and back covers, show the actual bulbs and the depths at which to plant. The life cycles of some of the more

---

[4]Jean S. Kennedy, Rev. of *The Complete Book of Bulbs,* by F. F. Rockwell and Esther Grayson. *Horticulture* LVI, no. 6 (1978), p. 14. Copyright © by Jean S. Kennedy. Used by permission.

common bulbs are presented in interesting circular diagrams easy to understand and of great help to the novice.

In the *Gardeners' Bulb Selector,* a very useful list in the back, many new varieties of tulips have been added, while the names of the species have been inexplicably omitted. The species are a delightful group — the perfect bulbs for a sunny rock garden. I miss, also, some photographs of bulbs which flowered at Gray Rock — home of the authors — but perhaps they were no longer available. These are minor criticisms, however, and I am glad to see one of my old favorites brought out in a new edition for a whole new generation of gardeners.

In almost every sentence the reviewer Jean Kennedy mentions a different use she makes of the book. From her recollections of an earlier edition, she can personally testify that the book is useful for beginners and remains an old and trusty reference. Even more, she immediately puts in focus the aim of the book — the pleasure of flowers. The final sentence of the first paragraph ties all these uses together.

With the mention of technical advances and of basic unchanging information, she points to the practical aspect of maintaining a garden — the digging around in the soil and the spraying of noxious chemicals. Besides commending the technical information, the reviewer lets us know the usefulness of the information on the life cycle of bulbs presented in the book. Thus she appreciates armchair theory as well as actual practice. Throughout, she reassures the reader that all the types of information are presented in a manner appropriate to the beginner's experience and knowledge.

The final paragraph returns to the particular pleasures of flowers: she mentions an expanded list of bulbs and a discussion of the photographs included in previous editions, but unfortunately missing from this one. She ends the review with her sense of delight in sharing one of her favorite books with new gardeners.

This review does its job well, even though its subject is of limited appeal and the prose seems quite ordinary. The review does convey all the levels on which the book operates: the book's content, the response it evokes, and the uses readers might make of it.

Popular Magazine Review

Books of more general interest are reviewed in Sunday newspaper supplements and general circulation magazines such as *Time* and *Newsweek*. For these publications, the reviewer must indicate the more generally shared interests to which the book appeals and must present her opinions in an energetic style that will hold the attention of the casual reader. The following review describes a book on a subject we all recognize, television news and news personalities. The review pinpoints the appeal of the book: the public's taste for the dirty truth behind the pristine image.

TELE-TATTLETALES[5]
Air Time: The Inside Story of CBS News.
By Gary Paul Gates.
440 pages. Harper & Row. $12.95.

by Betsy Carter

Inveterate gossips that they are, many journalists can't resist surrendering to a common fantasy: to write about the politics and pettiness of the organizations that employ them. Former CBS News writer Gary Paul Gates is no exception. His book, "Air Time: The Inside Story of CBS News," is a fascinating tattletale of power-hungry executives stabbing each other in the back for promotions, fiercely competitive vice presidents playing sophisticated war games with each other and ambitious correspondents desperately vying for precious air exposure.

Rich in tart quotes and juicy anecdotes, "Air Time" mischievously unwraps personalities carefully packaged by television and strips them of their glossy mystiques. Former correspondent Daniel Schorr is portrayed as a self-pitying "crybaby" with an oversize ego. Harry Reasoner is called "slipshod" and "nonchalant." Dan Rather is described as such an eager people pleaser that his former Washington bureau chief, William Small, once compared him to Hubert Humphrey. "If they were women," Small observed, "they'd be pregnant all the time." And former senior vice president Gordon Manning — "overbearing and meddlesome" — reigns like Lucifer in Gates's inferno.

Bawdy Parody: Not even Walter Cronkite emerges unscathed. Off-screen, he is far more egocentric and forbidding than his avuncular on-screen persona. Once, when an executive producer suggested sending letters of commendation to bureaus whenever they delivered outstanding stories, Cronkite scorned it as "a damn-fool idea" and decided that it would be much more effective to send them letters of reprimand when they fell down on the job. According to Gates, Cronkite warms up the annual Christmas party with a bawdy parody of a burlesque stripper.

While Gates is indiscriminate with the network's dirty linen, he is more selective in chronicling the coming of age of television from the Edward R. Murrow "See It Now" years through the Vietnam '60s to the Watergate '70s. Through these politically heated times, the network

[5]Betsy Carter, "Tele-Tattletales," Rev. of *Air Time* by Gary Paul Gates. *Newsweek,* 12 June 1978, pp. 102–103. Copyright © 1978 by Newsweek, Inc. All rights reserved. Reprinted by permission.

bore the wrath of angry presidents. President Johnson is depicted phoning CBS president Frank Stanton about the network's critical war coverage and telling him, "Frank, this is your President and yesterday your boys shat on the American flag." And after CBS aired a series on the Watergate scandal, Presidential aide Charles Colson telephoned Stanton to inform him that the Nixon Administration was going to use its power to attack CBS on Madison Avenue and Wall Street. "We'll break your network," Colson supposedly shouted.

Eye for Detail: Gates, a newswriter for the Cronkite show from 1969 until 1973, when he left to write "The Palace Guard" with Rather, is an indefatigable reporter with a jaundiced eye for detail and an easy conversational writing style. Unfortunately, he gets so intoxicated by minutiae that his critical judgment is often blurred. (Must we really know, for example, that playwright Arthur Miller attended the University of Michigan at the same time as CBS executive producer Bud Benjamin?)

Indeed, reading "Air Time" is a little like watching the evening news. At its best, the book is eye-opening and informative. At its worst, it trivializes a major electronic news-gathering operation into a series of gossipy — though highly amusing — anecdotes. Is that really the way it is?

Once Betsy Carter has informed readers of the gossipy nature of the book, she shares the fun by repeating — through quotation and paraphrase — some of the juiciest tidbits about newscasters and politicians. Her praise of technique, noticing the author's "jaundiced eye for detail and an easy conversational writing style," is consistent with what pleasures she finds in the book. However, by criticizing the writer as being "intoxicated by minutiae," she points to the book's limitations. A string of anecdotes about personalities does not provide her with enough information; she feels the need for a work of more serious purposes and more serious techniques to provide a well-rounded picture.

Betsy Carter's evaluation is not a scholarly judgment; she does not assume that truth must be explored and underlying principles discovered for science's sake. Instead her evaluation is based on her feeling that to come away satisfied from a book a reader needs the sense of a story fairly and realistically told. Readers who desire solid information and a sense of how the world operates may be insulted if they are only given random details intended to amuse them.

Scholarly Review

A scholarly review, on the other hand, must be concerned with truth, accuracy, and comprehensiveness rather than with only an

> **We read scholarly books with a different part of our knowledge, experience, and selves — the part that seeks firm answers to specific questions. We read scholarly books with all our critical faculties, with an attitude of "prove it to me."**

appearance of reality. We read scholarly books with a different part of our knowledge, experience, and selves — the part that seeks firm answers to specific questions. We read scholarly books with all our critical faculties, with an attitude of "prove it to me." The review below from the scholarly journal *Renaissance Quarterly* suggests that the book under consideration meets neither the criteria of a scholarly book nor those of a popular one.

TUDOR WOMEN: COMMONERS AND QUEENS[6]
by Pearl Hogrefe
Ames: Iowa State University Press.
1975. xiv+170 pp. $6.95
Review by Janis Butler Holm and Katherine M. Loring

Studies of women in their historical and cultural context in the English Renaissance have been scarce. Despite considerable scholarly attention to female characters in Elizabethan literature and to a handful of extraordinary historical female figures, one discovers little sophisticated enquiry into the social situation of sixteenth-century English women as a whole. There are some discussions of cosmetics, dress, and rules for ladylike behavior, some speculations about domestic life, but few of these reach beyond the descriptive to the analytical. The infrequent works attempting to demonstrate more fully the Elizabethan woman's place in society focus chiefly on traditional activities, and more recent studies reflecting current interest in women in nontraditional positions primarily consider women since 1700. Pearl Hogrefe's *Tudor Women: Commoners and Queens* is the first attempt to study closely the range of roles women played in English life from 1485 to 1603.

Sadly, *Tudor Women* fails to provide an examination from which many can profit. In her preface Professor Hogrefe explains that she has

---

[6]Janis Butler Holm and Katherine M. Loring, rev. of *Tudor Women: Commoners and Queens* by Pearl Hogrefe, *Renaissance Quarterly* XXX, no. 2 (1977), pp. 258–260. Copyright © 1977 by Renaissance Society of America. Used by permission.

attempted "to combine sound scholarship with simplicity of form," to interest both scholarly and general readers. Her intention is good — too much scholarship consists of specialists writing for other specialists. But *Tudor Women,* like Aesop's old man with the donkey, fails to satisfy every audience or, unfortunately, any audience. In trying to mesh the approaches of the social researcher and the historian of ideas, Hogrefe has isolated the least attractive tendencies of each, offering arid documentation interrupted occasionally by unfocused abstraction.

Although she has assembled much interesting and valuable information, her presentation often reduces the material's inherent interest and value, as promising themes are briefly introduced, then discarded. The book's subtitle, "Commoners and Queens," offers one possible shaping principle for the work. (Was there tension between commoners and queens? Mutual support? Did Elizabeth's strong rule advance the social position of her sex? If so, how?) But Hogrefe never pursues this; nor does she develop another focus suggested in the introduction — that Tudor women escaped their limitations through action and education.

Without focus, examples proliferate and grow tiresome. Hogrefe repeatedly fails to place her examples in a context, omitting important intellectual and social background and neglecting to provide a statistical basis of comparison for female achievements. Especially disappointing is her failure to explore the relationship between facts and their context. When she does attempt explanations, they are incomplete. Examining the decrease of women's participation in crafts and trade, she observes that it may be attributable in part to population growth in the sixteenth century and cites a number of gross population statistics. Here and elsewhere, we wish that Hogrefe had explored further the implications of her data. Is she suggesting that Elizabethan industry tolerated women when the number of positions available was less or equal to the number of men able to work? To what extent were sex-role expectations attributable to the economy, attributable to other related factors? Are we to see an irony in that Elizabeth, by keeping England fairly peaceful and prosperous, indirectly may have limited opportunities for other women to step outside traditional roles?

Hogrefe's poor grasp of the material as a whole creates many difficulties for the reader — poorly integrated examples, haphazardly placed information, aimless repetition. Her bibliographic citations are often arbitrary, and her failure always to mention her source creates problems for the scholarly reader. Certain questions of methodology, so important in a developing academic field, are never addressed in this book. When documents do not differentiate men and women in reporting certain activities, do we assume that no women participated or that their participation was taken for granted? Women's studies would be served by having such procedural problems brought to light; Hogrefe leaves the problems, and the reader, in the dark.

A lively manner may make faults of omission and illogic less notice-able, but Hogrefe presents her material in a dry textbook tone. It is doubtful that the general reader will find her catalogic manner intrigu-ing, while the specialist will feel that a presentation of seemingly unrelated factors, much in the mode of elementary recitation, consti-tutes inventory, not scholarship.

If our examination seems harsh, we must attribute that harshness to disappointed expectations. *Tudor Women* could have provided a long-needed context for Renaissance studies in several disciplines. It could have given coherence to a scattered lot of miscellaneous material by offering useful hypothesis and speculation. It does not do these things, and that is regrettable.

The two reviewers' main complaint is that the author, Pearl Hogrefe, does not adequately interpret the various facts offered the reader. This complaint clearly follows from their critical and scholarly viewpoint, which seeks patterns, causes, explanations, and synthesis. The demands of scholarly experience are more rigorous than those of other more familiar approaches to life. Janis Butler Holm and Katherine Loring are not willing to accept a random catalogue of facts: they are unhappy with an argument dropped before it is completed and are impatient with examples that fail to demonstrate the issue at hand. They seek a rational argument that takes into account all the specific evidence and that clarifies the *connection* between all the ideas used. The argument must be sup-ported by high standards of documentation and evidence, for otherwise a critical reader will remain in some doubt about the accuracy of state-ments. The scholar wants to eliminate doubt and establish knowledge with as much certainty as possible.

The two reviewers do consider an alternative — that the book may serve the less rigorous taste of the general public who might find the subject intriguing. Here, too, they find the book wanting: tediousness will not be popular, even as dullness is not the substance of scholarship.

The disappointment expressed by the reviewers reveals the inter-dependence of scholars, who need each other's work and thought to build on and support their own work. In both introduction and conclu-sion, the review complains of the lack of a serious study of "the social situation of sixteenth-century English women as a whole." Such a study is needed to make sense of scattered information and to provide a solid body of information that other scholars can develop. What these review-ers are looking for is known in scholarship as the *definitive work,* a work that settles specific questions to the satisfaction of experts in the area. A definitive work allows researchers to go on to more advanced questions on the basis of reasonable answers to the basic problems. As new information comes to light, a definitive work may lose its standing; but for as long as it is recognized, it simplifies the work of all scholars in the field. The reviewers here would like certain questions resolved so that other work can proceed; because the book under review — in their opinion — makes no serious attempt to address these questions, the keenness of their disappointment is understandable.

Writing a Book Review

In order to develop the fullest and most considered response to a book, your reading and thinking must go through several stages. The more questions of interest the book poses, the more time you should devote to developing your ideas prior to the actual writing of the review. When first reading the book for meaning, pay special attention to the preface or foreword and to any other information that will give a clue to the book's overall purpose and its general context. As you reread the book, annotate it with comments on the writer's technique and your own reactions. After having developed some thoughts through journal entries, look through the book one more time. Then clarify your thoughts by writing down answers to the following questions:

• What seems to be the author's main purpose or point?
• Is this purpose aimed at any particular group of readers?
• What information or knowledge does it convey?
• What personal or practical meaning does the book have for you?
• What are the most appropriate terms by which to evaluate the book?
• Based on the criteria you have just selected, how successful do you think the author was in carrying out the overall purposes of the book?

Once you know your reactions to what the book is and what it does, you are ready to outline and write the first draft of your review.

The Shape of Your Review

Beyond a few items that must appear in a review, what you include and how you organize it is up to you. Many reviews, however, do follow one general pattern that includes all the important elements of a review.

The required items are all a matter of common sense. First, the reader must know what book you are talking about, so at the top of the review give a *bibliographic entry*. Include not just author, title, and publication information but also the number of pages and the price of the book because readers like to know what kind of commitment in time and money it takes to read the book. The format of this entry, used throughout this chapter, is:

Author. Title. Place of publication: publisher, date of publication. Number of pages. Price.

Sometimes for the convenience of librarians the International Standard Book Number (ISBN) or Library of Congress (LC) code is listed. The first time you mention the book in the review you should repeat the author and title so that the reader does not have to jump back to the bibliographic entry.

The body of the review must give a clear overview of the contents of the book, the special purposes of and audience for the book, and the reviewer's reaction and evaluation. Though reviews show a wide variety of form and organization, a typical way of opening is with a direct statement of the kind of book and its main topic — followed by a few words of the reviewer's evaluations. If the book raises any special problem that the review will explore later, this may be briefly mentioned here. Thus, in the first few sentences, the reader knows where both the book and the review are headed.

The next paragraph or section often includes background that will help place the book in context, either by describing the general problem the book addresses or by mentioning earlier books by this or another author. This section is also an appropriate place to discuss the criteria by which to judge the book, for the context helps define what the book attempts to do.

Next, a summary of the main points of the book — highlighted by paraphrase and quotation — gives an overview of the actual content of the book. The reviewer's reactions may be included with the ongoing summary of the contents, as in J. H. Plumb's long review at the end of this chapter, or all the comments may be saved for the end, as in Betsy Carter's review on pages 129–130. Even where a personal reaction is withheld, the reviewer's manner of describing the contents often gives a clear impression of what he or she thinks. In any case, it is important to distinguish between the ideas of the author and those of the reviewer. Careful labeling (*George Orwell continues . . . ; This reviewer believes . . .*) keeps the reviewer's ideas separate from the author's ideas. Confusion between the two weakens the value of the review.

In the final part of the review, the reviewer is then free to carry on the discussion in a variety of ways, evaluating how well the book has achieved its goal, musing over the possibilities suggested by the book, arguing with specific points, discussing matters the book has left out, even exploring a personal experience related to the subject. No matter how far afield the comments stray, they usually return in the last few lines to a more direct comment on the book and tie together the issues raised in the review. Although some trick endings are clichés, a final statement that leaves the reader with a sense of completion — as with a musical cadence — gives a desirable graciousness to the review. That graciousness is important, for we should consider the evaluation of another person's work not as a cold measurement, but as a civilized act of human society.

Short Versus Long Reviews

The middle-length review of about five-hundred words, which we have been considering, is the most common in newspapers and magazines. It allows the reviewer room to present contents and reactions with substantial supporting examples and discussion. In any less space, the reviewer must get right to the core of the book's argument and to his or her reaction. Without space for lengthy support or involved explanations, the short review must rely on straightforward statements; precisely phrased judgments can be backed with only a few well-chosen examples. When the book is found wanting, the bluntness of a short review may produce a comic shock, as in the following capsule review from *Kirkus Reviews,* a semi-monthly guide to the new trade books for librarians and others in the book world.

RAINBOW:
Finding the Better Person Inside You[7]
by Dee Burton
Macmillan $7.95
SBN: 02-075740-9

Thirty-two banal prescriptions to improve your life, from "Engage in Altruistic Behavior on a Regular Basis" to "Make It a Point Always to Distinguish Between Low-Probability and Zero-Probability Events." No attempt is made to explain why these specific command-

---

[7]From *Kirkus Reviews,* 1 January 1980, p. 41. Copyright © 1980 by Kirkus Service, Inc. Used by permission.

ments are handed down, beyond the fact that they are "significant principles" for the author, or to synthesize them into any kind of coherent system; and their effect is uniformly assumed to be of a character-strengthening nature. However, the individual directives vary widely in potential merit: most would agree that we can all do with less rationalizing and stereotyping, for example, but few would be prepared to endorse some of the author's wild schemes to "Increase Your Psychological Risk-Taking" — as in "Tell your boss exactly what you think of him" or "Have an affair with a member of the sex to which you are not accustomed." The question is, why?

A few negative adjectives like "banal" and "wild" quickly convey the reviewer's negative opinion. The reviewer selects a few telling examples to make the point obvious and characterizes the book's lack of explanation and coherence in a single sentence. The final withering question "Why?" suggests that the book isn't worth serious attention. And many books aren't.

Another Capsule Review

Books worthy of serious consideration can be characterized well in a capsule review, so that the reader gains a sense of the content and value of the book. The following, also from *Kirkus Reviews,* in a relatively short space manages to give a taste of the book's complex moral argument and its unusual conclusion — and at the same time raises points of contention. The reviewer's admiration for the book is clear in the opening and closing sentences — but is made even clearer by the seriousness with which the reviewer takes the author's arguments.

PRACTICAL ETHICS[8]
by Peter Singer
Cambridge Univ. Press $27.50;
paper $6.95
SBN: 521-22920-0;
paper SBN: 521-29720-6

Singer (like Socrates) takes philosophy and puts it where it belongs — in the market place. In lucid, non-technical prose he tackles disputed moral questions — most notably abortion, euthanasia, civil disobedience, equality, animal rights, and the obligations of the haves to the have-nots — with a compelling blend of intellectual rigor and

[8]From *Kirkus Reviews,* 1 November 1979, p. 1313. Copyright © 1979 by Kirkus Service, Inc. Used by permission.

personal commitment. (An earlier, more limited example: *Animal Liberation,* 1975.) Singer calls himself a consequentialist, i.e., a utilitarian who measures acts against the norm of "what, on balance, furthers the interests of those affected" rather than with any simple calculus of pleasure and pain. He follows this guideline wherever it leads him — and sometimes winds up out on some pretty controversial limbs. He maintains, for instance, that some animals (chimpanzees, among others) are persons, because they are self-conscious, communicate, and have a notion of the future. Killing an adult, nonhuman primate, then, would be worse than killing a human baby, which is not a person in the strict sense. Singer is not promoting infanticide, but challenging this and other forms of "speciesism," a blind moral prejudice in favor of humanity. In another chapter he proposes with cool but passionate eloquence that withholding help from starving people (e.g., by spending money on luxuries instead of sending it to CARE) is "the moral equivalent of murder." Here and elsewhere Singer stops short of laying down any absolutes, but takes a bold stance that provokes the reader to respond, one way or another. Anti-abortionists will argue — with reason — that he does scant justice to the fetus' status as a potential human being. And ecologists will protest the narrowness of his view that only sentient beings are entitled to ethical consideration (so it's wrong to eat a hamburger, but all right to destroy a redwood forest?). Finally, professional philosophers will complain about the relative flimsiness of Singer's concluding chapter, "Why Act Morally?" on which, logically speaking, his whole case rests. But, whatever the objections, this is a superb performance, rich in substance and immaculately written: critical thinking at its creative best.

Writing capsule reviews will develop your ability to react to and place a book. You will learn to get to the core of your reaction in a few words, for otherwise the review will be finished before you get to your evaluation. By learning to characterize books succinctly and to make pointed estimates of their value, you will be able to find your way more easily among the variety of books available when you come to gather materials for your research paper. Even very short reviews — fifty words or less — will further sharpen your instincts about books and prepare you for placing books in relationship to each other, a skill needed for preparing *a review of the literature* (see Chapter 8).

Full Review

At the other extreme, the long review allows a full discussion of all aspects of a book and the reviewer's estimate of it. Not every book warrants detailed comment, but where the book raises interesting, complex questions or where the argument needs careful weighing, the long review permits all issues to be explored to their logical conclusion. To write an extended review that looks deeply into the issues of a book, the reviewer usually needs to have substantial knowledge of the subject, of the other books in the field, and of the previous work by the same author. The more deeply one looks into any book, the more important it is to understand how the book fits into earlier conversations.

Later parts of this text will deal with comparative evaluations of related books; however, at this stage, the following selection will reveal the usefulness of background knowledge in preparing a thoughtful review. Lawrence Stone, the author of the book, and J. H. Plumb, the reviewer, are among the most eminent of contemporary historians. Both have recently concerned themselves with the history of the family. In the review the seriousness of the conversation between them is evident as Plumb comes to grips with what his colleague has said. Plumb suggests limitations to what he finds in Stone's book and proposes answers for questions raised by the book.

At every stage of the review, Plumb's full understanding of the topic helps him evaluate data and deal with the larger issues of historical trends; at the same time, he is fair in reporting exactly what the original says and does. Plumb begins by characterizing Stone's approach to historical problems. He then defines the present level of scholarship on the family by describing what others have done and what kind of evidence is available. While providing this background, Plumb discusses methodological questions of the reliability and character of Stone's evidence. Thus, even before Plum gets to the real content of the book, he is reacting to the historical problem Stone has set for himself.

In the middle section, Plumb presents Stone's argument in detail, but he does much more than summarize. At each step Plumb evaluates the certainty of the evidence, the probability of Stone's speculations, and the overall solidity of the argument. Plumb even finds space for some personal reactions and comparisons to current family life. Yet throughout this web of comment, we never lose the thread of Stone's original argument.

In the last part of the review, Plumb addresses the most important issues that have emerged from the earlier discussion. Here he speaks directly to the reader, but even earlier, when he was reporting the ideas of others, we heard the reviewer's own voice and opinions.

This is reviewing at its most serious — one colleague answering another at length. Even though the substance is scholarly and the references and details may be unfamiliar, the review is lively, for we hear a genuine conversation going on here.

THE RISE OF LOVE[9]
The Family, Sex and Marriage in England: 1500–1800
by Lawrence Stone.
Harper & Row, 800 pp., $30.00

J. H. Plumb

Professor Stone may be the boldest historian alive. Certainly he seems almost recklessly brave by the timid standards of the profession. He can write large books or short ones, but he cannot write a book about a trivial theme. His first large book, *The Crisis of the Aristocracy, 1558–1641,* analyzed by dexterous use of social as well as economic history the collapse of the English aristocracy before the Civil War. It is an immense book, crowded with detail; here and there it may be faulted on minor matters, but it has established itself as a classic and its major thesis concerning the "rise of the gentry" is universally accepted.

Stone brought to bear the same qualities of rapid assimilation, analytical skill, and clarity of exposition to the causes of the Civil War in England, to the origins of the Industrial Revolution, to the questions of literacy, and to the history of the universities, in books of great power and vigor. He has also written with authority on medieval sculpture and eighteenth-century architecture. In all of his work one senses an almost feverish desire to master more and more fresh material. So a new major book by Lawrence Stone is always awaited with the most lively anticipation.

During the last decade, a new social history — one undreamed of by Trevelyan — has grown prodigiously: a history of birth, marriage, death, sex; of family relationships; of the role of the aged and the young within communities great and small. A multitude of subjects rarely touched on by historians of previous generations are now cluttered with active young historians. They delve into such arcane matters as homosexuality in Switzerland, breast-feeding in New England, *coitus interruptus* in Old England, swaddling in France, death not only in Venice but anywhere and everywhere. It is all fresh and exciting, and already the literature is immense.

Furthermore, immense sums are being poured into lavish computerized projects in the hope of settling statistically the problems of family size, age of marriage, the frequency of births, the age at death of children and adults, and the numbers in a household in seventeenth-century and eighteenth-century England. For this at least, there is evidence of a kind in bulk. But for the way the members of these families felt about each other or about their own fate, and about their hopes,

[9]J. H. Plumb, "The Rise of Love," rev. of *The Family, Sex and Marriage in England: 1500–1800* by Lawrence Stone. *New York Review of Books* 24 (24 November 1977), pp. 31–33. Copyright © 1977 by J. H. Plumb. Used by permission.

their aspirations, their satisfactions and frustrations, the evidence is thin, slippery in nature, and scattered here, there, and everywhere in autobiographies, diaries, prayers, confessions, household books, and family correspondence.

Imaginative literature — plays, novels, and poetry — is another source, plentiful in the fifteenth and sixteenth centuries and a flood in the eighteenth. And finally there are medical treatises, the handbooks of etiquette and advice, sermons, the propagandists of educational theory or of political philosophy. Yet the more voluminous the evidence becomes, the less reliable it is, particularly when it derives from the world of the imagination or the realms of theory and exhortation. Probably family correspondence is one of the surer guides to discovering the nature of family affection, but even here there are grave problems. Letters are usually written for a purpose, and fashion is often more responsible for modes of address than the dictates of the heart. And during most of the period that concerns Professor Stone writing was a difficult art for most men and women.

Professor Stone has read and digested vast quantities of such evidence for the three centuries with which he is concerned, and yet, even so, great quantities of family correspondence and accounts, let alone printed materials, have by the very nature of these sources eluded him. No human being, even if he lived as long as Enos, could ever cover them all. Professor Stone is well aware of this — and equally aware of all the dangers and pitfalls of the source material which he is using (except perhaps not quite as skeptical of some of the demographic statistics as he might be). He stresses in the first pages of his book that he faces formidable methodological problems in the data that he uses. "For one thing, many of the most . . . intimate habits of thought . . . do not usually find their way on to paper. One is therefore often obliged to infer hidden attitudes from overt actions, or even from gross statistical trends . . . a risky procedure." From time to time Professor Stone reminds his readers of the need for caution, but I expect that many of his colleagues will concentrate on the boldness of his speculations rather than on his plea to take care.

Basically Professor Stone presents two themes: one concerns the nuclear family, which he finds was established by 1500 — the family, that is, of mother, father, children, and (if rich enough), servants living in their own household. Newly married couples did not live with their parents; there were, in fact, no extended families in early modern Britain. The evidence for this is overwhelming and acceptable. Families were, however, held together in larger groups by kinship or clientage which became of less and less importance: strong in the sixteenth century, they are weak or have vanished by the eighteenth.

Stone then discusses the demographic structure of the nuclear family: the age of marriage, the number of children, their spacing, their survival rate, the age of death of parents. Here we enter more troubled waters. The evidence for his demographical data are the parish records. These probably ignore large quantities of births — maybe deliberately, since a pauper's child, or even a poor person's child, when registered, could claim settlement by birth and therefore be a potential burden on the poor-rate. Also many a poverty-stricken cottager might hesitate to pay the baptismal fees for a sickly child. There is also increasing evidence that a very considerable number of the poor failed to register their weddings. By the end of the seventeenth century it was very expensive for a poor person to be married in church, whereas he or she could get a piece of paper from a hedge-priest for as little as five shillings, or, if they could walk to London, and thousands did, they could get married in the Fleet by a parson in debt for more or less the same fee.

Professor Stone's figures are, however, probably fairly reliable for the well-to-do. They demonstrate that men and women were married in their late twenties and that births were fewer than one might expect, and were carefully spaced. Hence one can infer widespread *coitus interruptus* or other forms of nonreproductive sexual activity in marriage. Also bastardy rates were surprisingly low, leading Professor Stone to speculate — I think wrongly — that the huge gap between sexual maturity and marriage was a period of deep sexual frustration for males, leading to quick tempers, social aggression, violence, and apprentice riots. After all, one cannot believe that punk rockers and teddy-boys are overwhelmingly chaste any more than most youth groups of today, yet adolescent violence and mayhem is still rife.

However — to return to Professor Stone's main argument — the two outstanding facts of the nuclear family in the early modern period were that most marriages which involved property no matter how small were usually arranged marriages based on family and property needs, not on choice by affection. And secondly, these marriages were riddled with death to a degree which we find difficult to imagine. Children died as frequently, in towns certainly more frequently, than they survived. Parents often died before their children married. The number of aged people was comparatively small. The nonaffectionate marriage, the overwhelming authority of the husband, and the constant loss of infants led to a bleak family atmosphere — little affection between spouses, more discipline, beating, and subordination of children than love and tenderness for them.

These arguments of Professor Stone are richly illustrated in a wealth of anecdotal evidence that makes this very long book a pleasure to read. His evidence is drawn from a vast range of source material of every kind. Cold hearts, bleak mothers, formidable fathers, ever-present deaths, a decade or more of sexual frustration, arranged marriage — not much fun, it would seem, being an adolescent in seventeenth-century England, or in New England, where the pattern was largely the same.

Toward the end of the seventeenth century, Professor Stone, as well as many other tillers of his vineyard, discovers a change of attitude within the family. This is his second major theme. Parents, or rather some parents, ceased to beat their children as regularly and as savagely as their own parents had done them; swaddling clothes were given up, allowing the baby to be active; breast-feeding replaced wet-nursing so that motherly love was now directed to the child; more marriages were made on grounds of affection; a new world of family warmth was slowly being born.

The affectionate family became more permissive about sexuality, about self-indulgence, and was an easy target for the romantic conceptions of love. Professor Stone sees a connection — slight, maybe — with this new family attitude and the increasing survival of children after 1750. There was also at this time a greater attempt to keep them alive in all classes but the poorest. The rise in bastardy rates, too, he sees connected with new concepts of love, affection, and permissiveness. However, the permissive age of the late eighteenth century was quickly obliterated in the nineteenth century when the patriarchal family reasserted itself and puritan attitudes toward sexuality were given a new lease of life.

Professor Stone maintains that the "affective individualism" which grew up during the eighteenth century has little to do with the economic revolution in industry or the demographic changes that took place in the late eighteenth century, because it antedated both, even though both may have nurtured its growth. Once more, Professor Stone illustrates his theme of affective individualism with a fascinating display of erudition. Sometimes, as in the discussion of Pepys's sexual life and of Boswell's, he goes on too long about what is well known. Indeed, this long section on the case histories of gentlemanly sexual behavior, amusing and fascinating as it is to read, illustrates the difficulties and dangers besetting Professor Stone. Professor Stone uses six diaries or memoirs that exist between 1500 and 1800 which explicitly deal with the sexual activity of those who wrote them. He could have added a few more — William Hickey's memoirs for example — but even so the complete evidence would have remained slight — a dozen men or so in nearly 300 years! Even the outspoken Lord Hervey who had eight children by his wife but also was an active homosexual is never specific about his activities.

For the tens of thousands of married or unmarried men, indifferent to self-expression or revelation, we know absolutely nothing. We are totally ignorant of the activities of the illiterate poor who were the bulk of the population. What we do know from the experience of the last few generations is that sexuality is infinitely malleable; that public ideology, whether repressive or permissive, is a poor indication of actuality; that the long, curiously long, period between puberty and marriage does not make for chronic sexual frustration and deprivation, whether copulation is practiced or not.

One of the most dubious arguments of this book, and of most writers on demography, is that puberty at fourteen or fifteen and marriage at twenty-eight or twenty-nine means more than a decade of sexual deprivation. Equally dubious is the attempt made by many to quantify sexual activity from the records of ecclesiastical courts charged with the supervision of morals. One might as well judge the extent of homosexuality in nineteenth- and twentieth-century English boarding schools by the number of people sacked for it. I suspect that villages were more like the public schools described by Dr. Royston — some dominated by snooping prefects bent on routing out the mildest deviation, others rioting in lust, and most betwixt and between, moving in either direction according to the interests and will of a few powerful personalities. Speculate we may, but what we can be sure about is that we shall never now know. Alas, the more intimate problems of social history are far more insoluble than those of political history and, of course, far less important.

This does not mean that the attempt should not be made. Professor Stone's book presents a coherent picture of a social process that can be easily discerned. There is no doubt that there was a great change in social mood between 1600 and 1800, but whether this was caused primarily by changes in the emotional bonding of families is at the best merely speculative.

I wish Professor Stone had studied children's literature more closely: far from negligible before 1750, it rapidly proliferated in the late eighteenth century. This literature became from 1780 increasingly moralistic (not that it is very permissive before this date), and its burden was that children must obey their parents and honor them. It preached obedience, industry, honesty, avoidance of luxury and of sin. On the other hand, it stressed the need for compassion — particularly to the poor, to slaves, and to animals. But no one could discern in this torrent of literature, certainly after 1780, the slightest encouragement of permissiveness. Indeed, the ethic was very similar to that of the seventeenth century, even though its goal was different — success in life rather than avoidance of Hell.

Furthermore, I would argue that the change in family attitudes — in attitudes to woman, children, marriage, and to romantic love — is much more closely connected with the commercial prosperity of England which began to develop in the last decades of the seventeenth century. The growing wealth and security of the gentry and pseudo gentry after 1700 led them to indulge a passion for things, for earthly delights in ways that were neither available nor possible in the early seventeenth century except for a few very rich families. Affluence can create an atmosphere of relaxation, of self-indulgence, more quickly than any other social process: certainly it influenced the spread of a less terrifying theology and encouraged the pursuit of happiness on earth rather than in Heaven. And love and affection are surely central to material happiness.

As always, Professor Stone raises vast issues, settles them provocatively, and underpins his solutions with a wealth of illustration. Yet his book, by the very nature of his subject, must remain highly personal and in many places highly speculative. But it will be endlessly drawn on and will be endlessly discussed, which I am sure is what Professor Stone would expect.

Writing Assignments

1. Select a book that you remember enjoying as a child. Reread it and write a five-hundred-word review directed towards parents who are choosing books for their children.

2. Choose a book that you read recently and that had a strong impact on you. Review it in five hundred words for your college newspaper.

3. Write a one-hundred-fifty word review for your classmates about the worst book that you have read in the past year. Make clear why readers should stay away from this book.

4. Choose a subject about which you are knowledgeable. Then select three books that you have read on the subject and write a short fifty-word review of each. Direct your reviews to people just becoming interested in the subject and wanting to know which books are worth reading.

5. Choose a course you have taken that had several books on the required reading list. For each title assigned in the course, write a short fifty-word review to help your instructor decide whether to assign the same books in future semesters.

II
Using Sources Creatively

6

Comparing Your Reading to Your Personal Experiences

Preview

To understand any written work, you must recognize what in the real world it refers to. Further, to accept an idea, you must find it consistent with what you know about the world in general and in particular. Your knowledge of the world may come from previous experience, from common sense, from new observations, or from scientific experiments. By writing essays comparing your reading to your personal experiences, you will learn to evaluate ideas found in books and articles. You will be asked to write two types of papers: an *essay comparing reading and experience* and a *critical analysis of observations.*

The Sense of Reading

Written words are only ink marks on paper. Until you, the reader, gain a clear and sensible impression from the words, you literally have no sense of what the writer is attempting to convey. Based on everything you know about the real world, you must identify objects and concepts the writer symbolizes in language. In order to understand the writer's meaning and in order for a given piece of writing to extend your knowledge, you must already be familiar with most of what the writer presents. If writers use words that you do not know to describe objects you have never seen, they might as well be writing gibberish as far as you are concerned. You will experience a similar loss of meaning and sense if you look at an advanced book on physics or on horse racing — depending on where your ignorance lies.

Thus, whenever you read, you always measure the writer's words against those aspects of reality with which you are familiar. Even if you recognize all the words the writer is using, but the writer puts them together in a way that contradicts your knowledge, you will most likely reject the statement as *nonsense* — or as contrary to sense. You are not likely to accept a writer's construction of reality if he claims that "babies are found under cabbage leaves." You know better than to accept that as sense.

However, just because statements make sense to you — you understand them and they fit your perceptions of the world — does not guarantee that they are absolutely true. Your knowledge can grow by the conflict between what you have already accepted as sense and new claims that at first seem to be contrary to sense. To Europeans in 1492, Columbus's claim that he would sail around the globe violated both their sense of possibility and their sense of specific fact. Only when other navigators, following Columbus, sailed entirely around the world and returned alive did new possibilities and new facts replace the old. Evidence for a curved earth had been noticed by Greek astronomers two thousand years before Columbus; Anaximander could even calculate the earth's diameter. But the same evidence, easily observable without special equipment, was ignored by the astronomers of Columbus's time. Since they knew the world was flat, there was no point or motivation to look for evidence of roundness. Human beings tend only to observe what they already believe is there. Such examples point to a difficult situation: we must rely on what we know to understand and to judge what other people say, yet we must keep in mind that what we know may be eventually proved wrong.

> **By being attentive to a writer's claims, by doing our best
> to see what that writer wants us to see in the world —
> even though the writer's claims go against our prior
> knowledge — we may discover new ideas we can accept as
> part of our own view of the world.**

If we are to be thoughtful and critical as readers, we must rely on what we know to identify and to judge the ideas presented by the reading. Yet reliance on previous knowledge stands in the way of learning and accepting new ideas. There is no way to escape this dilemma. But by keeping it in mind and trying to accept a book *on its own terms* before judging it on our own, we can be both critical and open to new ideas. By being attentive to a writer's claims, by doing our best to see what that writer wants us to see — even though the writer's claims go against our prior knowledge — we may discover new ideas we can accept as part of our own view of the world. Finally, no matter how sympathetic a reading we give to any piece of writing, we must return to the question of whether it makes sense. The remainder of this chapter will be devoted to ways to judge the sense of any piece of reading by using common sense and experience, personal observations, and scientific experiments.

Experience, Memory, and Common Sense

To see both the value and the problems of that grab bag of personal experience and random knowledge we bring to any particular reading, let us look at the case of George Washington Plunkitt, the Tammany Hall politician. In the late nineteenth century, the government of New York City was run by a group of politicians known collectively as *Tammany Hall*. Under the leadership of Boss Tweed, they took advantage of the power they held for their own profit and the profit of their friends. Eventually a number of journalists, including Lincoln Steffens, exposed the Tammany Hall politicians as crooks; since then Tammany Hall has become the symbol for political corruption. However, from George Washington Plunkitt's inside view as a member of the Tammany organization, the situation didn't look nearly as bad as it appeared to the reforming journalists on the outside. When Plunkitt came to read Lincoln Steffens's exposé, *The Shame of the Cities*, he reacted by presenting his own insider's viewpoint. He expresses his down-to-earth thinking in down-to-earth language.

ON *THE SHAME OF THE CITIES*[1]

I've been readin' a book by Lincoln Steffens on *The Shame of the Cities*. Steffens means well but, like all reformers, he don't know how to make distinctions. He can't see no difference between honest graft and dishonest graft and, consequent, he gets things all mixed up. There's the biggest kind of a difference between political looters and politicians who make a fortune out of politics by keepin' their eyes wide open. The looter goes in for himself alone without considerin' his organization or his city. The politician looks after his own interests, the organization's interests, and the city's interests all at the same time. See the distinction? For instance, I ain't no looter. The looter hogs it. I never hogged. I made my pile in politics, but, at the same time, I served the organization and got more big improvements for New York City than any other livin' man. And I never monkeyed with the penal code.

The difference between a looter and a practical politician is the difference between the Philadelphia Republican gang and Tammany Hall. Steffens seems to think they're both about the same; but he's all wrong. The Philadelphia crowd runs up against the penal code. Tammany don't. The Philadelphians ain't satisfied with robbin' the bank of all its gold and paper money. They stay to pick up the nickels and pennies and the cop comes and nabs them. Tammany ain't no such fool. Why, I remember, about fifteen or twenty years ago, a Republican superintendent of the Philadelphia almshouse stole the zinc roof off the buildin' and sold it for junk. That was carryin' things to excess. There's a limit to everything, and the Philadelphia Republicans go beyond the limit. It seems like they can't be cool and moderate like real politicians. It ain't fair, therefore, to class Tammany men with the Philadelphia gang. Any man who undertakes to write political books should never for a moment lose sight of the distinction between honest graft and dishonest graft, which I explained in full in another talk. If he puts all kinds of graft on the same level, he'll make the fatal mistake that Steffens made and spoil his book.

A big city like New York or Philadelphia or Chicago might be compared to a sort of Garden of Eden, from a political point of view. It's an orchard full of beautiful apple trees. One of them has got a big sign on it, marked: "Penal Code Tree — Poison." The other trees have lots of apples on them for all. Yet the fools go to the Penal Code Tree. Why?

[1]From George Washington Plunkitt, *Plunkitt of Tammany Hall* (New York: Dutton, 1963), pp. 29–31.

For the reason, I guess, that a cranky child refuses to eat good food and chews up a box of matches with relish. I never had any temptation to touch the Penal Code Tree. The other apples are good enough for me, and O Lord! how many of them there are in a big city!

Steffens made one good point in his book. He said he found that Philadelphia, ruled almost entirely by Americans, was more corrupt than New York, where the Irish do almost all the governin'. I could have told him that before he did any investigatin' if he had come to me. The Irish was born to rule, and they're the honestest people in the world. Show me the Irishman who would steal a roof off an almhouse! He don't exist. Of course, if an Irishman had the political pull and the roof was much worn, he might get the city authorities to put on a new one and get the contract for it himself, and buy the old roof at a bargain — but that's honest graft. It's goin' about the thing like a gentleman, and there's more money in it than in tearin' down an old roof and cartin' it to the junkman's — more money and no penal code.

Tammany Hall on the Defense

Plunkitt's candid first-hand observations reveal some everyday facts about the political world of his time. His distinction between honest and dishonest graft amuses us because both types are crooked enough by our standards — particularly since we now have more stringent conflict-of-interest laws — but apparently he believed the distinction existed in his world. From his insider's view we also get a sympathetic portrait of the human desire to profit from situations. Plunkitt presents a working system that makes civic improvements by spreading the money around to friends. He even has some first-hand observations on ethnic and moral differences between New York and its rival in corruption, Philadelphia. If Plunkitt doesn't disprove Steffens's accusation that he and his friends are crooks, at least he lets us know the human workings of the corrupt system.

On the other hand, Plunkitt's comments are bigoted, self-interested, and narrow-minded. The whole point of the distinction between honest and dishonest graft is to show that he and his cronies are honest fellows, much better than those rascals in Philadelphia. To make his own crowd look better, he insults another ethnic group and flatters his own group. Since his whole life has been committed to the Tammany system, what he knows and thinks are mostly Tammany rationalizations and self-defense. For intellectual, emotional, and legal reasons, George Washington Plunkitt cannot step outside the Tammany viewpoint in order to consider the criticisms of reformers like Lincoln Steffens. He only finds some sense in Steffens when he can bend the reformer's statements to prove what he already believes — that Philadelphia is more corrupt than New York.

In Plunkitt's case the stakes are unusually high. To accept Steffens's book as making sense, the Tammany Hall politician would have to admit that he and his friends were dishonest. Very few people have that much intellectual honesty. Even under less extreme conditions, we tend to defend our existing opinions and commitments. We would rather not pay much attention to ideas that might upset our personal apple carts.

Yet a stubborn defense of our personal opinions is not simply narrowness; those apple carts we have constructed in the course of our experience are the sum of all we have come to know. We usually work to make sense of our past experiences, so that our generalizations — those structures of thought that form our common sense — are worth taking very seriously and should not be given up simply because a writer comes along with an opposite viewpoint.

The written essay in which we compare our experiences to the claims of an author allows us to develop in explicit form our knowledge about the accuracy of the writer's claims. With all the issues out in the open, we can see how much we agree or disagree, and we can begin to judge where the better sense lies. Intellectual honesty enters if we are able to rearrange or even add to our apple cart on the basis of some new and convincing thought we have read.

The Essay Comparing Reading and Experience

The *essay comparing reading and experience* is simply a paper in which you compare the ideas described in your reading to personal experiences that you are reminded of by the text. This essay is a more focused and formalized version of the informal *essay of response*, discussed in Chapter 3. The advice offered for the development of the essay of response applies here as well, but the thinking and organization throughout should be more specific and more rigorous. You should carry out the early steps of reading, annotating, and journal writing keeping in mind two key questions: "What experiences does this reading bring to mind?" and "How do the generalizations in this passage compare to what I have learned from personal experience?" In your marginal comments and journal, list as many related examples from your own life as you can.

When you read through your first responses and marginal comments, think about them in two ways: first, see whether your personal experiences generally agree with or contradict the ideas of the passage; second, see which of these personal associations presents your general train of thought most accurately. Follow through all the implications of your chosen comments — those that are most promising and forceful. Analyze in detail how your examples and ideas support or diverge from the statements in the reading. You can develop your thoughts through extended reading notes, journal entries, preliminary outlines, or even sketchy first drafts. Remember that you can always revise these first attempts to cut out digressions and tighten up organization and logic.

However, the final organization of the paper should be more formal and definite than the association of ideas, used to organize the *informal essay of response*. Here the specific tasks of *comparison* and *evaluation* suggest specific elements of organization.

In the early part of your essay, you should identify both the specific passage and the specific experiences or personal beliefs that you are comparing to that passage. Further, you should set up the general pattern of agreement, disagreement, or qualified agreement that will ultimately emerge from your comparison.

The main body of the essay will, of course, be comparative in structure. Because the reading stands independently of your essay — and can be referred to by the reader — you will probably devote more space to your personal experiences than to the reading. However, you need to summarize or paraphrase the passage with enough precision to enable your reader to know exactly what you are comparing from the original passage. Decide whether a short quotation, tight paraphrase, or compact summary will be most effective in informing your reader of the original. Exactly how much of the original you repeat will depend, to some extent, on how familiar your readers are with it; further guidance on methods of referring to the original appears on pages 331–334 in Chapter 10. In any case, the body of your paper should be devoted to those experiences that bear favorably or unfavorably on the reading. Always make sure that your experience is discussed in relation to the ideas from the reading; do not allow the narrative of your experiences to become an end in itself. The purpose of the essay is to illuminate and to evaluate the ideas of the reading through your experience.

Four Frameworks for Comparison

Your comparison may be organized in one of several ways. The first method is to use your personal experiences to explain and develop one or more of the important ideas in the original passage. If you use this method, your introduction will consist of a concise statement of the major ideas of the original. In the body of the essay, you will explore these ideas by examining carefully chosen, effective examples taken from your own life and experiences that illustrate these ideas. In the conclusion, you will reassert the general truths of the ideas as confirmed by your personal understanding of them. You may be familiar with this organization under the name of *exemplification*, or illustration.

A second organization is the traditional comparison, where ideas are compared on a point-by-point basis. The first point from the reading is discussed with your first related experience; the second point, with your second related experience; and so on. For the conclusion of this essay, you sum up all the smaller insights reached by the point-by-point comparisons.

A third method — still another form of comparison — is useful if the reading presents a consistent point of view that directly *contradicts* a consistent point of view suggested by your experience. In the first part of the essay, you draw together all the points from the reading to show the consistent pattern; then you draw together all the observations from your own experience to show the opposite pattern. In the conclusion, you discuss the specific differences between your point of view and the point of view of the original writer. The trick of this method is to maintain the comparative tension between the two points of view, even though you discuss them separately; otherwise, the essay may simply fall apart into two unrelated parts. Some techniques by which you can avoid this pitfall and keep your reader aware of the two opposing viewpoints are (1) by making clear cross-references and explicit comparisons between the two parts, (2) by repeating key phrases, and (3) by maintaining parallel order of points between the two parts.

Finally, if reading and experience are in agreement, you may use the reading to explain the experience. Then the essay will be a personal narrative punctuated by references to the reading in order to show the full meaning of the experience. You may then focus the conclusion directly on the usefulness of the ideas you have derived from the reading. This last method is particularly good for demonstrating how compelling ideas, presented persuasively by a writer, can reveal to the reader the order behind the apparently haphazard events of day-to-day life.

The following sample essay illustrates the first method of organization, exemplification. The student uses his memories of a childhood friendship as an example of the preadolescent intimacy that Harry Stack Sullivan discusses in the selection reprinted on pages 119–120. The student's essay begins with a summary of key features of preadolescent friendship identified by Sullivan. In the following paragraphs, the student reveals details of his friendship, exemplifying those features summarized in his opening paragraph. The student ends with the ways his friendship did not totally live up to Sullivan's ideal, but he relates even these limitations to Sullivan's model of social development.

My Friendship with Jesse

    The psychiatrist Harry Stack Sullivan in his discussion
of the "Need for Interpersonal Intimacy" describes the
close friendship that develops in preadolescence between
youths of the same sex. The friendship, or intimacy as
Sullivan calls it, is nonsexual, but it is marked by love.
Mutual sensitivity and concern for each other's feelings
lead the two friends to know each other well. They come
to respect each other's opinions and to rely on each other
for approval and validation of their personal worth. Even
more, they begin to collaborate in developing mutual satisfactions, and they share in each other's successes. Each
comes to consider the other as important as the self. When
stated in such abstract terms, Sullivan's concept of
friendship sounds too perfect, too pure--not at all like the
rough-and-tumble world of late childhood. Yet when I think
back on my childhood friendships, Sullivan's description
reminds me of my friendship with Jesse Hunt. The details
that I remember of our friendship help make Sullivan's idea
of friendship more plausible and familiar.

    Jesse and I were, I guess, a bit slow in developing our
friendship because we did not start to get close until we
were twelve, even though Sullivan says such friendships
can begin as early as the age of eight and one-half. Once
we were friends, however, we stayed close for almost five
years. Together we discovered books, girls, and the world
around us. Together we developed attitudes and values that

have lasted even though Jesse and I have lost contact over
the past two years.

Although Jesse and I had been neighbors and classmates
since we were nine years old, we did not get to know each
other well until we went off to junior high school. Every
day we walked the mile and one-half home together; we talked
about the teachers and the other students and what stupid
things we had to put up with. We communicated by nasty
jokes, making fun of the authority figures at school who
were trying to turn us into well-behaved, well-rounded, and
thoroughly boring young citizens. We satirized our classmates as phonies and straight arrows. We exchanged schemes
about how to get over, around, and through the seemingly
crazy requirements of school and the even crazier requirements of the social world in which we found ourselves. As
puberty started to overtake us, we also began plotting--
alas, unsuccessfully--against the virtue of the unsuspecting girls in our classes.

We built up a stock of private jokes, which we thought
were funny but which earned us reputations as cynics and
pessimists among our classmates. As our critical attitudes
developed and became public, the school authorities began
to consider us potential troublemakers. We liked our reputations because then we had a special identity. Our rejection of the phony world around us was the sign of our
intelligence and sensitivity. Even if others did not understand or approve, we knew we were right. We looked to
our shared reading to validate our socially critical point

of view. In eighth grade we read J. D. Salinger's <u>Catcher</u>
<u>in the Rye</u>; the main character, Holden Caulfield--a boy our
age who was disgusted by the "phoniness" around him--became
our hero. The next year we thought that Sinclair Lewis's
<u>Elmer Gantry</u>, with its portrait of a hypocritical gospel
preacher corrupted by lust and money, was the truth to end
all truths. From our reading, our jokes, and our shared
troubles with the school administration, we built up a
shared image of ourselves that gave us mutual respect and a
sense of self-worth, despite our being considered outsiders
by most of our peers.

Out of our shared respect for each other, we developed a
shared concern. Actually this concern was only expressed in
small ways because the crises that affected us were small.
If one of us had an argument with a teacher, the other would
carry on the argument in the next class. If a girl turned
one of us down for a date, the other would slyly insult her
later. Our behavior may have been childish, but it showed
us that we were aware of each other's feelings.

As time went on, we began to collaborate on more positive projects: we made some social studies presentations
together and then went on to become partners on the school
debate team. After we realized that the way to a girl's
heart was not through plots or insults, we double-dated
together.

There were, however, limits to our friendship. We were so
immature that we were embarrassed to express our feelings
directly. Instead Jesse would make jokes about my hair,

which he called a "rusty Brillo pad," and I would make
jokes about his laziness. I was in fact upset by the way
Jesse would let projects slide, but I did not know how to
help him, so I just made jokes. I could also never understand his strong feelings for his younger brother and sister; he never talked about them. On my side, I never talked
about the difficulties I was having with my family because
I thought he would not understand.

I only realized these limitations after I moved on to
other relationships. By the middle of our junior year in
high school, we both had steady girl friends and started to
lose contact. Without that first intimate friendship with
Jesse, I would not have been as well prepared to form
relationships with girls when the time for that came. As
Sullivan suggests, the preadolescent friendship is an
important stage in learning how to love other people.

Trying Ideas On for Size: An Expanded View of the World

When we take a book into ourselves and see what the writer is
talking about, we notice more of the world and therefore experience
reality from a new perspective. If the writer makes sense and we absorb
that sense, our personal sense of the world becomes enlarged. On the
other hand, if we observe the world looking for those things the writer
describes but do not find what the writer says we will find, then we may
doubt the writer's claims — and we will not accept these questionable
ideas into our view of the world. The next few pages will present examples — from the simple and concrete to the complex and abstract — of
how this process of evaluating another writer's ideas works.

New Parts to the World

Most simply, a writer may call our attention to a detail about the world we may not have known. If we enjoy stargazing, for example, the following comments in *Astronomy* by Robert Baker may lead us to plan a stargazing session.

> **Some Noteworthy Meteor Showers.** The Perseids furnish the most conspicuous and dependable of the annual showers. Their trails are visible through 2 or 3 weeks, with the greatest display about August 11.[2]

On a clear night in the second week of August, we can drive away from the city lights, lie back in an open field, and watch the "shooting stars." The book has made us aware of a part of reality that we have not before observed. If, however, we go out for three nights running but see no meteor showers, we may get frustrated with the book for not providing more accurate information. Certainly we would check other sources before we wasted any more gas or sleepless nights.

Reading for Advice

In addition to calling your attention to parts of reality, books offer advice: general statements about how to do specific tasks or the best ways to act in particular situations — or how to cook new dishes. A recipe may promise a delicious Dutch crumb apple pie if you use the proper ingredients and follow directions carefully. The evaluation of the advice, however, comes in the eating. If the recipe is good — and everyone asks for seconds and thirds — you keep the recipe in your file for future use. On the other hand, if the leftovers grow moldy in the refrigerator, you'll file the recipe in the garbage with the leftover pie. That is, after testing the advice, you decide whether to incorporate that advice into your permanent repertoire. According to the same criterion of whether the advice works, you can judge books on how to improve your tennis swing or your writing skills or your social life. Advice accepted becomes part of your life; advice rejected vanishes to some dead-letter office.

---

[2]From Robert H. Baker, *Astronomy* (Princeton, N. J.: D. Van Nostrand, 1959), p. 256.

Making Order of the World

Even more significant, reading can point out *patterns, relationships,* and *explanations* that can help you organize your thinking and notice various kinds of order in the world. The major ideas from your reading are frequently such statements of pattern, relationship, or explanation. One way to decide whether to accept or reject an idea is to test it out against new observations to see whether the idea points to patterns that really exist. For example, the elementary economic principle of supply and demand can be understood as a general relationship: if demand increases while supply decreases, prices will rise. After reading about supply and demand in your economics textbook, you might then start noticing price patterns of clothing at the local stores. You notice how popular styles are much more highly priced than more traditional clothes with the same amount of material and workmanship. Six months later, you notice that the stores are oversupplied with last season's fashion, and the price drops below that of more traditional clothes. Prices in your local stores will start to make economic sense to you: you will see individual prices as part of a larger relationship rather than random isolated numbers. Once you understand and accept the principle, you may be able to make some practical guidelines for yourself about the best bargains and the best time to buy. Thus you will have internalized and assimilated economic theory into your own economic behavior.

Concepts you come across in your reading may even start you observing whole new areas of reality. The first time students take courses in psychology they start to interpret the behavior of their friends and parents. Details of behavior that they previously ignored suddenly become very meaningful. One concept that almost always intrigues students is Freud's theory that a subconscious meaning lurks behind every slip of the tongue. Once students become acquainted with this idea, they start listening very carefully to Freudian slips in order to discover the psychological secrets of people they know. After they have accepted Freud's concept, no remark is ever again an innocent comment.

This absorption of new ideas from books into our daily perception of life is one of the deepest and most important ways our reading affects us. We build new ideas on knowledge of the old. In the following example of the work of Charles Darwin, we will explore at length how Darwin's assimilation of earlier ideas lies behind his educated observation of nature — even where his observations appeared radically original to his contemporaries. In this case study we will see the many ways an observant individual can make use of reading, even if the individual is not always aware of the process of assimilation of knowledge.

The Case of Charles Darwin

If any major advance in science seems to be totally original, based on the observations and thoughts of one person only, Darwin's *theory of evolution* would at first glance seem to be it. As a naturalist on the ship H.M.S. *Beagle*, Charles Darwin traveled to the far corners of the earth collecting samples and observing the varied forms of life on this planet. In 1836, after four years of travel, he settled back to a quiet life in England to make more observations and to think about the meaning of what he had seen. More than twenty years passed before he published his conclusions in *The Origin of Species by Means of Natural Selection* in 1859.

The first edition of this famous work made no mention of other writers who had worked on evolution and had come to similar conclusions; the few writers mentioned in passing were those with whom Darwin strongly disagreed. The material for the book seemed to come only from his own observations and thought — and seemed to go against almost everything that was written and taught at that time.

Darwin in his *Autobiography* claimed that he learned little from books, even though he attended Cambridge University:

> During the three years which I spent at Cambridge my time was wasted, as far as the academical studies were concerned, as completely as at Edinburgh and at school.[3]

What most absorbed his attention during his college years was walking in the woods to collect insects.

> But no pursuit at Cambridge was followed with nearly so much eagerness or gave me so much pleasure as collecting beetles. It was the mere passion for collecting, for I did not dissect them and rarely compared their external characters with published descriptions, but got them named anyhow.[4]

Yet when we look more deeply into the ideas developed by Darwin in *The Origin of Species*, we can see how he based his conclusions on the ideas of a number of writers who worked before and during his life — including the naturalists Linnaeus and Lamarck, the economic philosopher Malthus, the geologist Lyell, and Darwin's own grandfather Eras-

---

[3]Charles Darwin, *Autobiography* (New York: Norton, 1969), p. 58.
[4]Darwin, *Autobiography*, p. 62.

mus Darwin. Darwin drew on the ideas of these other thinkers to help him make sense of his own observations and point him toward new observations. Because the ideas Darwin worked with were publicly available in the books of earlier thinkers, other naturalists were also putting together similar theories of evolution. In fact, Alfred Wallace presented an almost identical theory at the same scientific meeting at which Darwin presented his. The ideas were available — ready to be put together by anyone with sufficient training, intelligence, and observational sharpness.

Linnaeus's Contribution

About a century before Darwin, Carolus Linnaeus classified plants and animals according to specific similarities and differences. Although Linnaeus himself did not express any belief in a theory of evolution, his classification system provided a framework that highlighted patterns of similarity and difference among life forms, and the system arranged plant forms from the simplest to the most complex. His classification helped Darwin to see family relationships between specific animals and to question if more complex forms had developed from simpler ones. Linnaeus's extensive arrangement of life forms — from most simple to complex — suggested to Darwin that the most advanced of animals were linked to the most simple of plants by a series of small gradual changes rather than by great leaps to entirely new types of life. Darwin himself states in *The Origin of Species* that classification reveals "some deeper bond . . . than mere resemblance . . . and that community of descent — the one known cause of close similarity in organic beings — is the bond."[5]

Jean Baptiste Lamarck, along with other naturalists, had developed a theory of evolution years before Charles Darwin. On the basis of his own observations, Darwin rejected many points of Lamarck's theory but kept one important aspect — the idea that certain characteristics will make an animal better able to survive in a particular environment.

Darwin combined this idea of adaptation with his observations of how plant and animal breeders improved their stock. Horse breeders, for example, would mate two very fast horses to produce better race horses; that is, the breeders select the traits that they want to foster. Perhaps nature also had a way, Darwin reasoned, to select the traits best adapted for survival. But how could selection take place in the wild where there were no humans to make the choice of animals to be mated?

[5]Charles Darwin, *The Origin of Species* (New York: New American Library, 1958), p. 387.

Malthus and the Struggle for Survival

The economist Malthus provided Darwin with the answer. In discussing human population, Malthus pointed out that population will tend to expand geometrically until the food supply runs out; then population will be limited by starvation, poverty, and natural disaster. In this struggle for existence in a crowded world, Darwin saw that only those specimens best adapted to the environment would survive; the method of natural selection was then survival of the best adapted.

In his *Autobiography*, Darwin describes the discovery of the final key:

> In October 1838, that is, fifteen months after I had begun my systematic enquiry, I happened to read for amusement Malthus on *Population*, and being well prepared to appreciate the struggle for existence which everywhere goes on from long-continued observation of the habits of animals and plants, it at once struck me that under these circumstances favourable variations would tend to be preserved, and unfavourable ones to be destroyed. The result of this would be the formation of a new species. Here, then, I had at last got a theory by which to work.[6]

Such a process of gradual selection of species through natural processes would require many millions of years to account for the wide variety of animals and plants that Darwin observed in his travels. Based on the Bible, most people of Darwin's time thought the world was only about six thousand years old. By studying rock formations, geologists were just beginning to find evidence that the earth had existed for a much longer period: in *The Principles of Geology*, Charles Lyell presented a theory of a world ancient enough to allow time for all the slow processes of selection that Darwin proposed. Lyell also presented an evolutionary theory concerning the gradual changes in rock formation.

Erasmus Darwin's Influence

Darwin, very aware of the major advance in knowledge he was proposing and very aware of the shortcomings he found in previous writings, tended to emphasize his own originality and to diminish the importance of the writers who influenced his thinking. He knew that he had rejected certain ideas of the same writers from whom he accepted other ideas — or parts of ideas. All these ideas were transformed by

---

[6]Darwin, *Autobiography*, p. 120.

Darwin as they were assimilated into his own new way of thinking. Even though he may have learned much from others, he knew he came to his major theories as a result of his own observations, thoughts, and evaluations. Thus he tended to undervalue the influence even of his own grandfather, Erasmus Darwin, who in 1794 had presented a theory of evolution in the book *Zoönomia*. Charles Darwin grants only a limited amount of influence in his *Autobiography*:

> I had previously read the *Zoönomia* of my grandfather, in which similar views are maintained, but without producing any effect on me. Nevertheless it is probable that the hearing rather early in life such views maintained and praised may have favoured my upholding them under a different form in my *Origin of Species*.[7]

The phrase *under a different form* is the key to understanding the feelings expressed in this passage. We have the perspective to see that Charles Darwin was, indeed, original, but his originality grew from the interaction between his own observations and the observations of others.

Charles Darwin's Influence

Just as Darwin was influenced by the thoughts of those who came before him, Darwin's observations and thoughts have, in the years since the publication of *The Origin of Species*, deeply influenced how later scientists have looked at life. The entire study of genetics, for example, grew directly out of Gregor Mendel's attempt to pinpoint the method by which evolutionary change is transmitted to offspring. Mendel read Darwin, accepted Darwin's ideas, and then designed experiments to explore the pattern of inheritance of traits. The current work with DNA and genetic structure has further specified the mechanisms of evolution.

Assimilating Ideas from Reading

The process of assimilating new ideas — new ways of looking at reality — from our reading is a slow one. We gradually accept or reject material on the basis of how it fits with our observations. Sometimes we interpret experience on the basis of ideas read so long ago that we no longer remember reading them; we think such ideas are entirely ours. At

[7]Darwin, *Autobiography*, p. 49.

other times we may accept parts of someone's thoughts but reject other parts; like Darwin we may remember more clearly how much we rejected than how much we kept. At other times we read without even thinking how the implications of the ideas may affect our present beliefs. Thus it is not always easy to pinpoint the direct influence of reading on our thoughts and observation. The more conscious we become about this assimilation process, the more control we have over it: we can choose which thoughts to accept or reject based on conscious evaluation of the ideas, and we can open ourselves to ideas that might strike us at first as strange.

One technique to make us more conscious of assimilating new ideas as we read is the writing of a *critical analysis of observation*, based on the ideas proposed in the reading. (*Analysis* means the division of something into its component parts, according to some scheme of categories; the word *critical* implies that there is a specific theory or set of ideas behind the categories.) The question behind the analysis is: "Do my own observations fall into the patterns or categories suggested by the reading?" If your observations agree with the ideas of the reading and the patterns from the reading help you understand your observations better, then the reading makes good sense to you and clarifies your ideas of reality. If your observations do not agree, you might then wonder whether your observations were appropriate or whether the ideas of the writer should be called into question.

A Student Looks at Tiredness

The process of assimilating ideas through reading might work as follows: a student who had not thought much about tiredness and had classed all forms of exhaustion in the same general category of "I'm wasted," might begin to think further after reading "The Psychology of Tiredness" from Ernest Hartmann's *The Functions of Sleep*, excerpted on pages 44–46. Hartmann, as you may remember, identifies two types of tiredness, one physical and the other mental. He attributes certain behavior patterns to each type and associates each type of tiredness with a different stage of sleep. He also states that the patterns aren't always pure but are sometimes mixed.

Our student, a female sophomore, at first reacted against Hartmann's ideas: "Tired is tired, and the only way it feels is no good." But the class discussion of different types of tiredness interested her, so she decided to observe herself and others to see whether she could spot Hartmann's categories of physical, mental, and mixed tiredness. She recorded her observations in a journal entry:

> Went home this weekend . . . what a pain to drive two hundred miles each way. Actually Cindy drove on Friday afternoon while I collapsed from the chem exam that morning. I can't believe it — I must have been up half the night studying!! In the car I sat there like some dumb cow gaping away, wanting to stop at every McDonald's we passed. I get so hungry after exams. And I want real greasy kid's food. The rest of the time I just sat there thinking about french fries. I bet I didn't say more than ten words the whole trip — except about stopping for food. Lucky Cindy didn't listen to me because otherwise I would have had to starve myself the rest of the weekend. Then she was playing a radio — all that dumbo country music she likes. And it seemed so loud; that trip was the worst. But I'm not the grouchy type so I just asked her to turn it down. She must have been tired too and since she was driving she had a right to choose the music. But did the music have to be so awful?
>
> Just looked over what I wrote — sounds like mental tiredness, doesn't it? Withdrawn, not willing to talk, childish desires — you know when I got home that night I played the stupidest games with my kid sister. I mean I was up half the night again, even though I thought I was so tired. I just kept putting off going to bed. Dumb. I knew I needed the sleep. Well, Hartmann says you do tend to lose control. And I guess I was pretty irritable and grouchy in the car, although I tried to hide it and be nice. But I don't know, I was sort of cheerier than the gloomy grouchpot Hartmann describes — especially when I got home. I was more silly; but I'm not the type to get depressed.

The journal helps her notice telling details about how she feels when tired. She starts to wonder whether those details fit into the patterns the psychologist suggests; his patterns, in turn, help her become even more aware of her own behavior.

After making a number of such entries, observing her own behavior and feelings when tired — as well as the activities causing the tiredness — this student would have a specific sense of the meaning of Hartmann's categories. She would also have specific personal observations on which to evaluate Hartmann's claims. Her journal entries, in fact, could become the raw material for an essay of critical analysis.

The Critical Analysis of Observation

When reading the selection that you will compare to your personal experience, pay particular attention to the categories into which the author separates the phenomena being discussed. By noting these categories and the kinds of examples the author uses, determine what kinds of observations you need to make. Then consider the best way to

pointed out earlier, an individual's observations are affected by that person's beliefs, prejudgments, and interests. To some extent, a person will see what she expects to see or thinks she should see. In an experiment, therefore, the experimenter tries to minimize personal factors by establishing objective measures that can be recorded without requiring interpretation by the observer. Statistical counts, machine readings, chemical tests, and descriptions using a specified technical vocabulary all reduce the interpretive role of the observer. The results produced by such techniques are less likely to be criticized as "just one person's way of looking at things." The results of the experiment have even better claims to objectivity if other experimenters in other laboratories produce the same results when they repeat the experiment.

make the observations and the best way to record them. For example, you might make a record of your own sensations of hunger or describe people meeting at a cocktail party or list the noises you can hear from your apartment window. Whether you make your observations over a long or a short period of time, keep an accurate record of what you find — through notes, tapes, or any other appropriate method. Don't rely on your memory; it may tend to tidy up the observations to make them fit more easily into the given categories.

After you have made all your observations, sit down with your notes, outline the analytical categories derived from the reading, and try to fit each observation into a category. Pay particular attention to those observations that seem anomalous — that is, that don't fit into a specific category. These anomalies will help you think about the limitations of

be changed, and it no longer would be the Civil War. Even in the field of psychology, where there is a substantial tradition of precise experiment, some psychologists suggest that you cannot fully understand human behavior divorced from everday activities and the very personal combination of motives, thoughts, and experiences peculiar to each individual.

The Certainty of Facts

The problem of designing, interpreting, and applying experiments lead back to an ancient problem that has vexed philosophers since the beginning of knowledge: what is a statement of fact and how does one verify fact? The common-sense distinction between a statement of fact and a statement of opinion is that a statement of fact reports a particular thing that actually happened, whereas a statement of opinion presents one person's thoughts about what happened — with no guarantee that such was the case. Facts depend upon observational certainty. In different fields, however, there are different possible levels of observational certainty; that is, the guarantee that a statement represents what truly happens varies from discipline to discipline. Any literate person can read the digital count on a Geiger counter, recording radioactive events of a specified range, and can get the same results as another person reading that same digital count. But consider social scientists observing two people exchanging words. Is the interchange a discussion, a disagreement, an argument, or an economic class confrontation? In history, how do you know that the Romans fought the Carthaginians at a particular time in a particular place except by the written word of ancient historians and by a few questionable archeological fragments? Thus the criteria for statement of fact and for verification — the verification that one needs to accept a report as fact — necessarily differ from field to field.

As you become more involved in a particular discipline, you will recognize the different possibilities for experimental observation, the criteria for verifying statements of fact, and the methods for reporting observations. You may even have a course explicitly teaching the experimental methods of the discipline. Learning the design, use, and limits of observation and experimentation in your chosen field may be as much a part of your professional training as becoming familiar with the theories and facts already developed.

Experimental Reports

Even though experimentation varies from field to field, a few general features of the writing of experimental results are common

> **Reports of experiments almost always include these steps:
> (1) a statement of the researcher's purpose and hypothesis,
> (2) a description of procedure, materials, and apparatus,
> (3) a report of results, (4) a discussion of the meaning of the
> results, and (5) a conclusion about the validity of the
> hypothesis and the implications for further study.**

throughout most disciplines. Reports of experiments almost always include these steps: (1) a statement of the researcher's purpose and hypothesis, (2) a description of procedure, materials, and apparatus, (3) a report of results, (4) a discussion of the meaning of the results, (5) a conclusion about the validity of the hypothesis and the implications for further study. Sometimes these parts are further broken down and expanded; sometimes they are presented in a continuous narrative. No matter what form they take, these parts are usually found in the experimental report.

The introduction presents the background of previous work — both in theory and experiment — that led to the current hypothesis being tested. The hypothesis may be an original one or one taken from a previous writer in the field. In college laboratory courses, you will usually be given a hypothesis to test; as you advance to more independent work, you will most likely have to develop hypotheses of your own. The introduction, establishing the logic and purpose of the experiment in terms of prior work published in the field, helps the reader see exactly what you are trying to prove by the experiment.

The experimental design should be explained in the section on procedure, materials, and apparatus in order to indicate how the experiment isolates those factors to be measured and eliminates any possible interfering factors. The description of the experimental design should also indicate a method of observation and measurement that will achieve precision and decrease personal bias. Finally, the description should be clear and precise enough to allow another experimenter to re-create the experiment and confirm your results.

The report of results should, of course, be as accurate as the experiment allows: you should indicate the degree of accuracy of your claims, and you should never claim to have found more than you actually did find. In some cases a narrative of the actual progress of the experiment helps put the results in better perspective.

The results, however, are not sufficient in themselves: they must be discussed and interpreted. What kinds of patterns emerged? Were the results as anticipated? Were there any anomalies? How do these results compare with those of previous experiments? How strongly do the results support or contradict the original hypothesis? Do they suggest some other theoretical possibility? Would information from another kind of experiment or a repeat of this one be useful in verifying the hypothesis further? Answers to these and similar questions will draw out the full meaning of the experiment and contribute to advancing knowledge in the field.

Thus, although researchers may, to the uninitiated, seem to gain knowledge entirely on the basis of first-hand experience, the experiments only make sense in a framework of theory, verification, and criticism presented in the literature of the field. Study of published research helps the new researcher define problems that need investigation and provides the information necessary to carry on that investigation profitably. Afterwards, the research report connects the results of the experiment with the rest of what is known in the field, making the work available for future researchers. In this way scientists build on one another's work — checking and developing the findings of all the separate researchers.

Writing Assignments

1. Write an essay comparing your own social experiences as a teen-ager with the following analysis of the adolescent peer group by Luella Cole. The excerpt is from *The Psychology of Adolescence,* a textbook used in the training of junior high school and high school teachers. Consider the audience for your own essay to be your own high school teachers — to let them know whether what they learned in their courses on education truly reflected teen-age experience.

THE ADOLESCENT PEER GROUP[9]

The unit of social life during adolescence is a small group that is often referred to by adolescents as "the crowd" but by psychologists as the "peer group." It is typically composed of an equal number of boys and girls. The core of it contains six to eight members, with perhaps another half-dozen adolescents around the fringes. Those who are steady members of the group customarily live within short driving distance of each other, attend the same school, and come from roughly the same socioeconomic background.

[9]From *Psychology of Adolescence,* Seventh Edition by Luella Cole and Irma Nelson Hall, pp. 346–348. Copyright 1936, 1942, 1948, 1954, © 1959, 1964, 1970 by Holt, Rinehart and Winston, Inc. Reprinted by permission of Holt, Rinehart and Winston.

The activities of the crowd vary somewhat from one season of the year to another; at almost any season they include listening to the radio, watching TV, occasionally going to a movie, eating, dancing together at the home of some member, and listening to phonograph records. In the summer they go on picnics together or they sit on someone's porch and talk — with at least one trip each evening to the neighborhood drive-in — or they go swimming and so on. In the winter the group sits around the home of a member, watches TV, and raids the icebox from time to time. None of this comes under the heading of adventure as seen through the eyes of late childhood, but it is apparently exciting to the adolescent. It is adventure, not into the world of things but into the world of social relationships. An adult listening to the conversation of such a crowd for an evening can hardly see that the chatter has been worthwhile. It does not seem to start anywhere, to go anywhere, or to be about anything. It is, however, satisfactory to the participants. It obviously gives them an opportunity to develop their conversational powers on other people whose abilities are no better than their own. Other values obtained from such a crowd include experiences in getting along with other people, practice in social skills, development of loyalty to a group, practice in judging people, assistance in the emancipation-from-home procedure, and experience in love-making under circumstances in which the participants are protected from serious consequences. Moreover, the group gives its members a feeling of social security, of "belonging."

The peer group plays such an important role in the lives of adolescents that a teacher should understand its nature and its values to the members. It should be remembered that adolescent boys and girls are very uncertain of themselves because they are changing so rapidly. One function of the peer group is to defend the adolescent from his own uncertainty through the security of his membership in a group. It also provides a chance for him to achieve status on his own merits — not those of his family — in terms of the values held by his age-mates. It gives him an opportunity for further developing his self-image, especially as regards the behavior that differentiates him or her from members of the opposite sex. And, as any group can do, the peer group helps the adolescent to develop the qualities that he will need in adult life. It is necessary for the school to work in terms of this spontaneous organization of youth and not try to work against it, since it has more authority over adolescent behavior than adults have.

The "peer culture," the sum total of spontaneous social manifestations among age-mates, is most clearly defined and most influential during the middle years of adolescence. At this time, adult values have less power to produce behavior than peer values. That is, if "everyone" is wearing berets, it is almost impossible to persuade an adolescent to wear any other sort of headgear, no matter how formal the occasion or how inappropriate the beret; if "no one" is wearing berets, then an adolescent will not wear one even to keep the hair out of his eyes while he is sailing a boat. Apparently, one of the deepest of adolescent needs is the need to be supported and approved by his peers. Deviations of any sort from the mode of the group are painful. An adolescent cannot afford to risk the ridicule of his intimate friends because he is too dependent upon them for approval. The peer group is a powerful force in setting standards of behavior and attitudes toward various problems. As long as the individual adolescent conforms in the main to the standards and opinions of his group, he is accepted. If he does not conform, he tends to see his group as less attractive than it was earlier, and his age-mates tend to reject him. As the years pass, the values of the crowd gradually mature and approach the adult norm for their social group. Also, the crowd tends to disintegrate under the pressures of later adolescence and early maturity. But while it endures, it is the most formative influence in the life of the average boy or girl.

On the debit side, it is probable that the crowd encourages some degree of snobbery and that it has an undesirable effect upon those who belong to no crowd at all. Sometimes an intense rivalry springs up between two crowds and leads to extremely silly behavior and occasional outbreaks of violence in some communities under economic or social stress, but such situations do not usually last long. If some observant and tactful older person can bring about an attachment to an existing crowd for the isolates or can influence the growth of a new crowd among those who belong to none and can manage to curb the occasional excesses of loyalty, this spontaneous social group could become even more valuable than it is naturally. Even as it is, the crowd probably does more to bring about normal social growth than do teachers and parents combined.

The spontaneous groupings of the adolescent population can be, and have been, studied and classified in a number of ways. One set of groupings is based upon consideration of socioeconomic status, preferred activities, and self-identification as to role. Four groups to be found in almost any high school are the following:

1. A group, largely lower-class and of low ability, emancipated from home, and playing adult roles.
2. A higher socioeconomic group of high moral code, moderate emancipation, and conforming to the demands of home and school but carrying on independent activities.
3. A group that is not emancipated from home and centers its activities around home, school, and community.
4. A group whose ways are those of people in the lowest socioeconomic levels.

In this study there was a total of ten groups, each reflecting a way of life that was derived from common backgrounds, common interests and activities, and common concepts of role.

The pupil who does not belong to a crowd is miserable. Few youngsters are self-reliant enough to stand alone. The sense of belonging is an indispensable ingredient for their happiness. Sometimes social isolation springs from deep-seated factors of personality but usually from relatively superficial matters of dress, manners, and attitudes. A teacher can often help such adolescents to become acceptable by persuading them to alter their appearance, to conform better to superficial social requirements, and to drop one or two annoying mannerisms. If the causes of isolation lie in a distortion of personality, a teacher can still provide sympathy and understanding, and he can try to bring the pupil into contact with those who can help him directly with his basic problems.

2. Basing your observations on ideas derived from Ernest L. Hartmann's chapter on "The Psychology of Tiredness," excerpted on pages 44–46, record in a journal your own patterns of tiredness. Then write a short critical analysis — length to be specified by your instructor — directed to an audience of your classmates, who are making similar observations about their own patterns of tiredness.

3. Write a critical analysis based on ideas from the following passage in Erving Goffman's *Relations in Public*. The passage discusses ways people keep from bumping into one another as they walk down the street. Using Goffman's comments, develop categories of body gestures, patterns of movement, and other activities that people employ while walking through crowded places; then make observations according to those categories. The final essay of critical analysis should be long enough to present the categories, to describe and to explain the data, and to develop conclusions. The audience for this essay will be your classmates, who are making similar observations.

PEDESTRIAN TRAFFIC[10]

A few comments about pedestrian traffic seem possible. In American downtown streets, traffic tends to sort itself out into two opposite-going sides. The dividing line is somewhere near the middle of the sidewalk but is subject to momentary shifting (to accommodate sudden bunching of traffic in one direction) and to longer term displacement caused by the tendency for the journey to and from work to involve a large volume going in one direction in the morning and the reverse at night. As in road traffic, the side going in one's direction tends to be on the right of the dividing line. However, pedestrians on either side who desire to walk quickly sometimes move to the curb and

[10]From Erving Goffman, *Relations in Public*, pp. 9–13. Copyright © 1971 by Erving Goffman, Basic Books, Inc., Publishers, New York.

there manage two-way flow. The innermost part of the street tends to be slowest, perhaps because of the obstruction produced by window shoppers and those entering and leaving buildings. Apart from these considerations, lane formation *within* the right- or left-hand side tends not to be marked, although when an individual momentarily shifts from a lane to facilitate traffic flow, he is apparently likely to shift back into it after the interference is past. It might also be added that at crosswalks the side-division tends to break down, and those going in one direction will take up both sides at the curb, thus facing across the street a broad front of others ready to come toward them. Contrariwise, there are steps and tunnels that physically mark and thereby consolidate two-lane flow.

When routing by divided two-way flow is not used to avoid collision during opposite-direction passing, pedestrians tend (in America) to use the road traffic device of veering to the right, although this practice is breached for many reasons, among which are the principled ones that males should take the road side when passing females and that pedestrians have the right to cut across the sidewalk at any point, there being no full equivalent of periodic road intersections.

The workability of lane and passing rules is based upon two processes important in the organization of public life: externalization and scanning.

By the term "externalization," or "body gloss," I refer to the process whereby an individual pointedly uses over-all body gesture to make otherwise unavailable facts about his situation gleanable. Thus, in driving and walking the individual conducts himself — or rather his vehicular shell — so that the direction, rate, and resoluteness of his proposed course will be readable. In ethological terms, he provides an "intention display." By providing this gestural prefigurement and committing himself to what it foretells, the individual makes himself into something that others can read and predict from; by employing this device at proper strategic junctures — ones where his indicated course will be perceived as a promise or warning or threat but not as a challenge — he becomes something to which they can adapt without loss of self-respect.

The term "scanning" does not have to be defined, but the way it is done in pedestrian traffic needs to be described. When a pedestrian in American society walks down the street, he seems to make an assumption that those to the front of a close circle around him are ones whose course he must check up on, and those who are a person or two away or moving behind his sight-line can be tuned out. In brief, the individual, as he moves along, tends to maintain a scanning or check-out area. (By angling his own head so as not to be directly obstructed visually by the head of the pedestrian ahead of him, he can ensure his maintenance of this view.) As oncomers enter the individual's scanning range — something like three or four sidewalk squares away — they are commonly glanced at briefly and thereafter disattended because their distance from him and their indicated rate and direction of movement imply that collision is not likely and that no perception by them of him is necessary for his easily avoiding collision. A simple "body check" is involved, albeit one performed more circumspectly (at present) by women than by men. This check tends to occur when the individual making it can introduce a large directional change through a small and therefore undemeaning angular correction. Once others have been checked out satisfactorily, they can be allowed to come close without this being cause for concern. Thus the individual can generally cease to concern himself with others as soon as they have come close enough abreast of him so that any interference from them would require a very abrupt turn. And further, since he apparently does not concern himself with oncomers who are separated from him by others, he can, in dense traffic, be unconcerned about persons who are actually very close to him. Therefore, the scanning area is not a circle but an elongated oval, narrow to either side of the individual and longest in front of him, constantly changing in area depending on traffic density around him. Note that even as the individual is checking out those who are just coming into range, so they will be checking him out, which means that oncomers will be eyeing each other at something of the same moment and that this moment will be similarly located in the course of both; yet this act is almost entirely out of awareness.

When an individual deems that a simple body-check is not sufficient, as when a collision course is apparent or there is no clear indication of the other's course, then additional assurances are likely to be sought. He can ostentatiously take or hold a course, waiting to do this until he can be sure that the other is checking him out. If he wants to be still more careful, he can engage in a "checked-body-check"; after he has given a course indication, he can make sure the signal has been picked up by the other, either by meeting the other's eyes (although not for engagement) or by noting the other's direction of vision, in either case establishing that his own course gesture has not likely been overlooked. In brief, he can check up on the other's eye check on him, the assumption here being that the other can be relied on to act safely providing only that he has perceived the situation. Finally, a brief face engagement may be inititated in which one party signals what he proposes they do and the other party signals agreement. (A strategic device here is to signal a collaborative routing in which the other has a slight advantage, this usually assuring agreement.) In all of this maneuvering, two special moments can be found. First, there is the "critical sign": the act on the part of the other that finally allows the individual to discover what it is the other proposes to do. Second, there is the "establishment point": the moment both parties can feel that critical signs have been exchanged regarding compatible directions and timing, and that both appreciate that they both appreciate that this has occurred. It is then that movements can be executed with full security and confidence; it is then that those involved can feel fully at ease and fully turn their attention elsewhere.

4. The following excerpt, from an article in *Psychology Today* by Joyce Dudney Fleming (January, 1974), reports the results of an experiment in teaching language to an ape. The investigation into the language-learning abilities of animals is one of the legacies of Darwin's work, for evolution emphasizes the similarities between humans and other animals. Researchers had to accept and assimilate evolutionary ideas about such similarities before they could seriously imagine that apes could learn language.

This excerpt is written as a journalistic narrative; nevertheless, it contains all the main parts of a formal experimental report. Identify and summarize the main points of each part of the experimental report as given in this excerpt: (1) introduction, (2) procedure, methods, and apparatus, (3) results, (4) discussion, and (5) conclusion.

THE STATE OF THE APES[11]

Man is not unique; the belief that he is has been with us forever. The foreshadowing of the death of that belief is almost as old. It may have started when ancient physicians discovered the extensive similarity between the bodies of men and other animals. It certainly was evident when Darwin's theory of evolution attained general scientific acceptance. Now the end is in sight as man is forced to concede the last significant attribute that was his and his alone — language.

The animal reaching for our holy title, only user of language, is the chimpanzee. Not one that performs like a trained seal. Not one that dutifully repeats exactly what is taught. Not one at all, but a dozen chimps, in Reno, in Santa Barbara, in Norman, Oklahoma, and in Atlanta. They have vocabularies of substantial size. They combine symbols to produce appropriate combinations that they have never before seen. They use language to manipulate their environments. They mystify their experienced teachers with unexpected abilities and insights.

The Failure of the Spoken Word. For many years we believed that chimps must be smart enough to learn a language. Yet all attempts to teach them to talk have been failures by even the most generous standards. The world's record for number of words spoken by a chimp is held by Viki, who managed to learn four words in the 1950s. Her problem was speaking. Chimpanzees cannot learn to talk, but they can learn to use a complex set of symbols to convey information. The symbols can be hand signals, pieces of plastic in different shapes and colors, geometric designs on typewriter keys; anything they can manipulate with their hands.

The record of failure turned to a record of success when Beatrice and Allen Gardner at the University of Nevada looked at communication among chimps in the wild, noticed that they used many more hand signals than vocal signals, and decided to try teaching a gestural language instead of a verbal one. They chose Washoe as their first pupil.

Washoe is a female chimpanzee who was born in the wild. She was about a year old when her language training began in June 1966. At this age her development and her needs were much like those of a human baby who is one or one and a half years old. She slept a lot, had just begun to crawl, did not have either her first canines or molars. During the first few months her daily routine was centered around diapers, bottles, and making friends with her human companions.

The Gardners chose a chimpanzee instead of one of the other higher primates because of the chimp's capacity for forming strong attachments to human beings. They believe that this high degree of sociability may be essential for the development of language. The language they chose for Washoe was American Sign Language (ASL).

ASL is a system of communication developed for deaf people and used extensively throughout North America. It is a set of hand gestures that corresponds to individual words. (The other system for the deaf, finger spelling, is not used in this research.) Many of the signs are iconic, visual representations of their meaning. For example:

drink — the thumb is extended from the fisted hand and touches the mouth,

up — the arms are extended upwards and the index finger may also point in that direction,

smell — the palm is held in front of the nose and moved slightly upward several times,

cat — the thumb and index finger come together near the corner of the mouth and are moved outward representing the cat's whiskers. This close association between sign and meaning makes it easy to learn to read some of the simple and frequently used messages.

Think Doctor. A wide range of expression is possible within this system. While learning to sign, the Gardners practiced translating songs and poems, and found that any material could be accurately signed. When technical terms and proper names present a problem they are designated by an arbitrary sign agreed upon by the community of signers. Washoe's teachers chose the signs *think doctor* and *think science* for the words psychologist and psychology.

The fact that ASL is used by human beings allows for some comparison between Washoe's signing and that seen in deaf children of deaf parents. The Gardners report that deaf parents see many similarities between Washoe's early performance, some of which was filmed, and that of deaf children learning to sign.

Washoe lived in a fully-equipped house trailer. The Gardners designed her living arrangements to exploit the possibility that she would engage in conversations — ask questions as well as answer them, describe objects as well as request them. They gave her a stimulus-rich environment, minimal restraint, constant human companionship while she was awake, and lots of games that promoted interaction between Washoe and human beings. Her teachers used no language except ASL in her presence.

Flower and Smell. The results of combining this pupil and this language in this environment are remarkable. Her teachers taught her the sign for *more* in the context of tickling, a romping, wrestling game Washoe played with them. She generalized its use to all activities and all objects. They taught her the sign for *open* using only three particular doors in her house trailer. She transferred its use to all doors, containers, drawers, the refrigerator and, finally, to water faucets. They taught her the sign for *flower*. She used it for all flowers and for a number of situations in which an odor was prominent, such as opening a tobacco pouch or entering a kitchen where food was cooking. So they gave her the sign for *smell*. She differentiated the two signs and uses each appropriately, but the error she makes in odor contexts is frequently *flower*.

When she makes mistakes, Washoe often tells her teacher more about what she knows than when she signs correctly. The Gardners started using pictures of objects to test Washoe's vocabulary after she spontaneously transferred her signs from objects to pictures of similar objects. However, if they used a photograph of a replica of the object, she made a lot of mistakes. She called them *baby*. In response to a picture of a cat she signed *cat* on almost 90 percent of the trials; to a picture of a replica of a cat she signed *cat* on 60 percent of the trials and *baby* on 40 percent. Her teachers used *baby* to refer to dolls and to human babies. To Washoe it meant something different, something like miniaturization, or replication in some artificial sense.

The First Sentence. In April 1967, less than a year after her training began, she produced her first combination of signs, a kind of sentence. Though no lessons on combinations had ever been given, her teachers had signed to her in strings. As soon as Washoe had learned eight or 10 signs she started putting them together in sets of two or three, much as small children learn to combine words. She learned some of her combinations from her teachers, but others she made up herself. For example, Washoe invented *gimme tickle* to request tickling and *open food* *drink* to ask that the refrigerator be opened. Her teachers had always used the signs *cold box* for this appliance.

With just 10 signs there is a large number of possible two- and three-sign combinations, but Washoe did not make sentences from random groups of signs. The ones she used were usually the ones that made sense. The signs she used in front of a locked door included *gimme key, open key, open key please,* and *open key help hurry.* The Gardners analyzed Washoe's two-sign combinations using a method like the one Roger Brown, a psycholinguist from Harvard, developed for children. They found that her earliest combinations were comparable to the earliest combinations of children in terms of the meanings expressed and of the semantic classes used. These classes express relationships such as the agent of an action (*Roger tickle*), the location of a state, action or process (*in hat*), the experiencer of a state or emotion (*Washoe sorry*).

At the end of 21 months of training, she had 34 signs that met a rigorous set of accuracy and frequency criteria. The Gardners imposed these criteria to be sure she really knew a sign before they added it to her list. Not all of Washoe's early signs referred to objects or to actions. She used *hurt, sorry* and *funny* in appropriate situations. She acquired four signs during the first seven months of training, nine during the second, and 21 during the third. Instead of becoming bogged down by all of this new material, she processed it at a faster and faster rate. After three years of training, her total vocabulary was 85 signs. After another year, it had almost doubled.

Washoe probably could have gone on this way forever, but her human friends had other plans. Several of her teachers were leaving the project. It would be difficult for Washoe to get used to a whole new set of teachers, so the Gardners chose another plan. In October 1970, they gave up Washoe and her 160-sign vocabulary to Roger Fouts, one of their most promising graduate students, who was going to Oklahoma to continue this research. . . .

The Evidence Piles Up. The scientific community is justifiably skeptical about the idea of talking chimps. All reported attempts to teach them a verbal language have been failures. But little by little the all-important evidence is piling up.

The Gardners, who pioneered with Washoe, are very conscientious about distributing information to other psychologists. In the early years of Washoe's training they periodically sent out summaries of her linguistic development. The usual response was that it was all very interesting, but that her performance would not be scientifically important until she:

1 demonstrated an extensive system of names for objects in her environment;

2 signed about objects that are not physically present;
3 used signs for concepts, not just objects, agents and actions;
4 invented semantically appropriate combinations; and
5 used proper order when it is semantically necessary.

All of these are reasonable criteria. All are demonstrated by at least one chimp, most by several. But as the type of data demanded as evidence for language becomes more complex, it is increasingly difficult to decide which criteria are reasonable.

This difficulty arises because we have no definition that allows us to recognize language outside the context of vocal human communication. This is an unusual situation.

The definition for a particular function is usually a set of principles that are common to all the systems that perform that function. Reproduction is a good example. All animals have a system of reproduction. These systems are very different from each other, but all have some principles in common. These principles allow us to recognize, and correctly label, all the different systems. But the only naturally occurring system of language belongs to human beings. What can we compare it with? How can we recognize a language that is not exactly like human language?

There is no final answer to this question, but the possibility of one becomes stronger each time Booee signs to Bruno, or Peony solves another linguistic problem. Perhaps we will get our answer if Lucy becomes pregnant from the artificial insemination planned for her, and if she bears a healthy infant, and if she teaches that infant signs. I know this is a lot of ifs, but I would like to add another one. If it happens, it will be dynamite.

7

Comparing and Synthesizing Sources

Preview

Once you start comparing the statements of different books, you may discover many problems in fitting the sources together. Books may cover the same subject but with different foci and with different purposes. Books may disagree over facts, ideas, and basic viewpoints. Large gaps of knowledge may exist, not covered by any available source. In this chapter, we will study ways of fitting parts together and evaluating differences between writers. Two types of essays, the *comparative analysis of sources* and the *synthesis of sources,* will help you develop the skills of comparing and evaluating sources.

The Myth of Wall-to-Wall Knowledge

A library presents an imposing vision: books neatly arranged according to reference numbers on endless rows of metal shelves. Initially, the wall-to-wall books make you feel that any fact you want to know must be in one of them and that the ideas in these books should fit together as neatly as the books fit together on the shelves. You have a comforting feeling that all knowledge in books interlocks to provide a smooth carpet of learning — everywhere even and consistent under foot, no matter where you may tread.

When you actually start to look for specific information or try to find agreement between the books on a particular topic, you are more likely to feel that you have stepped into the badlands of the Dakotas or the swamps of Florida. You cannot always find what you are looking for; what you do find may be contradictory or confusing. On the positive side, you may uncover some wonderful surprises — ideas and information that you had no idea existed.

If you stop to consider why and how books are written, the unevenness of ground may not take you so much by surprise. Each person who writes a book makes a particular statement, based on individual thoughts and perceptions about a subject of personal interest; moreover, each writer shapes his or her particular statement around particular purposes, as discussed in Chapter 4. Each writer does build on what came before — on the other books in the library — but each builds in an individual way to serve different functions and to speak to different readers. In some disciplines, particularly in science and technology, knowledge has been organized or codified. But even in fields with high degrees of codification, there are still major areas of disagreement, large gaps in knowledge, and different approaches to problem areas.

Think of a conversation involving a large number of people. Each person has a different viewpoint, different interests, and different points to make. Perhaps after much talk, the group may achieve a consensus on some limited facts, certain shared principles, and perhaps specific lines of action. More often there are disagreements, unresolved issues, misunderstandings, and only partial interest in what other people say.

Once you as a reader move beyond the coherent world of a single book in order to gain the wisdom of several authors on a single subject, you will have to make sense of the diversity of statements you will find. To make your own informed statement on a subject that other writers have discussed, you need to sort out agreement and disagreement, fact and opinion, and ideas you accept and those you reject. This chapter presents techniques and criteria for making choices between opposing statements and presents ways of bringing diverse materials together. In this chapter, you are asked to write two types of essay: the analytical comparison of two pieces of writing and the composite library report. These two types of essays provide practice in the skills of intelligently drawing together material from different sources.

A first task, however, is to sort out the different levels at which books may either converge or diverge — in regard to subjects, facts, ideas, and underlying perceptions.

Finding the Common Ground Between Two Books

The first condition for a successful conversation, whether spoken by party-goers at a college mixer or written by various scholars, each alone at a desk, is that the participants be talking about the same subject. If one person talks about unemployment and the other talks about television ratings, two separate monologues are taking place but no conversation — unless they have discovered a common ground between the two subjects, such as possible effects of economic downturns on television production. Topics must coincide, overlap, or intersect to allow meaningful discussion.

By bringing two books or articles together for comparison, you are suggesting some common ground between them — some relationship between the two statements. Perhaps one of the writers explicitly recognizes that such a relationship exists by citing and discussing the earlier writer's work. At times, writers deliberately answer each other. However, you may find many cases where two writers have not explicitly joined issue even though they are clearly writing about the same topic. In fact, you may bring together writers who may never have heard of each other — because *you* have perceived that their subjects are the same.

Even before you begin comparing two pieces of writing to see whether they are at peace or war over the common ground, you must locate and define that common ground. This is not always an easy task. At one extreme, you may find books that appear to take on the same subject and to have similar purposes. All biographies of Henry Ford attempt to present a true picture of the life of the great automobile

> **Because the connections between books can be so wide-ranging and different in kind, and because no two books cover exactly the same ground in exactly the same way, the more specific you are in localizing the precise areas of overlap and shared concern between books, the more you will gain by bringing them together. You will then know exactly what the discussion is about.**

industrialist, and most cover his entire life — from birth and childhood to death. Predictably, each of these books presents facts and statements about the major events in Ford's life: the building of his first car, the opening of his first factory, the creation of the assembly line, the introduction of the Model T, his libel suit against the *Chicago Tribune*, and his attempt to run for president of the United States in 1924. Other events, such as the patent battle with Selden, who had filed a patent application on the design of an automobile as early as 1879, are covered in only some of the biographies. In addition to varying on the events covered, the books vary greatly in their amount of interpretation, criticism, praise, and discussion of causes and effects. Thus, even when several books seem to be taking on precisely the same subject, you must be careful to identify the overlap, topic by topic.

In the middle ground, you will compare books that have substantial overlap even though they take on different overall subjects. Any history of the automobile industry would, necessarily, discuss many topics involving Henry Ford's life, just as any biography of him would have to discuss his role in the growth of the industry. Again you must specifically identify the exact topics and extent of overlap; parts of each book will have little to do with the other.

At the other extreme are books or articles that are not primarily concerned with the same topics but that do have some bearing on a particular topic. The life of William C. Durant, the founder of General Motors, at several points touched on Ford's life; a biography of Durant might, therefore, shed some additional light on their relationship, discussed only briefly in a biography of Ford. By identifying such intersection between two books, you may be making connections no one else has made. By making, for example, connections between a history of advertising in the early part of the century and Ford's merchandising policies as presented in a Ford biography, you may find an explanation of Ford's great success.

Because the connections between books can be so wide-ranging and different in kind, and because no two books cover exactly the same ground in exactly the same way, the more specific you are in localizing the precise areas of overlap and shared concern between books, the more you will gain by bringing them together. You will then know exactly what the discussion is about.

Do Books Differ on Facts?

In 1892 I completed my first motor car, but it was not until the spring of the following year that it ran to my satisfaction.

—Henry Ford, *My Life and Work* (in collaboration with Samuel Crowther)[1]

The last days of May, 1896, saw the quadricycle almost completed. Ford and Bishop were working every night. "We often wondered when Henry Ford slept," remarked Charles T. Bush of the Strelinger company, "because he was putting in long hours working [at the Edison plant] and when he went home at night he was always experimenting or reading." Clara worried about his loss of sleep, but did not let him guess that she feared that his efforts might culminate in a breakdown. For the last forty-eight hours before the vehicle was ready he hardly slept at all. Finally early in the morning of June 4 — between 2 and 4 A.M. — the task was finished, and the builder was ready to take his car out for a trial run.

—Allan Nevins, *Ford: The Times, The Man, The Company*[2]

Sometimes we can judge the truth of a statement of fact on the basis of our own observations. Often, however, we must rely entirely on second-hand reports. If all the written sources agree about the facts of a particular event, and if you have no other cause for suspicion, reliance on written reports should present few problems. You can generally assume that the facts were just as all the sources report them. For example, if all biographies of Henry Ford and all histories of the Ford company agree that the lowest retail price of the Model T Touring Car was $360 and that this was the price during 1916 and 1917, you may take these facts as true. Further, if company and dealer records, contemporary advertisements,

[1]Garden City, N.Y.: Garden City Publishing Co., 1922, p. 30.
[2]New York: Scribner's, 1954, p. 316.

and public announcements *all* confirm the facts, you have no reason to doubt them.

Conflicting Facts

What happens if written sources disagree about what happened? If different observers report different statements of fact, how can you tell which has the facts right? Here we are not talking about the meaning or the interpretation of events — that will be discussed later in this chapter — but only about the directly observable phenomenon: What happened? When did it happen? Where did it happen? Who was involved? If sources disagree, you may become justifiably confused about what the actual events were. The two quotations at the beginning of this section present just such a conflict over facts. Henry Ford himself states he built his first working car in 1892; Allan Nevins, the historian, writes that Ford did not build his first working automobile (called a *quadricycle*) until 1896. Obviously Ford could have only built his first automobile once, but who are we to believe about when it happened — Ford himself or a reputed scholar?

Your first reaction to such a conflict may be "What does it matter? Who cares?" That is, you believe the difference is minor and does not bear directly upon the issues you are interested in. In some cases this response may be appropriate. If, for example, you were looking into Ford's career only as a background to studying the development of early assembly-line techniques, the exact date of Ford's first car may not matter. If you have to refer to the date, you could simply cite both sources and leave the dispute unresolved. Not all conflicts must be resolved, but you should notice when they do occur.

One reason you should make note of conflicts — no matter how minor they at first seem — is that they may later point to more important issues. If in studying Ford's statements about the development of assembly lines you find Ford has a tendency to stretch the truth to make himself look better, this earlier conflict over dates may help you *confirm a pattern*.

For many questions about Ford's contribution, however, the date of his first car is crucial, for the difference of four years determines whether Ford was one of the leaders in auto invention and design or whether he just made use of what others did before him. If Ford built a working car in 1892, it would have been the first in this country, since there is no record of an operating car in the United States prior to that year — despite Selden's design on paper for well over a decade. The date determines whether Ford, in addition to being a business genius, was an inventive genius as well.

Resolving Conflicts

The significance of the date makes the conflict an important one to resolve, but — as anyone who has watched a courtroom drama on TV can tell you — it is not easy to determine the facts from the conflicting testimony of two witnesses. The difficulties in evaluating testimony in a courtroom come from two major sources. First, testimony is given by people — people with fallible memories, limited or distorted perceptions, and personal interests. There are many reasons why a person may not have clearly seen what happened — and even more reasons why that person might not state exactly what he or she saw. Therefore legal procedure defines who may testify about what and in what manner in order to reduce personal factors, limited memory, and self-interest and to increase specificity and accuracy.

The second difficulty is that many of the facts — often the most important ones — have not been observed by anyone who will or can testify. Nobody but the dead victim may have seen the accused pull the trigger. Thus the trial may have to depend on *secondary evidence* in order to establish the most vital facts. The victim's friend, for example, may testify that she was talking on the phone with the victim at 12:14 A.M. Suddenly the victim stopped talking, and the friend heard a scuffle, a shot — then silence. The police testify that they found the body dead of bullet wounds at 12:30 A.M. From this evidence the jury can infer a murder took place. The defense then calls as witness a bartender from the next city who testifies that the accused was in his bar from 10 P.M. until 2:00 A.M. Unless the prosecution can discredit the bartender's story by other testimony, the jury can only infer that someone else committed the crime. The main facts are pieced together indirectly, based on the interpretation and quality of the secondary evidence.

Ford Versus Nevins

Now let us evaluate the dispute over the date of Ford's first car, using as criteria the credibility of the witnesses and the strength of the evidence. First, we must ask how good are Ford and Nevins as witnesses. Henry Ford, in one respect, should be a very good witness: he was there when it happened and should know more precise information than an outsider like Nevins, who must rely on other people's reports. On the other hand, Ford is speaking from his memory, thirty years after the actual events. Over that long a period, recollection can get quite hazy, reflecting how Ford would like it to have been rather than how it actually was. Ford, moreover, has much to gain by reporting the earlier date: the 1892 date would make him a pioneer of auto invention. So we may wonder whether Ford is an accurate and unbiased observer.

Allan Nevins also has some pluses and minuses as a witness. On the minus side, he wrote sixty years after the events; he was not even born when the first cars were being tested. Further, as the preface to his book states, Nevins's research on Henry Ford was funded by the Ford Foundation. Yet this funding by a potentially interested party ultimately makes Nevins's dating more credible, because the later date goes directly against the interests of the sponsor. Even more to Nevins's credit is his substantial reputation as a historical scholar, more dedicated to truth than to private bias. Thus, although Nevins is more distant from the actual events, he is probably less biased as a witness.

It is on the question of evidence, however, that the real difference between the accounts of Ford and Nevins becomes quite apparent. Ford relies only on his recollection. He does not present the testimony of other witnesses on the scene at the same time nor does he include any documentary support — such as bills for raw materials. We have only his word and memory to go on. Nevins, on the other hand, offers — in the pages around the quoted passages — substantial evidence in support of two claims for the later date. First, to support the claim that Ford's tinkering with engines did not lead to an operable car prior to 1895, Nevins cites the testimony of three people who discussed Ford's work with him at that time. All three agree that Ford's work was only at the beginning stages. Moreover, the dates used by these witnesses are substantiated by the dates of magazine articles that entered into their discussions with Ford. Furthermore, Nevins cites Ford's wife, who claims that as of Christmas, 1893, Ford had only a partially assembled engine and no other parts of a car. Once again, her date is correlated with the birth of a child, whose birth certificate is a matter of public record.

In support of his second claim that Ford did complete a working car in 1896, Nevins cites the testimony of individuals close to the events. These witnesses confirm many secondary supporting circumstances: Ford's difficult financial condition because of the cost of materials and Ford's physical and mental exhaustion from working on the car while still maintaining a full-time job. The statements of one particular witness, Charles King, are particularly persuasive. King helped Ford in the last stages of building the car and had previously worked on one of his own. Thus he was both an expert — skilled enough to evaluate Ford's progress — and a first-hand witness, very close to the events. Nevins's evidence confirms that Henry Ford did build his first car in 1896.

Criteria for Evaluation

What characteristics make a good observer and what qualifies as convincing evidence vary substantially from field to field (see pages 171–172). Moreover, each particular conflict over facts brings in individual factors that must be considered. The following suggestions should be used flexibly; keep in mind the specifics of each case and the special criteria of the disciplines involved. These criteria, nonetheless, do provide a starting point for the evaluation and resolution of conflicts over fact.

Criteria for evaluating sources or witnesses

• Generally, the closer the witness was in time and place to the original events, the better. If the writer was not there, he or she may cite reliable sources who were.
• The more the writer or primary witness knows about the subject or events he or she is describing, the more he or she will know what to look for, what to report, and what to conclude.
• The fewer biases or prejudgments writers or witnesses have about the matters they are reporting on, the more likely they will give an undistorted account.

Criteria for evaluating evidence

• The more *specific* and *complete* the evidence is, the more likely it is to present a clear and precise picture.
• The more *internally consistent* the evidence is, the more likely the report is accurate. Internal consistency means that one part of the evidence does not contradict another part and that all parts support a single interpretation. Be cautious: in some cases, too consistent evidence may mean oversimplification or fudging of observations.
• The more the evidence was recorded at the time of the events reported, the fewer problems with distorted memory will occur.
• The more the evidence is tied to matters of public record — such as contemporary newspaper accounts, government documents, or widely acknowledged facts — the more credible the evidence is.
• The less indication of bias, or fraudulence, or of false statements, the more reliable the evidence is.

At times you may not be able to make a clear-cut choice between two conflicting reports of fact: the witnesses and evidence may be equally good — or equally poor — on both sides, or you may lack enough background information to judge. In such cases all you can do is acknowledge the conflict and suggest what the *implications* of either report being true might be. Tracing the logical implications of each report may give you an indirect indication of which side may be more likely to be true. At least you will learn the consequences of favoring one report over the other.

Working Out the Implications

Suppose, for example, that Ford did build a car in 1892 and that nobody but Ford and his employee Sam Huff (who later backed up the claim) knew about it. What would the implications of this be? One implication is that we have lost traces of the early history of the automobile — which is possible. Another implication is that Ford was able to keep the car secret from those around him, including his wife — a bit less likely. A third implication is that Ford was a pioneer of auto design as well as production. This last idea might be checked against the pattern of the rest of his life to see whether he displayed as much engineering genius as business genius. Did he tend to borrow engineering advances or did he make them himself?

On the other hand, if Nevins's date of 1896 is correct, we can see other implications: first, that Ford had a flexible, if not a fabricating, memory. We could check the accuracy of his memory against other claims that Ford made. Second, when Ford made his claim in 1926, he had reasons for wanting to date his first car as early as possible. And finally, Ford's skill was more in adapting other people's inventions than in developing his own; thus his real talents emerged only when he began the production and sales of his car.

The more you know about the 1890s, automobiles, and Ford, the more you will be able to judge these implications against the conflicting facts. These implications move us toward the realm of ideas, interpretations, and conclusions.

Do Books Differ on Ideas?

Ideas tell us what a writer thinks about a subject and not just what he or she is describing as facts. The writer's ideas may be about causes, effects, similarities, motivation, meaning, or any other kind of abstraction that goes beyond the immediately verifiable.

It is, for example, a matter of fact — verifiable in company records, newspaper accounts, and history books — that on January 5, 1914, Henry Ford announced a wage policy for Ford Motor Company, more than doubling the minimum wage of his workers from $.26 an hour to $5 for a full eight-hour workday. However, that policy gives rise to many questions whose answers are in the realm of ideas and open to a variety of opinions: what caused the company to increase wages so greatly? Why did the announcement receive such wide publicity? Why was it criticized? What was the effect of the increase for all American workers? Was the policy a success? The answers to these questions can only be found by *interpreting* the factual evidence — and not just by collecting more facts.

Even though ideas differ from facts, they are still very dependent on facts because the facts are the basic material upon which you must base your thinking. You have already seen how a disagreement over facts can lead to a disagreement over conclusions: the evaluation of Ford's achievements, in part, depends on which date is correct for his first working model. Even if two writers agree on facts, they may come to opposing conclusions by choosing different facts on which to base their ideas. Finally, writers may come to different conclusions based on the same facts by using different reasoning processes. Thus, to evaluate conflicting ideas, you must evaluate both the facts they are based on and the reasoning by which the writer developed ideas out of facts.

The Meeting of Ideas

Before we begin to consider ways of resolving contradictory ideas, we must identify whether the ideas in question agree or disagree — or have little to do with each other. Unlike statements of fact, which usually present contradictions in obvious ways, statements of ideas are not as easily compared. Two statements of fact either make a claim about the date of a salary increase or they do not. However, ideas interpreting that same event may take off in many different directions from the simple fact. For example, referring to the date of Ford's wage announcement, one writer says that the date was held up because Ford wanted to make sure that profits were great enough to support the increased costs of higher wages; another claims that the date was far in advance of the liberalization of wage policies of other American corporations; another notes that the date marked the beginning of a number of Ford policies concerned with worker welfare. Each of these ideas may be plausible, but they have nothing to do with each other. They explore entirely separate issues — even though they all concern the single fact of date. Each operates in a different realm.

So the first task in comparing ideas is to define the realm each idea operates in. The more common *realms of ideas* include

causes
effects
intentions of statements and actions
implicit meanings
relationships between facts
statements of value

You will notice many others in the course of your reading. Further, the writer's idea may be limited — a discussion of only a part of the issue within a single realm. In explaining the reasons for Ford's dramatic wage increase, you may note the causes within the mind of Henry Ford, the causes within the company, and the causes in the political and social climate of the period. Statements about causes within each of these areas do not necessarily contradict statements about causes in the others. Only when statements exist in the same realm with the same limits can you find direct agreement or disagreement.

Nevins Versus Sward

A direct conflict of ideas occurs between Keith Sward in *The Legend of Henry Ford* and Allan Nevins in *Ford: The Times, The Man, The Company* over the issues that led to the Ford Company's change in wage policy. Sward cites fear of labor unrest, employee radicalization, and unionization as the main cause of the managerial decision to raise wages dramatically. Nevins directly contradicts this idea by claiming the company's main concerns were a sense of fairness and a desire for increased quality of work — through increased morale and improved home life for the workers. Sward sees the company reasoning from fear; Nevins sees the company reasoning from good business practice and moral equity.

Nevins and Sward present ideas about the company management that are mutually exclusive, for each claims to be presenting the single most important motivation. If they each claimed to be suggesting only one out of many possible motivations, then it might be possible to accept both statements; some of the company executives may have responded to fear, and others may have acted from a sense of fairness. Even one person may have mixed motives and mixed feelings. Because the two writers each claim to isolate the single most important factor, their statements are mutually contradictory. Both motivations cannot be the most important. Further, each writer explicitly scoffs at the opposite idea: Sward states that Ford showed little regard for the welfare of workers, whereas Nevins argues that labor unrest and radical feeling were much less significant than they were later made out to be. In other words, you cannot explain what they both say without pointing out the conflict.

Mutual Compatability

The concept of *mutual compatability* of ideas and its negative counterpart, *mutual exclusivity* of ideas, are the keys to finding relationships between ideas. Ideas of two authors are usually not so directly opposed that one says yes while the other says no. More usually, you will have to determine whether the statements of two authors can reasonably fit together. Writers who make claims using extreme words like *only, most, primary, always,* and *never* will frequently conflict with each other; writers who make claims that concede other possibilities — through phrases such as *in part, along with, one of several,* or *sometimes* — are more apt to be mutually compatible. One writer's claim that Ford's large salary increase worked smoothly *in all its aspects* is not compatible with another writer's negative claim that the riots of job seekers outside the Ford factory after the announcement were a direct result of the false hopes raised by Ford. However, the negative evaluation, pointing to the riots, would be compatible with the more moderate claim that the Ford managers did their best to anticipate the effects of the wage increase. This qualified statement allows for the possibility that — despite the best efforts of the Ford planners — certain effects may have resulted from factors beyond their awareness.

Evaluating Disputes over Ideas

Once you have spotted disagreement of ideas — either by direct or indirect contradiction — you can then turn to analyzing and evaluating the disagreement. Examine the causes of the disagreement. Does the disagreement come from conflicting evidence, a different selection of evidence, or from different reasoning processes? Does the conflict come from the facts or what the writer does with the facts?

Disputes over Facts

Conflicting facts give rise to different ideas. As we noticed in the last section, the date of Ford's first car has many consequences for evaluating his contribution to the development of the automobile — and even for the evaluation of his personality. If you can resolve the conflict of facts, you can usually resolve the conflict between two writer's resulting ideas. Thus, once we determined that Nevins's later date of 1896 was the correct one, many consequences — Ford's greater skill in business than invention, his fallible memory, and his desire for increasing his reputation beyond the facts — fall into place. Therefore, whenever you come across an idea conflict based on a fact conflict, you should try to resolve the fact conflict, according to the criteria presented on pages 189–194.

Disputes over Selection of Facts

Since frequently there are more facts available than anyone can make full use of in any single book or article, each writer must make a choice of what he or she considers the most important or relevant facts; thus the different choice of facts may lead to different conclusions. Each writer may have access to different facts or may be more or less careful about paying attention to all the available facts. At times, deeper differences between the thinking of different writers may predispose them to pay more attention to one fact rather than another. The writer's selection of specific facts — from all those available — affects the ideas the writer eventually develops from the facts.

A typical conflict of ideas arising from a different selection of facts occurs between Sward and Nevins over the consequences of the Ford wage policy for the workers. Sward focuses attention on the number of workers who did not complete the six-month probationary period to become eligible for the five-dollar-a-day minimum. Sward cites many statistics concerning the rapid turnover of new employees and concludes that the Ford policy was not as generous as it first appeared to be and that Ford kept down labor costs by a deliberate policy of rapid turnover, enabling the company to pay the lower probationary wage to a large part of the work force. Nevins, on the other hand, focuses attention on the 70 to 80 percent of workers who did complete the probationary period and profited from the higher wage. Nevins, citing many instances of how workers' lives improved, comes to the conclusion that the program was generous and beneficial to the workers. Sward concludes that, as far as the workers were concerned, the program was a fraud.

Which Set of Facts?

In this case, none of the facts are in dispute; neither writer presents any statistic or claim of fact that contradicts those cited by the other writer. The differences only are in the facts they choose to attend to:

the facts about the probationary employees versus the facts about the long-term employees. How can you evaluate the merit of conclusions made on such different bases of fact? The answer lies in evaluating how appropriate the initial choice of facts is in each case.

First, you should consider which of the authors gives a more complete picture by basing conclusions on a wider cross section of the available facts. An author who limits himself to a narrow range of facts, ignoring many other obvious aspects of the situation, is more likely to come to a partial and distorted conclusion. In this respect, both Sward and Nevins share some degree of irresponsibility; each ignores half the picture. Sward, by focusing on the workers who did not meet company standards for permanent employment, entirely ignores the benefits to the workers who did make the grade. The permanent workers for him become only the exploited tools of manipulative company policy. Nevins, on the other hand, is only concerned with the benefits to the permanent workers, which included many handicapped workers. In determining that the company demands were not excessive, Nevins, in essence, dismisses those who could not meet the company standards of discipline: they simply did not deserve the job. It appears that neither author looked carefully at both sides of the picture. Later we will explore some deeper reasons why this might have happened.

The Complete Picture

Sometimes one author is able to present a fuller picture because he or she has fuller access to facts. Perhaps one author was able to interview a key figure in the story — a figure that no other author was able to interview. Perhaps a later author is working with documents only recently discovered. Perhaps one author is a more careful scholar than another, searching harder for and paying closer attention to the facts available. If you find any of these situations, obviously you should give more credence to the author with fuller access to the facts.

Even if both authors paint equally complete pictures, you can ask which author tends to use the more representative and typical facts and which relies on obscure, unusual facts. This distinction can, actually, cut both ways. At times the obscure facts may be the most important: a writer who wishes to expose hidden corruption will call into question all the more obvious and public acts of a famous politician by uncovering damaging data. At other times the obscure facts may simply be unrepresentative and distorting; for example, a lengthy exploration of the childhood friendship between Abraham Lincoln and another boy who grew up to be a shady character would not present a fair portrait of Lincoln's development. In determining whether the more obvious or the more

> **The more you know about the subject, the more you can judge whether a particular writer's selection of facts is fair and representative.**

obscure facts are the most relevant, your own background knowledge of the subject enters the picture. The more you know about the subject, the more you can judge whether a particular writer's selection of facts is fair and representative.

Toward a Synthesis

In comparing ideas based on different facts, you may decide that neither writer's set of facts adequately presents the true picture and that fair conclusions should be based on both sets of facts. You would then reject the extreme conclusions of each author and would develop your own *synthesis* — or conclusion based on a combination of facts. In the conflict over whether or not workers benefited from the Ford wage policy, you might develop the following synthesis: "Although Ford's strict, perhaps meddlesome, regulations hurt some workers who could or would not fit the company mold, the substantial number or workers who did comply with company regulations benefited by both higher salary and an improved quality of life."

Different Reasoning

In other cases, both writers agree on the facts and make roughly the same selection of facts — but still disagree on the conclusions to be drawn from the facts. Here, as your criterion for evaluation, you should observe what the writers do with the facts. Both Sward and Nevins, for example, agree on the facts of the riot after the announcement of the wage policy: within a day of the announcement, ten- to fifteen-thousand unemployed workers gathered outside the factory gates looking for work. After a few days, the crowd turned violent; the rioting ended only after police turned fire hoses on the men standing outside in the frigid weather. Although both writers agree on these facts, Sward takes the incident as another example that Ford could not have had the workers in mind when he formulated the policy, whereas Nevins simply blames the company's lack of awareness of the large numbers of unemployed within a short distance of Detroit.

By examining the reasoning process that leads from facts to conclusions, you can make some determination over which writer presents the more careful and logical argument. Sward's argument, in simplest form, is that workers were hurt; therefore, Ford could not have been concerned with the welfare of workers. Such an argument assumes, however, that what a person intends is the same thing that ultimately happens and that events always turn out according to plan. But we all know that things do not always turn out as we intend, that plans go awry. Even though intentions may be good, the results may be bad. Sward, in order to make his case about Ford's lack of concern, would have to show that Ford was aware ahead of time of the strong possibility that large crowds of unemployed would gather and riot. If Sward could present evidence to this effect and show that Ford still went ahead with his plans, disregarding the potential harm to workers, then his argument would be more convincing. Sward, however, presents no such evidence. Nevins relies on the more reasonable assumption that people do not always have complete control over the consequences of their acts and that sometimes events do not turn out quite as planned. The events were simply the result of a good idea that temporarily grew out of control.

In examining the reasoning behind conclusions, you may in some cases be able to apply the rules of formal syllogistic logic; in other cases you may have to rely on more common-sense guidelines, such as the appropriateness of different assumptions to the circumstances. The varieties of logic available to writers and appropriate to different situations will be discussed in greater detail in Chapter 9 on pages 297–303.

Different Viewpoints

At times you will sense that differences of opinion come from deeper sources than just finite differences of fact or logic. Differences of opinion can arise from basic differences in the way people look at issues. You must already have sensed, for instance, that the disagreement between Sward and Nevins is part of some larger pattern than the detailed differences so far discussed. These deeper, more basic patterns are the subject of the next section. Even where such deeper, more systematic differences exist, you should — insofar as you can — evaluate and resolve specific conflicts of fact or logic. The more specific and precise you can make your evaluation of two conflicting opinions, the more persuasive your analysis and your conclusions will be.

Do Writers Differ in Perceptions?

The disagreement between two writers may be more than a matter of isolated facts and ideas. The disagreement may appear in consistent patterns that you can identify throughout both pieces of writing. Two writers may have such consistently different views that you may wonder whether they are actually discussing the same subject. Keith Sward's book, *The Legend of Henry Ford,* consistently makes Ford out to be a villain, whereas Allan Nevins's *Ford: The Times, The Man, The Company* presents a complex man of talent and, at times, compassion. How can both books be talking about the same man?

If you examine these large differences, however, you can find a pattern to them. You will come to understand how different writers come to view the same subject differently; and you should be able to determine which viewpoint is the more accurate — or at least more acceptable to your own perspective. The following pages will present four types of deep-seated differences; you may discover others when you come to analyze conflicting sources in the course of your own research.

Same Evidence; Different Conclusions

First, after researching a subject and thinking about their research, all writers come to general conclusions about their subjects. These conclusions then help them shape the argument of their entire writing on the subject. As you know from your own writing — and as we will explore in the next chapter — your thoughts on a subject help you select and interpret the evidence you find. The entire process of research and writing is in fact an interaction between the thoughts you are developing and the evidence you are amassing.

Once a writer starts to understand a subject in a particular way, the writer wants to share this perception and make as clear and convincing a case for it as possible — without distorting the material. A writer who has studied Ford's life and has come to see Ford as a social innovator who never lost touch with his grassroots origins may pay special attention to Ford's effect on American society and to his down-home opinions. Another writer, of equal integrity and intelligence, may come to understand Ford's distinctive qualities only as business shrewdness helped by luck. This writer will be sensitive to Ford's corporate manipulations and good fortune in being in the right place at the right time.

The best way to evaluate this type of basic difference is to see which writer has made the best case. A point-by-point comparison of the books will help you judge whose evidence seems better, who gives a more complete and balanced view of the facts, and who comes to the more reasonable conclusions from the evidence. When you sum up this point-by-point comparison, you may find that one author has indeed found the better pattern or interpretation. Or you may find that one book seems more accurate and perceptive on some points whereas the other book makes more sense on other points. Using the evidence and ideas from both books, you may come to a synthesis, such as the following: Ford's shrewdness lay in adopting the innovations of others; although his grass-roots attitudes sometimes worked against his business sense, they more frequently led him to make the right business decisions.

The more you know about a subject, the better you will be able to judge whose evidence and conclusions are better. For this reason, if you find basic differences of interpretation between two sources, you should look at additional sources if possible. These third and fourth sources may not provide easy answers, but they will give you a wider background of knowledge on which to base your own judgments.

The Viewpoint of Special Interests

Authors who have a special interest in promoting a predetermined view will frequently present a systematic pattern of bias in their writing. *Advocacy writing* — that is, writing to support one view and to attack its opposite rather than to determine the truth of the matter — occurs frequently during political campaigns and in social conflict situations when two groups clash over rights or power. The commitment to promote the cause at issue may outweigh the commitment to truth. Campaign biographies of candidates for the presidency are notorious for their flattering portrayal of the writer's chosen candidate and their systematic destruction of the opponent. In fact, in 1922 and 1923, when Ford was considering running for the presidency, a number of flattering biographies of him appeared, including *The Truth About Henry Ford* by Sarah T. Bushnell (Reilly and Lee, 1922), *The Amazing Story of Henry Ford* by James M. Miller (M. A. Donahue, 1922), and *Henry Ford: The Man and His Motives* by William R. Stidger (Doran, 1923). At the same time a highly critical pamphlet *The Real Henry Ford* by E. G. Pipp (Detroit: Pipp's Weekly, 1923) tore into the candidate. Curiously enough, when Ford was no longer running for office and Pipp no longer perceived him as a political danger, Pipp wrote another more

balanced pamphlet, *Henry Ford: Both Sides of Him* (Detroit: Pipp's
Weekly, 1926). Political and social issues do much to obscure objectivity.

Once you discover a pattern of advocacy in a piece of writing, you will
find the explanation for many differences of fact and opinion compared
to other sources, which either advocate a different side of the issue or do
not have any advocacy purposes. Once you understand the advocacy
purpose, you should become extremely cautious about accepting statements of fact and idea from an advocacy source at face value. The arguments made and the facts cited in advocacy literature often do not come
from deep research and careful thought.

The differences between two opposing pieces of advocacy writing
may not provide the basis for an intelligent and careful judgment of the
facts and issues but may rather present a battle in full swing. Advocacy
literature often relies on unsupported assertions and unsubstantiated
claims of evidence. Evidence may be distorted or falsified, and the reasoning may be slippery — designed to be immediately appealing and
superficially sensible rather than logical and tightly argued. In comparing
two conflicting pieces of advocacy writing, you may find large patterns
of difference but little substantive material on which to base an evaluation.

Nonetheless, some advocacy literature does attempt to present accurate facts and careful reasoning following the philosophy that the best
way to gain support is through convincing readers of the truth. So at
times you may gain important information from such sources, but you
must be very cautious in weighing what is said against other less interested sources.

Although advocacy sources may not present much objective truth,
they are the living documents of actual political and social struggles. By
reading the 1976 campaign biographies of Jimmy Carter and Gerald
Ford, you may not learn who was truly the better candidate, but you will
learn how the candidates wanted themselves presented, the issues they
used in the campaign, and the kinds of voters to whom they were trying
to appeal.

Writers with Different Purposes

Different purposes will lead writers to focus on different facts
and to develop different kinds of ideas, as discussed and illustrated in
Chapter 4. Different purposes raise different questions for the writer to
explore. Although advocacy is the most obvious and transparent kind of
purpose, writers have many other purposes that involve fewer temptations to distortion of facts and to slippery logic. The differences between

writers may simply be the result of the pursuit of different issues. For example, a writer who wants to study some general principle of business management will want to find out how Ford succeeded in business. A writer who wants to study American social history will want to analyze Ford's almost legendary public image during the Model T years. Each writer will come up with very different data and ideas. For the most part, the statements of these two authors will neither agree nor disagree; they will simply draw different lessons from different material. In passing, they may touch on a few shared issues — but only in passing. An analysis of social history will not tell you much about the development of the corporate structure within the Ford Motor Company, but it may give you some clues on why the Model T was initially such a success and why it eventually did lose popularity.

Different Views of Life

Finally, writers may differ in very fundamental ways of looking at and interpreting life. At times, basic differences in intellectual commitment, religious belief, philosophic outlook, cultural background, and even personality type can lead to different judgments about which data and ideas are most significant, how life is organized, and how human beings act.

A writer who believes in a particular school of psychological analysis may insist that the only way to understand the decisions made by an adult is to examine the basic structure of personality formed in childhood. This writer will pay close attention to any material that deals with the subject's childhood. Such is the case in Anne Jardim's *The First Henry Ford: A Study in Personality and Business Leadership* (Cambridge, Mass.: MIT Press, 1970). On the other hand, an author like Keith Sward, who believes that we can only understand an individual's decisions as part of large economic trends in the entire society, will pay close attention to material on financial interests and business cycles. Each writer will use different facts, ask different questions, interpret by different methods, and reach different conclusions. Jardim offers a psychological interpretation; Sward offers an economic interpretation.

In comparing the writings of two authors who have such basically different outlooks, you may be able to make some judgments about whose evidence is more accurate and complete and whose conclusions are more reasonable, but frequently the opposing material will not meet on enough specific points to allow such judgments. Examining the economic and psychological theories behind each writer's thinking will probably take more time and knowledge than you have. Of course, as you become more involved in a specific discipline that interests you, you will grow more familiar with the more important theories and approaches, and you may then come to some informed judgments about them. Bear in mind that some theories remain unresolved questions — even among the most knowledgeable. In the end, you may simply have to recognize the large differences of interpretation among writers.

Basic Patterns of Thought

By recognizing basic patterns of thought, you may not always discover which is right, but you can usually recognize which assumptions and approaches are close to the ones you can accept. Even more important, you may be able to understand how writers with beliefs that radically differ from yours perceive issues quite differently. Such recognition of basic differences may help you understand ideas you might otherwise reject as useless or absurd. With a broadened perspective, you can then view conflicts impartially. Such an impartial overview is needed to understand the dispute that arose from Ford's famous statement that "history is more or less the bunk." Ford saw himself as a pragmatic man, interested in making life better for the average person now. Despite his success, he still included himself among the common people. He had a rural distrust of journalists, fancy learning, "big shots," and international politics — all of which only made trouble for the ordinary person. When he rejected textbook history, he felt it described only the wars created by kings and queens and forgot the common people who actually fought the wars. Ford believed "official" history did not reflect real day-to-day life; consequently, he never paid much attention to the facts of history.

When Ford made his famous comments on history, the newspapers treated him as a country dolt. The educated people of the time were struggling to create in America an intellectual life to compete with Europe's; they were quick to disown what they considered Ford's ignorant, know-nothing attitudes.

When we consider the dispute impartially, we can see that Ford was far from ignorant about those things he considered important, such as manufacturing automobiles. Given the level of success he had reached and given the great changes in society that he felt were the result of practical inventions, his practical, antiintellectual attitude is understandable. At the same time, the journalists and other writers, concerned about the development of an American intellectual life, felt they were not out to hoodwink the common people with fancy words. Each side saw an opposite way to improve American life and perceived the other way as misleading and dangerous. Ford saw the issue as a practical concern for ordinary life versus the empty rhetoric of intellectuals; the journalists saw it as ignorance versus education. Both sides were unable to develop sufficient impartiality to see the entire picture. With historical perspective, we are able to rise above this dispute to understand the attitudes and perceptions motivating each side.

The remainder of this chapter is devoted to writing assignments that will require you to resolve differences between authors. The first — an analytical comparison between two passages on the same topic — requires you to map out the difficulties of a small but confusing spot. The second — a synthesis of what several writers have to say on a subject — gives you a larger challenge.

Writing an Analytical Comparison of Two Sources

In examining two sources that cover the same subject, you need to do two separate tasks: first, identify the specific agreements and disagreements between the two sources; second, analyze the patterns of agreement and disagreement. The first task will let you know how much difference exists between them, and the second will help you resolve the differences. In the preparation of an *essay of analytical comparison,* the first step has to be completed before the second step is begun because you must know the differences precisely and explicitly before you can analyze them. In your final version of the paper, the results of the two tasks may be intermixed as part of an overall evaluation of the two sources.

Selecting Two Passages

Unless two matched passages are handed to you by your teacher, you must first select the two pieces of writing that you will compare and analyze. This is no easy task. The passages should be short enough to allow detailed discussion; often well-matched passages of only a few paragraphs will provide enough material for a five- to ten-page discussion. In order to provide sharp comparisons, the passages should have more than a vague similarity: they should cover exactly the same issues within exactly the same limits. (One example would be the development of assembly-line techniques at the Ford Company from the time of the introduction of the Model T until 1914.) Moreover, both passages should make directly comparable statements; for example, both should discuss Henry Ford's role in the introduction of assembly-line techniques.

Sometimes you can find short, self-contained selections in two separate versions of a news story published in various newspapers or contemporary affairs magazines. Or you might excerpt matched selections from longer works, such as biographies of Ford or sociological analyses of the role of the car in American life. When working with excerpts, your decisions on where to begin and end the selection are crucial: try to match the subjects, the limits, and the claims of the two passages.

Occasionally, if you find some deeper comparison you wish to make — such as between basic ways of thinking — you may pick two selections that do not appear to resemble each other very much on the surface but do raise a basic issue sharply. For example, if you want to see just how much an economic interpretation of the decline of the Model T differs from a sociological one, you might compare two rather different passages from two rather different books. Such a comparison, however, is difficult, requiring much knowledge of the subject and clarity in defining the issues.

Whether you choose passages that offer many surface comparisons or that join issues on a deeper level, the best passages to select are those you come across in researching a paper for one of your courses. Then the conflict will be real to you — one whose resolution will clarify some issues of interest and use to you.

Making Apt Comparisons

Having chosen the two selections, you should try to understand each as fully as possible in its own terms. To do this, you may use any or all of the techniques presented earlier — reading journal, paraphrase, and so forth. If you are working with selections from longer works, it usually helps to become familiar with the surrounding contexts as well.

Then identify the specific areas of correspondence between the two passages. For each claim or statement made in the first selection, take note of any corresponding claims in the second. You may keep track of these correspondences by numbering comparable claims of both writers with the same number or by annotating ("see line 24 of other"). Or you may want to compile a comparative chart of correspondences.

As you collect these correspondences, you will already be noticing patterns of agreement and disagreement; once you have all of them collected, you can organize the various agreements and disagreements according to the categories presented earlier in this chapter. The following chart may be useful to you:

I. Facts
   A. Agreements
      1.
      2.
      3.
   B. Disagreements
      1.
      2.
      3.
II. Ideas
   A. Agreements
      1.
      2.
      3.
   B. Disagreements
      1.
      2.
      3.
III. Basic viewpoints and patterns of thought
   A. Agreements
      1.
      2.
      3.
   B. Disagreements
      1.
      2.
      3.
IV. Conclusions

As you sort out the matching items, you may start to see patterns emerge, such as the two authors agree that specific events took place but disagree on the dates and order of the events. Or you may find absolute agreement on facts and total disagreement on conclusions. Or you may notice crucial issues on which the two writers turn to entirely different types of evidence. As patterns emerge, you will also gain more insight into the major differences between the writers regarding their purposes and their conclusions. The patterns you discover — of similarities and differences between the sources — will become the bases for your essay.

If the pattern is one of basic similarity, you might consider whether shared assumptions, common sources of information, or common purposes lie behind the similarity. If there is a mixed pattern of agreement and disagreement, you might try to determine whether the similarities or dissimilarities dominate — or whether the dissimilarities seem random and minor.

If many major disagreements leave you confused about the truth of the subject, you should try to evaluate which writer presents the more credible or persuasive case. In each instance, you will have to determine what are the appropriate criteria for judging the kind of dispute before you; these criteria were discussed earlier in the chapter.

In the special case of two writers consciously arguing with each other — that is, each knows and discusses the other's views — you may also consider how effectively they argue against each other. Does each one answer the other's objections adequately? Does each successfully confront the other's main points? Or do they talk past each other, avoiding direct confrontations or missing the other's main objections?

You should explore these issues in journal entries, notes, outlines, or other informal ways until you come to some firm conclusions. At that point you are ready to begin writing the rough draft of the final paper.

The Final Essay

The final paper should begin by clearly identifying the two passages being compared by title, author, and publication information. If you are using excerpts of longer pieces, identify precisely where your excerpts begin and end. If the readers of your paper are not likely to be familiar with the material you are discussing, you would do well to include copies of both selections in their entirety as an appendix to the essay.

The introduction to the paper should present, in general terms, the overall pattern that will emerge in your comparison and possibly what you intend to prove about the relative value of the two selections. In other words, you should indicate to the reader where the comparison leads and what kind of analysis you will pursue.

The Body

The body of the paper should present the substance of the agreements and disagreements: you should expose the patterns and analyze the examples you have found. You need not discuss all the details from both selections, but you must use enough specific examples to support your general characterizations. You may refer to details in the two originals by quotation, paraphrase, summary — or line number if you have included copies of the originals. Whatever method you use, accuracy and fairness in representing the originals are particularly important because you will be setting details from two separate sources against each other. If too much gets changed between the originals and the discussion, you may wind up comparing products of your own imagination rather than the actual sources. Chapter 10 will present more complete discussion of appropriate and accurate reference.

Organization

The development and organization of the paper will, of course, vary with what you have to say. You may want to present the whole pattern of agreement and disagreement first, halting only to fill in representative details, and to follow later with a detailed analysis of underlying causes for the pattern. Or you may want to analyze and evaluate each disagreement as you come to it, and add up the total pattern at the end. If the sources describe a series of events, you may want to discuss the points of your comparison chronologically. Or you may find that you can produce a clearer comparison by separating differences of factual evidence from differences of interpretation. For example, you may want to compare the two authors' factual representations of Ford's campaign for president before comparing their interpretations of Ford's motives. Since there is no one way to organize such a comparison, you should derive your organization from the patterns you have come to identify in the particular material before you.

Comparative Focus

You must take care, however, to keep your focus on *the comparison between the two sources.* Don't fall into the error of simply summarizing the two separate pieces — one after the other — or of just recounting facts about the subject covered in the two sources. Remember that your main subject is the relationship between two pieces of writing. Two techniques of sentence style should help you keep this task in mind. First, whenever you refer to details from one source, repeat the author or the title of the source — and do not continue the example for more than a few lines. For example, by repeating Henry Ford's name as author, you are constantly emphasizing that this is only *his* way of presenting the subject — only his claims about the events.

The second technique is to include many sentences that compare two ideas within the same sentence, as in this example: "Although Sward's view that assembly line techniques developed gradually does not permit him to set a specific date for the 'invention' of the assembly line, Nevins's emphasis on the continuous movement of the main product along the line allows him to point to the installation of a conveyer system in 1913 as the key date." This placing of statements side by side within the same sentence will help you maintain the comparison throughout the essay.

The conclusion of the essay should develop from the issues you have raised in the body of the paper and should sum up the results of your analysis. Depending on the body of your essay, you might then sum up all the points of comparison to make an overall evaluation of the relative trustworthiness of the two sources. Alternatively, you might observe how two writers, coming from such different standpoints, wind up with the same conclusions.

The Synthesis of Multiple Sources

The purpose of the *essay of synthesis* is to combine what a number of sources have to say into a coherent overview of the subject. In preparing the synthesis, you have to compare and analyze multiple sources in order to choose between conflicting statements, but the final paper presents your final understanding of the subject — not your gropings. If, for example, you want to synthesize all that was known about the astronomy of the Aztecs of ancient Mexico, you would have to draw on facts, ideas, and interpretations from a number of different souces about the Aztecs, premodern astronomy, architecture of sun temples, and mythology. Your main focus, however, would be what you discovered about Aztec astronomy — and not the differences among your sources.

In the past, the essay of synthesis might have struck you as an easy task, much like the library report you may have done in junior high school. But by now you are much more aware of the problems of fitting multiple sources together in any coherent, consistent way. Not only do sources conflict but also they often omit just the information you are seeking. You become very significant at this point: only you can make the connections between the information provided in different sources; only you can search out additional sources to fill in the gaps; only you can put together the pieces into an intelligent whole. The sources remain quite separate until you bring them together.

In particular, the essay of synthesis will present you with five separate tasks: (1) to frame a subject, (2) to gather material from varied sources, (3) to fit the parts together, (4) to achieve a synthesis, and (5) to unify the style.

> You become very significant at this point: only you can make the connections between the information provided in different sources; only you can search out additional sources to fill in the gaps; only you can put together the pieces into an intelligent whole. The sources remain quite separate until you bring them together.

Framing a Subject

To frame a subject on which there is enough — but not too much — source material, you must find a question, issue, or subject on which a number of people have written, presenting facts and interpretations; but the number of sources should not be so great as to create a confusion of material. In other words, you have to find a limited topic that forms the center for a cluster of writing.

One place to look for such topics is within the structure of different academic disciplines. Each academic discipline is defined by a series of research questions that focus the attention of researchers in that field. For example, in anthropology much investigation centers on determining social roles within different societies. By selecting one type of society and one social role — such as the role of the shaman in American Indian tribes — you can define a cluster of research materials with which to work.

Sometimes a dispute over a controversial theory may excite much interest and lead to a flurry of new publications in support of one theory or the other. For example, much geological writing in the late 1960s argued for and against the controversial idea of continental drift. At other times a discovery or an invention may affect the work of many scholars and scientists, so that much new writing centers on the meaning of the discovery or the consequences of the invention. A major new discovery may have widespread consequences for an entire discipline. Such, for example, was the enormous effect of the discovery of the structure of DNA on all biological studies. Thus, within academic subjects, you can look for clusters of sources around topics defined by the structure of the field, around controversial theories, or around new discoveries and inventions.

In more popular writing, such as newspapers, general circulation magazines, and general nonfiction books, you can often find clusters of interest around social problems (juvenile delinquency in the 1950s or inflation in the 1970s), major historical figures and events (Abraham Lincoln or Pearl Harbor), social institutions (changes in the nuclear family), trends and fads (toga parties), or matters of political and public debate (the merits of national health insurance). In such areas of public interest and excitement, the different pieces of writing may not fit together in such clear-cut ways as they do in more organized academic disciplines. By sorting out the ways that these different sources do relate to one another, you will find out much about the different attitudes behind the public interest.

Gathering Material from Varied Sources

Since you are trying to gather a composite view of the subject, you need to go beyond the most obvious sources for your topic and draw on the information and insights of a number of different viewpoints. If, for example, you are interested in what TV programming was like in the mid-1960s, you will get only a very limited view if you rely totally on the program descriptions in *TV Guide*. However, in an article in one of the old issues you may find mention of some criticism of TV quality. If you then follow up by finding out who these critics were and what their complaints were, you might discover the large public debate set off by Newton Minnow's remark that TV programming was a "vast wasteland." And you might also be led to find out about the movement that resulted in the Public Broadcast System. *One source will lead you to another* until you get many different ways of looking at the topic.

Fitting the Parts Together

If you find conflicting statements between sources, you need to judge which is the more reliable, according to the methods and criteria presented earlier in this chapter. A more frequent problem results when sources do not have any points easily compared — either points of agreement or disagreement. So it will be up to you to discover these correspondences. You may have to point out the relationship between the broad theoretical statement of one writer and the details of a case study by another. Or you may have to make explicit an indirect connection between two separate sources. Or you may have to identify a pattern that shows the similarity between the viewpoints of two articles.

This connection between facts and interpretations has been discussed throughout this chapter; however, in the final writing of your synthesis it is not enough for you, the writer, to understand the connections: you must explain these connections to your readers. To make the connection clear to someone who may have not recognized it before, transitions between sections are extremely useful. A transitional phrase or sentence, describing the connection between one idea and the next, can tie together seemingly diverse material, fill in gaps, and put the facts and ideas in sensible relationship. A careful writer will help the reader follow all the steps of his or her presentation.

Achieving a Synthesis

At this stage, you must add up all the information to discover significant patterns and to come to conclusions. These patterns and conclusions will be the shaping forces behind your organization of the final synthesis. You cannot simply rely on the patterns, and the conclusions, of your sources, for the limitations of purpose of each source determine the organization and ideas of that piece of writing. Since you are combining material from several sources — and you may well be broadening the scope of the subject — your own conclusions and organization will necessarily take on a new shape.

Informal and formal outlines are, as always, useful as attempts to make coherent sense of all your journal notes and annotations. By trying different outlines, you can see in which way the information fits together best. As you approach a satisfactory outline integrating the ideas and information from the sources, you will be able to formulate an overview of the subject. A direct statement describing this overview — tying together the various parts of your synthesis — can serve as a thesis statement for your paper.

Unifying the Style

Unifying the writing style while remaining true to the sources will be your final task. Because the sources you use have their own separate purposes, the material in each may be presented in very different ways — from numerical statistics to anecdotes to highly detailed analyses. When you bring together such varying material, you must present all materials in a way that will be consistent with the overall design of your paper, the synthesis. For example, if you are collecting information on the effects of the Supreme Court's Bakke decision, you may be drawing on a wide variety of materials: statistical charts of college enrollments by ethnic background, direct comments on the decision by college admissions officers, general policy statements by college boards of trustees, straight news reports, and analyses by journalists. You must bring together all these different kinds of writing into a single readable whole. Instead of copying an entire statistical table — with much unnecessary material — you must pull out the most relevant statistics and explain their bearing on your topic. You cannot simply string together statements of college officials; you must rather bring out the official positions and hidden attitudes behind them. In other words, you must translate the separate kinds of language used in the various sources into a uniform style appropriate to your synthesis.

Even though you will often need to rephrase and rearrange the material from the original sources, you must be careful not to distort the original meanings. When you pull out only selected statistics and explain their meaning, you must be careful not to leave out other important statistics that might give rise to conflicting interpretations. In summarizing the argument of a newspaper column, you should not leave out so much of the context that the article appears to say something it could not possibly have meant. Chapter 10 gives more specific advice on how to present the ideas of other writers as part of your own coherent argument — without distorting the original meanings. Chapter 10 also covers the various methods for documenting the sources of your information; in a synthesis you must document your sources fully and carefully so that the reader can judge the credibility of your material.

One Student's Synthesis

Each time you have to synthesize material from a number of sources — whether as a separate *essay of synthesis* or as part of some larger project — the tasks just described will appear in varying guises. Each time you will have to find different ways to handle them so that the advice we have given should serve as only the most general guidelines. The following sample paper, titled "Protest and Violence," will present the way one student solved these problems in one particular case.

The assignment was to characterize any single social trend that took place in 1968 during a period of about a week. To do this, the student was to synthesize magazine and newspaper articles written during the specific week that she had selected. Since everyone in the class was doing the same task for a different week within that year, the papers combined to form a social history of the period, which all the students then read as background for their future research.

Our student found the focus for her paper in the violence that erupted out of the social protest movements of late March and early April, 1968.

Once she had found her theme, she was able to select a few relevant sources out of the immense number of newspaper and magazine articles on that subject. She interpreted the different instances of violent activities she found as examples of different responses by protesters and government officials to the same event. She was thus able to show a connection between many different incidents and the contrasting attitudes reflected in them. She was even able to fit in a campaign article by a political candidate, which on the surface seems quite dissimilar to the reports of incidents that provided the bulk of her sources. In the introduction to each section, she was careful to link one part with the next and to reassert the main focus of the paper.

All the varied material adds up to support her main synthesis: during the ten-day period, expression of dissent "led to increasing confrontation and violence." Although she uses several different kinds of sources, she maintains a consistent expository style to present her overall vision of the pattern of events. The reader never doubts that she is in control of her sources.

Sample Essay

Protest and Violence

The decade of the 1960s was a period when the young people of this nation expressed their political and social ideas through public protest. They made their voices heard demanding an end to racial segregation, an end to the war in Vietnam, and a new concern for the environment. Desiring rapid change, they stated their demands in radical ways. The controversies caused by these radical demands led to increasing confrontation and violence. The ten days from March 28, 1968, to April 6, 1968, were a time when the violence was reaching its peak.

The period began with peaceful intentions of protest as Martin Luther King prepared a march in Memphis, Tennessee. The demonstration on March 28 was to protest a garbage

strike that affected the black population of the city--but
not the white. The Reverend Martin Luther King believed in
nonviolence and intended to lead his 4500 followers in a
peaceful march; however, a band of radical young blacks,
calling themselves the Invaders, infiltrated the parade
and began throwing stones and glass. The police reacted,
made mass arrests, and shot a sixteen-year-old boy to death.
Rioting followed, and the Memphis National Guard had to be
called in to enforce a curfew.[1]

This escalation of peaceful protest into violent confrontation distressed the entire nation. President Lyn-
don B. Johnson's reaction was typical of the despairing
hopes of most people: "The tragic events in Memphis yesterday remind us of the grave peril rioting poses. This
nation must seek change within the rule of law in an
environment of social order. Rioting, violence, and
repression can only divide our people."[2]

The sad cycle of demonstration, violence, repression,
and division recurred in a smaller incident involving a
white radical group called the Yippies. Three thousand
Yippies were on their way to a celebration of spring in New
York City's Central Park when a few became violent as they
passed through Grand Central Station. Arrests followed and
the demonstration was broken up. Since the Yippies were
already planning a similar gathering to be held in Chicago
at the time of the Democratic National Convention in
August, this incident increased police fears that the
Chicago gathering would turn into an ugly confrontation.[3]

In an atmosphere of confrontation and violence,
unexplained incidents appear frightening. On March 29,
four large fires were set at Chicago department stores,
Carson Pirie and Scott, Montgomery Ward, Wieboldt's, and
Goldblatt's.[4] The next day suspicious fires or unexploded
fire bombs were discovered in four major New York department stores (Bloomingdale's, Klein's, Macy's, and
Gimbels'). At the same time, two other store fires were
reported in Chicago. Although all these fires were suspicious, no direct evidence of conspiracy appeared, and no
radical group was implicated.[5]

Violence seemed uncontainable. President Johnson decided
that the only way he could bring peace to a divided country
was to end the war in Vietnam. On the evening of March 31,
he announced in a TV speech that he was halting all bombing
raids on North Vietnam and calling for negotiations to end
the war. In order to keep the peace negotiations out of
politics, he announced that he would not run for re-elec-
tion.[6]

National unity was not that easy to regain. On April 4,
Martin Luther King was murdered in Memphis.[7] In reaction, a
wave of violent rioting swept the cities of this country.
Looting, arson, and general civil disorder tore apart
Memphis, Chicago, Detroit, Boston, and Washington. The
week ended with the National Guard patrolling American
cities.[8]

Even out of such destruction and disorder, some good came
about. Within a week, the Civil Rights Act of 1968, ending

racial discrimination in housing, was passed by Congress
and signed by the president.[9] A small bit of justice was
born out of great injustice. In addition some members of
the establishment were making themselves available to the
radicals and were trying to encourage young people to
involve themselves in organized politics. Senator Eugene
McCarthy, running for the Democratic nomination for the
presidency, wrote that he placed great faith in the youth
of this country. He called them a "concerned generation"
that, despite their "exotic hairdos and occasionally
eccentric behavior," demonstrated a deep moral concern.[10]
He believed that their rebellion came from "their sense of
social commitment and their urge for involvement."[11]

During those few days of March and April, 1968, this
"urge for involvement" led to violent conflicts that seemed
to be moving beyond control. It was a time when young people were expressing their ideas actively--no matter what
the consequences.

Notes

[1]"Memphis Blues," *Time*, 5 April 1968, p. 25.

[2]Max Frankel, "President Offers U.S. Aid on Riots,"
New York Times, 30 March 1968, p. 30.

[3]"The Politics of Yip," *Time*, 5 April 1968, p. 61.

[4]"Chicagoans Flee 4 Fires in Loop," *New York Times*, 30
March 1968, p. 1.

[5]Murray Schumach, "Fires Set in Bloomingdale's and
Klein's," *New York Times*, 31 March 1968, p. 1.

[6]Tom Wicker, "Johnson Says He Won't Run; Halts North Vietnam Raids; Bids Hanoi Join Peace Moves," New York Times, 1 April 1968, p. 1.

[7]Earl Caldwell, "Martin Luther Is Slain in Memphis," New York Times, 5 April 1968, p. 1.

[8]Ben A. Franklin, "Army Troops in Capital As Negroes Riot; Guard Sent to Chicago, Detroit, Boston," New York Times, 6 April 1968, p. 1.

[9]"Opening the Doors," Time, 19 April 1968, p. 20.

[10]Eugene McCarthy, "Opinion: On the Concerned Generation," Mademoiselle, April 1968, p. 98.

[11]McCarthy, p. 98.

Writing Assignments

1. From an area in which you are now doing or have done some research, select two passages from different sources covering the same topic. Write an analytical comparison of at least five hundred words — or as long as necessary to cover all the pertinent issues. Your audience will be other researchers in the area, who will be concerned with the degree of agreement between these sources.

2. Excerpt two short passages for analytical comparison from the following three discussions, which all deal with Henry Ford's attempt to intervene in international politics just before the United States entered World War I. Write an analytical comparison of over five hundred words. Your audience will be your classmates, who by now know something about Henry Ford and something about an analytical comparison of sources.

HENRY FORD AND GRASS ROOTS AMERICA[3]

The role of Henry Ford in American politics in 1916 cannot be evaluated without reference to the "Peace Ship" episode. Although the

---

[3]From Reynold M. Wik, *Henry Ford and Grass Roots America*, pp. 165–167. Copyright © 1972 by The University of Michigan Press. Used by permission.

basic facts in this venture are well known, the significance of these events needs further interpretation.

Henry Ford had grown up in a family that hated violence and war, and it was not surprising that he joined the American Peace Society in the fall of 1915. There he met Rosika Schwimmer, the Hungarian pacifist, in November of that year. Madam Schwimmer believed that any war which ended in a complete military victory for one side would eventually lead to further conflict. Therefore she wanted to stop the European war before the militarists were ready to quit fighting. She urged the establishment of an organization which would provide a forum for continuous mediation of international disputes. Neutral countries could provide this service by calling a conference. When Woodrow Wilson refused to call such a meeting, Madam Schwimmer and other pacifists toured the United States soliciting support for the idea. It was on one of these tours that Madam Schwimmer met Henry Ford, who was eager to help implement some program of direct action. Later in a meeting in New York, the Peace Ship venture was born. A group of delegates would go to Europe as negotiators to offer mediation to the warring parties.

Since the expedition needed passengers, telegrams were addressed to prominent people such as Thomas Edison, William Howard Taft, Luther Burbank, William Jennings Bryan, David Starr Jordan, and Ben Lindsey. Many refused the invitation, but the *Oscar II* pushed away from a Hoboken dock on December 5, 1915, with 83 delegates, 54 reporters, 50 technical advisers, 18 college students, and three photographers — an array which Charles E. Sorensen called the "strangest assortment of living creatures since the voyage of Noah's Ark."

Losing sight of the pilgrims' real mission, journalists stressed the bizarre, such as the prankster who sent two caged squirrels to Ford; the newsmen who organized themselves into the Friendly Sons of St. Vitus, and the cable to Rome to get the blessing of Pope Pius VII, who happened to have died in 983 A.D. Editors tossed off such phrases as "Ford's Folly," the "jitney-peace excursion," and "more innocents abroad." The Boston *Traveler* commented: "It is not Mr. Ford's purpose to make peace. He will assemble it."

During the fourteen-day voyage, morale plummeted. Here was a divided reaction to President Wilson's message to Congress on December 7 which called for military preparedness; Henry Ford, the stabilizing influence among the leaders, came down with a cold and spent much of the time in his cabin; and Madam Schwimmer proved rather dictatorial and domineering. When the *Oscar II* reached Oslo, after surviving submarine-infested waters, Ford left the party on December 23 and returned to the United States on the *Bergensfjord*. This gave the impression that *he* was trying to get out of Europe by Christmas. The peace delegation visited Sweden and Denmark, however, and then received permission to cross Germany by train to Holland. A committee for continuous mediation scheduled other meetings in Stockholm and at the Hague. But by January 15 the peace party disbanded, with students and delegates returning to New York.

Obviously the Peace Ship adventure suffered from hasty planning, questionable actions, and a bad press on both sides of the Atlantic. The London *Times* referred to the members of the Ford Mission as faddists, propagandists-socialists, suffragists, and social reformers who tried to turn disgust into approbation. One news item merely announced that the Ford Peace Party arrived in the Hague to hold its meetings in the Zoological Gardens.

Although this mission was vilified in many quarters, the venture is now beginning to be seen in better perspective. The endeavor contained genuine idealism, with a desire to save humanity from war and death. One of the college students who made the trip, Christian A. Sorenson, of Grand Island College in Nebraska, spoke for youth when he gave a speech aboard the *Oscar II*. He warned against making America an armed camp, he opposed military conscription, he decried the wasted bodies on battlefields. Speaking metaphorically, he suggested gathering all the skulls of Europe's dead and building a pyramid a mile square and reaching to the clouds. With a giant pen dipped in the blood of Verdun he would write militarism as a monument to greed and war. He pleaded:

> Let us hear from the wives who will be widows and the young maidens who die of broken hearts. Let us hear from young men in shops and farms who will fall in trenches, there to die like cattle and be burned like piles of rubbish. The English verse puts it aptly; "Damn the army; damn the war. Oh what bloody fools we are."

More recently, Walter Millis saw the ridicule of the Ford Peace Ship as the "undying shame of American journalism." The idea of continuous mediation relied on the concept that the building of a new world depended on how the war ended. If one could read history backward and envision a negotiated peace in 1916 with neither Allies or Central Powers defeated, perhaps the postwar collapse of Europe might have been avoided. Had this occurred, governments might have been spared the forces of Communism, Fascism, and Nazism. Today the concept of continuous mediation lives in the charter of the United Nations. In this sense, Ford and his associates were ahead of the times. Perhaps Ford's expenditure of nearly half a million dollars in behalf of his principles did not represent failure. He could take consolation in the words of Rabbi Joseph Krauskopf of Philadelphia who attacked the critics of Ford in 1915, saying, he would "rather a thousand times be branded a fool in the service of humanity than be hailed a hero for having shed rivers of blood."

HENRY FORD[4]

From the outbreak, in Europe, of the First World War, Ford had grown increasingly pacifist. His particular kind of success had depended on a free economy impossible in wartime. The interest in the country's development that Model T's exploits had aroused in him was sincere; it was unbearable to him that this progress should be interrupted. He had the aloof contempt that most citizens of what was then an isolationist stronghold felt for European politics. Finally, he had a very genuine hatred of killing in any form and, not having the equipment for the historical analysis of international behavior, the normal performance of an army was, to him, just plain murder.

His opinions were known to several prominent pacifists of the time. David Starr Jordan and Louis Lochner were anxious for the United States to carry on "continuous mediation" in Europe and, when President Wilson was cool to this proposal, they looked for a millionaire to finance a publicity campaign for the project. The Hungarian pacifist Rosika Schwimmer had already gained Ford's ear on the subject and when — after several luncheon meetings, in which Lochner and Mme Schwimmer were joined by Jane Addams, Oswald Garrison Villard, and a number of educators, editors, and clergymen — it was suggested that American delegates to a neutral commission in Europe proceed by special ship, Ford announced that he would finance the expedition.

> If I can be of any service whatever [he said] in helping end this war and keeping America out of it, I shall do it if it costs me every dollar and every friend I have.

He tried, personally, to persuade the President to give the pilgrimage official sanction and, upon Wilson's natural refusal, he released the full story to the press, with appalling results. Whether or not Ford himself made the promise to "get the boys out of the trenches by Christmas," the slogan was roundly ridiculed by the newspapers of the country — especially as November was then already well advanced.

The *Oscar II*, chartered by Ford, was scheduled to sail on December 4. In the weeks before the sailing a corps of stenographers in the Biltmore Hotel in New York who had sent out invitations to the voyage were busy opening declinations. Persons Ford and Mme Schwimmer had counted on sent late regrets: Bryan, Edison, John Burroughs, Ida Tarbell, and others. But the Biltmore suite was besieged, as Mark Sullivan tells, by "star-eyed enthusiasts as well as cranks, fanatics, butters-in and joy-riders of all sorts." And the reporters, the newspaper wags, the cartoonists were everywhere. "It was the answer," Walter Millis writes, "to an editor's prayer," and he adds:

[4]From *Henry Ford*, by Roger Burlingame, pp. 82–86. Copyright 1954 by Roger Burlingame. Reprinted by permission of Alfred A. Knopf, Inc.

The famous "Peace Ship" had been launched, to the undying shame of American journalism, upon one vast wave of ridicule.

Other writers have since thought the laughter of the press shameful. Yet at the time, with the widespread pro-Allies feeling following upon the sinking of the *Lusitania* in May, and as some of the incidents of the preparation were unmistakably absurd, the often cruel laughter could hardly have been avoided. The American press is rarely gentle with such naïve idealism.

The *Oscar II* left on the fourth in a chaos that has repeatedly been described as "indescribable," with every sort of comedian on the dock and Henry Ford standing at the rail waving quite seriously and throwing American Beauty roses to the crowd. The whole affair was undoubtedly insulting to our future allies, thousands of whose young men were dying daily in the worst possible conditions of filth and horror. Its plan-lessness, its hurried, haphazard organization, its execrable publicity have since been thought by many earnest and intelligent pacifists to have put a stop to any possible peace movements later in the war. Yet, in retrospect, there is something deeply moving about the impulses behind it. Twenty-five years later, as William Simonds tells in his biog-raphy of Ford, the *Detroit Free Press*, on the December anniversary, said editorially:

> But we do not laugh any more, nor joke, when that unique argosy is mentioned. We mourn rather the disappearance of times when men could still believe in progress in human enlightenment, and thought that even those in the throes of blood lust might be led to reason. . . .
> No peace ship has sailed since the Second World War began. It could find no port either geographically or in the hearts of men.

In the Ford party was one who was strongly opposed to the whole affair. This was a prominent and intelligent clergyman, Dean Marquis, of Detroit's Episcopal cathedral. Marquis, a friend of the Ford family and Mrs. Ford's spiritual adviser, had left the church in order to accept employment in the company. At the request of Mrs. Ford and several of the company's executives he had pleaded with Ford not to go on the Peace Ship. It had been useless, so Marquis went along, hoping to persuade him to leave the pilgrimage and come back as soon as possi-ble. His opportunity came when Ford, drenched by a wave on deck, got a severe cold and was confined to his stateroom. Marquis invaded it and again brought his persuasion to bear.

Until the party landed in Norway, however, Ford was adamant. In Christiania he added to his cold by insisting on walking to the hotel through a snowstorm. Finally, weak and tired, he gave in and admitted to Louis Lochner: "I guess I had better go home to mother. You've got this thing started now and can go along without me."

They went — to Stockholm, Copenhagen, and The Hague — and elected a permanent delegation, which Ford continued to finance until the break with Germany in 1917.

Ford returned to Detroit, where at the moment his company was producing two thousand Model T's a day. Late in the year the millionth Ford car had come off the line. Nothing quite like this production had ever been seen in the industrial history of the world.

THE LEGEND OF HENRY FORD[5]

In his first effort as knight errant, Ford ran up the standard of a militant pacifist. His debut in world politics began in the summer of 1915 when the European war was entering its second year. His first skirmishes over the new terrain were purely verbal. They took the form of statements to the press that were studded with passionate denunciations of war. Most of these bristling manifestos were, in reality, the work of Theodore Delavigne, a Detroit newspaper reporter, whom Ford engaged as his pamphleteer and "peace secretary." Issued in the name of his distinguished patron, Delavigne's broadsides were all the more noteworthy in that Ford was swimming upstream. Wall Street had already forged an alliance with France and Britain. Pro-British sentiment was deep-seated in America. The advocates of military preparedness were in the saddle. Against such a combination of social forces, Ford flung himself headlong.

His interviews and statements of 1915 read like socialist handbills. Hot with fervor, they branded Europe's war a capitalists' war. The instigators of the conflict, Ford said, were the money-lenders, the absentee owners and the parasites of Wall Street. At one press conference he exclaimed, "New York wants war, but not the United States." In another broadside he characterized the professional soldier as either "lazy or crazy." On the day that Couzens tendered his resignation at Highland Park, after having broken with Ford over this same issue, Ford released a statement on the causes of war that was the most trenchant thing he had yet uttered on the subject. This time he named names. With consummate scorn he denounced the Morgan firm for sponsoring a half-billion dollar war loan to the Allies. The Anglo-French bankers who were then negotiating with the Morgan syndicate, he said, "ought to be tin-canned out of the country."

Ford proposed a course of action. First, he castigated the war profiteers of America by saying what he would do in the event the conflict abroad were to spread to the United States. Under such condi-

[5]From *The Legend of Henry Ford* by Keith Sward, pp. 83–90. Copyright 1948, © 1976 by Keith Sward. Reprinted by permission of Holt, Rinehart and Winston, Publishers.

tions, he prophesied, before accepting a single order for cars that might be used for military purposes — even though he were offered three times the normal price — he would burn his factory to the ground. Next he issued a call to "the people" to stop the war by taking things into their own hands. He offered in August 1915 to pledge his entire "life and fortune" to the cause of peace.

Before long Ford's peace plans took more specific form, thanks to the persistence and colorful personality of Rosika Schwimmer, an American feminist of Hungarian origin. Brilliant, handsome and persuasive, Mme. Schwimmer was courting support for a movement to end the European war by mediation. It was her belief, shared by a number of notable colleagues, that the conflict in Europe could be halted through the intervention of a congress of peace delegates drawn from the neutral countries. The mediators whom she hoped to enlist were to convene continuously in some neutral capital until peace terms could be drawn up that would prove acceptable to the belligerents. Before they could hope to win recognition or any official standing, the proponents of the "Schwimmer" plan were well aware of the fact that they would first have to rally popular support in each of the participating neutral nations.

As the ablest and most energetic advocate of this proposal, Mme. Schwimmer went to Detroit in the hopes of enlisting Ford's aid. Her plan and the declarations of her prospective patron had much in common. Both were predicated on direct action and the will of the people. Both hoped to cut through the red tape of diplomacy and to do what no neutral nation either dared or cared to initiate officially. Nothing seemed more fitting to Mme. Schwimmer than an attempt on her part to solicit the support of America's most celebrated and most highly regarded millionaire. In November 1915, therefore, she proceeded to Detroit, determined to see Henry Ford in person.

On the alert, none of Ford's intimates, particularly the secretary Ernest Liebold, would permit any such interview. These social censors could readily identify Mme. Schwimmer as one of the "inadmissibles." The feminist was just about to give up in disgust when Liebold left the city on a business trip. Then she slipped through what remained of the protective cordon, with the aid of a newspaperman. Once admitted to Ford's office, Mme. Schwimmer made the most of her opportunity. She put her case so convincingly that Ford invited her to have lunch at his home the following day. This second engagement fell on November 17, 1915.

At the Dearborn luncheon, not all the guests gave a friendly ear to Mme. Schwimmer's eloquent pleading. Her sketch of the projected Conference of Neutrals struck a responsive chord in her host and in the mind of Louis Lochner, then a Chicago pacifist who had been included in the party, but it did not impress Ford's wife and two other important guests. The principal listeners whom Mme. Schwimmer was unable to sway were two intimates of the Ford family, William Livingstone, a local banker, and the Very Rev. Samuel S. Marquis, then Dean of the Episcopal Cathedral of the city of Detroit. Pulled this way and that in the table conversation, Ford was none too comfortable, Lochner reported later. He was ill at ease and seemed afraid to express any opinions of his own. When he spoke at all he took aim at "a certain banker" who he felt was responsible for the war. To Mme. Schwimmer, herself a Jewess, Ford offered the opinion that "the Jews" were the promulgators of the war. As he dropped this hint, he airily tapped one of his pockets and said he "had the papers" to prove it.

But despite the charged atmosphere of the reception at Dearborn, and despite the vagaries of her host, Mme. Schwimmer carried the day. Her triumph was complete and instantaneous. Ford was so impressed that he rushed pellmell to carry her scheme into execution. At her suggestion he leaped at the idea of financing a "Peace Ship" for the purpose of transporting a delegation of American pacifists to a projected Conference of Neutrals. At the same time he resolved to go direct to the President to solicit for the expedition either official sanction or at least the blessings of the United States Government. Moving with vigor and confidence, Ford left for New York several days later in order to prepare for the coming pilgrimage. Quartered at the Belmont in what a certain New York newspaper soon caricatured as "the nut suite," he chartered a private steamer, the *Oscar II*. Lochner, Mme. Schwimmer and their colleagues, meanwhile, were busy trying to give the *Oscar II* an impressive passenger list.

The quixotic voyage of the *Oscar II* could not have hoped for a favorable press, on any terms. The American economy was already deeply committed to the cause of the Allies. After having floated a $500,000,000 Franco-British loan in the United States, the Morgan firm was acting as purchasing agent for the beneficiaries of this credit. American corporations were about to reap a harvest of war orders. Adroit British publicists were winning American sympathies. Against so powerful a coalition of forces, Ford was now flaunting his wealth as well as his heresy. None of his current utterances was calculated to soften the blows that were about to rain down upon him. Shortly before putting out to sea, he suggested that the soldiers in the trenches should call a general strike. No conscientious objector could have excoriated the cause of war in more vitriolic terms. In a previous statement to the Detroit *News*, Ford had exclaimed, "Do you want to know the cause of war? It is capitalism, greed, the dirty hunger for dollars. Take away the capitalist," he said, "and you will sweep war from the earth."

Taking its bearings from such a compass, the Peace Ship was doomed before it lifted anchor. It set sail, moreover, in the face of an organized campaign of derision for which Ford himself unwittingly supplied the themes. His every gesture served to provoke a press that was only waiting for the kill. To Oswald Garrison Villard, then editor of

the New York *Evening Post*, Ford averred, "All you need is a slogan."
Villard said, "Yes, Mr. Ford, what kind of a slogan?" "Oh, something
like — 'We'll get the boys in the trenches home by Christmas.' What do
you think of that?" Villard was one of the few editors in New York who
was not scoffing at the expedition. He pointed out to Ford that the
Oscar II was one of the slowest steamers on the Atlantic, and that if the
war ended the moment this vessel docked in Europe, the feat of moving
10,000,000 soldiers back to their homes by Christmas would have to be
over and done with within a period of nine days. Grateful for Villard's
correction, Ford said, "Oh, I hadn't thought of that. Well, we'll make it,
we'll get the boys out of the trenches by Christmas."

Sheathed in innocence and self-assurance, Ford blithely set out for
Washington to see the President. With Lochner, he arrived in the capital
hoping to get an endorsement from the White House. The audience
with Wilson was described some years later in *America's Don Quixote*,
Lochner's memoirs of the Ford expedition. The President carefully re-
frained from making any commitments. He was polite but evasive.
When his guests were finally dismissed, they left empty-handed. Most of
the time, said Lochner, Ford had sat in Wilson's presence, swinging his
leg back and forth over the side of an armchair. Irritated because of the
President's noncommittal attitude, he had held his tongue until Lochner and he were alone outside on the steps of the White House. Then
in a rage, Ford told his companion what he thought of Wilson. He
snapped, "He's a small man."

Graciously rebuffed by the chief executive of the nation, the two men
repaired to a theater in Washington for the purpose of addressing a
women's peace rally. Here Ford made his second appearance as a public speaker. He managed to get out a single sentence. He said, "I simply
want to ask you to remember the slogan, 'Out of the trenches before
Christmas, and never go back,' and I thank you for your attention."
Flustered by the applause, the manufacturer reddened and retreated to
the rear of the stage.

Such artless behavior on Ford's part was rich material for a metro-
politan press that was both cynical and pro-British. It was fodder for a
merciless effort to make the peace mission sound like comic opera. For
purposes of caricaturing the "rich fool" or the "rustic innocent," nothing was handier than Ford's own homely, unaffected speech. It was in
the mouth of a rural oaf that hostile reporters at the Belmont put Ford's
prophecy that when the war was over, Europe would "grow up as quick
as an onion" or his ingenuous remark, "The Lord is with us . . . and we
are going to follow the sunbeam right to the end."

Into the hodgepodge of reporting and editorial writing at Ford's expense went every bizarre incident that occurred at the Belmont. This
patchwork-quilt of hostility included the reported visit of a woman who
offered to contribute what purported to be a patent medicine guaranteed to heal wounded soldiers. Another reporter told of an odd charac-

ter who wandered into the Belmont headquarters, flippantly greeting its principal occupant as "the champion bug hunter." No journalistic art was required to burlesque what happened when some practical joker forged an invitation from Ford and sent it to Dr. Charles G. Pease, then a notorious anti-nicotine crusader with a penchant for haunting public places and snatching cigars out of people's mouths. Pease never joined the Ford party, but he accepted the fabricated invitation and his acknowledgment was duly reported by the press.

Men of substance added their voices to the chorus of ridicule. Col. Theodore Roosevelt lambasted the peace ship as the "most discreditable" exploit in history. On the floor of the upper house, Senator Thomas of Colorado characterized Ford's delegation as "an aggregation of neurotics." Arthur Vandenberg, then a newspaper editor in Michigan, referred to the *Oscar II* as a "loon ship."

Mocked and pilloried on every side, Ford of necessity lost much of the support which might have graced his expedition with prestige and dignity. Most of the substantial liberals and intellectuals on whom Mme. Schwimmer had been counting, discreetly snubbed an invitation to book passage on the *Oscar II* at Ford's expense. Many distinguished Americans wired their regrets: Jane Addams, Julius Rosenwald, Zona Gale, Charles P. Steinmetz, William Dean Howells, Ida Tarbell, Thomas Mott Osborne, David Starr Jordan, Cardinal Gibbons, Morris Hillquit and Margaret Wilson, the President's daughter. From the roster of outstanding public figures, even Ford's closest friends refused to enlist as co-mediators of peace. John Burroughs, John Wanamaker, Luther Burbank and Thomas Edison respectfully declined Ford's invitation. Not a single college president would come forward, though nearly every one of consequence was invited. Of the forty-eight governors who were sought as guests, only Gov. Hanna of North Dakota saw fit to accept the offer.

On the final passenger list there were, consequently, few names of note. The guests included eighty-three peace delegates drawn somewhat at random from the tiers of the less renowned in public life. Outside of a determined minority, the passengers were by no means even agreed on the object of their undertaking as it had been projected by Mme. Schwimmer. The bulk of the delegates the New York *Times* characterized as "rainbow chasers," "crack-brained dreamers" and "tourists." For full measure, and all at Ford's expense, the formal delegation was accompanied by a body of fellow-travelers: eighteen college students, fifty clerks and technical attachés, and fifty-seven members of the press.

As the *Oscar II* prepared to sail on December 4, 1915, comedy continued to plague her. At the dock someone handed Ford a cage that enclosed within its wrapper two squirrels. Caviling newspaper reporters promptly christened the little animals "Henry F. Acorn" and "William H. Chestnut." When William Jennings Bryan came to see the boat off, he was kissed by an elderly woman who wore white streamers reading "Peace At Any Price." Edison's brief reception was every bit as droll. When the inventor put in an appearance, Lloyd Bingham, an actor and one of the passengers, installed himself on the deck, megaphone in hand, acting as unofficial master of ceremonies. At Bingham's command, the crowd of 10,000 on the pier first honored Ford with a "hip-hip, hooray" salute. The same tribute was repeated for Edison as the cheerleader called out, "Here's the fellow who makes the light for you to see by. Three cheers for Edison." A "hobo" poet and magazine writer who was an accredited member of the press corps boarded ship with his bride-to-be. They were wedded at once in the ship's salon, with the captain of the *Oscar II* officiating at the ceremony. Ford and Bryan signed the certificate of marriage. These solemn rites had to be repeated in mid-ocean because the first ceremony was illegal. The couple's marriage license had been issued by the State of New York and the first union, to which Bryan and Ford attested, had been consummated while the *Oscar II* was still moored at the port of Hoboken, New Jersey.

Still other grotesque events marred the sailing of Ford's vessel. A band concert alternated with hymn singing on shore. As Ford stood quietly acknowledging the cheers of the crowd, a dozen women gathered around him singing "America." When the steamer was a few hundred feet from the pier, Urban J. Ledoux, who chose to call himself "Mr. Zero," dived in after it. When the crew of a river tug fished him out of the Hudson, Ledoux explained that he had only wanted to swim after the *Oscar II* "to ward off torpedoes."

Up to the final moment of embarkation, Ford's wife and advisers tried every expedient at their command to keep the peace ship from sailing under Ford's auspices. Most of the night before he sailed, Ford spent in the company of his friends Livingstone, the banker, and Marquis, the Episcopal dean, both of whom had opposed Mme. Schwimmer's proposals from the start. Imploring their wealthy friend to desert at the last moment, neither of these family intimates had the least success. Unmoved by their appeals, Ford the following morning assigned his power-of-attorney to his son, Edsel, to provide for any emergency that might arise while he himself was at sea. Blocked on land, Mrs. Ford and several frantic Ford executives carried the fight to the Atlantic. They delegated to Marquis the task of weaning Ford from his fellow-travelers while the *Oscar II* was in passage. This practical-minded minister was promptly quartered in the King and Queen's suite of the *Oscar II*. He was to share this space with Ford and with Ford's bodyguard, Ray Dahlinger.

3. Write an *essay of synthesis* of about eight hundred words characterizing the social trends mentioned in print during one week out of the last fifty years. Use material from newspapers, news magazines, and at least one other kind of periodical. All members of the class should choose weeks within the same year, so that they will then be informed readers of one another's papers.

4. Choose a minor historical event or a short period in the life of a famous person. Find what four reputable sources say on the subject and write a narrative combining the information. Imagine your reader to be a high school student with a strong interest in history.

5. Choose a news story that is currently breaking. Taking your information from several newspapers and magazines, write a narrative of the events as they might appear in a year-end summary of major news events. Direct your paper to a college-educated audience.

8

Writing the Research Paper

Preview

The research paper is an original essay presenting your ideas in response to information found in library sources. As you gather research material, your ever-increasing knowledge of a topic will allow you to make informed judgments and original interpretations. At each stage of research, you will have a more complete idea of what you have already found and what you are still looking for. Midway in the process, the writing tasks of the *review of the literature* and of the *proposal* will help you focus the direction of your research. This chapter presents both the technical skills of finding and recording information and the intellectual skills of understanding the material, developing original ideas, and making informed judgments.

Your Ideas and the Library's Information

Writing a research paper is a process of interaction between the materials you find in printed sources and the ideas you develop in yourself. Your ideas lead you to search out additional materials, and these new-found materials lead you to new ideas. Throughout this process it is you who decides what materials you need, discovers the connections between different pieces of information, evaluates the information, frames the questions you will answer, and comes to original conclusions. Before you begin, you cannot know what you will find or what your conclusions will be; but as you proceed, your emerging sense of direction will give shape to the entire project.

In order to gain information and to discover other writers' thoughts on your subject, you will have to become acquainted with how material is arranged in libraries. Library classification systems, card catalogues, periodical indexes and abstracts, computer data banks, and similar information retrieval systems will tell you whether information is located on library shelves or on microfilm reels. But only your own growing knowledge of the subject can tell you what information is useful and how that information relates to questions you are raising. The secret to library research is to remember that the organization of material in books, journals, and reference documents differs from the new organization of facts and ideas that you will eventually achieve by your own thinking on the subject.

Writing an essay based on library sources takes time. You will spend time initially finding sources; you will spend additional time reading these sources and taking notes. Even more time will be needed for your thinking to go through many stages: you will need to identify subjects, raise questions, develop focus, formulate and reformulate ideas on the basis of new information, come to understand the subject, and reach conclusions. The vision of what your paper should cover will only gradually emerge in your mind. You will find your subject not in any book or card catalogue but only in your own thoughts — and only after you have begun to investigate what the library books have to offer.

This chapter will present the typical stages you will pass through in preparing an original library research essay — that is, an essay in which you develop your own thoughts based on library research materials. The purpose of these stages is to separate some of the complex tasks that go into the assignment and to allow you to focus on each skill one at a time.

In reality these stages are not so clearly separable: everyone has an individual way of working, and the development of each essay follows a different course. To give an idea of the way the various stages interact in the development of one particular paper, I will describe how a hypothetical student might develop the ideas for a research essay assigned in a writing course.

First Step: Finding a Direction

Before you can do any research, you must set yourself in a direction. That direction can, and probably will, change with time and knowledge — at the least it will become more specific and focused. But with the first step, as the cliché goes, begins the journey.

How can you set that first direction?

Interest Your Reader

The immediate context in which you are writing the paper provides one set of clues. If you are writing the research paper as part of an academic course, the issues raised in class and the particulars of the assignment given by the teacher establish the direction. If the teacher gives a detailed sheet of instructions defining the major research assignment, these instructions will suggest specific kinds of topics.

In addition to the appropriate topic and the stated expectations of the teacher, you should also consider the intended audience as part of the context. In some courses the teacher is the only reader; that teacher, already well informed about the topic you choose, may read your paper to judge how well you have grasped what you have learned and how well you express your understanding of the material. If such is the case, you would be wise to choose a topic in which you can demonstrate just those things. At other times the teacher, still the only audience, may request papers on topics about which he or she has only limited familiarity. In another class, the teacher may ask you to imagine yourself a practicing scholar writing for a well-informed professional community; your classmates may in fact be your primary audience — the community to which you report back your findings. Careful consideration of which topics might interest each of these audiences may help you choose an initial direction.

Interest Yourself

You should also look into yourself and into the materials to help you choose a general area of research. If you choose an area in which you already have some background knowledge, you will have some insight into the meaning and importance of the new materials you find. Some acquaintance with a subject will also give you a headstart in identifying useful sources. Even more important, if you already have an interest in the subject, you will have more motivation to learn the subject in depth and to understand it more completely. If your interest in the subject makes you feel your questions are worth answering, that conviction will carry across to your eventual readers. On the other hand, if you pick a subject that is tedious to you from the start, not only will you probably drag your heels in doing the research, but also you will have a hard time convincing your readers that reading your paper is worth their time.

As you search for topics that will interest your audience and yourself, you must check to see whether enough of the right kinds of materials are available to make the topic possible. If there is too little information — if you have to use every scrap available — you will have no flexibility or selectivity in the development of your essay. You need a larger stock of information than you will finally use, so that you can select, focus, interpret, and consolidate the material in a new way. On the other hand, if material appears plentiful, the task of wading through all the relevant documents will require careful planning and strategy so that you can identify the most useful sources and use your time efficiently. You should also be careful about choosing topics that have already been treated from every conceivable angle: unless you are remarkably ingenious, you may wind up only parroting the extensive work already done.

Two Quick Checks

Two types of preliminary checks will help you get a sense of how large your topic is. First, you should find an overview of the subject to read. A short, clearly written book, an article synthesizing current knowledge in a nontechnical journal, or an article in a specialized encyclopedia can give you — without too much investment of time — a sense of the range and possibilities of the subject. You will also start to see the difficult areas you may run into as your research develops.

Second, you should make a preliminary search of your library. By looking under the most obvious subject headings in the card catalogue, in any specialized bibliographies, in periodical indexes, and in the indexes of microform materials, you can rapidly survey how much material is available on the subject. From the titles listed, you may also get some idea of the approaches taken in the various sources. These bibliographic library tools are discussed in detail on pages 239–243.

One Student's Progress

As a typical hypothetical example, let us follow the progress of Fred Carmino, a sophomore science major — with particular interests in astronomy and science fiction — who is developing a topic for a research paper in a writing course. His teacher's only stipulation was that the topic had to grow out of some issues that came to public attention during the 1950s. The audience for the final paper was to be other students in the class, all of whom were simultaneously becoming expert in some other major issue of that period. The assigned length of the paper was ten pages or approximately 2500 words, typed and double-spaced.

Our student immediately remembered that the first space satellites were launched in the late 1950s. He thought he personally would be interested in finding out more about the development of the space program. He also suspected that many people had written on the topic and that — unless he found a very unusual angle on the subject — he would only be rehashing what was already written. A few minutes with the card catalogue, the *Readers' Guide to Periodical Literature*, and *Physics Abstracts* convinced him that there was too much material for him to sort out in a reasonable period and that his own particular interest in the area had already been well covered. He noted the names of a few books and promised himself he would get to them when he had some spare time.

While walking home, somewhat dejected — sensing a lack of progress — he remembered hearing about some strange theories that were proposed in the early 1950s, theories about a planet almost crashing into the earth back in Biblical times. He had never heard these theories mentioned in regular science classes, but one of his friends had told him about a book — *Worlds in Collision* by Immanuel Velikovsky. Since the idea sounded potentially interesting, he later checked to see whether enough material was available to risk going further.

Checking the card catalogue under *Velikovsky*, our student found several books by Immanuel Velikovsky: *Worlds in Collision* (New York: Doubleday, 1950), *Earth in Upheaval* (New York: Doubleday, 1955), and a multivolumed set, *Ages in Chaos*, issued by Doubleday over a period of years (1952–1979). Going to the library shelves and skimming through the introductions, he could see that all the books were detailed expansions of the basic ideas presented in the earliest one, which he then decided to look at in greater detail.

In the catalogue he had also discovered two books about Velikovsky: *Velikovsky Reconsidered,* edited by the editors of *Penseé* magazine (New York: Doubleday, 1976), and *Scientists Confront Velikovsky*, edited by Donald Goldsmith (Ithaca: Cornell University Press, 1977). Quickly skimming the introduction and table of contents of each book, he found that the first was a collection of articles supporting Velikovsky's theories; and the second contained papers by well-known scientists criticizing his work. Both these books seemed directed toward a general rather than a scientific audience.

When he looked into the *Readers' Guide*, starting with the 1950 edition — again under the subject heading "Velikovsky" — he found even sharper evidence of controversy. The earliest articles, from general circulation magazines such as *Harper's* and *Collier's*, generally had positive-sounding titles, but soon more negative articles from such scientific magazines as *Science News Letter* and *Science* appeared. The titles of these later articles clearly showed sharp criticism and rejection of Velikovsky's ideas. By mid-1951, articles of both kinds had vanished: both scientific and general readers appeared to have lost interest. But then every few years — in 1955, 1963, 1971, and 1974 — a cluster of articles appeared whose titles gave signs of renewed controversy. So it became clear to our student that Velikovsky was still pressing his ideas and that heated conflicts persisted in an on–off way at least through 1977. He began to read *Worlds in Collision*, curious to see what the fuss was all about. He sensed enough intriguing material to hold promise for an interesting bit of future research.

Finding the Needed Information

Because even the smaller libraries have more material than users can locate by memory, librarians have devised various techniques for filing documents and for helping you find the information you need. Although a description of the more common information storage and retrieval devices follows, remember that each library has its own selection of techniques.

Whenever you begin work in an unfamiliar library, take a few minutes to orient yourself by reading orientation pamphlets or signs prepared by the local librarian. Furthermore, do not feel hesitant about bringing specific research problems to the reference librarian, who will know the special resources of the particular library as well as more general information-finding techniques. The more specifically you can define your research problem to the librarian, the more exact and creative solutions he or she can suggest. Although you will be working in your college library most frequently, you should also acquaint yourself with other libraries in your region, particularly those that have specialized collections in areas that interest you.

Locating the Source You Want

The problem of finding materials in the library falls into two parts: you must discover what materials you want to examine, and then you must find where in the library these materials are stored. Since the second task is the easier, we will discuss it first.

If you already know either the author or the title of a particular work — whether book, article, government publication, or other document — the various catalogs in the library will let you know whether the library has it and, if so, where and how it is stored. The main card catalog lists all books alphabetically in several places: under author, under title, and under one or more subject areas. Each entry card contains extensive bibliographic and descriptive information, as in the sample that follows. The most important piece of information is the *shelf* or *call number* usually listed in the upper left corner of the card; this number tells you where you can find the item on the library's shelves.

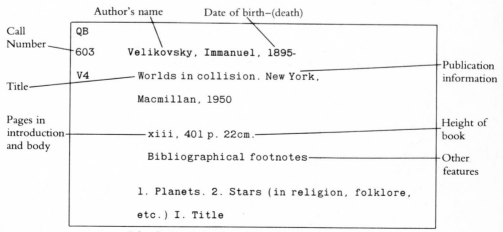

Library of Congress System

The call number on the sample card — QB 603 V4 — is from the Library of Congress Classification System, now used in most larger libraries in this country. In this system the first letter indicates the main category and the second letter, a major subdivision. The additional numbers and letters indicate further subdivisions. The main categories of the Library of Congress System are as follows:

A General Works (such as general encyclopedias, almanacs)
B Philosophy. Psychology. Religion.
C Auxiliary sciences of history (such as archeology, heraldry)
D History: General and Old World
E History: America (general)
F History: America (local, Canada, Mexico, South America)
G Geography. Anthropology. Recreation.
H Social Sciences
J Political Science
K Law
L Education
M Music
N Fine Arts
P Language and Literature
Q Science
R Medicine
S Agriculture
T Technology
U Military Science
V Naval Science
Z Bibliography and Library Science

Dewey Decimal System

Smaller libraries tend to use the Dewey Decimal Classification System, based on a simpler and less differentiated all-numerical classification. The major categories are as follows:

000 General works
100 Philosophy and related disciplines
200 Religion
300 Social sciences
400 Language
500 Pure sciences
600 Technology

700 The arts
800 Literature
900 Geography and history

Some old and large libraries, such as the New York Public Library Research Collection, have their own numerical systems, which do not indicate any systematic subject classification but rather reflect the order in which the documents were received.

Serials File

Some libraries list entries for newspapers, magazines, and other periodicals in a separate *serials file*; this file will list which issues of the periodical are available and whether the issues are loose, bound, or microform. The serials file entry will also give reference letters or call numbers, where appropriate. Since the serials listings offer only the titles and issues of the periodicals — and not the authors and titles of specific articles — you will usually have to consult the appropriate *periodical index* to find out exactly where and when any particular article appeared. You will usually also need to consult a specialized index to locate a government publication or any microform material. Each library offers a different selection of the many available indexes; some of the more common are in the following list.

Indexes of General Circulation Periodicals

Readers' Guide to Periodical Literature
Public Affairs Information Service
Humanities Index
Social Sciences Index
General Science Index

Indexes of Newspapers

New York Times Index
The Times Index (London)
Wall Street Journal Index
Washington Post Index

Indexes of Government Publications

Monthly Catalog of U.S. Government Publications
American Statistics Index

Indexes to Specialized Journals

Humanities

Art Index
Index to Art Periodicals
Film Literature Index
International Guide to Classical Studies
International Bibliography of Historical Sciences
Analecta Linguistica
MLA International Bibliography
Index to Little Magazines
Music Article Index
Popular Music Periodical Index
Index to Religious Periodical Literature
Philosopher's Index
Humanities Citation Index

Social Sciences

Anthropological Index
Accountants' Index
Business Periodicals Index
Criminology Index
Population Index
International Bibliography of Economics
Education Index
British Education Index
Current Index to Journals in Education
Resources in Education
International Bibliography of Political Science
Environment Index
Psychological Abstracts
Sociological Abstracts
International Bibliography of Sociology
Index to Current Urban Documents
Women Studies Abstracts
Social Sciences Citation Index

Sciences

Biological and Agricultural Index
Biological Abstracts
BioResearch Index
Chemical Abstracts
Computer and Control Abstracts

Bibliography and Index of Geology
Hospital Literature Index
Hospital Abstracts
Index Medicus
Physics Abstracts
Science Citation Index

Once you have the journal and the issue containing the article you want, you need to return to the serials file to get the shelf number; then locate the issue, microfilm, or bound volume on the library shelf. In some larger libraries you may not be allowed to fetch the materials directly from the shelves; instead you must file a request slip and an attendant will get the material for you. This closed stack system, although making it harder for you to browse, does allow librarians to maintain order in complex collections.

Pursuing Leads

The more difficult problem is to know what material you want in the first place. More ingenuity, imagination, and dogged persistence are involved than the simple following of procedures. The procedures below can only serve as starting points that may lead you into many false directions before they lead you to a few good ones. You will probably have to look through much material before you find the few items that are directly relevant to your search.

Subject Headings

The first place to look is under the subject headings in the catalogs, indexes, and bibliographies described above. Almost all are either arranged or cross-indexed according to subject. The trick is to find the right subject heading, since each topic can be described in many ways — and the catalogs and bibliographies only have a limited number of subject headings.

If you have trouble locating an appropriate subject heading, you may find the publication *Subject Headings Used in the Dictionary Catalogs of the Library of Congress* useful. Most libraries follow its system of headings. Sometimes you may have to try several different terms to describe your subject before you hit on the one used in the card catalog or in a periodical index. Sometimes merely rearranging the terms of a long subject heading may be enough to help you find the listings. For example, the subject of social aspects of American science would be phrased in a card catalog as "Science — Social aspects — United States."

Computer Search

Increasingly, research librarians have access to computer search systems that allow the researcher to find most listings in a particular subject area. Among data now computerized are items from *Biological Abstracts, Chemical Abstracts, Index Medicus, Physics Abstracts,* and *Resources in Education.* The titles of articles on a subject are retrieved through the use of *keywords* or *descriptors*; each data system has its own set of descriptors so that again the most important task is to find the right subject headings. You will be aided in your search by publications listing the current keywords used in each system. For example, the ERIC system — the Educational Resources Information Center — provides a frequently revised list of subject headings in *The Thesaurus of ERIC Descriptors*.

Newspaper Search

Since only a few of the major newspapers are fully indexed, you may need to begin your subject search with a newspaper — the *New York Times*, the *Washington Post* — that is fully indexed. Once you have identified the days when news stories appeared in the indexed papers, you can then check those dates — and check a few days forward and backward — in unindexed newspapers.

These first subject searches will give you an entry into the topic, but most likely they will not provide all the material you will eventually need. Much of what you find will not be directly relevant to your interests, and you'll return these volumes to the shelves after a few moments of skimming. The material that you find relevant probably won't tell the full story and may only serve to lead you to further material.

At this point, you require real ingenuity — to let the material you have already found lead you to more material.

One Book Leads to Another

First, one book or article can lead you to another through the references cited by the author. In footnotes, bibliographies, and passing mentions, authors will indicate the work of other authors on which their own work is based. If you find a particular book or article important for your topic, it is likely that the earlier sources referred to will also be of some importance. Just because footnotes and bibliographies are sometimes in small print and tucked away in the back, don't ignore them.

Sometimes the most fruitful thing a book will give you is the title of another book that turns out to give you just the information you were looking for.

In your search, you should also develop the skill of selective browsing. If you find a few books on your subject clustered around a particular shelf number, browsing through nearby shelves — both before and after the shelf number — may help you turn up some related items. Similarly, if you find a particular journal that has published several articles over a short period of time dealing with your topic, skimming the tables of contents of earlier and later years may turn up a choice find.

After reading a few sources, you may discover that one or two scholars have written the major studies on which most other researchers have based their work. If this is the case, you may be able to locate other sources by finding out which other researchers have referred to these seminal writers. The *Science Citation Index, Social Science Citation Index*, and *Humanities Citation Index* will direct you to articles in professional journals that cite any particular earlier book or article by seminal writers. (The listings are arranged according to the work cited.)

Since each source teaches you more and more about your subject, you will be able to judge with ever-increasing precision the usefulness and value of any prospective source. In other words, the more you know about the subject, the more precisely you can identify what you still must find out. You will also become more aware of what other secondary subjects you need to investigate as background. As you move into your research, you will know more specific topics, key terms, and major figures; you can then return to the subject headings of the indexes, catalogues, and bibliographies for another round of more precise searching for sources. At some point, of course, you will have to stop looking and decide that you have enough information. But that decision is a story for later in this chapter.

Record Keeping

Throughout the long process of gathering raw material, you will need to keep track of specific sources, much varied information, and your developing reactions and ideas. While working on shorter papers based on just a few sources, you may be able to keep all the materials on the desk in front of you and store all your thoughts in your mind. But as research projects grow bigger and more complex, haphazard methods of record keeping will lead to loss of materials, to loss of valuable ideas, and to general confusion.

Listing Sources

First, you need to keep careful account of the sources you use, not only because you will need to document them in the final paper but also because you may want to refer back to one or another — for a piece of information you later realize is valuable. Depending on the size of the project and your own habits, you may record the sources on a continuous list or on separate index cards. The separate cards have these advantages: they allow you to sort out sources according to topic and to alphabetize the list for the bibliography; they also allow you to pull out individual titles to bring with you to the library.

Whatever form the list takes, it should include (1) all the information you need to write the documentation for the paper, (2) all the information you need to locate the item in the library, and (3) enough of a description so that you will be able to remember what kind of work each source is. Book documentation requires

> author(s) — full name
> publication information — city (state), publisher, year

Periodical documentation requires

> author(s) — full name
> title of periodical
> specific issue by date (or volume number)
> inclusive pages

Other materials may require slightly different information; for detailed instructions, see pages 343–357.

To be able to relocate the information, you should record the library — or other place you found the material — and the shelf number. To help you remember the kind of information in the book, you should add a few descriptive and evaluative phrases. All this information will lead to a listing much like the one on the sample bibliography card on page 247.

On another list or another set of cards, you can keep track of sources you have not yet examined — promising leads from footnotes and bibliographies. Make sure to record any data that may help you locate a potential source. In addition to specific titles, you can record your future plans: types of information you still need and possible sources you might look into. For example, our researcher thought he might investigate how much publicity Velikovsky's theories received in the mass media, so he added this comment to his list of future research prospects: "How big a

> **By maintaining a list of potential leads and sources, you gain a sense of the direction in which your research is going, and you can organize the work ahead of you.**

public splash did V's first book make? Check newspapers for reviews, advertisements."

By maintaining a list of potential leads and sources, you gain a sense of the direction in which your research is going, and you can organize the work ahead of you.

Note Taking

You must, of course, keep track of the relevant information you find in the sources — by taking some form of notes. The most precise form of note is an exact quotation: whenever you suspect that you may later wish to quote the writer's exact words, make sure you copy the quotation correctly. Whenever you decide to copy exact words down in your notes — even if only a passing phrase — make sure you identify them by *quotation marks*. In this way you can avoid inadvertent plagiarism when you are working from your notes.

Paraphrase, summary, and outline offer more selective forms of note taking than straight quotation. You can record only the most relevant information, and you can focus on giving your reader the essential ideas

Author —— Kazin, Alfred

Title of article —— "On The Brink"

Title of periodical —— The New Yorker, April 29, 1950, pp. 103-105

Location —— College library -- bound periodicals —— Shelf

Descriptive evaluation —— Review of Worlds in Collision: strongly negative, critical of V's evidence and logic; reviewer wonders about book's appeal from the source rather than the author's complete argument. In each case, make sure your notes accurately reflect the meaning of the original, even though you are using your own words. In taking notes from any one source, you may use each of these forms of note taking — depending on how directly the passage bears on your subject. Again, if you borrow a phrase or even a key word from the original, identify it as original wording by quotation marks.

Early Notes

In the early stages of your research, before you have a specific idea of your final topic, you should record a wide range of information — even though you will not use all of it. In this way, you should not have to return to the source to pick up some useful data or detail that you ignored the first time around. As your topic gains focus, you may become more selective; in the last stages of research, you may simply be interested in a single fact to fill a gap in your argument.

Whatever form your notes take, make sure that you keep an accurate record of where each piece of information comes from. Since you should be keeping a separate complete list of sources, you need only identify the source in your notes by a key word from the title followed by a specific page reference.

An easy — but potentially dangerous — way to retain information from sources is to keep hold of the sources, either by borrowing books from the library or by making photocopies. The danger in keeping the original or photocopy is that once you have the information on your desk at home, you may never look at it until you begin writing the paper. In order for the information to be incorporated into your thinking on the subject, it has to be in your mind — and not just on your desk.

The process of understanding the relationships among the many ideas that you read requires that you make sense of each bit of information as you discover it. If you own a particularly useful book or have made a photocopy of pertinent pages, you should read and annotate the material at the time you find it. By staying on top of the reading, you will think about the material at the proper time, and you will have complete, well-organized notes when you are ready to gather together all your information for the paper.

Notes on Your Own Reactions

Finally, you need to keep track of your own developing thoughts on the subject. Your thoughts will range from specific evaluations of particular sources, to redefinitions of your topic, to emerging conclusions that may become the thesis of your final paper. Hold on to these thoughts, however tentative: they cover the essence of what you have already learned about the subject, and they will provide the direction for what you do next. What at first may seem a minor curious idea may develop into a central idea. In the notes, recording your own thoughts as they develop, you will find the seeds of the internal organization of your material, and this new organization will make your paper original.

While you are still searching for sources, periodic attempts to restate your subject, to develop an outline, and even to write tentative opening paragraphs — long before you are actually ready to write the paper — will help you focus your thinking. The *proposal,* discussed later in this chapter, presents a more formal opportunity to gather your thoughts and to focus your direction.

Closing In on the Subject

After reading on a subject for a time, you become familiar with both the subject itself and the writing on the subject. Both types of knowledge should help you define your specific approach to further research. Knowledge of the subject itself lets you know what issues exist and which issues are important. While becoming increasingly familiar with your subject, you gain substantive material upon which to base your thinking. Simultaneously, your knowledge of the prior writing, or the *literature* on the subject, lets you know which issues have been fully discussed and which have not. In addition to helping you evaluate the early information you have come across, a study of the literature helps you sort out what kinds of data are available, what biases exist in the writing, what purposes other writers have had, and what areas of agreement exist between sources.

After several days or weeks of research, you may find that the questions that interest you have already been fully discussed in the literature, or you may find — quite to the contrary — that no previous writer has had exactly your interest in the subject. You will also learn whether the available literature can provide you with enough information to pursue the questions that interest you. By seeing what approaches other writers have taken, you may discover a new approach to the subject that will lead to original questions. A study of the literature also may give rise to questions about why other writers have treated the subject in the way they have.

After this overview of both the literature and the subject, you are ready to choose a more specific direction for your research. The questions that you want to work on and that have promising sources will become more evident. Your research questions will help you decide what new information you need to locate and what kinds of sources you still need to seek out.

On the Right Track

The example of our student researching the theories of Velikovsky will illustrate how increasing knowledge leads to more precise definition of the research question. After reading *Worlds in Collision,* our student was surprised by Velikovsky's astounding claims that the planet Venus was once part of Jupiter but broke away to form a comet that passed close to earth before it settled down in Venus's present orbit. When Venus in the form of a comet passed close to earth in about the fifteenth century B.C., it caused great catastrophes: rains of fire, magnetic storms, rock storms, blackened skies, floods, and wrenching of the earth's motion.

Velikovsky supported these dramatic claims with accounts from the legends and the sacred books of ancient peoples all over the earth. Velikovsky's version of the history of the planets and of the events on earth was so different from anything our student had learned in science or history classes — or had read anywhere except in science fiction stories — that he wondered how it could possibly be true. Velikovsky's use of myth seemed impressive, but his theories didn't seem scientifically sound. At the same time, Velikovsky's account appealed to our student's sense of imagination. Whether or not the story was true, he felt it would make a first-class science fiction movie — filled with literally earth-shaking events.

The next book our student looked at, *Velikovsky Reconsidered,* made him consider the possibility that Velikovsky's ideas might be right. The book, a collection of articles in support of Velikovsky's theory, presented new evidence that seemed to back up his claims. Particularly provoking were findings from recent space probes that were contrary to orthodox scientific expectations but consistent with Velikovsky's theory. These findings included the discovery of electromagnetic fields surrounding the earth and the measurements of Venus's temperature and rotation. In several articles, our student read that members of the scientific establishment not only refused to listen to Velikovsky but also used unprofessional tactics in an attempt to censor his publication. This reaction aroused our researcher's curiosity even more; however, he remained suspicious because he knew he was receiving only the supporters' side of the story.

Therefore, he turned to the hostile scientists and their discussion of Velikovsky. He first checked standard astronomical textbooks and reference works on the planets but could find no mention of Velikovsky. Nor could he find any catastrophic theory like Velikovsky's — no matter how many indexes he checked. He next looked at the reviews and articles on Velikovsky that had first appeared in scientific journals. Most of these were general condemnations, calling Velikovsky a quack and a charlatan who knew nothing about scientific methods. However, he found little specific criticism in any of the earlier articles. By the mid-sixties, a few scientists began to call for a closer examination of Velikovsky's ideas. Their interest led to a debate at the 1974 meeting of the American Association for the Advancement of Science. The scientific side of that debate was published in *The Humanist* magazine and the book *Scientists Confront Velikovsky*.

Sidetracked

After reading the analyses of the professional astronomers, our student was very confused: although the refutations seemed quite convincing, he himself didn't have enough technical knowledge to evaluate the arguments in detail — or to decide whether some other valid criteria might be used to judge Velikovsky's work. He tended to believe the scientists and felt that they had finally given Velikovsky a fair hearing.

At this point, our student judged that he could add little to the debate directly; if he made an evaluation of Velikovsky's findings the main subject of his paper, he would wind up repeating existing arguments. A second issue — whether scientists had treated Velikovsky poorly — no longer seemed promising, since that controversy was already well documented. Many scientists had admitted to the lack of fairness; the debate of 1974 had seemed, in part, to make amends for this treatment. The issue seemed closed. Our student was discouraged; he had reached a dead end.

A New Track

The next day our student realized that one issue still remained open. The nonscientific reception of Velikovsky's books had been discussed only lightly, yet there was much available evidence for him to explore — to determine why Velikovsky was so popular with general readers even while he was totally rejected by scientists.

By coincidence, the kind of coincidence that often happens when one is in the middle of research and sensitive to any mention of the topic, he came across two further indications that Velikovsky remained part of the popular imagination. First, he went to see a recent remake of the movie *The Invasion of the Body Snatchers;* in the movie a minor character — who may have already been taken over by creatures from outer space — was reading *Worlds in Collision,* perhaps to make him seem suspicious. Second, when reading that day's *New York Times,* he came across an interview of Velikovsky that painted an attractive picture of a quiet, aging scholar working in an isolated house on an island off the New Jersey coast. Although the article did not address any scientific issues, it did indicate to our student that almost thirty years after the start of the controversy, Velikovsky remained a personality of public interest.

Formalizing the Subject

Somewhere in the middle of your research — once you have a solid feel for what information is available — your attention should shift from what has been previously said about the subject to the questions you set for yourself. Are any answers in sight? Your mind will be turning from other writers' statements to your own gradually forming ideas.

At this point you are ready to formalize the final topic of the project through a review of the literature and a proposal. The *review of the literature* sketches in the sources and background of your project; the *proposal* specifies the nature of your anticipated contribution to the subject. These two short pieces of writing will help clarify the direction and the purpose of the research in your own mind, and they will reveal your research plans to others who might be able to give you useful advice — classmates, teachers, thesis supervisors, or research committees. They may provide titles of valuable sources you may not have come across or suggest ways you might focus your thinking and research even more.

The Review of the Literature

The *review of the literature* surveys the available writing on a subject, indicating the patterns of current thought that the researcher has discovered. The review of a particular topic usually includes short sum-

> **The *review of the literature* surveys the available writing on a subject, indicating the patterns of current thought that the researcher has discovered.**

maries of the major pieces of literature and even shorter characterizations of less important material. The review also covers the connection or lack of connection among the various works in the literature.

In writing a review of the literature, cluster the discussion of similar books and articles. Explain as explicitly as possible the similarities within each cluster and the differences between clusters. Note such patterns as historical changes in thinking or conflicts between opposing groups of scientists. All the major opinions you have come across should be represented in the review. In this manner you will both organize the literature for your own purposes and you will demonstrate to the readers of the review that you are familiar with most of the material on your subject.

In some academic disciplines, the review of the literature may stand as an independent piece of writing, both at undergraduate and more advanced levels. In these disciplines, the literature may be so technical and may require so much detailed study that simply gaining a grasp of it is enough of a task for any student at any one time. Thus teachers in the sciences and the social sciences may assign reviews of literature on specific topics to familiarize their students with the most recent professional findings. Active scholars may write reviews of the literature for professional journals to keep their colleagues informed on proliferating research. When the review stands as a separate piece of writing, it may be quite extensive — upwards of twenty pages — and deal with the major sources in some detail.

Even the separate review of literature, in the long run, is in the service of new, original research. In the case of the undergraduate in a technical discipline, such original research may be postponed until the student gains a wider range of skills and concepts necessary to make a contribution at current levels of work; the review of the literature is a way of making the student aware of that level. In the case of practicing researchers, the professional review of the literature provides the starting point for future work by themselves or their colleagues.

When written as the introduction to a proposal for original research, the review of the literature can be concise, stressing the broad outlines of information available rather than revealing all the important details. The review serves as a background and a justification for the proposal.

Sometimes a review of the literature is needed as part of the final research paper or report on an experiment. In this case, the writer should be highly selective, raising only those issues and presenting only those findings necessary to understand the new work that follows.

The Proposal

The proposal states how you intend to build on, fill in, answer, or extend the literature you have just reviewed. In other words, the proposal should define a task that will result in something different from what has already been written. The proposal should also indicate how you intend to accomplish the task and your best estimate of the kinds of results you expect.

Identifying an Original Task

The setting of an original task for yourself in the proposal will lead to a final essay that goes beyond what others previously have written. Sometimes you may find your particular task by applying new information to an old question: applying modern psychological theories to existing biographical facts may lead to an entirely new view of some notable person's work — for example, a re-evaluation of Darwin or Woodrow Wilson. Or newly reported data about crime in urban areas may be helpful in re-evaluating long-standing theories about the relationship between crime and unemployment.

You may take a new approach to a long-standing controversy. You may realize, for example, that one new approach to the question of whether TV has hurt children's reading skills is to compare the best-selling children's books before and after the advent of TV. Although all the information and the basic question are not new, your new combination will lead to new answers.

You may also find an entirely new question to ask. This alternative is particularly attractive when you are at some distance in time from the other writers on the issue. The distance often results in seeing the subject from a different perspective — and that different perspective leads to new issues. For example, during the early sixties, most discussions on armaments in this country focused on immediate questions of practical defense, such as whether we were ahead of the Russians in the arms race or whether we had an adequate deterrent. Looking back on that period now, you will no longer be so caught up in the practical issues; you might now ask whether the level of international fear during that period led to a special relationship between the United States government and the de-

> **However you develop an original task for your paper, you
> need to keep in mind the limits of the resources available
> to you — in terms of both source materials and your own
> level of skills.**

fense industry. By asking entirely new questions, you can examine the earlier source material and develop whole new lines of investigation.

In your preliminary research, you may also have discovered important areas of your subject that have been neglected or only half-explored. Such is the case with our student working on Velikovsky. He found that, aside from the speculations of an earlier reviewer and a few passing comments from scientists, no one had explored the reasons for the obvious popularity of Velikovsky's theories among nonscientists.

Practical Considerations

However you develop an original task for your paper, you need to keep in mind the limits of the resources available to you — in terms of both source materials and your own level of skills. From your review of the literature, you should be able to recognize the topics that would be extremely difficult to handle because of lack of substantive information; for example, any discussion about the Viking contact with American Indians would probably be very speculative and very short for the simple reason that so little conclusive evidence remains. Similarly, if you are a student taking an introductory survey of psychology, you would be wise not to propose an entirely new theory of schizophrenia. A more limited task — the application of one existing theory to several published case histories — would allow you range for original thought but not overburden you with a task beyond your present skills.

Implementing Your Task

Having set yourself an appropriate original task, you need to explain in your proposal how you are going to accomplish it. This means indicating the sources you know you will use and the additional information you still need to seek out. If the additional information is to come from library sources, you should indicate what sources seem promising. If you need to conduct a survey, an interview, or an experiment — provided, of course, that it is appropriate to the course and possible within the assigned time — you should describe the precise purpose and the methods. You should also indicate the kinds of analyses you will apply to the findings you generate. At some point, you should indicate the general organization of your final argument. Thus the proposal will reveal all the issues you will deal with and all the means you will employ to accomplish your task.

Even though you have not yet completed your research, you should by now have some idea of the kinds of answers you are likely to find. These emerging answers will serve as tentative hypotheses, which you can evaluate as you gather and organize your evidence. These emerging answers will focus your thinking and lead you to consider the final shape of the paper.

Finally, you should discuss your interest in, or the importance of, the subject as defined in your proposal — to convince the reader and possibly yourself that the subject is indeed worthwhile. The more clearly you understand the value of your work, the more focused and motivated your work will be.

Sample Review of the Literature

Immanuel Velikovsky's Theory of

Interplanetary Catastrophe

Immanuel Velikovsky's theory describing the near collision thirty-five centuries ago between the earth and Venus
and the coming together of the orbits of Venus, Mars, and
the earth twenty-seven centuries ago has aroused a nonstop
controversy. The professional scientific community rejects
the theory almost totally, whereas the supporters of the
theory are almost all from outside the scientific establishment. The literature on the subject is essentially
a record of that controversy.

The debate began shortly before the publication of
Velikovsky's Worlds in Collision in 1950. Although
summaries and excerpts of the book appeared in general

circulation magazines--<u>Harper's</u>, <u>Collier's</u>, and <u>Reader's</u>
<u>Digest</u>--in the months before the book's publication,
the book was the first complete statement of the theory.
The book opens with a discussion of some astronomical
observations that were not explained by current theory;
Velikovsky then presents his own novel theory that Venus
was once part of Jupiter but broke away to become a comet.
As a comet, Venus passed through the orbits of earth and
Mars before settling down into its present planetary orbit.
These wanderings of Venus had many catastrophic effects on
earth, as recorded in the stories of the Old Testament and
in traditional stories set down by other peoples around the
earth. Most of the book is devoted to correlating the effects of the near collisions with the traditional accounts
of mythology.

    Velikovsky later elaborated the geological evidence in
<u>Earth in Upheaval</u> and the mythological evidence in the
four volumes of the <u>Ages in Chaos</u> series (<u>From the Exodus</u>
<u>to King Akhnaton</u>, <u>The Age of Homer and Isaiah</u>, <u>Ramses II</u>
<u>and His Time</u>, and <u>Peoples of the Sea</u>). These later books
added details to his theory but almost all of the subsequent debate centered on his first book.

    The reviews of <u>Worlds in Collision</u> (as excerpted in <u>Book</u>
<u>Review Digest</u>, 1950, p. 930) indicate that the two sides of
the controversy formed quickly. On one side were those who
rejected the theory on scientific and scholarly grounds;
on the other were those who found the book exciting and a
challenge to conventional ideas. Articles in such maga-
zines as <u>Science News Letter</u>, <u>Science Digest</u>, and <u>Science</u>

reported the scientific attack on Velikovsky's ideas. Although all the attacks were general condemnations of Velikovsky's lack of scientific procedures and thinking, there
was little evaluation of specific evidence. After this initial rejection, scientists seemed to ignore his theory; and
no mention of it can be found in standard works and textbooks on astronomy and the solar system.

Support, however, came from favorable articles in Time
and Newsweek as well as from the previously mentioned
reviews and excerpts. These supportive articles were
written by nonscientists for nonscientists. In particular,
Eric Larrabee, an editor of Harper's, continued to write
articles in support of Velikovsky. In the 1970s new support
came from two small journals, Pensée and Kronos, published
on college campuses. Many of the articles from Pensée are
republished in Velikovsky Reconsidered. This recent
support centers on two themes: first, measurements and
discoveries made by space probes that confirm some of
Velikovsky's predictions; second, the unprofessional
behavior of scientists in attempting to suppress Velikovsky's views and in refusing to give him a fair hearing. These latter charges of unscientific behavior are
documented in The Velikovsky Affair.

Some professional scientists, impressed by the confirmation of some of Velikovsky's predictions (see Motz
and Bargmann) and recognizing the lack of fair treatment,
called for a more complete examination of the evidence. As
a result, a debate was held in 1974 at a conference of the

American Academy for the Advancement of Science; some of
the debate was republished in The Humanist magazine, and
a larger selection was published as the book Scientists
Confront Velikovsky. The arguments presented by the scientists, particularly by Carl Sagan, offer detailed refutations based on mathematical calculations.

  But this careful scientific refutation has not seemed to
resolve anything. Velikovsky, although he participated in
the debate, refused to cooperate in the publication of the
conference proceedings. He instead has continued to press
his theories in the last three volumes of the Ages in Chaos
series. His followers have continued to argue his case in
books such as The Age of Velikovsky and in articles, mainly
in small journals such as Kronos.

Bibliography

I. Books by Immanuel Velikovsky

Worlds in Collision. New York: Macmillan, 1950;
    rpt. New York: Doubleday, 1950.

Earth in Upheaval. New York: Doubleday, 1955.

Ages in Chaos (4 volumes):

Vol. I. From the Exodus to King Akhnaton. New York:
  Doubleday, 1952.

Vol. II. The Age of Homer and Isaiah. New York:
  Doubleday, 1979.

Vol. III. Ramses II and His Time. New York: Doubleday,
  1978.

Vol. IV. Peoples of the Sea. New York: Doubleday, 1979.

II. Books and Articles on Velikovsky's Theory

"Book Arouses Controversy." <u>Science News Letter</u>, 15
   April 1950, p. 229.

Brown, Harrison. "Books." <u>Scientific American</u>, March
   1956, pp. 127-128 ff.

de Grazia, Alfred, ed. <u>The Velikovsky Affair</u>. New Hyde
   Park, N.Y.: University Books, 1966.

Goldsmith, Donald, ed. <u>Scientists Confront Velikovsky</u>.
   Ithaca: Cornell Univ. Press, 1977. (Partial
   Proceedings of 1974 AAAS Convention; appeared in
   abbreviated form in <u>The Humanist</u>, November-
   December 1977.)

Kazin, Alfred. "On The Brink." <u>New Yorker</u>, 29 April
   1950, pp. 103-105.

LaFleur, L. J. "Cranks and Scientists." <u>Science</u>,
   November 1951, pp. 284-290.

Larrabee, Eric. "The Day the Sun Stood Still."
   <u>Harper's</u>, January 1950, pp. 19-26 and March 1950, pp.
   18-19.

----------. "Letter." <u>Science</u>, 7 August 1953, p. 167.

----------. "Reply." <u>Scientific American</u>, May 1956, p.
   12 ff.

Motz, Lloyd, and V. Bargmann. "On the Recent Discoveries Concerning Jupiter and Venus." <u>Science</u>, 21 December 1962, p. 1350 ff.

Oursler, F. "Why the Sun Stood Still." <u>Reader's
   Digest</u>, March 1950, pp. 139-148.

<u>Pensée</u>, editors. <u>Velikovsky Reconsidered</u>. New York:
   Doubleday, 1976.

Pfeiffer, John. "Letter." <u>Science</u>, 13 July 1951, p.
  47.

"Professors as Suppressors." <u>Newsweek</u>, 3 July 1950, p.
  15-16.

"Retort to Velikovsky." <u>Science News Letter</u>, 25 March
  1950, p. 181.

"Scientists in Collision." <u>Newsweek</u>, 25 February 1974,
  p. 58 ff.

"Theories Denounced." <u>Science News Letter</u>, 25 February 1950, p. 119.

Velikovsky, Immanuel. "Answer to My Critics."
  <u>Harper's</u>, June 1951, pp. 63-66.

----------. "<u>Worlds in Collision</u>: Author Comments on
  Controversy." <u>Publisher's Weekly</u>, May 1950, p. 2739.

"Velikovsky Controversy." <u>Chemistry</u>, October 1971, p.
  17.

Sample Proposal

Proposal for a Paper: The Reasons for

Velikovsky's Popularity Among

Nonscientists

Although the scientific opposition to Velikovsky's ideas
has been well documented, both from the standpoint of scientific doubts about his theory and from the standpoint of
the unfair treatment and attempts at suppression, there
has not been much study of the nonscientific support for
his ideas. I propose to examine how popular Velikovsky's
ideas have become and what reasons account for that popularity. I will focus primarily on the first wave of popular-

ity that followed publication of his first book, <u>Worlds
in Collision</u>, which became one of the best-selling books
of 1950. I will also examine how that early support led to
the longer-lasting support that continues even to the
present.

The <u>New York Times</u> best-seller list should give one
indication of how popular the book was. Reflections of
ideas similar to Velikovsky's in such popular media as the
movies should also indicate how well those ideas took hold
in the popular imagination. Some of the reasons explaining
his popularity may be found in the favorable reviews. Advertisements for the book will show what kind of appeal
the publishers were trying to make. Even some of the negative reviews and articles about the controversy may contain indirect evidence. Looking into the background of cultural attitudes toward science may also indicate how the
book fit in with a national mood. In other words, I will be
looking for nonscientific reasons for the popularity of the
book.

Such an investigation should tell much about the motivation of the supporters, even though the paper will not
discuss the issue of which side is wrong or right. The essay may also reveal something about the nonscientists'
attitudes toward science at the midpoint of this century.

Completing the Research

The proposal limits the research tasks remaining. The specific
issues outlined in it define the amount and type of information you still

need to find. In the course of completing the research, you may find a few new leads, but you need to pursue them only if the new information seems essential to an intelligent response to the issues. One of the skills of research is knowing when you have enough information; in considering too many side issues or too many perspectives, you may lose the main thread of your subject. A well-conceived proposal will, in most cases, mark the boundaries of your task.

At this point, the student working on the Velikovsky project is only interested in information that will explain the appeal of the planets-in-collision theories to a nonscientific audience. All the material on the hostile scientific response or the subsequent debate is no longer of direct interest. The attitudes expressed in the popular media and the general cultural currents of the period become the main focus of research.

As the last few pieces of information fill in the picture, it is time to test out specific ways of piecing the information together. Depending on your temperament, your habits, and the subject, the final shape of the paper may come to you in different ways. This is the time for heavy use of scrap paper for jotting down your ideas, associations, trial sentences, and outlines. Some specific techniques that you may find useful follow:

• Write trial thesis sentences
What does all this information lead to?
What are you trying to say in this paper?

• Write trial introductions
Where does the subject begin?
How does it relate to other issues?
What will interest your readers about this subject?
How can you get the main argument of the paper moving?

• Make sketchy outlines
What are the main points?
How do they fit together and in what order?
How do they lead to your conclusion?
How do the details of the research support your ideas?

• Phrase difficult ideas
How do you state your key points?
Will certain ways of phrasing your ideas bring them more into focus?

• Let your thoughts flow freely in journal entries
What is your relationship to your readers?
What will they want to know about the subject?
What do you want them to find out?
What will they find difficult or controversial?

Although you may not use any of these trial attempts directly in the final paper, each attempt will help you evolve the kinds of language, reasoning, and organization you will eventually use.

Outlining the Argument

On shorter, less complex papers, a few organizational notes may be enough to fix the structure of the argument in your mind before you begin writing, but research papers are usually too long and too complex to organize by haphazard methods. An essay of anywhere from ten to fifty or more pages, incorporating a range of ideas and information from many sources, requires conscious, careful planning. Preparing a full outline will let you think over your plans, consider them from several perspectives, and revise them accordingly.

The outline places in schematic form the main topic and issues you will discuss in the paper and arranges the subtopics and specifics underneath the major statements. It is the bare bones, the skeleton, of the paper you will write. As such, you should neither take it lightly nor arrange the material in a mechanical, automatic fashion. Rather you should consider what are the essentials of what you want to convey and what will be the most effective arrangement of the material.

The outline is your way of putting the subject together. Your major statements and arrangement of them, although built out of your reading of sources, should *not* resemble the pattern of any source. If you borrow the skeleton of someone else's work, it will look like that earlier piece of work, no matter how you flesh it out. But having consulted many sources — and compared, evaluated, and synthesized them — your vision of the subject will not resemble anyone else's: your outline will be the result of a long line of original inquiry.

You are probably familiar with the mechanics of the outline. At the top is a thesis statement, a statement that the entire paper argues for and supports. Listed underneath the thesis are the major statements that support or subdivide that thesis; these major statements are identified by Roman numerals. In turn, each major statement is supported or subdivided into secondary statements, listed beneath it, and identified by upper-case letters. This subdivision continues as long as the material warrants, the smaller units being marked successively by arabic numerals, lower-case letters, numerals in parentheses, and letters in parentheses. Successive indentations visually separate the main points from the minor ones. Schematically, this is the framework of your outline:

Thesis statement
I. First major statement
   A. Secondary statement
      1. Supporting claim
         a. Specific evidence
         b. Specific evidence
         c. Specific evidence
      2. Supporting claim
         a. Specific evidence
         b. Specific evidence
            (1) Example
            (2) Example
      3. Supporting claim
      4. Supporting claim
   B. Secondary statement . . .
II. Second major statement
   A. . . .

Usually the more major divisions will present ideas or generalized material; the smaller divisions will cover details, evidence, or references to supporting source material.

As a convenience in preparation for the final writing stage, you may want to cross-reference your notes to the numbers on the outline. In preparing the outline, you will also discover whether you need to seek out a few additional pieces of information to complete your argument.

The importance of the outline is that it forces you to arrange your thoughts in some order and then to consider the arrangement. As you outline and revise the outline, you should keep the following points in mind:

• Support your thesis
Does every part of the outline directly relate to the thesis by presenting your case, explaining an idea, or filling in *necessary* background?
Do all the entries add up to a convincing argument for your thesis claim?
Is the thesis broad enough to encompass all the important issues in your topic?
• Clarify the order and relationship of the major points
Are the statements in the most logical or effective order?
Does one statement lead to the next?
Does the argument maintain a consistent direction — or does it backtrack or even contradict itself?
• Establish the relationship of major and minor statements
Does each group of subheadings adequately develop the major heading?

Does each piece of specific evidence have a clear relationship to some larger claim you are making?

• Establish your task in the introduction

Does the introduction show your awareness of the prior writing on the subject?

Is a review of the literature necessary — to fill in the reader on background?

Does the introduction raise the major issue you will discuss in the paper?

Does it reveal how you will pursue that issue?

Does the introduction indicate the importance and interest of your topic?

• Frame an effective conclusion

Does the conclusion grow out of the major ideas you have discussed in the paper?

Does the conclusion reinforce your main thoughts?

Do you indicate how your findings relate to the findings of previous writers?

Do you suggest possible ways of pursuing the issue in future writing?

Does the conclusion show awareness that your own writing is part of a continuing conversation on the subject?

• Check for coherence

Does the outline reveal a paper that holds together?

Will the final paper make the impact you desire?

Creating the Full Statement: Drafting, Revision, and Final Form

The writing of a research paper employs all the skills discussed in this book, for the research paper is the synthesis of everything you can find from your reading and all the ideas you develop based on that reading. During the period of library research and the preliminary tasks of the proposal and outline, you will come to tentative conclusions. Reaching these early conclusions does not mean that you can put your concentrated thinking to rest and go through a mechanical task of filling in words to fit the outline. Quite to the contrary, all your powers of thought must remain alive until you have created the exact and final words of your message. That struggle to find the right words will lead you to new thoughts about the subject and cause you to reconsider — and perhaps make more precise — many of your earlier conclusions. You never know fully what you will write until you finally write it. The outline can serve only as a partial guide — a stage in your thinking. Even having a complete first draft does not complete the active consideration of your subject, because the refinement of language through revision will lead you to new meanings.

The remaining two chapters of this book, Chapters 9 and 10, are devoted to the thought processes and mechanical skills that come into play during the actual writing and revision of any essay. They apply in the fullest to the research paper. The next few paragraphs introduce the last chapters by presenting a few of the topics — logic, word choice, transitions — that apply in particular to the research paper.

First, because the research paper rests on such a variety of source material and requires such an extended development, the step-by-step organization of your thoughts as they appear in the final paper is exceedingly important. You do not want your reader to get lost in the mass of information or the range of ideas you present. Beyond preventing confusion, you also need the reader to see the issues and subject from the perspective which you have finally reached. The pattern of your organization should reflect some real pattern you have discovered in the material. The orderly arrangement of ideas in a way appropriate to the material is the essence of the broader meaning of logic, as will be discussed on pages 297–303.

Once you have come to an organizational logic for your paper, you need to make that logic explicit for the readers, so that they know what you are trying to do. The longer and more complex the paper is, the more you need transitions — bridging phrases and sentences — in order to show the connection between one idea and the next. The importance of transitional phrases has already been discussed in other chapters that emphasize structure and connections — the summary and the synthesis — and will be discussed further in the next chapter.

Since the reader does not know your earlier thought processes, your final choice of words fixes the meaning that will be conveyed to the reader. Because the statements of the research paper are the results of long work and long thinking, they should be among your most informed and thoughtful statements; naturally you want them to be understood precisely. Since the medium of presentation is words, the clarity of your ideas, the precision of your argument, and the seriousness of your intentions can only be transmitted through your choice of words. The discussion of revision in the next chapter includes more detailed comments on style.

Because the research paper is a structure of your own thought built upon the written statements of others, you need to be aware of the most effective method of presenting the material from each source and the proper ways of giving credit to the sources you use. These skills of referring to sources and documentation are the subject of Chapter 10. The techniques of referring to original sources discussed there will help you use the material to best advantage, while allowing you to develop your own thoughts. The research paper must have, of course, a complete set of footnotes and a bibliography, as described on pages 339–354.

The last stage of preparing your paper for public presentation is the creation of a handsome final manuscript — neatly typed with generous margins. Absolutely essential is a careful proofreading of the final manuscript. These elements of formality and care are in themselves signs that you are making a well-considered public statement on a subject you have wrestled with long in private. Your thoughts deserve the best possible presentation.

Sample Research Paper

Fred Carmino

Writing II

Professor Bars

April 31, 1979

THE VELIKOVSKY PHENOMENON:

The Appeal of <u>Worlds in Collision</u>

Outline

Thesis: Popular attitudes in 1950 about science, religion, scholarship, and impending catastrophe accounted for Velikovsky's original high sales, but the negative scientific reaction changed the nature of the support.

I. Introduction--the problem

  A. Velikovsky's ideas

    1. Summary of theory

    2. Velikovsky's background and approach

  B. Reaction

    1. Scientific rejection

    2. General popularity

  C. Statement of thesis

II. General attitudes toward science

  A. Respect for recent accomplishments

  B. Low level of knowledge and specific interest

    1. Little science education before Sputnik

    2. Science fiction just becoming popular

    C. <u>Worlds in Collision</u> fits situation

       1. Discussed scientific topics in vivid stories

       2. Made large impressive claims

       3. Paralleled growth of science-fiction film

         a. Increase of films since 1950

         b. Films influenced by <u>Worlds in Collision</u>

III. Religious influence

    A. Book explains Biblical events, part of long tra-
dition

    B. Many religious best-sellers

    C. Reviews in religious publications recognized
appeal

  IV. Respect for scholarship

    A. Book shows wide learning

    B. Example of interview impressed with Velikovsky's
scholarship

   V. Fears of catastrophe

    A. World War II, cold war, atomic arms race

    B. Pessimism about catastrophes

       1. Kazin's comments

       2. Qualification

 VI. Effects of criticism by scientists and scholars

    A. Controversy becomes appeal

    B. Eventual discrediting of Velikovsky

    C. Reaction against scientific rejection

       1. Objections

         a. Lack of fair hearing

         b. Attempts at suppression

In 1950 Immanuel Velikovsky published <u>Worlds in Colli-</u><u>sion</u>, a book that presented an astronomical explanation for many of the catastrophic events described in the Old Testament.[1] Velikovsky claimed that the extraordinary events at the time of the Israelites' departure from Egypt and their arrival in the Promised Land were caused by the near collision of the earth and a comet. This comet, he theorized, was a part of Jupiter until it broke away and eventually settled into an orbit to become the planet Venus. Before settling into a planetary orbit, however, the comet so disturbed Mars's orbit that Mars nearly collided with the earth at the time of the founding of Rome.

Despite the broad scientific claims of the book, Immanuel Velikovsky was not trained as an astronomer; his professional training was in medicine and psychiatry.[2] Nor did he present his arguments in a typically scientific way with measurable data and equations; instead he relied on the stories of mythology and sacred books. His discussion of scientific material, such as geological evidence and the motions of planets, was general and descriptive rather than specific and statistical.

Worlds in Collision opens with a direct challenge to "certain notions now regarded as sacred laws in science,"[3] but scientists, by and large, have not taken the challenge seriously. Even before the book's publication, articles in scientific journals denounced the book as "nonsense and rubbish."[4] Throughout the years scientific rejection has been, with very few exceptions, consistent, although in recent years some scientists have felt it necessary to give a more complete and careful analysis of their reasons for rejecting Velikovsky's ideas.

Despite scientific skepticism, Velikovsky found an audience outside the scientific community. Worlds in Collision spent more than six months on the New York Times Book Review best-seller list, with eleven weeks as the leading nonfiction best-seller.[5] Sales of this book and a sequel, Earth in Upheavel, continued throughout the fifties and sixties; both were released in paperback editions in 1977.[6] At least two small magazines, Pensée and Kronos, have published many articles in support of Velikovsky's theory, and several books have appeared in his defense.[7]

Thus, even though few scientists have shown much interest in Velikovsky's ideas, his theory of interplanetary catastrophe has had immediate and continuing popularity among nonscientists. This paper will investigate the source of that immediate popularity and will suggest how that early popularity changed into the later cultlike support. Reasons for the early popularity can be found in public attitudes concerning science, religion, scholarship, and international disaster; all these elements entered into the original response to the book. The totally negative reaction of scientists had, oddly enough, the consequence of turning the early popularity into permanent support.

The end of World War II marked the beginning of the atomic age with the nuclear explosions at Hiroshima and Nagasaki. The power of science must have seemed awesome, for it had unlocked the secret of matter itself to produce energies surpassed only on the sun and other stars. There was talk of nuclear power being used for peaceful purposes, and the bombs produced became larger and larger. At the same time other inventions made possible by science were becoming everyday facts of life: airplanes, television, radar. Science seemed capable of doing anything; the common person was naturally led to respect science.

Even though science was well regarded by the average individual, the general level of specific information and detailed interest was quite low. In America science education for all students did not become a priority until after 1957, when the United States was stirred to competition by the Soviet achievement of orbiting the first artificial satellite, Sputnik.[8] Another indication of the low level of interest in anything scientific was the lack of popularity of science fiction before 1949. Although a few science-fiction magazines were published as early as 1926, not until 1949--with the publication of The Magazine of

Fantasy and Science Fiction and a year later with the publication of Galaxy Magazine--did science fiction truly
begin its rise to its current level of popularity.[9]

Worlds in Collision thus appeared at a time when interest in science was just beginning to awaken in the popular
imagination, but when ignorance of science was still great.
The book played into that awakening but uneducated taste
quite well. It presented claims about an obviously scientific subject--the motions of planets--but stated in a
way most people could understand, through familiar Biblical and mythological stories and by vivid descriptions
of catastropic events, such as in this short excerpt:

> A phenomenon that has not been observed in modern
> times is an electrical discharge between a planet
> and a comet and also between the head of a comet
> and its trailing part.
>
> The events in the sky were viewed by the peo-
> ples of the world as a fight between an evil mon-
> ster in the form of a serpent and the light-god
> who engaged the monster in battle and thus saved
> the world. The tail of the comet, leaping back and
> forth under the discharges of the flaming globe,
> was regarded as a separate body, inimical to the
> globe of the comet.[10]

Velikovsky's claims were broad and astounding, just the
kinds of claims people were coming to expect from science,
for science seemed to be turning common sense on its head.

Turning matter into energy, traveling through the air, seeing pictures transmitted from miles away were the kinds of
extraordinary ideas that science was making commonplace.
The very idea that Velikovsky appeared to challenge major
beliefs was enough to validate his work as science to many
nonscientists. We see this kind of reaction in the review
by Elaine Lambert that appeared in <u>Library Journal</u>:

> These exciting theories challenge Darwin, Newton
> and many modern cosmological tenets. . . . may
> well inspire re-examination of physical and so-
> cial sciences--so sound and stimulating are his
> points and so related to new atomic and universal
> discoveries.[11]

Science to this reviewer seemed to mean revolutionary
theoretical changes.

One can see the growing appeal of such vivid and sci-
entific-seeming claims by examining the feature films of
the period. In 1949 no feature films appeared with a
scientific or futuristic theme, but in 1950 there were
three science fiction films (<u>Rocketship X-M</u>, <u>Destination
Moon</u>, and <u>The Flying Saucer</u>) and three scientific docu-
mentaries (<u>Ivan Pavlov</u>, <u>Secrets of Nature</u>, and <u>The Flying
Missile</u>). In 1951 and 1952, not only did the trend of science and science-fiction movies continue, but also some
films seemed specifically influenced by Velikovsky's book,
probably to capitalize on the book's popularity. <u>The Day
the Earth Stood Still</u> (1951) obviously takes its name from

the events described in <u>Worlds in Collision</u>, even though
the movie plot has little to do with the book. <u>The Man
from Planet X</u> (1951) uses the plot device of a newly formed
planet passing near to the earth. <u>When Worlds Collide</u>
(1952) takes its title and plot from an earlier novel
but so closely resembles Velikovsky's book in many aspects
that it seems a clear case of capitalizing on the popularity of <u>Worlds in Collision</u>.[12]

The advertising for <u>Worlds in Collision</u> played upon
the same themes of fantastic interplanetary events as the
movies. An advertisement in the April 2, 1950, issue of the
<u>New York Times Book Review</u>, for example, shows shooting
stars and lists these questions in bold type:

> Is it true . . .
>> That "the Sun stood still in the midst of
>> heaven"?
>> That Venus and the Earth almost collided?
>> That the Red Sea really parted to let the
>> Israelites pass?[13]

The advertisement not only raises the possibility of
incredible events but also suggests that the presentation of Velikovsky's ideas is a major event in scientific
history--equivalent to the revolutionary ideas of Darwin
and Einstein. To sell the book, the advertisement plays
upon the idea that science deals with extraordinary events
and presents revolutionary claims. Even though many
recognized scientists reject Velikovsky, he is made to

appear to the general reader as the essence of a true
scientist.

The advertisement also makes an appeal to religious
feeling through the quotation from the Bible about the sun
standing still and through reference to the parting of the
Red Sea. Since modern science began, some people have
continually tried to show that its findings confirm the
events described in the Bible. Velikovsky's argument
certainly fits in with this tradition since he explains
not only the parting of the Red Sea but also the plagues
of Egypt, the manna that fell from heaven, and the
earthshaking events described by the prophets. Books on
religious themes were popular when <u>Worlds in Collision</u> was
published. In 1949, for example, best-sellers included
these nonfiction religious books: <u>The Greatest Story Ever</u>
<u>Told</u> by Fulton Oursler, <u>The Seven Storey Mountain</u> by
Thomas Merton, <u>A Guide to Confident Living</u> by Norman
Vincent Peale, and <u>The Peace of Saul</u> by Fulton J. Sheen.
Several of the works of fiction also had a religious theme,
such as <u>The Big Fisherman</u> by Lloyd Douglas.[14]

Because of the religious interest, <u>Worlds in Collision</u>
was reviewed in several Christian periodicals: <u>The</u>
<u>Christian Science Monitor</u>, <u>Christian Century</u>, and <u>The</u>
<u>Catholic World</u>.[15] Although the reviewers were critical of
his theology, they did recognize that some religious be-
lievers would turn to Velikovsky for confirmation of the
Bible. As W. E. Garrison comments in the <u>Christian Century</u>,
"Some religious conservatives have gone into spasms of
delight over this reinforcement of their position."[16]

Not only did Velikovsky appear to be a true scientist to some and a confirmer of the faith to others, but also he appeared to many as the ideal of humanistic scholarship. Worlds in Collision made evident his wide learning in all the mythologies and ancient writings of the world. The popular respect for Velikovsky's scholarship is shown in an interview by Harvey Breit, which appeared in the New York Times Book Review. Harvey Breit admires Velikovsky's far-ranging intellectual experience--from the study of econ-omy, law, and history in Moscow to the study of medicine in Germany and psychiatry in Palestine. The interview paints a picture of an impressive scholar, having "a strong-boned face that has a touch of a student's pallor."[17] The inter-viewer seems particularly impressed with Velikovsky's insistence that the publisher place footnotes on the page rather than at the ends of chapters. The article ends with a discussion of intellectual courage. Curiously, this praise-filled interview appears in the same issue as a scathing review of the book. While Breit was showing such respect for the superficial appearance of scholarship, Waldemar Kaempffert was asking on his front-page review of Worlds in Collision "if this quasi-erudite outpouring is not an elaborate hoax."[18]

Beyond these three roles--scientist, defender of the faith, and scholar--that would lead ordinary people to look up to Velikovsky, there was another reason his book ap-pealed to Americans in 1950: a general anxiety about plane-tary catastrophe was somehow the mood of the time, and this anxiety may have generated interest in his ideas. Americans

had just experienced the terrible destruction of World War
II; they were newly involved in a cold war and atomic arms
race; and they were living under the fear of atomic war-
fare. The thought of atomic bombs destroying the world may
have led to a kind of pessimism about catastrophes; it
would therefore not be too far-fetched to imagine earlier
periods of great destruction. Alfred Kazin discusses this
mood in a review appearing in the <u>New Yorker</u>:

> The one point his book makes is that the primary
> events in history are global catastrophes and
> cataclysms, that man is always on the brink of
> universal destruction, and that the most he can
> be is a recording agent of these prodigious
> calamities. Hence, nothing in the whole human
> record is significant except as it reflects the
> power of great outside forces to clean us out. And
> this is just what many people do think today; it
> plays right into the small talk about universal
> destruction that is all around us now . . .
>
> The scare warnings . . . play upon our super-
> ficial pessimism and our passivity; they make
> it easier for us not to feel individual respon-
> sibility about anything.[19]

Kazin sees people adopting Velikovsky's vision of human
powerlessness just because they do not want to face up to
the difficulty of acting to improve the terrible situation;
it is easier to accept the role of victim of large uncon-

trollable forces. Whether or not Kazin's extreme conclusions are warranted, there certainly seems some connection
between fear of atomic catastrophe and the story of another
ancient catastrophe. The same fears of catastrophe are frequently thought to lie behind the science-fiction disaster
movies of the fifties, and we have already seen how the
themes of Worlds in Collision were picked up by the movies.

   The strong negative reaction from scientific and scholarly reviewers eventually did undercut the popular impression that Velikovsky was a true scientist and scholar--
but not until after Worlds in Collision had topped the best-
seller lists for many weeks. For a period, the controversy
became the book's main selling point. As the advertisement
of April 23 said, it was "the book everyone is talking
about."[20] But the follow-up books--the first volume of Ages
in Chaos (1952) and Earth in Upheaval (1955)--were not
reviewed widely, received only negative comment, and did
not make the best-seller list. The controversy seemed to be
settled on the side of the scientific establishment. Even
during the few months it took for Worlds in Collision to
appear on the other side of the Atlantic, it had become
little more than the butt of some mildly sneering British
humor in a review in the London Times Literary Supplement.[21] From the British perspective, the book did not seem
to be raising any serious issues for anyone.

   The scientific rejection of Velikovsky in the United
States, however, was so total and so heavy-handed that a
few brave people continued to support his cause. These
supporters were not sure Velikovsky was right, but they

objected to the way he was being treated. They objected to
the pressure some scientists put on the first publisher,
Macmillan, to make the company drop the book, and they
objected to his scientific opponents not bothering to
explain their negative views carefully.[22] In particular,
Eric Larrabee, an editor at Harper's, kept insisting on
Velikovsky's right to a fair hearing and civilized
treatment. As Larrabee wrote in a letter to Scientific
American (May 1956), the issue had changed from the
correctness or incorrectness of Velikovsky's ideas to
a question of intellectual treatment:

> The question at issue is how to handle icono-
> clasm--how the iconoclast is to behave, how those
> confronted with him are to behave. As one who
> has participated in this affair from an early
> stage, I am of the opinion that Dr. Velikovsky has
> behaved better than his detractors.[23]

Larrabee wrote similar comments on a number of other occasions.[24] To at least a few supporters, Velikovsky remained
someone worthy of serious scholarly consideration--at
least until he was given a full hearing.

When the space probes of the late 1950s and early 1960s
coincided with a few of Velikovsky's predictions (about
radiation belts around the earth and Jupiter and about
the temperature of Venus), the feeling grew that Velikovsky deserved a more careful and complete hearing by the

scientific community. The astronomer Lloyd Motz and the physicist V. Bargmann wrote a letter to <u>Science</u> in 1962 urging that, even though they "disagree with Velikovsky's theories . . . his other conclusions [should] be objectively reexamined."[25] Still, most of the scientific establishment remained totally set against treating Velikovsky with any seriousness. <u>Science</u> printed another letter in reply to the Motz-Bargmann suggestion, simply mocking the idea that Velikovsky could be taken seriously.[26]

As the counterculture of the 1960s developed its distrust of any establishment figures, Velikovsky became a likely hero. He appeared to be a person who was discriminated against by the scientific establishment but one who still continued to press his views. Velikovsky came to represent a challenge to authority and orthodox belief. As an apparent threat to the establishment--a threat that the establishment tried to suppress--Velikovsky came to symbolize to members of the counterculture the limitless possibilities of the world that the establishment was trying to close off and make narrow. Gradually Velikovsky regained some of the luster as scholar and scientist that he had attained before <u>Worlds in Collision</u> was so heavily criticized. But now he had the added appeal of the challenger and the prophet, who was trying to make the closed establishment hear his message. Further research is required on the subject of this later support for Velikovsky.[27] This counterculture support finally forced the scientific community to provide a fuller hearing on Velikovsky's work;

in 1974 a debate was held at the Conference of the Ameri-

can Academy for the Advancement of Science.[28]

Despite the strong scientific and scholarly arguments

made against Velikovsky at that conference, he still

remains a figure commanding some popular respect, and his

books keep selling. The New York Times recently ran an

interview with the eighty-three-year-old writer. The inter-

viewer presented him as a quiet, scholarly man, still deep

in his studies, and still the focal point for supporters

who "rally round his books, asking him for the latest,

writing long letters and cheering him on."[29] Over the last

three years, the final three volumes of his Ages in Chaos

series have been published, and the string of pamphlets

and magazines from small presses in support of him keep

appearing.[30]

The man who began as the popular reader's idea of the

bold scientist in 1950 remains that for many readers to-

day--despite years of rejection by reputed scientists and

scholars. His support, if anything, has become more intense

the more vehemently he is rejected by scientists. Perhaps

the only conclusion to be drawn is that what scientists

consider valid science is very different from what the

general public thinks of as science. The gap between the

two ideas of scientific thinking may be very large.

Notes

[1]Immanuel Velikovsky, Worlds in Collision (New York:

Macmillan, 1950). After pressure from some scientists, the

book was transferred from Macmillan to Doubleday, which had no scholarly or textbook publications.

[2]David Stove, "The Scientific Mafia," in <u>Velikovsky Reconsidered</u>, ed. by the editors of <u>Pensée</u>. (New York: Doubleday, 1976), p. 6.

[3]Velikovsky, <u>Worlds</u>, p. 5.

[4]"Theories Denounced," <u>Science News Letter</u>, 25 February 1950, p. 119.

[5]<u>New York Times Book Review</u>, April-November, 1950.

[6]Immanuel Velikovsky, <u>Earth in Upheaval</u> (1955; rpt. New York: Dell, 1977).

[7]Most of the items in support of Velikovsky are published by small presses, but two books that have been released by major publishers are <u>Velikovsky Reconsidered</u> and C. J. Ransom, <u>The Age of Velikovsky</u> (New York: Delta, 1976).

[8]Robert H. Kargon, ed., <u>The Maturing of American Science</u> (Washington, D.C.: American Association for the Advancement of Science, 1974), p. 101.

[9]Anthony Boucher, "The Publishing of Science Fiction," in <u>Modern Science Fiction</u>, ed. Reginald Bretnor (New York: Coward, McCann & Geoghegan, 1953), p. 30-34.

[10]Velikovsky, <u>Worlds</u>, p. 78.

[11]Elaine Lambert, rev. of <u>Worlds in Collision</u>, <u>Library Journal</u>, April 1950, p. 559.

[12]<u>New York Times Film Reviews: 1949-1958</u> (New York: Arno Press, 1970).

[13]<u>New York Times Book Review</u>, 2 April 1950, p. 14.

[14]Harry Hansen, ed., <u>World Almanac and Book of Facts</u> <u>for 1950</u> (New York: N.Y. World Telegram, 1950), p. 909.

[15]R. C. Cowen, rev. of <u>Worlds in Collision</u>, <u>Christian</u> <u>Science Monitor</u>, 15 April 1950, p. 14; W. E. Garrison, rev. of <u>Worlds in Collision</u>, <u>Christian Century</u>, 7 June 1950, pp. 703-704; Ben Hunt, rev. of <u>Worlds in Collision</u>, <u>Catholic</u> <u>World</u>, September 1950, p. 476.

[16]Garrison, p. 704.

[17]Harvey Breit, "Talk with Mr. Velikovsky," <u>New York</u> <u>Times Book Review</u>, 2 April 1950, p. 12.

[18]Waldemar Kaempffert, rev. of <u>Worlds in Collision</u>, <u>New York Times Book Review</u>, 2 April 1950, p. 1.

[19]Alfred Kazin, "On the Brink," rev. of <u>Worlds in</u> <u>Collision</u>, <u>New Yorker</u>, 29 April 1950, pp. 104-105.

[20]<u>New York Times Book Review</u>, 23 April 1950, p. 14.

[21]"Scientific Speculation," rev. of <u>Worlds in</u> <u>Collision</u>, <u>Times Literary Supplement</u>, 22 September 1950, p. 591.

[22]The behavior of the scientific community is described at length in Alfred de Grazia, ed., <u>The</u> <u>Velikovsky Affair</u> (New Hyde Park, N.Y.: University Books, 1966). The incident is analyzed in Norman Storer, "The Sociological Context of the Velikovsky Controversy" in <u>Scientists Confront Velikovsky</u> (Ithaca, Cornell Univ. Press, 1977).

[23]Eric Larrabee, "Reply," <u>Scientific American</u>, May 1956, p. 12.

[24]See also <u>Science</u>, 7 August 1953, p. 167, and <u>Har-</u> <u>per's</u>, August 1963, pp. 48-50.

[25]Lloyd Motz and V. Bargmann, "On the Recent Discoveries Concerning Jupiter and Venus," <u>Science</u>, 21 Decem—
ber 1962, p. 1352.

[26]Paul Anderson, "Reply," <u>Science</u>, 15 February 1963,
p. 670.

[27]The key documents for this analysis are the two
books listed in note 8 and the issues of <u>Kronos</u> from
January 1976 to Summer 1978, published at Glassboro State
College, Glassboro, N.J.

[28]Excerpts of the proceedings were published in <u>The
Humanist</u>, November-December 1977. For an expanded version,
see Donald Goldsmith, ed., <u>Scientists Confront Velikovsky</u>
(Ithaca: Cornell Univ. Press, 1977). Although Velikovsky
did participate in the conference, he refused to let his
remarks be published in either of the documents.

[29]Francis X. Clines, "Velikovsky, The Venus Probe and
Ideas in Collision," <u>New York Times</u>, 1 March 1979, p. B1.

[30]Vol. II. <u>The Age of Homer and Isaiah</u> (New York: Dou-
bleday, 1979); Vol. III. <u>Ramses II and His Time</u> (New York:
Doubleday, 1978); Vol. IV. <u>Peoples of the Sea</u> (New York:
Doubleday, 1977); a recent addition to the small press
pamphlets is Shane Mage, <u>Velikovsky and His Critics</u> (Grand
Haven, Mich.: Cornelius Press, 1978).

Bibliography -- Works Cited

Anderson, Paul. "Reply." <u>Science</u>, 15 February 1963, p. 670.
Boucher, Anthony. "The Publishing of Science Fiction." In
     <u>Modern Science Fiction</u>. Ed. Reginald Bretnor, New
     York: Coward, McCann & Geoghegan, 1953, pp. 23-45.

Breit, Harvey. "Talk with Mr. Velikovsky." <u>New York Times</u>
     <u>Book Review</u>, 2 April 1950, p. 12.

Clines, Francis X. "Velikovsky, The Venus Probe and Ideas
     in Collision." <u>New York Times</u>, 1 March 1979, p. B1.

de Grazia, Alfred, ed. <u>The Velikovsky Affair</u>. New Hyde
     Park, N.Y.: University Books, 1966.

Garrison, W. E. Rev. of <u>Worlds in Collision</u>. <u>Christian</u>
     <u>Century</u>, 7 June 1950, pp. 703-704.

Goldsmith, Donald, ed. <u>Scientists Confront Velikovsky</u>.
     Ithaca: Cornell Univ. Press, 1977. Originally pub-
     lished in shorter form in <u>The Humanist</u>, November-
     December 1977.

Hansen, Harry, ed. <u>The World Almanac and Book of Facts</u>
     <u>for 1950</u>. New York: N.Y. World Telegram, 1950.

Hunt, Ben. Rev. of <u>Worlds in Collision</u>. <u>Catholic World</u>,
     September 1950, p. 476.

Kaempffert, Waldemar. Rev. of <u>Worlds in Collision</u>. <u>New</u>
     <u>York Times Book Review</u>, 2 April 1950, p. 1.

Kargon, Robert H., ed. <u>The Maturing of American Science</u>.
     Washington, D.C.: American Academy for the Advancement
     of Science, 1974.

Kazin, Alfred. "On the Brink." Rev. of <u>Worlds in Col-</u>
     <u>lision</u>. <u>New Yorker</u>, 29 April 1950, pp. 103-105.

<u>Kronos</u>, January 1976-Summer 1978.

Lambert, Elaine. Rev. of <u>Worlds in Collision</u>. <u>Library</u>
     <u>Journal</u>, April 1950, p. 559.

Larrabee, Eric. "Letter." <u>Science</u>, 7 August 1953,
     p. 167.

----------. "Reply." <u>Scientific American</u>, May 1956, p. 12.

----------. "Scientists in Collision." Harper's, August 1963,
     pp. 48-50.

Mage, Shane. Velikovsky and His Critics. Grand Haven,
     Mich: Cornelius Press, 1978.

Motz, Lloyd, and V. Bargmann. "On the Recent Discoveries
     Concerning Jupiter and Venus." Science, 21 December
     1962, pp. 1350-1352.

New York Times Book Review, April-November 1950.

New York Times Film Reviews: 1949-1958. New York: Arno
     Press, 1970.

Pensée, May 1972-Winter 1974. Available from Student Aca-
     demic Freedom Forum, P.O. Box 414, Portland, Oregon.

Pensée, editors. Velikovsky Reconsidered. New York:
     Doubleday, 1976.

Ransom, C. J. The Age of Velikovsky. New York: Delta, 1976.

"Scientific Speculation." Rev. of Worlds in Collision.
     Times Literary Supplement, 22 September 1950, p. 591.

"Theories Denounced." Science News Letter, 25 February
     1950, p. 119.

Velikovsky, Immanuel. Ages In Chaos. 4 vols. New York:
     Doubleday, 1952-1979. Vol. I. From the Exodus to King
     Akhnaton, 1952; Vol. II. The Age of Homer and Isaiah,
     1979; Vol. III. Ramses II and His Time, 1978; Vol. IV.
     Peoples of the Sea, 1977.

----------. Earth in Upheaval. New York: Doubleday, 1955.

----------. Worlds in Collision. New York: Macmillan, 1950.

Writing Assignment

1. Write a research paper of 2,500 to 3,000 words (approximately ten typed pages, double-spaced); include notes and bibliography. The audience for the paper will be the other students in your class, who will be researching related topics. The teacher may present you with a list of specific topics or may ask you to develop an original paper from one of the following:

a. The class will be asked to investigate a specific year; members of the class will first gather background material, perhaps by each student writing a synthesis of events for a week of the year selected (see pages 212–221). Each student will then pick an event, person, or issue in that year to investigate further. The scope of the final paper need not be limited to the original year but may trace the topic back or forward in time — as appropriate.

b. Each student will choose a local public or private agency, corporation, or other institution to explore, such as a local plastics company or day-care center. After gaining some background about similar institutions (for example, the development of the plastics industry or recent legislation affecting day-care programs), you should gather specific information about your chosen institution and then contact the institution directly to see whether you can obtain an interview or any additional information. For the final paper you may focus on any issue, process, or problem that you may discover in the institution.

c. Interview a person who has spent time in another region or country. Find out if he or she has observed customs, attitudes, or ways of life significantly different from those where you live. Choose one of these differences to explore in your research.

Near the beginning of your research, you should submit to the teacher a short statement (one or two sentences) defining your intended research area. Midway through your research, after your topic has become focused, submit a formal review of the literature (of three hundred to five hundred words) and a formal proposal (of at least two hundred words). Before you begin writing the rough draft, the teacher may also wish to see your research notes and outline.

III
The Craft of Writing

9

Writing Techniques: Process and Patience

Preview

Writing is a process with many parts. Not only does the overall process of learning to write take time but also each individual paper takes time to develop and perfect. Many steps lie between the first idea and the finished writing. The previous chapters of this book have concentrated on the preliminary steps of gathering and evaluating information, thinking through responses, developing ideas, and organizing the ideas into an orderly framework. This chapter concentrates on the later steps of putting words together to make an effective statement. Drafts and revisions will help you focus attention on one writing task at a time.

Writing Takes Time

No one is born an accomplished writer. Beginning with the time you first learn to identify the letters of the alphabet and your fingers gain the muscular control necessary to write by scribbling, you learn to write in many stages — each stage adding new layers of complexity and control. The advanced skills of consciously integrating reading and writing, which you are asked to do in this book, rely on a wide base of previously acquired skills. Greater mastery of skills does not necessarily make writing easier, but it does allow you to write at a more advanced level and have more control over what you write. The more you become aware of the resources of language and the possibility of greater control, the more success you can have writing: expressing yourself — joining the conversation — can become a source of great pleasure.

In one way, the task of writing at your best level is an endless struggle; even a professional writer can never look forward to a golden day when writing no longer takes great effort. On the other hand, at any stage of your writing development, you can only write as well as you can write. If you work hard, spend reasonable time, and apply intelligence to any writing task, you need not berate yourself for not meeting your perhaps too high standards. Nor need you despair because the words and thoughts are not totally under your control. You should do the best you can, and a few years from now you will do better.

You must realize by now that the process of learning to write is a long one; so is the process of writing any individual piece. Few essays pop into a writer's head fully developed, word for word, as they appear in the final paper. Unlike speech, which often seems to flow spontaneously and where the first thought is rarely far from public utterance, writing needs time, thought, and many conscious choices to move from your first conception to a public document. Writing can be extremely frustrating as you try to turn vague ideas into a full statement that will mean what you want it to mean to the reader. Because you do not start out with anything that resembles a completed statement, you may doubt that you have anything to say, but you will find that you are frequently mistaken. If you gather the courage to put down your beginning thoughts and if you have the patience to work through the many stages of developing these thoughts, that vague beginning will lead to a precise and full final statement. You may also mistakenly assume that your first thoughts are adequate for the final statement that will communicate with and convince your reader. Good writing requires you to apply yourself on many levels.

> **Each writing task is an individual problem, and the final piece of writing is your solution to the problem. Unlike a math problem, many solutions are possible and acceptable. No one knows what your essay will be like until you create it. It is in the process of developing and revising your writing that you invent a new solution.**

If you neglect any of these levels, you may find that you are communicating less than you thought you were.

It is fortunate that writing is something of a private act, even though its goal is public communication. You can think about your writing for a while, correct it, revise it, and put it through several stages. You may show early versions of your writing to friends and advisers for help, but in the end only the final version is the one that counts. Not only can you use the earlier versions of your writing to develop and clarify your meaning gradually, but also you can experiment in the early drafts, trying out ideas, organizations, and various ways of constructing sentences to find the most effective one. If the experiment fails, you can always rework the passage before you reach the final version.

Each writing task is an individual problem, and the final version is your solution to the problem. Unlike a math problem, many solutions are possible and acceptable. No one knows what your essay will be like until you create it: it is in the process of developing and revising your writing that you invent a new solution. It is only by tackling new writing problems resourcefully and by developing new solutions to these new problems that your skill as a writer will grow.

Drafting

Drafting — writing an essay in several versions, each time limiting your attention to only a few factors — is necessary for good writing because writing is both a complex competence and a demanding art. You have by now acquired many skills that go into writing, from the mechanics of spelling to the formal rules of grammar to the strategic use of examples — to the logical organization of the entire paper. Even if some of these skills are second nature to you, it is quite difficult to keep them all in mind simultaneously while you are trying to write. Even a professional juggler can keep only a limited number of objects in the air at one time. Even if you could pay full attention to all the skills at once, that effort would leave you very little mental room to devote to the actual subject of the writing — your individual ideas on a topic and the invention of new ways of developing your topic. The more you can totally devote your mind to each of these tasks, one at a time, the more you are likely to discover a good solution to each. Your writing will develop most efficiently if you limit yourself to one problem at each stage, starting with the basic issue of developing ideas and working through to the final task of neat typing according to conventional formats.

The techniques of gathering notes, developing ideas, and organizing an outline, techniques presented throughout this book, are frequently classified as prewriting activities, but they are, in a very real sense, early *writing* activities, because you are already shaping what you read, see, and think into written words. These early written materials may even be thought of as fragmentary rough drafts because they will become the substance of the final paper after they are transformed into more polished drafts. The previous chapters of this book have offered extensive advice on these early stages of writing. The remainder of this chapter will discuss the later, more polished drafts that you will work toward, after you have developed your initial ideas and approximate organization. These later stages of developing a full written statement consist of

1. fleshing out the thoughts in words
2. tightening the relationships between statements
3. defining the relationship to the audience
4. sharpening the language
5. satisfying the formalities of public presentation

One additional stage occurs after you are finished with the writing, but it is as much part of the writing process as the earlier stages:

6. dealing with response to your writing

The actual separation of these stages into drafts — and revisions of these drafts — will vary depending on the kind of writing you are doing, its difficulty, your own skills, and your preferences and habits. In actual practice the stages often overlap. No matter how your own drafting methods vary from the idealized stages presented here, you should follow the general pattern of working on the deeper structural issues first — your ideas and their organization — and moving gradually toward the more surface issues, such as polishing the language.

The First Full Draft: Fleshing Out Thoughts in Words

No matter how complete and formal, an outline can only provide a loose scheme for your writing — an anticipated order of major and subordinate thoughts. Only when you turn the approximate plans of an outline into a continuous and complete first draft will you discover all that you want to say on the subject. Only then will you need to clarify the precise relationship of all the parts to the whole; only then can you judge the appropriateness of your specific examples for illustrating the points you wish to make.

In writing the first complete draft, the most important consideration is to create a continuous line of words — a thread of argument that covers all you feel must be said on the subject. This first full draft may be ungrammatical, inelegant, redundant, even a bit obscure, because you should concentrate mainly on setting down on paper everything you have to say on the subject. This objective will be met if you follow these three guidelines:

• Be as complete as possible. Don't worry about being too long, overly explicit, or repetitious. Write something as many times and in as many ways as you need to until you feel you have stated it correctly. You can always choose the best of these options later and cut out the excess at that point. Right now, you just need to make sure you have a full set of words to work with later. If you try to be complete in the first draft, you won't have to worry later that you have left something important out.

• Try to support every generalization through detailed examples and make sure that each specific detail is closely related to a general statement of the paper. Specific examples help tie down the meaning of your generalizations, helping both you and your reader see exactly what you have in mind. This procedure will not only help you bring out your ideas more sharply but also will force you to look more carefully at those ideas you have only vaguely formulated. Conversely, by making sure every specific is related to a generalization, you will make certain that your paper never loses its point. Details can sometimes be so all-consuming in themselves that they may cause you to forget the main direction of the paper. Generalizations give meaning to the specifics. Again, don't worry about too many examples and too much explicit explanation making your paper repetitious; you can always eliminate the excess in later drafts.

• Pay attention to step-by-step continuity. Justify to yourself why one point should follow another. Decide how each individual piece fits in with the overall design. Then bring out the connections between points as explicitly as possible by using transitional words or phrases, by referring back to other related points, or by repeating the main points of the argument. Don't worry if these connecting devices seem obvious, self-evident, or cumbersome; you can always either delete them or make them less obtrusive later.

Logic: Tightening the Relationships Between Statements

The continuity of your essay should be more than the connections of a kite's tail, where one scrap of cloth is tied to another unmatched scrap of cloth to form a long chain held together only by bulky knots. The statements of your essay should bear important structural relationships to one another — more like the parts of the well-defined body of a kite than the scraps of its haphazard, trailing tail. The study of the relationship of statements is *logic* in its broadest sense, and the logic of an essay is the way in which its parts fit together.

There are many different kinds of logic — many different rationales for drawing statements together in a coherent essay. Each of these logics is an entire study in itself, far beyond the scope of this book. One type, formal logic, you may have studied in school; another type, associative logic, you may have seen incorporated into some of your reading; you may have acquired a practical understanding of transactional logic from your daily interactions with other people. Obviously, the more you know about each type of logic, the more effectively you can use and control logical statements in your writing.

In revising your first draft, you must recognize what kind of logic is most applicable to the kind of writing you are doing, and then you must attempt to bring out that logic sharply and consistently throughout the piece of writing. That is, you must choose the most appropriate kind of logic, adhere to it throughout the piece (unless you have a strong rationale for shifting), and finally let the reader know exactly what connections are being made and why.

Formal Logic

Formal logic (or *deductive logic*) is governed by a set of rules that define what conclusions follow precisely from a given set of propositions. In their most familiar form, deductive arguments appear as *syllogisms* or a series of *premises* and a *conclusion* that follows from the premises, as in this example:

> No human being has feathers.
> Johnson is a human being.
> Therefore, Johnson does not have feathers.

Actually, there are four types of deductive arguments. The above example is called a *categorical argument* (where the conclusion is based on the general category to which the specific example belongs). The next example is a *hypothetical argument* (in which the conclusion depends on some hypothetical condition being true):

> If gas supplies are short, gas prices will rise.
> Gas supplies are short.
> Therefore, gas prices will rise.

The third type is the *alternative argument* (which is based on the elimination of a limited number of possible alternatives):

> Either Jones is evil or he is stupid.
> Jones is not stupid.
> Therefore, Jones is evil.

The final type of deductive argument is the *disjunctive argument* (where a situation is shown to be impossible):

> A person cannot be in two places at one time.
> Lucretia was in Washington last Saturday evening at 10 P.M.
> She was not in Boston last Saturday evening at 10 P.M.

Such syllogistic logic serves very well for determining all that can be properly inferred from a given set of *propositions,* or first statements. In abstract fields of study, such as mathematics and formal logic itself, chains of syllogistic logic can produce complex conclusions of great certainty. Deduction plays a role in most areas of study.

However, formal logic does not help you in judging the truth of first propositions nor in making statements beyond those things implicit in the first propositions. That is, formal logic will not help you prove whether, indeed, human beings do or do not have feathers or whether Johnson is the name someone has given to a pet parakeet. Moreover, such a set of propositions will not help you discover why human beings do not have feathers. Formal logic does not, in reality, cover most arguments and questions and statements people actually are interested in making. In practice, formal logic at most tells you what you cannot do — what is a breach of basic ground rules of rational argument — rather than what you should do.

Further, there are dangers in relying too heavily on deductive logic in any but the most abstract disciplines. Although some mathematical propositions — such as *parallel lines never meet* — are true by definition, most propositions about actual things in the world are only simplifications and approximations, such as *politicians must pay attention to the interests of their constituents if they hope to be re-elected.* The specifics of any situation referred to by this general statement are much more complex than the general words indicate; for example, the politician's constituency may include many conflicting interests. Even in such an abstract field as theoretical physics, the basic propositions of Newtonian mechanics were found to be only approximations that did not apply under extreme conditions, such as speeds approaching the speed of light. Even Einstein's revisions of the propositions of mechanics are held by many physicists to be still only simplifications and approximations. Now if you take these approximate statements and combine them with other approximate statements and run them all through many deductive operations, the possible errors will add up — so that you may wind up with conclusions that are not at all reasonable. Thus you should not try to deduce too much from simplified statements about the world.

Inductive Logic

Inductive logic is reasoning from observed events rather than from abstract propositions and is, consequently, the main logic of experimental science. The principle of induction is that if, every time you observe a particular thing, you notice that it behaves in a certain way, then after many such observations, you can assume that the next time it will behave the same as before. That is, if you have seen Johnson many times and never once was he growing feathers, you can assume that the next time you see him he still will not be growing feathers. In even more general terms, if Johnson is a human being and if you have never observed any human being growing feathers, you can assume — even before seeing this particular human called Johnson — that he is not growing feathers. The limitation of induction is that Johnson may be a freak of nature, but given all the accumulated observations of science on this subject, such an aberration is extremely unlikely. Induction is very useful for developing generalized descriptions of repeating and patterned events. Induction keeps your attention on the actual shared characteristics of phenomena. If, however, you are describing random, unpatterned, or unique events, induction is useless, if not misleading. Further, induction, by itself, leaves you close to the surface of things as they appear and may not be appropriate for inquiry into deeper causes or meanings.

Analogical Reasoning

Analogical reasoning is the drawing of conclusions on the basis of the similarity between two things. It is a way of applying what you know about one thing to another. Thus, if you notice that a corporation is in some ways organized like a sports team, you may be able to understand some of the more confusing aspects of the company's organizational structure through the more clear-cut sports example. All analogies, however, are imperfect: a corporation is not a sports team, and the two differ in significant aspects. Thus you should be precise on exactly what the similarities are, and you should limit the conclusions you can draw from the similarities. Analogies may be useful as an early stage to help you gain an understanding of an unfamiliar subject; you can find your bearings by making comparisons to things you already know. However, an argument based purely on analogy is weak, for it does not establish the distinctiveness of the new subject under investigation. Analogies, therefore, are best used only to introduce your readers to a topic with which they are unfamiliar; since you would by then already know the subject quite well, you would know just how far you should legitimately extend the analogy.

Ordinary Argumentation

Ordinary argumentation, according to philosopher Stephen Toulmin, follows none of the patterns already described but rather draws conclusions from given data by means of *warrants*, which act as bridges between data and conclusions. For example, starting with the data that Marianne Hodge has made *A*'s throughout the semester in her writing course, we make the usual conclusion that she will receive an *A* as the course grade. The warrant that allows us to go from data to conclusion is that students who receive *A*'s all semester long receive a final grade of *A*. If we were pressed to give *backing* for this warrant, we might further say that the final grade in this particular course is based on a straight average of all grades for the semester, except for special circumstances that do not occur more than one time in a hundred. The last phrase "except for . . . " gives the necessary qualification to the conclusion. Schematically, the argument would appear as follows:

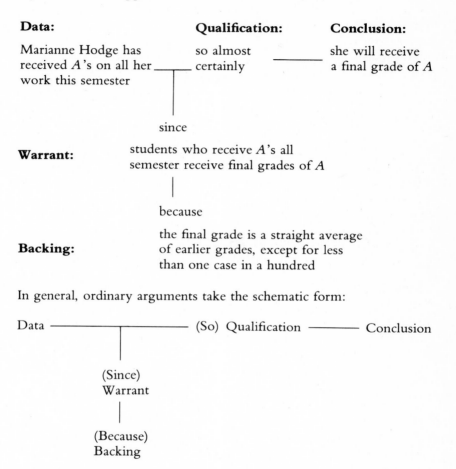

Data: **Qualification:**   **Conclusion:**

Marianne Hodge has   so almost   she will receive
received *A*'s on all her _____ certainly _____   a final grade of *A*
work this semester

since

Warrant: students who receive *A*'s all
                        semester receive final grades of *A*

because

Backing: the final grade is a straight average
                        of earlier grades, except for less
                        than one case in a hundred

In general, ordinary arguments take the schematic form:

Data ——————————— (So) Qualification ——————— Conclusion

(Since)
Warrant

(Because)
Backing

In trying to convince someone of an argument, you must have warrant and backing for your argument that your particular audience finds acceptable. If, for example, a student believes that Professor Jones assigns final grades by randomly pulling grades from a fishbowl and not by taking an average of the grades, our warrant and the conclusion that follows will not be convincing to that student. In writing arguments for any of the academic disciplines, you must therefore use warrants and backings accepted as valid and relevant by the appropriate discipline.

Persuasive Logics

At times your purpose may not be to convince the reader through reason. Instead you may want to persuade your readers through appeals to their emotions, beliefs, or interests. The *logic of persuasion* requires you to consider what moves the reader and then build your argument around that. The order and relationship of the statements in such a persuasive essay will be based on getting the reader more and more involved with your side of the issue — rather than on laying out an impersonal argument. This kind of persuasion is useful when you want others to act with you or support your cause, provided it is not important that you achieve intellectual agreement. However, since most academic writing presumably aims at intellectual agreement, you would be unwise to write your next paper in economics as an appeal to your professor's emotions.

In one academic situation, it may make sense to pay some attention to the attitudes of your readers. If you foresee that your readers may be so set against your ideas that they will not see your point or pay attention to your arguments, you might first try to establish some common ground of agreement with them. You should try to imagine how they will receive your ideas; put yourself in their position. Then state the ways in which you agree with them. In this way a sense of trust and communication will be established before you try to convince them of more controversial matters. This attempt to remove threat and hostility from communication is the essence of *transactional logic*, as presented by the psychologist Carl Rogers.[1]

Other Logics

At other times, you may not be attempting to convince your reader of anything. You may instead be presenting a set of feelings or a state of mind, perhaps yours or perhaps another individual's. You may, for example, be trying to re-create for a history paper how an eighteenth-century Englishman would have responded to news of the rebellious colonialists in America. Here you would have to pay some attention to the *logic of emotions*.

In writing a narrative of the growth of the French-speaking separatist movement in Quebec, you would have to pay attention to the *logic of*

[1]Carl Rogers, "Communication: Its Blocking and Facilitation" in Richard Young, Alton Becker, and Kenneth Pike, *Rhetoric: Discovery and Change* (New York: Harcourt Brace Jovanovich, 1970), pp. 284–289.

events, the *logic of group dynamics,* and the *logic of nationalist sentiment.* Indeed, the connection and sequence of statements in your own paper may necessarily follow these logics rather than more traditional logics discussed earlier. One may even speak of something as strange as *dream logic* where events, disordered by waking standards, perhaps make sense in some deep symbolic way. If your psychology teacher or perhaps your creative writing teacher asks you to keep a record of your dreams, your writing will have to reflect dream logic.

If you are writing an informal essay where you are speculating on connections between ideas, events, and feelings, the relationship of statements may follow only an *associational logic.* For this type of essay, you will only have to show that there is some tangential connection between two statements — but not necessarily an ironclad structural link. If you are interpreting a piece of writing, *interpretive logic* demands that you explain explicitly the structure and meaning of each part of the original.

Different kinds of essays call for different kinds of logic. In each case you must decide which is the appropriate form of logic to connect and integrate all your statements into a whole. When you revise for logic, you must then clarify and bring out the specific type so that your readers will know which of these many forms of logic governs your thinking. The most exquisite logic in the world will remain unconvincing unless your readers can follow it.

Defining Your Relationship to the Audience

The audience — the ultimate readers of your writing — should be kept clearly in mind throughout the writing process, for without an audience to communicate with, you would have little motivation even to start to imagine writing. Moreover, your reasons for communicating with a particular audience should shape the piece of writing as it develops. In revision, however, you need to consciously define your relationship to the audience so that you can rework your paper to have maximum effect on your readers. Not only for persuasive writing but for all writing, the more you know of your readers' attitudes, dispositions, and knowledge, the more effectively you will be able to communicate with them.

Your Responsibility

The first aspect of your relationship to your readers is your responsibility to them. And the first responsibility is not to write nonsense, lies, or unwarranted statements. For each statement you make in your paper, you should ask yourself if it is a true statement and if it makes sense. If the reader discovers you being less than truthful or sensible, you will lose that reader's trust and patience. You may have a hard time getting either back. Part of truthfulness is letting the reader know how certain or uncertain you are of any claim you make. Ask yourself how much you need to know, or what kind of proof you should have, to make any particular claim with absolute certainty. If you have that knowledge and proof, you should present them to the reader. If you don't have either, don't bluff. You can still make the statement, but let the reader know either that you are not yet certain of it, or that you are only mentioning the idea to raise questions, or that you are only presenting a speculation open to further evaluation. The more you are honest about the strength of your proof, the more the reader will respect those times you write with absolute certainty.

Another part of responsibility to the readers is to take into consideration their expectations. This does not mean you always have to give them what they want or expect; often you will want to — and should — tell them something quite different. But it does mean you should recognize and, if necessary, explain the way in which you are disregarding reader expectation and your reasons for so doing. You can see how reader expectation operates, for example, when you write an essay in answer to a test question. The grader, or reader, of the essay expects to find a direct and full answer to the stated question; any failure to meet that expectation will be reflected in your grade. If you believe that the question is improperly framed — and you feel you can get to the most important issues by answering a different question — you had better begin your answer with a very clear and convincing explanation of how and why you are changing the question. In almost all writing situations, you must pay attention to some reader expectation, whether it is your supervisor's desire for a clear-cut recommendation in a business report or the mystery fanatic's anticipation of being amused and baffled by your detective story.

The final responsibility to your readers is that you make good on all that you promised. The title and introduction of a piece of writing are usually filled with implicit promises. If you title a paper "A Comparison of Mass Transit in New York, San Francisco, and Dallas," you are promising to give a comprehensive overview of all forms of mass transit — bus, subway, and train — in the three cities, to make specific comparisons among the systems, and finally to draw conclusions about the advantages and disadvantages of each city's system. If you intend to do less — to tell only about the buses in each city — you need to choose a less ambitious title. Similarly, if in your introduction you write "the importance of speech act philosophy for understanding spoken agreements cannot be underestimated," you are obligated to explain what speech act philosophy is, what it has to do with spoken agreements, and why it is so important to the subject of spoken agreements. Promises can even be implicit in the tone of your language; for example, if you initially adopt a humorous tone, you had better live up to it by actually being funny. If you choose to write with unusual words and long, intricate sentences, you are implying that your subject is so difficult and complex that any less tortuous language could not convey your precise meaning; your actual content had better live up to this elaborate technique — unless you want to be thought pompous and obfuscating.

Your Opportunities

In addition to your responsibilities, you have opportunities to enlighten and convince your reader. To enlighten the reader, you must carefully consider what the reader needs to know in order to understand everything you discuss in your writing. To increase the reader's understanding, you may have to provide more background or you may have to offer more specificity — persuasive examples or telling details. In order to judge how much background or specificity your audience can profitably use, you have to draw on your knowledge of the audience — what your readers already know, what they believe, and how they think. You can gain some sense of what a professional audience is likely to know from seeing what ideas and information are common in the professional literature of the discipline. For a more general audience, you can look to the cultural beliefs, educational level, and common experiences of your anticipated readers. If you are writing for an instructor, you probably have substantial personal knowledge to go on; what students call "psyching out" a teacher is worthwhile if it is done in the spirit of figuring out how best to communicate to a teacher whose views differ from your own.

Introductions and conclusions are particularly useful places for letting the reader know the significance of your subject. A well-written introduction can draw your readers into the subject and let them know how the subject relates to the surrounding issues and to their personal interests. With professional audiences, a review of the literature immediately following the introduction will help place your subject against the relevant background so that the reader can see what you are hoping to accomplish in the essay. The conclusion can drive home the major ideas of the paper and pinpoint their importance and essential implications. The conclusion can help readers see what meaning they should take away from the writing and what action, if any, they should consider.

Finally, you must ask yourself what will convince this particular audience of your ideas. What kind of evidence is most compelling with this audience — statistics, theoretical analyses, personal experience, introspection, or what? Do readers hold to ideas that conflict with yours so that you have to demolish these competing ideas before you can argue for yours? Are there certain objections readers are likely to raise, so that you can anticipate the objections? It is important to remember that just because readers understand your argument does not mean that they will be convinced by it. Also remember that just because certain evidence convinces you does not mean that it will convince all readers — whether they are reasonable or otherwise.

Fine-Grained Revision: Sharpening the Language

By this stage you should know what your paper will say and how you would like it to affect the reader. But until you have pored over each sentence, each phrase, and each word, your meanings may be much murkier to the reader than you imagine. Writing communicates only through language. Only detailed attention to language makes your message precise and clear. This painstaking and detailed revision of language may at first seem unrewarding, but in struggling with obstinate words and sentences, you may create a more sharply defined statement than you had thought possible. As with people you know well, the beauty, character, and interest of writing are expressed through details.

A skillful writer attends to the details of language on three levels: the intelligent and logical progression of statements within the paragraph; the clear, concise, and graceful phrasing of sentences; and the choice of precise words. Although we will treat the three separately, in practice they are interrelated. By finding a single right word, you may eliminate a long awkward phrase; by showing the relationship of statements through well-controlled sentence structure, you may solve problems of paragraph organization. You may solve problems of clarity, precision, and gracefulness at any of the three levels.

> **Each well-written paragraph contains a number of sentences brought together because they share a common element. The art of writing paragraphs is to make evident this common element by the arrangement and connection of sentences.**

Anatomy of a Paragraph

Each well-written paragraph contains a number of sentences brought together because they share a *common element*. The art of writing paragraphs is to make evident this common element by the arrangement and connection of the sentences. Then each statement will shed light on the previous one, and each will carry forward the meaning of the whole.

Sometimes the common element is obvious, particularly if the paragraph is built around a well-developed topic sentence placed in the most prominent position. The topic sentence may then be exemplified, proved, explained, or otherwise supported in the remainder of the paragraph. In earlier writing courses, you may have studied a series of paragraph types built around a topic sentence in lead position. Some common paragraph types are commonly known as comparison and contrast, cause and effect, classification, statement supported by multiple arguments, and statement supported by extended example. You may also have studied easily recognizable patterns for organizing details within a paragraph: time order, space order, and order of importance. All these are good and useful tools for making order out of otherwise disorganized statements.

By now, your writing and thinking may have advanced to a stage where what you have to organize is more complex than these simple patterns will allow. What brings your statements together may be more subtle than simple support of an explicit topic sentence: you may now wish to establish a cluster of different relationships within a single paragraph. To move beyond the basic patterns you have learned, you need to create new patterns to fit your new, more complex meanings. Paragraph structure does not have to be rigid or limiting; it just has to make sense.

The early chapters of this book contain examples and analyses of paragraph structures that appear in professional writing. These examples appear as part of the discussion of such tasks as paraphrase, summary, and analysis of writing technique. Understanding the organizational structure of other writers' work is part of intelligent reading. If you expect your readers to pay close attention to your most serious statements, you should work toward a control of paragraph structure that will reward close attention by revealing precision of meaning. You must write intelligently to deserve intelligent reading.

More advanced forms of paragraph structure are frequently hybrid combinations of simpler, more easily recognized patterns. As you become more adept at reading and writing, you can blend several kinds of organization together in a single paragraph and still maintain a common core of meaning. If you create such hybrid structures, it is especially important to keep relationships clear; otherwise, the reader may not see any reason behind what appears to be a muddle of very different types of statements. In the following sample paragraph from Leon Edel's biography of the novelist Henry James, the writer maintains coherence, flow, and clarity as he introduces many kinds of background information about the relationship between Henry James and the writer Oscar Wilde.

The bulky figure of Oscar Wilde had crossed Henry James's path at infrequent intervals during the previous decade. They had met long before — in 1882 — in a drawing room in Washington, during Oscar's circus-like tour of America. James had confided to friends at the time that he thought Wilde "an unclean beast," and found him "repulsive and fatuous." Thereafter he referred to him usually in terms of the animal kingdom. There was however no ill will or animosity between them. Oscar simply irritated James; and the novelist regarded with curiosity and a certain amused condescension the public antics and public wit of the younger man. Wilde on his side spoke with respect but with understandable reservations concerning the fastidious American. His own relaxed amateurism, his emphasis on talk and performance rather than on creation, caused him to feel that James treated art as "a painful duty" rather than as one of the amusements of life. They had no common bonds of temperament; and they represented two diametrically opposed attitudes toward life and the imagination. If Wilde insisted on putting his talent into his art and his genius into his life (as he later told André Gide), Henry James did exactly the opposite. James's drawing-room wit was merely the surplus of his genius — and he lived for his art. He was eleven years older than Wilde; he worked hard and was highly productive. Wilde had a lazy facility that James found "cheap" — the cheapness of the actor who knows how to provoke applause: he had written very little and the American deplored the public display which had made the young Wilde the subject of Gilbert and Sullivan and of George du Maurier in *Punch*. There has been speculation that Gabriel Nash, the talkative aesthete in *The Tragic Muse*, incorporated some of Wilde's qualities: if this was so, James had drawn a singularly generous portrait. Nash's cultivated ineffectuality might be that of Wilde; his wit is that of Henry James, and so is his sentience. Whether James read *The Picture of Dorian Gray* when it came out in 1891 we do not know. What we do know is that Wilde turned to the theatre at the very time that James did; and from this moment on, they were — from James's point of view — rivals, or fellow-contenders in the same arena.[2]

The paragraph begins with what can only be very loosely called a topic sentence; the first sentence is more like an introduction to a story of many parts. The second sentence seems to be leading into a retrospective narrative, but the next few sentences turn first to the effect of the first meeting and then to James's general opinions about Wilde. After presenting Wilde's opinions of James, Edel redirects the paragraph into a comparison of the two men. The comparison leads back to James's distaste for Wilde, which Edel links to a character analysis of a Wilde-like character in James's writing. The character analysis raises the historical question of how much James knew of Wilde's writing. The paragraph ends with the last moment of a chronological sequence, but the information conveyed is more like the logical conclusion of all that came before it. Although this last sentence is not the total topic of the paragraph, it does demonstrate the consequence of all that came before it — like the conclusion of a story.

Despite the complexity of the paragraph structure and its lack of an explicit topic sentence, the meaning, coherence, and progress of the paragraph are clear. We gain a many-sided picture of how things stood between Wilde and James up to the time they both began writing plays. The paragraph, in fact, serves as an introduction to a chapter discussing the period when they both were writing plays.

The Well-Arranged Sentence

Sentences bring words together. The art of writing sentences is in bringing out the connections among the words essential to the intended meaning — while at the same time keeping the sentence as simple and easy to understand as possible. Your control of sentence structure largely determines your control of meaning. Carelessly thought-out sentences may present irrelevant or even false ideas; tangled sentences may convey little of your meaning to the reader. On the other hand, a well-shaped sentence can clarify a previously murky concept or can create a vivid and sharply defined impression for the reader.

[2]From pp. 43–44 in *Henry James — The Treacherous Years: 1895–1901* by Leon Edel (J. B. Lippincott). Copyright © 1969 by Leon Edel. Reprinted by permission of Harper & Row, Publishers, Inc.

The main tools for your artful control of sentence structure are the rules of syntax, for they define the well-established ways of putting words together. Syntactical rules are the means by which your readers will recognize the relationships you are establishing in your sentences. Even if you occasionally break the rules for a particular stylistic effect, the shock effect only works against a background of conventional sentences. The shock of the unusual. In the next few paragraphs, we will present some of the uses and strengths of various syntactic forms.

The Key Spots

The subject and the verb are the most important parts of any sentence; do not squander them on anything less than the most important words of your statement. Subject and verb can, by themselves, often carry a very complete message.

Ralph yawns.
Philosophy lives.
I came. I saw. I conquered.

Words other than the subject and verb typically modify or complete the primary statement of the subject and verb. Consider, for example, this sentence:

Net profits after taxes dropped slightly this year.

The central meaning is contained within the subject and verb: *profits dropped*. The other words only let us know what kinds of profits (*net, after taxes*), how much (*slightly*), and when (*this year*).

In a poorly constructed sentence, the writer places the less important words in the more important positions and pushes the important words into spaces that should hold only minor modifiers. The writer allows many meaningless words to creep in, and the reader has a harder time figuring out what the sentence says — or is trying to say. See what happens when we take the previous example and push the main words to the far corners of the sentence.

Concerning the post-tax remainder of net profits during the current annual period, our ledger books reveal a change of small proportions downward.

The subject and verb tell us only that *books reveal*. What do they reveal? A change, but what kind of change? Of small proportions, but in which direction? Downward. We only get the key information at the end of a long string of modifying phrases.

If you search for the key words to convey your idea and then put these words in the most important positions in your sentences, your meanings will become clearer and your sentences simpler. Short, simple sentences — with strong subjects and verbs — can frequently convey your full meaning.

However, you will also find need to put two or more statements into a specific relationship with one another within the same sentence. In time, the complexity of your thoughts will inevitably require the use of more complex sentence structures. The first point to remember in combining two statements is that you must know the exact purpose of the combination: a loose continuity between two ideas ("and another point is . . .") is not enough to warrant combining them. You must have a specific and substantial reason for combining sentences.

Coordination

In *coordination,* two or more sentences are brought together to emphasize their equality:

> Jack is taking notes on the statistics lecture, *and* Carol is outlining the textbook.

> You can spend the money for repairs, *or* you can learn to live without a car.

> I want very much to go to the concert, *but* I have already promised to go to the play.

As in these examples the two statements can be additive, alternative, or contrary.

Coordination through the use of a semicolon emphasizes the parallel nature of two statements:

> Economics is now one of the more popular courses of study; fifteen years ago literature courses had the largest enrollments.

This parallelism of meaning can be further emphasized by parallelism of phrasing:

> Premedical programs require a concentration in science; prelegal programs require a concentration in liberal arts.

Technically, the first three shortened versions contain participial phrases of different kinds; the last two shortened examples contain appositives. A participial phrase is a modifying phrase built on either the present participle of a verb (the *-ing* form) or the past participle (the *-ed* form for regular verbs). An appositive is additional information placed directly after a noun and is usually set off by commas. These constructions allow you to bring in modifying information while keeping a simple sentence structure.

Gerunds

The present participle of a verb (that is, the *-ing* form) can be used as a noun:

Running tires a person.

The technical name of this verb form used as a noun is *gerund*. Gerund phrases can include all the objects and modifiers the verb could have in an independent clause, so that gerund phrases can operate much like the shortened subordinate clauses discussed in the last paragraph. The following example from baseball shows how complex a situation you can describe by using a gerund phrase as subject:

Intentionally dropping a fly ball when there are two or more runners on base was eliminated by the infield fly rule.

The subject of the sentence is the gerund phrase *intentionally dropping a fly ball when there are two or more runners on base*. This subject includes the gerund *dropping*, the object of the gerund (*a fly ball*), and the adverb *intentionally;* moreover, the gerund is modified by an entire subordinate clause, *when there are two or more runners on base*. The entire complex gerund phrase serves as the subject of the main clause; this entire complex situation "was eliminated by the infield fly rule."

Colon

One often neglected — but powerful — tool of sentence combining is the colon. When used to connect two sentences, the colon indicates that the second sentence explains or sums up the first, as in the following examples:

Group membership imposes responsibilities: club members must pay dues, attend meetings, and owe obligations of loyalty and mutual help.

The four people living in the apartment share work, decisions, and concern for one another's welfare: they form a voluntary family.

The colon also serves to introduce quotations and lists or series. In all cases, the items after the colon should fill out the statement before the colon.

In the fully revised essay, each sentence should make a specific contribution to the overall argument. Each sentence's contribution should be expressed in as clear, direct, and readable form as possible. Complex thoughts may require lengthy, complex sentences for their accurate presentation, but you have a responsibility to the reader to make the sentences no more difficult than they need be. And no matter how complex the sentences may be, they should never be confusing. If, after many attempts to tighten your sentences, they remain tortured and murky, the problem may be with the thought and not the phrasing. To help yourself, try to express the thought by using an entirely different kind of sentence; if you still are baffled, rethink the thought from the very beginning. If you cannot state your idea clearly, you may not know yet what it is you want to say.

The Right Word

Choosing the right words can be frustrating. Ernest Hemingway rewrote the ending of *A Farewell to Arms* thirty-nine times; the problem was, he explained, "getting the words right." Either you cannot pinpoint the words for the idea you want to express, or you think of too many alternatives and cannot choose which one. To make matters worse, there are no absolute guidelines to tell you what choice is right in all circumstances. What is the right choice in one sentence may be the wrong choice further down the page — and certainly wrong in another paper.

The three things that will most help you choose the best word for each circumstance are knowing your subject well, knowing what you want to write about it, and knowing what words other writers use to discuss the subject. In other words, you need to know the subject, your mind, and the relevant vocabulary. Rarely does anyone come to the end of any part of this tall order. Given what you do know at the time you are writing, you do have to make your choices; consider the factors discussed below when choosing.

Dead Wood

Your first consideration should be to evaluate how much each word adds to your overall statement. Words that take up space without contributing anything should be eliminated — except where they are necessary to avoid awkwardness or confusion. Two common groups of words that can usually be eliminated without loss are vague intensifiers (such as *really, very,* and *quite*) and weak subjects (such as *the fact that, there are,* and *one of the things that*). Repetitious words, covering material already covered elsewhere, also should be deleted. Words that provide information irrelevant to the point of your writing should also be eliminated. You may, for example, be proud of the thirty-eight miles per gallon obtained by your car, but mention of the mileage would be out of place when describing how much your dog loves to ride.

Some phrases add only a little information at the expense of many words. By isolating the few bits of substance, you may be able to state the point more concisely. Consider, for example, this sentence:

Being of grouchy disposition, I lacked the patience to listen to the entire story to the end.

Only a few words — *grouchy, I, lacked, story* — convey all the substance. The sentence can be phrased more concisely:

My grouchiness kept me from hearing the full story.

Concrete or Abstract

You also want to consider how concrete or abstract a word is. The more concrete a word is, the more it identifies an actual thing that exists in the world; the more abstract a word, the more it refers to an idea or quality rather than to an actual thing. The word *strawberry* is more concrete than the word *fruit;* the word *food* is even more abstract than *fruit.* The more concrete the words you use, the less likely they will be misunderstood. For example, *strawberries* cannot be mistaken for *blueberries,* and neither can be confused with *apples.* But the abstract word *food* gives the reader only a vague picture of what you have in mind. In using abstract terms, you run the danger that your reader will not understand what you are referring to exactly. The grand abstractions, such as *freedom, truth,* and *justice* — unless well defined and used with the greatest care — can result in gross misunderstandings and confusions.

Concrete words also leave readers with more vivid impressions than abstractions. A reader can easily imagine the taste, texture, sight, and smell of a strawberry, but what can the reader imagine from the un-specific word *food*? On the other hand, it is very difficult to discuss ideas without abstractions. Without the abstract term *food,* agricultural econo-mists would have difficulties discussing how to provide something to eat for everyone in the world. Thus, in choosing between abstract and con-crete words, you must decide whether unmistakable, vivid impress-sion of an actual object or the idea behind the object is more appropriate for your discussion.

Specificity and generality are closely related to concreteness and ab-straction, but there is a difference. The more specific a word is, the more it pinpoints the items it refers to. The specific phrase *the strawberry I am holding in my hand* refers to one, and only one strawberry, but the concrete word *strawberry* by itself is general, for it can potentially refer to billions of strawberries — not just in this year's crop, but throughout the history of agriculture. Specific words tend to be more vivid and less mistakable than general words, but general words are useful for discuss-ing repeating phenomena or categories of things.

Word Precision

In most circumstances you will want to choose precise words — that is, words that offer clear limits to their meaning. As we have just seen, words that are concrete and specific tend, by their nature, to be precise. *Abraham Lincoln* is obviously more precise than *president* or *leader*. Problems of precision are more likely to occur with words that are abstract, general, or both. Make sure that you know exactly what you mean whenever you use a general or abstract word, and then let the reader know. Sometimes you can achieve this precision by being careful to use the troublesome word in exactly the same way each time you use it. At other times, giving more concrete or specific examples of your more abstract or general statements will help tie down the difficult words. If the problem is very sticky, you can give explicit definitions of all the important terms you will use in the paper; however, you must make sure that your usage throughout the essay is consistent with your definitions. Technical terms are especially useful for increasing precision, but only if you are writing for a professional audience familiar with the technical language; otherwise, the unknown terminology will serve as a barrier — rather than as an aid — to communication.

Another aspect of precision is identifying with what certainty you are making the statement and how absolutely the statement holds for all cases. You need to take care in choosing words that accurately express

your degree of certainty about the claims you are making. In the following example, whichever word in the parentheses you select implies a
specific level of certainty — how complete you feel the evidence is.

This paper (*suggests, identifies, describes, demonstrates*) factors influencing
the onset of viral diabetes.

Even the choice of *a, the,* or *one of the* indicates a level of definiteness.
Such qualifying words as *tendency, partial, under some circumstances,* and
almost help limit the extent to which a statement can be held true.

Hedging

As necessary as qualification is for precision, it can be improperly used to hedge statements that should be made with more certainty.
Unless you can justify your every use of words like *perhaps, possible,* and
probable, you are hiding behind these weak words. You should have, as
the saying goes, the courage of your own foolishness.

Another kind of hedging is for the writer to use a more general word or
phrase than is necessary. In particular, words like *relate, depend,* and *connect* can apply to a host of situations. Do not use the general word to
avoid thinking out the specific word or to avoid committing yourself to a
definite statement. Only use the general term when you mean precisely
the entire large category of things encompassed by the general word.
When used to avoid making a clear-cut statement, both overly general
words and uncalled-for qualifiers go by the name of weasel words — and
for good reason.

Emotions and Judgments

Another scale against which to judge your choice of words is
the continuum from highly emotional to impersonal words. At times it is
perfectly appropriate to report on your own emotions, as in autobiography and — less obtrusively — in reviews of art and literature. In some
situations you may want to report on the feelings of others — in analyzing some of the personal motivations behind a historical event. In other
circumstances, comments reflecting your own or others' feelings are
totally inappropriate — in describing the behavior of subjects in a psychological experiment.

The continuum of judgmental and nonjudgmental words, in part,
overlaps with the emotional-impersonal continuum, for reports on your
emotions often reflect your values. *Values* are those deeply held principles
and beliefs upon which you base your opinions of worth and quality.
Judgments of value and morality are carried in such words as *good, bad,*

virtuous, and *evil;* judgments are also carried in expressions of causes ("His negligence caused the accident."), nonobservable connections ("Where there is life, there is hope."), and imposed categories ("He is a painter of the decadent romantic school."). Much intellectual discourse would be impossible without these judgments; nonetheless, if you are writing within any of the scientific disciplines, you must eliminate such judgmental statements and rely as much as possible only on what can be observed or can be directly deduced from observations.

Denotation and Connotation

A final continuum against which to consider the impact of your words is the scale from purely denotative meaning to heavily connotative or associative meaning. Denotative meaning is the explicit, defined reference of a word; for example, *snake* denotes a scaly, legless reptile with a long, cylindrical body. Connotative meaning, on the other hand, refers to all those other associations we have about a word beyond its literal meaning; for example, *snake* connotes something untrustworthy, sneaky, poisonous, and generally evil. At times you will want to use words with strong connotations in order to evoke a mood or a reaction on the reader's part. Elsewhere you may have to make sure that the connotations of a word do not conflict with the tone or attitude of the whole paper; for example, whether you call a particular ancient king an *absolute monarch*, a *dictator*, or a *tyrant* depends on how benevolent a picture you wish to draw. If you have previously described him as enlightened, well-intentioned, and successful, the word *tyrant* would evoke connotations contrary to the image you are creating. In situations where you want to keep the meaning as explicit and denotative as possible — in certain kinds of philosophical and scientific argument — you will want to choose words that have very little connotation. Much of the unusual technical language of the social sciences is an attempt to describe the facts of everyday life in a way that will not evoke the everyday connotations.

Consistency of Style

The three levels of attention to language that have been discussed on the past few pages — paragraph, sentence, and word — are the major elements of style. But style is not a fancy decoration pasted on during the final revision; style is the natural outgrowth of the process of addressing individual writing tasks. A clear conception of the purposes of any piece of writing should lead you to a consistent style — a way of telling your story to your audience. After you have set the basic style of your paper through initial work on the details of paragraphs, sentences, and words, you need to make a further revision for *stylistic consistency,* in which you look for and work on those spots that are not yet up to the high level you have achieved in the rest of the paper. Be particularly suspicious of those spots where you are proud of turning a phrase or making a clever joke, for those may be just the spots where you bring in considerations irrelevant to the main task of the paper — no matter how amusing or pleasing to your own mind. All the language of the paper must work together.

Public Presentation of Your Paper

Throughout the process of finding your thoughts, organizing them, and setting them into words, your mind will be more than fully occupied. You probably will have little time for or interest in such matters as correct spelling, punctuation, grammar, and footnote form. By this point in your writing career, such mechanics should be largely automatic, but people do make mistakes, especially if they have heavier matters — like creating a statement — on their minds. I know that in my own rough drafts I become so involved in setting down my thoughts that I seem to forget the basic mechanics: I write down *there* when I mean *their* or I drop a verb ending. Such errors don't matter much in the early drafts, for the drafts are only for my own use. But if such silly errors stayed in my final copy, I'd be more than embarrassed. I'd probably have to turn in my red pen and badge as an English teacher. Nevertheless, I would not want to break the trend of my thought by checking every spelling I was unsure of or by proofreading every half-formed phrase in early drafts. I might not even use those words and phrases in the final paper.

The solution is, of course, a final revision with grammar in mind and dictionary in hand. With your full attention on the basic mechanical skills, the revision for correctness should clear up all remaining mistakes. Knowing that you will revise for correctness at the end of the writing process will free your mind for the more important thinking and organizing earlier on.

During this final revision, you should also mark where footnotes are required and then write a draft of the notes according to the appropriate format, as described in the next chapter.

After the final revision, everything going into the paper should be set, so that making a clean copy is only a matter of accurate typing. No matter how accurate your typing is, however, you need to *proofread* the final copy to correct any errors that may have slipped in. If you must make minor corrections, write them in as neatly as possible. The clean copy is the public presentation of your work: it should present as few obstacles to the reader as possible. Generous and consistent margins and a generally neat appearance make the paper more inviting to the reader. However, excessive prettiness, such as unusual typefaces or colored paper, is as much of a barrier to objective reading as smudged and crumpled pages.

Dealing with Response to Your Writing

After you have placed the clean copy in your teacher's hands — or put the report on the boss's desk or slipped the manuscript into an envelope addressed to the publisher — you breathe the usual sigh of relief, let the subject slip to the back of your mind, and turn to new endeavors. You feel you have made your statement, and the cycle of writing is complete.

At a later time, the conversation is reopened: comments come back to you. In school, papers return with a grade and comments evaluating where you went right and where you went wrong. Using marginal annotations, the teacher may begin a discussion about ideas that you raise. A friend who has read your paper may want to argue with you. Response can come to you in many ways.

Writers at all levels have two common reactions to the response of readers. The writer may either react too strongly to the reactions of others — despairing at criticism and rejoicing at praise — or the writer may discount anything a reader may have to say — on the theory that the writer knows what he or she was trying to do and knows the best way to do it.

Much more is to be gained from a middle course, a serious but measured consideration of readers' responses. If someone makes a criticism or suggests a change, consider whether the criticism may be justified. Ask yourself whether the reader understood what you were doing; ask yourself from what perspective did the reader make the comment. You may conclude that the critical comment was right, in whole or in part; with this new perspective, you may begin to rethink the subject or just revise a few words. Even if you reject the criticism, you may learn much: if the reader misunderstood your meaning, you might ask whether the fault was in your writing.

It is part of the writing process to learn how your writing appears to different readers. Although gaining approval is always pleasant, you should be more concerned with whether you have communicated fully. To a writer, response from readers is a very special kind of information, for it alone can tell you what you have and have not achieved through your writing.

Writing Assignments

1. For each of the following passages, analyze how one statement leads to the next. Can you categorize each connection according to one kind of logic or another? Explain how the logic used in each case is appropriate to the situation.

   a. The opening of the Declaration of Independence on page 30
   b. Newton's three laws of motion on pages 30–31
   c. The passage by Thomas Kuhn on page 29
   d. Orwell's essay "You and the Atom Bomb" on pages 84–86
   e. The sample paper of synthesis on pages 217–221
   f. One of your own essays

2. Write short statements (two or three sentences each) on the topic of either fear or joy, using each of the following logics:

   a. deductive logic
   b. inductive logic
   c. ordinary argumentation
   d. analogy
   e. associative logic
   f. narrative logic
   g. dream logic

3. Identify the ways in which the following paragraph violates reader expectations or otherwise acts irresponsibly toward the audience. Then rewrite the paragraph to correct these problems.

> The four reasons for the popularity of television soap operas all derive from the lack of social experience people have today. First, because young people lack social experience, they are unsure about what they can expect from life as they take on adult roles. The soap operas provide a picture of the world, which the young people can imagine as their futures. Using the TV image as the model for the world the viewers also learn about how they might behave in society. They aren't confident about their own behavior and about how to interpret other people's behavior. They let TV tell them what they should have learned on their own more realistically in actual life. But that's all a big joke,

isn't it? I mean real people don't act like those cardboard idiots on the tube, always staring off in space wondering about what will happen to an illegitimate twelve-year-old sister now that she has run off with a disbarred lawyer who is accused of murdering his wife. I mean, is that any way to behave? What a joke. But back to my main point, I've heard people say they even look at soap operas to see how the people dress and how they furnish the houses. People, old and young, must have pretty empty lives to need that to fill up their imaginations. I guess soap operas give them make-believe communities to worry about, just like when they were kids and had make-believe friends to play with. It's all fantasy.

4. Identify the ways in which each of the following writers shows awareness of the audience.

a. Dale Carnegie in an excerpt from *How to Win Friends and Influence People* on pages 82–83

b. Betsy Carter, book review on pages 129–130

c. John Maynard Keynes, preface on pages 95–96

5. Analyze the paragraph structure in each of the following:

a. The excerpt by Patrick Moore on page 28

b. The passage by Margaret Mead on pages 6–7

c. The selection by William C. Dement on pages 53–55

d. A few paragraphs from one of your own essays

6. In the excerpts by Susan Wagner on page 106 and by Maurice Corina on page 107, underline the main subject and main verb of each sentence; then circle the words conveying the most important information in each sentence. Do the subject and verb coincide with the most important information? If not, try revising each sentence to make better use of the main positions.

7. Using any techniques that are grammatical and appropriate, combine the sentences in each group below. Also shorten the combined sentences if no important information will be lost.

a. The network was faced with a dilemma.

It could report on the secret negotiations.

The government would accuse it of irresponsibility.

It could bury the story.

The public would accuse it of irresponsibility.

b. It is difficult to shoot a science fiction movie.

You must coordinate special effects and acting.

Large budgets are expended on special effects.

The actors must make totally imaginary scenes seem plausible.

c. Sergei Eisenstein was a great Russian filmmaker.

He coined the term *montage*.

Montage is an important film technique.

One shot follows another.
The image on the screen changes abruptly.
The viewer sees a connection between images.
A new meaning develops from the combination of the shots.
d. Old movies challenge new moviemakers.
The new moviemakers try to outdo scenes in the old movies.
Woody Allen saw an old slapstick joke in many old movies.
An unsuspecting character slips on a banana peel.
Woody Allen made a movie called *Sleeper*.
Sleeper is set in the future.
The fruits and vegetables of the future are giant-sized.
Woody Allen slips on a fifteen-foot banana peel.

8. The following passage is based on an essay by Winston Churchill, the famous British political leader, discussing the movies of Charlie Chaplin. In the original passage Churchill compares British and American tramps, but here Churchill's complex polished sentences have been broken into choppy little statements. You are to rewrite the passage, recombining the statements to re-create all the connections between the statements.

> Charlie Chaplin portrays tramps. People go to the cinema. Every one of these people is familiar with these tramps. I wonder about something. How many of these people have reflected about an idea? These tramps are homeless wanderers. These tramps are characteristically American. The English tramps are dwindling in number. In their ranks one finds all sorts of people. One finds the varsity graduate. His career has ended in ruin and disgrace. One finds the illiterate. This illiterate is a half-imbecile. He has been unemployable since boyhood. But they have one thing in common. They belong to a great army. The army is defeated. They still pretend to look for work. They do not expect to find work. They are spiritless and hopeless.
>
> The American hobo existed twenty-five years ago. He was of an entirely different type. Often he was not much of an outcast. He was not cast out from society. Rather he was a rebel against society. He could not settle down in a home. He could not settle down in a job. He hated routine. Regular employment was a routine. He loved the road. The road had changes and chances. He had an old adventurous urge. This urge was behind his wanderings. The same urge sent covered wagons. Covered wagons lumbered across the prairie. They went towards the sunset.[3]

9. Revise the following sentences to make more appropriate word choices and to eliminate unnecessary words.

[3]Adapted from *Collier's*, 26 October 1935, p. 24.

a. It is a fact that in the experiment scientists observed an evil-looking, snarling rodent devour three heads of Boston lettuce, which comprised the entire harvest of the garden grown by the seven-year-old daughter of one of the scientists.

b. This guy placed an order for some stuff, which the pharmacist refused to sell without a prescription, probably because he didn't want to do anything that was illegal or otherwise against the law.

c. Somebody wanted to learn charcoal sketching, water colors, oil painting, sculpting, design, space relations, color, scale, proportions, graphics, etching, wood blocks, and other things like that, but he had to support his parents, so he got a job listing numbers in columns in order to see how much the company took in and spent.

d. Carol thought Kevin's habitual slacking of the mandibular muscles to produce an invariable three centimeter aperture between his upper and lower facial labial flesh was the most sensual thing she had ever seen.

10. Select an essay written by you earlier this semester that has been heavily marked and annotated by a teacher. For each comment or correction, either write an answer defending your original statement or revise the original to conform to the suggestions.

10

Preparing References and Documentation

Preview

By making explicit the sources of your ideas and information, you let the reader know the full extent of the conversation in which you are taking part. You may use sources for many purposes; the ways in which you refer to the source materials depend on those purposes. Whenever you cite another writer's work, whether by paraphrase, summary, or direct quote, you must document it. Proper documentation — through in-text mention, footnote, and bibliography — legitimates your use of source materials and allows the reader access to those sources.

Revealing Sources

The informed writer draws on knowledge gained from many sources. In part writers use existing knowledge as a storehouse that provides examples, evidence, and quotations as support for their ideas from respected authorities. The writer also uses existing knowledge as a foundation upon which to construct an orderly base of facts and ideas that most educated people will accept as reasonable — so that the writer doesn't have to prove every point from the beginning. On this shared foundation the writer can build new and ambitious structures. If the writer ignores the solid foundation of existing knowledge and builds instead on the shifting sands of fad and whim, the structure is likely to collapse and few readers will put much faith in it.

The uses of knowledge go beyond metaphorical storehouses and foundations: the statements of knowledge you discover in sources provide the context and much of the content for your informed writing. Other writers' ideas can inspire you to continue your research or rouse you to debate their points in your writing. As we have pointed out, you must decide whether sources should be accepted, rejected, or compared to other sources. Several authors can provide multiple perspectives on your one subject, or your research can put the writings of these authors into new perspective. Perhaps you have not considered that your writing may serve as an entry for the reader into the ideas of previous writers. In short, informed writing takes place within a complex world of continuing reading and writing.

The people who read your writing may not be aware of all the facts and ideas you have discovered through your own reading; in fact, they may have come in contact with very different information through other books. For this reason you need to make explicit what source materials you are relying on. You must identify through reference and documentation those points of connection between your thoughts and the thoughts of other writers who came before you. *Reference* is the art of mentioning other writers' words, ideas, or information in the course of your own argument; *documentation* is the technique of accurate identification of the precise source of these words, ideas, and information. Through skillful reference and correct documentation, you can demonstrate the relationship of your own comments to the ongoing written conversation, making it easier for you to say what you want to say and easier for your reader to understand your meaning. Your reader will come to see the full discussion instead of being just an eavesdropper of one disconnected fragment.

> **You must identify through reference and documentation those points of connection between your thoughts and the thoughts of other writers who came before you.**

There are other narrower — but still important — reasons for proper reference and documentation. First, you will be more likely to convince your readers of the validity of your ideas if you can show that you are building on the solid foundation of respected earlier work and that you are taking into account what is already known about your subject. Second, you should repay a debt of gratitude to those earlier writers whose work you have used; they are the ones who stocked the storehouse for you. Finally, intellectual borrowing without giving credit is theft, called *plagiarism*. Plagiarism is passing off someone else's work — whether in the exact words or paraphrase — as your own. There should, however, be no need to hide any of your sources if you are actively working with the material and are using the sources to develop your own thoughts. Indeed the more clearly you identify what others have said, the more sharply your own contribution will stand out.

Reference

The Uses of References

During the periods when you are selecting a subject, gathering information, and developing your thoughts, you will look at many sources with only a vague idea of the eventual use you will make of the material in your final paper. Many of those sources you may, in fact, never use directly. As you give shape to your final statement, you must decide not only what source material you will mention but also the purpose of each reference. You must know how each bit of cited material advances the argument of your paper, for if you lack a clear idea of why you are mentioning someone else's work, your paper is in danger of losing direction. You do not want your paper to deteriorate into a pointless string of quotations that leaves your readers wondering what you are trying to say.

The purpose of any reference must fit in with the argument you are making and with the kind of paper you are writing. Otherwise the reference is an intrusion, distracting the reader from understanding and evaluating your main point. For example, in the middle of a technical paper reporting the chemical analysis of a new pesticide, it would not be appropriate to quote the political statements of the producer or of environmental groups. But you might want to mention — and even describe in detail — a new method of chemical analysis developed by another chemist, particularly if that new method allowed the user to obtain more precise and trustworthy results. The reference must be more than loosely connected to the subject: it must fit the exact logic of the argument you are making at the place where the reference is made.

In the past, you probably have used references most frequently to quote or paraphrase the words of some authority who agrees with a statement you have made. In political debates and other situations where you are trying to persuade the audience on less than totally rational grounds, the fact that a respected person has said something similar to what you have said — only perhaps more elegantly — may lend some acceptability or believability to your claims. However, persuasion through passing mention of an authority will not lend strength to a scholarly analysis for a professional audience; for a scholarly paper your argument must stand up to scrutiny on its own merits without regard for the graceful words of poets or the reputation of the idea's supporters. In persuasive debate, however, the citing of authority remains an effective tool, particularly if you can embarrass the opposition by showing that one of their heroes really supports your side on this issue. Political journalists delight in such tactics.

In more serious academic writing, you can use the authenticated findings of other researchers to support your own findings — but only in carefully limited ways. One way is to follow your general point with another researcher's specific data or a case study as evidence. Another way is to present all your own evidence and reasoning, and then compare your conclusions to those of other researchers, showing how both studies — yours and theirs — are consistent and confirm each other. In both these situations you retain primary responsibility for your argument and only use other studies to show that your conclusions agree with what others have found.

As you look to other writers for support, you may turn on them — to attack what you consider wrong-headed nonsense. In persuasive debate situations, where destroying your opponent's arguments is almost as good as making your own case, quoting the opposition's ideas as the first step in tearing them apart is often a good tactic. While attacking, you may sometimes have the opportunity to bring in you own, more praiseworthy ideas. But in academic or professional writing, where your purpose is in establishing the truth and not in gaining votes, you should only attack in limited circumstances, such as when an error is so convincing and so firmly believed by most experts that it stands in the way of more accurate thought. Then you should only show why the cited ideas are wrong — but not ridicule them as outrageous or foolish. Ridicule may be an effective political tool, but it destroys the cooperative community necessary for rational discourse. The insults traded by nineteenth-century German philosophers may be amusing to read in retrospect, but they only created deeper divisions among philosophers than were necessary. If, however, you do find a fair critique of another writer's argument a useful way to advance your own argument, you shoud refer as precisely as possible to the specific ideas you are criticizing — even to the extent of lengthy quotation. This detailed reference should then become the starting point for specific and carefully argued criticisms.

At times your essay may call for interpretation or analysis of primary source material. One example would be a paper in which you were trying to understand Thomas Jefferson's thinking through an examination of his letters. In this kind of textual analysis, as with critiques, you need to make specific reference to the exact ideas or passages being analyzed, by quotation, paraphrase, or summary, along with page and line reference. This reference identifies exactly what material you are working with and allows the reader to compare your interpretation and analysis to the original in order to judge whether your arguments are convincing. Similarly, if you are comparing the thoughts of two or more writers, you need to present enough indication of the originals so that the reader can understand and evaluate your comparison. Put yourself in your readers' position and analyze how much they need to know of the originals. Such specific comparisons of two arguments can serve as the basis for your own synthesis, resolving the conflicts between the two earlier writers. Extensive comparison, interpretation, and analysis of the thoughts of a number of writers may be necessary if you are tracing the evolution of ideas on a particular issue. In all the uses of reference mentioned in this paragraph, opinions expressed in the sources are what is being studied; that is, you are analyzing the opinions rather than just citing them in support of your idea. The sources are part of the subject you are discussing.

At other times, various writers' works may serve as a general background for your own ideas: you may be building upon someone else's theory; or your own findings may be understood fully only when they are set against other research findings; or you may borrow a method of analysis from another writer. In all such cases you may have to discuss the original sources at some length in order for your readers to understand the ideas, assumptions, information, and methods that lie behind your own approach. Even more specifically your paper may present an experiment or argument testing someone else's theory; you must then certainly let the reader know the source of the theory in question.

In the course of your own reading and writing, you may discover many other uses for mentioning the work of others. You will also develop a sense of the most effective and important places to bring in references. Always in citing source material, you must know why you are citing it and how it fits most effectively into your ongoing argument. You must never let your use of sources overwhelm the forward impetus of the main statements of your paper.

Maintaining Forward Motion

Two structural devices can help you maintain the forward motion of your writing while still discussing all the relevant references: a review-of-the-literature section and the content footnote. In many essays, a review of the literature, limited to only those items specifically relevant to the essay, can provide most of the necessary background (see pp. 252–254). Such a review, usually presented early in the essay — perhaps directly after the introduction — frees the writer to follow his or her own line of thought with fewer interruptions later in the essay.

If some sources develop interesting sidelights to your main issue or if other sources make points you want to answer, the discussion of either might interrupt the flow of your main argument. In that case, you can place the secondary discussion in a content footnote. Such footnotes can also be the place to discuss detailed problems with evidence, further complexities of background, and additional reviews of literature limited to a specific point made in passing. For examples of content footnotes, see the notes at the end of the sample research paper on pp. 283–288.

Reference Techniques

Each time you refer to another writer's work, you need to decide in how much detail to report the content of that reference. You have a range of options varying in explicitness from the identification of a thought or concept by its name only (Freudian Oedipus complex) to the lengthy quotation of the writer's original words. Each option has advantages and disadvantages that must be weighed in each separate reference situation. The decision of which option to use should be based on the nature of the material cited, the need to provide your reader with a precise understanding, and the role the reference takes within your larger argument. The following more specific considerations may help you choose among the alternatives.

Reference by Name Only

In each field the writings of certain key individuals are so well known that any person familiar with the field will recognize a concept — or even a whole series of findings — just from a short *tag name.* Sometimes the tag names include the name of the original author or researcher, as in *Bernoulli's effect* or the *Michelson-Morley experiment;* at other times the name is more generalized, as in *the second law of thermodynamics.* The three examples just cited all have complete and precise meanings to trained physicists. Similarly *Turner's thesis* has a definite meaning to any historian, and *Grimm's law* is recognized by any linguist. Such tag names allow you to bring in a concept quickly without any halt in the forward motion of your ideas.

However, you must consider not only if all your readers will recognize the reference but also if they will understand it exactly the way you do and the way you are applying it to the subject under discussion. Philosophers will recognize Plato's *allegory of the cave,* but they will most likely disagree on its meaning. Turner presented his thesis concerning the role of the frontier in American history in several different versions. The reader may easily mistake which aspect of Turner's thought you have in mind and therefore misinterpret how that thought fits in with the point you are making. If the references used are even more indefinite, the potential for confusion increases. Just think of the grab bag of different meanings different readers may understand by the term *constitutional guarantees of freedom* or by a reference to *President Carter's foreign policy.* Thus you should rely on tag names only when the meaning is so limited and self-evident in the context of your argument that the reader will not mistake your meaning. If any possibility for confusion exists, you should use a more explicit means of reference.

Summary

As described fully in Chapter 2, a summary allows you to explain in a short space those aspects of the source material relevant to your argument. You can focus on the most important points pertaining to your discussion, letting the reader know how you understand the ideas you are referring to. You can also adapt the summary to fit into the continuity of your prose and the organization of your essay. The summary is particularly useful for establishing background information, for reviewing an established theory, and for reporting supporting data from other studies. In these situations the reader frequently will not need all the details of the original and will not be likely to question your interpretation of the original. However, in those situations that require a detailed examination of the source material or where you are presenting a controversial interpretation or critique of the original, you may need to give a more complete paraphrase — or even a direct quotation. Particularly if you are using the summary to introduce a source you will then attack, you must not make your task too easy by exaggerating the weaker parts of the original and leaving out the stronger points, the qualifications, and the explanations necessary for an accurate assessment. Such "straw man" tactics keep you from confronting the more basic points of dispute and will lead readers to suspect the integrity of your argument.

Paraphrase

Detailed restatement of a passage in the form of a paraphrase allows you to keep control of the style and continuity of the writing (see Chapter 1). Paraphrase allows you to move smoothly from your own points to the source material, preventing the disconcerting shifts of tone of voice that often result from excessive quotation. You can also keep the focus on your main argument through emphasis in the paraphrase. Paraphrase is indispensible when the original source never makes an explicit and complete statement of the relevant ideas in one place; you must then reconstruct the important material in a single coherent paraphrase. Two other kinds of special material, transcripts of spoken conversation and the condensed prose of reference books, also usually need to be paraphrased in order to be easily readable. Because of the importance of sustaining the logical order of your argument and keeping your own statement sharply in focus, you should generally prefer paraphrase to exact quotation for reporting sources in detail.

Quotation

Direct quotation is the most obvious and most abused form of referring to another writer's thoughts. It should be reserved only for those times when you will later analyze the exact words of the original text or when the meaning is so open to interpretation that any change of words would lead to possible distortion. Occasionally you may want the direct testimony of other writers if their phrasing is so precise and stirring that the rhetorical effect strengthens your own argument or if you need to recreate the mood of some historic confrontation. In any case, it is not enough just to quote and move on: you must work the quotation into the line of your argument. You need to point out to the reader the relevance of the quotation to the point you are making and to indicate what the reader should understand from the quotation; you must therefore select the quotation carefully to make the point you wish to make — and no more. Keep the quotations short and relevant; always explicitly point out the relevance. Unless you can give good reasons for reading the quotation, the reader may skip over it. The greatest danger of quotations is that they may remain foreign, undigested lumps interrupting your ongoing argument.

Depending on the needs of your paper, you may want to use several methods of reference within a short space; for example, you may use a summary to introduce the context of a reference, followed by a paraphrase of the key points and a quotation of an important phrase you will analyze later. Such a mixture of reference methods occurs in the sample passage from Freud's *On the Interpretation of Dreams,* reproduced on page 51.

Whatever methods you use to refer to source materials, you should give an accurate representation of the original; moreover, you should use the material in ways consistent with the original form, intent, and context. The greater the detail in which you present the source material, the less chance there is for you — unintentionally or intentionally — to distort, twist, or unfairly deride the material. Even direct quotation can turn a meaning around by leaving out an important context or a few key words. Reasons of intellectual honesty should keep you on guard against the possible unfair use of sources. More practically, if the reader knows the original and catches you distorting it, the penalty is steep: loss of the reader's trust in your judgment and honesty. In matters of communication, losing the reader's trust is losing the whole game.

Punctuating References

When you refer to sources by name, summary, or paraphrase, you are using words and sentences that are your own and are therefore punctuated in the same style as the rest of your writing — except for the documentation of bibliographic information, discussed later in this chapter. You need to be careful, however, to make clear through the phrasing of your sentences exactly where the borrowed material begins and ends. It is necessary to distinguish your own thoughts and ideas from those obtained from other sources.

Direct quotation, because it promises accurate reproduction of the words of the original source, does present special problems of punctuation. First, the other writer's words need to be set off from your own. Whenever you use the exact words of your source, even for just a short phrase, you must set off the quoted words. For short quotations — that is, quotations of five typed lines or less — this may be done through quotation marks, as I am now doing in quoting the theoretical physicist John Ziman, "A scientific laboratory without a library is like a decorticated cat: the motor activities continue to function, but lack coordination of memory and purpose."[1]

For quotations within short quotations, the interior quotation should be marked with *single* quotation marks, as in the following example: "Toulmin shares Kuhn's view that there are periods in science when knowledge does not cumulate. He calls them 'recurrent periods of self doubt,' during which scientists tend to question whether science can explain anything."[2]

Longer quotations need to be set off from the main body of your writing by triple-spacing, indenting ten spaces, and double-spacing the entire quoted passage. Triple-space before returning to your own words. This form of quotation is called a *block quotation*. When you set off the quoted material in this way, do *not* use quotation marks to begin or end the quotation, for they would be redundant. Note the typing of block quotations in the student research paper, Chapter 8. As another example, I will quote what the sociologist Robert Merton has to say about the use of reading in his field.

> No great mystery shrouds the affinity of sociologists for the works of their predecessors. There is a degree of immediacy about much of the sociological theory generated by the more recent members of this distinguished lineage, and current theory has a degree of resonance to many of the still unsolved problems identified by the earlier forerunners.
>
> However, interest in classical writings of the past has also given rise to intellectually degenerative tendencies in the history of thought. The first is an uncritical reverence toward almost any statement made by illustrious ancestors. This has often been expressed in the dedicated but, for science, largely sterile exegesis of the commentator. It is to this practice that Whitehead refers in the epigraph to this chapter: "A science which hesitates to forget its founders is lost." The second degenerative form is banalization. For one way a truth can become a worn and increasingly dubious commonplace is simply by being frequently expressed, preferably in unconscious caricature, by those who do not understand it. (An example is the frequent assertion that Durkheim

[1]John Ziman, *Public Knowledge* (Cambridge: Cambridge University Press, 1968), p. 102.
[2]Diana Crane, *Invisible Colleges: Diffusion of Knowledge in Scientific Communities* (Chicago: University of Chicago Press, 1972), p.28.

assigned a great place to coercion in social life by developing his conception of "constraint" as one attribute of social facts.) Banalization is
an excellent device for drying up a truth by sponging upon it.

In short, the study of classical writings can be either deplorably useless or wonderfully useful. It all depends on the form that study takes.
For a vast difference separates the anemic practices of mere commentary or banalization from the active practice of following up and
developing the theoretical leads of significant predecessors. It is this
difference that underlies the scientists' ambivalence toward extensive
reading in past writings.[3]

Notice that the beginnings of paragraphs within the quotation are doubly
indented and that the quotation from Whitehead within the block quotation is set off by double quotation marks. For quotations within a quotation typed in block form, use single or double quotations — as in the
original.

Because you are claiming to present the exact words of the original,
you must clearly mark any changes you make. If you delete some words
from the quotation because they are not relevant to your argument, you
must indicate the deletion by an *ellipsis,* that is three dots (. . .). If the
ellipsis begins at the end of a complete sentence, you must use a fourth
dot — where it normally belongs — to indicate the end of the complete
sentence. The material deleted from the following quotation by the anthropologist Jack Goody requires the use of both three-dot and four-dot
ellipses:

> There are two main functions of writing. One is the storage function
> that permits communication over time and space, and provides man
> with a marking, mnemonic and recording device. . . . The second func-
> tion of writing . . . shifts language from the aural to the visual domain,
> and makes possible a different kind of inspection, the reordering and
> refining not only of sentences, but of individual words.[4]

In the original text this quotation was preceded by the phrase "We have
seen that . . ." but because the deletion did not come in the middle of the
quotation, it did not require an ellipsis. Further, since the remaining part
of the sentence could stand independently as a grammatical sentence, the *t*
of the first word, *there,* was capitalized. You may also have noticed that
there was no double indentation for the paragraph beginning; double

[3]From *Social Theory and Social Structure,* 1968 Enlarged Edition, by Robert K. Merton. Copyright ©
1968 and 1967 by Robert K. Merton. Used by permission of Macmillan Publishing Company, Inc.
[4]Jack Goody, *The Domestication of the Savage Mind* (Cambridge: Cambridge University Press, 1977),
p. 78.

indenting is needed at the beginning of a quoted paragraph only when the quotation extends to a second paragraph.

You should avoid adding anything to the exact quotation. Your comments on the quoted material should be placed either before or after the quotation. However, you may occasionally have to add a word or two of explanation to clarify the meaning of the quotation, either because the quotation uses material clarified earlier in the original text or because you need to summarize deleted material to bridge two parts of the quotation. All added material must be put in square brackets — [interpolation]. Since typewriters do not have brackets, add them by hand. Do not use parentheses, as they may be confused with parentheses used by the original writer. The historian Elizabeth Eisenstein, for example, in discussing the chilling effect of censorship on scholarship, notes that on "hearing of Galileo's fate in 1633, he [Descartes] stopped working on his grand cosmological treatise and perhaps clipped the wings of his own imagination by this negative act."[5]

On rare occasions you may wish to emphasize a word or phrase in a quotation by underlining or italicizing it. If you do, you must indicate that you — and not the original author — is placing the emphasis, as in the following quotation from the political scientist Paul Boller: "Quotemanship — the utilization of quotations to prove a particular point — has in recent years become a highly *skilled* art (emphasis added.)"[6]

Making the Most of References

Beyond you yourself knowing why and how you are using a reference, the reader must understand what you want to show by the reference and what conclusions you have drawn from it. A reader may find material drawn from sources puzzling or interesting for the wrong reasons; therefore, you must give the reader specific guidance as to the relevance of the material for your argument and the full set of implications for your thought. You need to introduce the reference — that is, to show how the material fits into the continuity of your essay — and then you need to follow the reference with interpretation, analysis, or other discussion.

The introduction to the reference serves as a transition between the ideas you were developing at this point and the material you are bringing

[5]Elizabeth Eisenstein, *The Printing Press as an Agent of Social Change* (Cambridge: Cambridge University Press, 1979) II, p. 663.
[6]Paul F. Boller, *Quotemanship* (Dallas: Southern Methodist University Press, 1967), p. 3.

> **You need to introduce the reference — that is, to show how the material fits into the continuity of your essay — and then you need to follow the reference with interpretation, analysis, or other discussion.**

in from the outside. You need to connect the material with your previous statements and then to indicate where the material comes from. Even though the details of the source may be fully stated in a footnote, the reader usually needs to be given at least a general idea of the source in the text in order to evaluate the material. So that the reader may properly understand the reference, you may also have to include some background information in the introduction.

Transitions are, of course, necessary throughout your writing, but they are unusually important before references because you are bringing in material foreign to your own statement. That external material, particularly if it is quoted in its original form, may seem to be quite distant from what you are saying unless you show the reader the point of connection. In fact, unless you make the justification for the material obvious to the reader, the material may appear so digressive that the reader will skim over it to get back to what seems to be the main line of the argument. Further, the inserted material may have a number of possible interpretations for your statement so that you must indicate which interpretation you want the reader to attend to.

Depending on the material and the function of the reference, the introduction may be short and direct, such as: "These findings concerning growth rates are confirmed by a similar experiment conducted by Jones." Or the introduction can be quite complex, incorporating much background, interpretation, and directiveness, as in this:

> This long-standing ambivalence Smith felt towards authority figures can be seen even in his letters as a teen-ager. The following passage from a letter to his father, written when Smith was only fourteen, shows his desire to be respectfully at odds about his father's opinions. Notice particularly how the polite phrases at the beginning of sentences almost seem ironic by the end when he starts to assert his own contrary opinion.

Here the introduction was lengthened by the necessity of indicating the exact feeling "at odds" and the particular features of the quoted material that indicate the conflict.

Once you have presented the reference, you should not leave the reader in the dark about the specific conclusions or implications you want to draw from it. You must draw out the conclusions and relate them to the larger points of your essay. If you include a quotation to be interpreted or analyzed, you must carry out those tasks in full detail — and not simply rely on a few brief general comments. Similarly, if you cite a set of detailed data, you must let the reader know exactly what you have found in the mass of specifics. Since you have gone to the trouble of presenting quotations or data, you should take just a bit more trouble to wring all the meaning out of them that you can. Often you will find that in the process of making your analysis or conclusions explicit for your reader, you yourself will become more precise about the consequences of the cited material. Only rarely will the meaning of the reference be so clear-cut and self-evident that no discussion is needed. What you may at first consider tedious belaboring of the obvious may turn out to be the kind of attention to detail that leads to interesting new thoughts.

The introduction and discussion of sources are the main means you have of showing how other writers' thoughts and information can be assimilated into your own argument. No matter how much you have thought through your reading, unless you tie your references directly into your argument, they will appear only pedantic quote-dropping to your reader. Only through thoughtful transitions and discussions of the material can you keep the continuity of your thoughts and keep everything under the control of your main argument. No matter how many sources you use, yours must be the controlling intelligence of the paper.

Documentation

What Must You Document?

You must give full documentation — that is, specifically identify the source you are using — each time you directly refer to the work of another writer and each time you use material — facts, statistics, charts, ideas, interpretations, theories, or the like — from another writer, even though you do not directly mention the writer's name. In other words, whenever someone else's work appears within your writing — whether undisguised through direct reference and quotation or submerged through paraphrase and summary into your own argument — you must give credit to the specific source, either in the form of in-text documentation or in footnotes.

You can decide for yourself whether or not to document those sources that you have not explicitly used in the final version of your essay. If certain ideas or information from other sources lie behind your own original ideas, you may want to identify such sources in a bibliographical discussion within a footnote. In the bibliography, you may mention all the books you have consulted, or only those you have found of use, or all those other readers may find useful, or only those that you have actually cited in your essay. The choice of which kind of bibliography is appropriate to each piece of writing will be discussed later.

There are only two exceptions to these general rules: common knowledge and deep sources of your thinking. *Common knowledge* is the information that most people familiar with your subject would already know and which few experts would dispute. For example, most people know — and few would dispute — that separation of powers is one of the principles behind the United States Constitution. If a number of your sources mention the same fact or idea with little discussion and with no disagreement among them, you can generally assume that the fact or idea is part of common knowledge and therefore does not need documentation.

What you should consider common knowledge does depend, to some extent, on the particular audience. In addition to the general shared knowledge of our culture, each subgroup has its own shared common knowledge, which may be unknown to other groups. To students of English literature, for example, it is common knowledge that T. S. Eliot was, in part, responsible for the revival of metaphysical poetry in this century. But readers without a specialized interest in English literature might not even know what metaphysical poetry is, let alone whether it was revived by T. S. Eliot, whoever he might be. Thus if you were writing as one expert to another, you would not need to document your claim about Eliot; but if you were writing as a non-expert to other non-experts, you would need to document the claim and to indicate the expert you are relying on.

The deep sources of your thinking are those ideas and information that you came in contact with long before you began work on the essay in question. Even though you did not have your current project in mind when you read those materials — perhaps even years ago — they may have influenced how you approached the current problem and how you interpreted the material you did search out particularly for this project. However, such influences may be so far in the back of your memory that there is no way to identify which writers helped shape your thinking with respect to your current project.

At some point in your intellectual growth, you may find it interesting and enlightening to try to reconstruct your intellectual autobiography and to identify how your thoughts and interests grew in relationship to the books that you read at various points in your life. Such self-searching may lead you to reread and rethink the sources of your ideas. But for most of your writing, you need not go back to these earlier sources; such a deep search may be, in fact, distracting to the more immediate task of the essay. So it remains a matter of judgment whether or not to include any deep sources, even in cases where you know them. Include them only if they will increase the strength and clarity of your argument. Generally you only have a direct responsibility to document those sources that you directly sought out and used for the current project.

Documentation of Specifics — In-text Mention and Notes

Every time that you mention or quote a source — or any idea, fact, or piece of information from that source — you must indicate at that point in the text the documentation of the reference. The documentation includes author, title, and publication information for general references to a work; if the reference is to a specific fact, idea, or piece of information, you must also include the exact page of the original item.

If the bibliographic information is concise and can be incorporated smoothly into the text of your writing, you may do so and thereby avoid excessive footnoting. Notice that in the following example of in-text documentation, the information fits naturally into the flow of the discussion.

> The publication in 1962 of Thomas Kuhn's challenging study *The Structure of Scientific Revolutions* (Chicago: University of Chicago Press) caused historians and philosophers of science to re-evaluate their ideas about how scientific knowledge advances. From the very first page of the book, Kuhn takes issue with the traditional view of scientific growth, which he claims derives from "the unhistorical stereotype drawn from science texts."

In some research sciences and social sciences, concise in-text documentation can be made through shortened parenthetical information linked to fuller information in the bibliography. Three such systems of parenthetical documentation linked to bibliography are commonly in use. The most common is the *author-date system* where the in-text parenthesis lists the author, date of publication, and specific page reference (if necessary):

Some studies have indicated that perceptual distortion is multi-causal (Jones, 1958; Smith and Smith, 1965; Brown, 1972), but one recent work claims that "only a single cause stands behind all the perceptual distortion observed in the earlier studies" (Green, 1979, p. 158).

Also used are the *author-title system* (Kinney, "New Evidence on Hinckley's Theory," p. 357) and the *numerical system* (*35*, 357). In the numerical system, each item in the bibliography is given a reference number; this reference number is underlined in the parentheses to distinguish it from the page reference that follows. Only use these parenthetical styles if your instructor or the journal for which you are writing indicates that one of them is the accepted form.

In many fields, particularly in the humanities, parenthetical reference is not currently an accepted form; nor is full documentation acceptable within the text because it interrupts the continuity of writing. For these reasons, most detailed documentation should be placed in notes — either footnotes or endnotes — and thereby separated from the main body of the text. Sometimes the stated policy of your teacher or of the journal in which you hope to publish will determine whether the notes should be placed at the bottom of each page as *footnotes* or gathered together at the end of the essay (or chapter) as *endnotes*. Frequently you yourself can choose. Endnotes create a less cluttered-looking text and are easier to type; footnotes make the notes more accessible to the reader.

In either system, the notes are numbered, the same number linking the note to a specific place in the main text of your writing. The reference number in the main text should be placed *after* the material to be documented, usually after a final period or the closing quotation mark, and typed slightly above the line, as in these examples:

```
Stephen Toulmin observes that the difference between

thoughts and concepts is the difference between the per-

sonal and publicly shared.[7]

Stephen Toulmin discusses the distinction between

thoughts and concepts: "Each of us thinks his own

thoughts; our concepts we share with our fellow-men. For

what we believe we are answerable as individuals; but
```

[7]Stephen Toulmin, *Human Understanding* (Princeton: Princeton University Press, 1972), p. 35.

```
the language in which our beliefs are articulated is pub-
lic property."⁸ We may consider such a distinction . . .
```

If several references occur within a single sentence, you may combine the citations into a single footnote and put the single reference number at the end of the sentence. If the combined footnote will lead to confusion about who should receive credit for which ideas, place the reference number at the end of an appropriate phrase — just after the mark of punctuation. The reference numbers in the next example separate source material from the new commentary added by the writer of the paper.

```
Toulmin's distinction between private thoughts and pub-
lic concepts necessarily articulated in the common lan-
guage⁹ on the surface appears to be consistent with Pop-
per's view that sciences strive toward "objective
knowledge,"¹⁰ but public language does not guarantee ob-
jectivity.
```

If you are using the endnote system, the notes should be numbered consecutively throughout the entire article or chapter; if you are using the footnote system, you may either start the numbering from the beginning on each page or you may keep the numbers consecutive throughout.

Note Format

The documentation in notes should contain, as mentioned earlier, four kinds of information: author, title, publication information, and specific page reference, where applicable. For books, publication information consists of city of publication (and abbreviation of state if city is not well known), publisher, and year. For articles in periodicals, publication information is the name of periodical, volume number, and date of periodical. This book follows the style prescribed by the Modern Language Association in the *MLA Handbook* for both notes and bibliography. In most other note styles, the order and content of the information in the note is similar; variations are primarily in preferred punctuation.

[8]Toulmin, p. 35.
[9]Toulmin, p. 35.
[10]Karl R. Popper, *Objective Knowledge* (Oxford: Oxford University Press, 1972).

Other commonly used style sheets — for use in specialized disciplines — are prepared by the American Chemical Society, the American Institute of Physics, the American Mathematical Association, the American Psychological Association, and the Council of Biology Editors.

Basic Note Punctuation

For a book

- First line indented
- Reference number elevated slightly
- Commas between main parts
- Publication information in parentheses
- Word *page* is abbreviated p. (*pages*, pp.)
- Period at end

[1]Jane Author, <u>Any Old Title</u> (Metropolis: Metropolis Univ. Press, 1980), p. 17.

For an article in an anthology

- Article title in quotation marks
- Book title underlined (note the word *in*)
- Editor after book title (ed. abbreviated)

[2]Jane Author, "The Articulate Article," in <u>The Scholarly Collection</u>, ed. Joseph Editor (Metropolis, Metropolis Univ. Press, 1980), p. 17.

For an article in a periodical

- Article title in quotation marks
- Periodical title underlined
- Volume number included
- Date of issue in parentheses

[3]Jane Author, "This Month's Title," <u>Metropolis Monthly</u>, 35 (June 1980), p. 17.

Modifications of Basic Form

Depending on the bibliographic information of your sources, you may have to modify the basic models above in the following ways:

Author

If no author is given, begin directly with title.

If two authors: **Jane Author and John Writer,**

If three authors: **Jane Author, Joan Scribbler, and John Writer,**

If four or more authors: **Jane Author et al.,**

Multivolume set

If part of a multivolume set, include the volume number after the book title. Also list the set title if different from the volume title.

Author, *My Childhood,* **Vol. I of** *My Life* (publication information), p. 73.

Edition

If other than the first edition, list edition number or edition name after the title and set information.

Author, title, **2nd ed**. (publication information), p. 4.

Translator and/or editor

List after edition.

Author, title, edition, **trans. Jane Jones, ed. John Jones** (publication information), pp. 2–6.

Series

If book or set is part of a series, list series title, editor, and number of this volume in the series after all the above additions, but just before the publication information.

Author, title, edition, translator, editor, **American Biographical Classics, ed. Donna Edwards, No. 37** (publication information), pages.

Date of Publication

This is the date of the first edition unless another edition is specified. Reprint date should be placed after the primary date.

Author, title (**1957; rpt.** City, state if city unfamiliar: Publisher, **1976**), pages.

Type of Periodical

For popular magazines and newspapers, delete the volume number and set off the date of issue in commas instead of parentheses. For scholarly journals with continuous pagination throughout the volume, delete the date and give only the year.

Author, "Title of Article," ***Time,* 17 June 1968,** pages.

Author, "Title of Article," ***Renaissance Quarterly,* 33 (1979),** pages.

Book Review

If an article is a book review, directly after the title place *rev. of* followed by title of book and author. If the article has no title, simply use *rev. of.*

Author, "Title of Article," **rev. of *Disaster,* by S. Smith,** periodical information, pages.

Specific samples of book and periodical notes appear at the end of this chapter.

Second and Later Mention

You need to give the complete bibliographical information only the first time you cite a work. In later citations you need only indicate in short form which document you are citing and the specific page reference. Usually you can indicate the document by using only the last name of the author.

[6]Toulmin, p. 39.

If you cite two authors with the same last name, you should distinguish them by first initial as well.

[7]R. Cole, p. 456.
[8]S. Cole, p. 123.

Similarly if you cite more than one work by the same author, you should add a shortened form of the appropriate title in second and later references.

[9]Kuhn, <u>Structure</u>, p. 24.
[10]Kuhn, <u>Tension</u>, p. 143.

Generalized Documentation — Bibliographies

Bibliographies are lists of sources related to the subject of your writing; however, you do not indicate the specific information you have used or the location of that information in the sources. Thus a bibliography serves only as a general listing of the sources that you have used or that your readers may wish to use.

Because bibliographies can vary in completeness and selectivity, it is better to label the bibliography in your paper with one of the more specific names presented below rather than the loose overall term *bibliography*.

The two most common types of bibliography indicate the sources you actually used in preparing your paper. A *Works Consulted* bibliography lists all the materials you looked at in the course of your research on the subject, although you will most likely omit the titles that turned out to be irrelevant to your subject. A *Works Cited* bibliography presents only those sources which you actually refer to in the course of your paper. Both the *Works Consulted* and the *Works Cited* demonstrate the quality of your research and the bases of your own work; they also allow readers to search out any of your references that seem of potential use for their purposes. These two kinds of bibliography are those most usually attached to formal essays.

Bibliography for the Reader

The other kinds of bibliographies are more fully directed toward reader use. The *Complete Bibliography* includes all works on the subject — even if you did not consult them for the present project and even if you have never seen the publications. The preparation of such a complete listing requires such an exhaustive and extensive search for materials that it frequently is a project in itself. The primary purpose of a *Complete Bibliography* is as a service to future scholars on the subject, so that they may quickly discover the materials relevant to their new projects. Thus a *Complete Bibliography* must meet high standards for completeness and reliability.

The kind of bibliography usually titled *For Further Reading* is directed more toward the nonscholarly reader who would like to know more about the subject but who does not intend to go into the subject as deeply as the writer. The list of books *For Further Reading* is therefore usually short and selective, presenting those books that expand topics raised in the preceding work but that are not too technical for the general reader.

If you feel that a few comments on each source listed might make either the *Complete Bibliography* or the *For Further Reading* list more useful to the reader, you can turn either into an *Annotated Bibliography*. The annotations may comment on the content, quality, special features, viewpoints, or potential uses of each source. The annotations should come right after the formal bibliographic listing of each book; the comments may range from a few fragmentary phrases to a full paragraph. The following examples of annotated entries are from the bibliography at the end of H. C. Baldry, *The Greek Tragic Theatre* (New York: Norton, 1971).

> R. C. Flickinger, *The Greek Theater and its Drama* (Chicago University Press, 1918; 4th edition 1936, reprinted 1965). Greek Drama explained through its environment. Detailed discussion of technical problems.
> A. E. Haigh, *The Attic Theatre* (Oxford University Press, 1889; 3rd edition revised by A. W. Pickard-Cambridge, 1907; New York, Haskell House, 1968). Still useful in part, but out of date on many aspects.
> A. W. Pickard-Cambridge, *The Theatre of Dionysus in Athens* (London & New York, Oxford University Press, 1946). The standard work, fully documented and illustrated, on the history of this theatre down to the Roman Empire.

If you wish to discuss relationships between works or problems that arise in a number of sources, you may wish to write a *Bibliographic Essay* instead of simply presenting a list. The bibliographic essay is closely related to the *review of the literature* discussed on pages 252–254, except that the bibliographic essay is done after the project is completed rather than in the early stages. As such, it should focus on either the usefulness of particular sources for the completion of your project or the potential usefulness of the sources for future readers — either scholarly or non-professional.

Bibliography Format

Bibliographies are basically organized as alphabetized lists by the last name of author (or the first word of the title for anonymous works). For the sake of clarity and usefulness, the bibliography sometimes can be broken up into several titled categories — with the items still alphabetized within each category. For example, the works by an author who is the main subject of the study may be separated from critical and biographical works about the author, as illustrated on p. 259. Or extensive archival sources may be listed separately from more conventional print sources. The bibliographic essay is, of course, organized around the topics discussed and is the only exception to the general rule of alphabetical listing.

Each bibliographic entry contains three kinds of information: author, title, and publication information. Thus it contains the same information as the footnote or endnote, except that the bibliographic entry does not have the final item of specific page location. The main differences between bibliographic entries and footnotes are in the order of the author's name and the consequent changes in punctuation. Because bibliographies are alphabetized, the author's last name must be put first; a comma follows the last name to show that the order is reversed. Since the comma has that function, *periods* must be used between the major divisions of information.

Basic Bibliography Punctuation

For a book

- First line flush with left margin; second and following lines indented
- Author's last name first, followed by comma and first name
- Book title underlined
- Periods between major parts and at end

```
Author, Jane. Any Old Title. Metropolis: Metropolis Univ.

     Press, 1980.
```

For an article in an anthology

- Article title in quotation marks; book title underlined
- Editor after book title, name in normal order
- Inclusive pagination of article at end

```
Author, Jane. "The Articulate Article." In The Scholarly

     Collection. Ed. Joseph Editor. Metropolis: Metropolis

     Univ. Press, 1980, pp. 12-26.
```

For an article in a periodical

- Article title in quotation marks; periodical title underlined
- Date of issue in parentheses
- Inclusive pagination of article at end

```
Author, Jane. "This Month's Title." Metropolis Monthly, 35

     (June 1980), pp. 12-26.
```

Modifications of Basic Form

Depending on the bibliographic information of your sources, you may have to modify the basic models above in the following ways:

Author

If no author is given, begin directly with title.

If two authors: **Author, Jane, and John Writer.**

If three authors: **Author, Jane, Joan Scribbler, and John Writer.**

If four or more authors: **Author, Jane, et al.**

Multivolume set

If multivolume set, use title of entire set for main entry, followed by number of volumes; use inclusive dates for main publication date. List separate volume titles and dates at end of entry.

Author. *My Life*. **3 vols.** City: Publisher, **1962—1968. Vol. I.** *My Childhood*, **1962; Vol. II.** *Youth*, **1965; Vol. III.** *Middle Age*, **1968.**

Edition

If other than the first edition, list edition number or name after the main title.

Author. Title. **2nd ed.** Publication information.

Translator and/or editor

List after edition information.

Author. Title. Edition. **Trans. Jane Jones. Ed. John Jones.** Publication information.

Series

List series title, editor, and number of this volume in this series just before the publication information.

Author. Title. Edition. Translator. Editor. **American Biographical Classics, ed. Donna Edwards, No. 37.** Publication information.

Date of Publication

This is the first edition date unless another edition is specified. Reprint date should follow the primary date.

Author. Title. **1957; rpt.** City: Publisher, **1976.**

Type of Periodical

For popular magazines and newspapers, delete volume number and set off date of issue with commas instead of parentheses. For scholarly journals with continuous pagination throughout the volume, give only the year for date.

Author. "Title of Article." ***Time*, 17 June 1968,** pages.

Author. "Title of Article." ***Renaissance Quarterly*, 33 (1979),** pages.

Book Review

Directly after article title, place *Rev. of,* then title of book and author. If the article has no title simply use *Rev. of.*

Author. "Title of Article." **Rev. of *Disaster*, by S. Smith.** Periodical information, pages.

Samples of Documentation

Forms of notes compared to forms used in bibliographies:

Book, Single Author

note   [1]Bruno Bettelheim, *The Uses of Enchantment* (New York: Knopf, 1976), p. 285.

bib.   Bettelheim, Bruno. *The Uses of Enchantment.* New York: Knopf, 1976.

Book, Two Authors, Translator, Part of Series

note   [2]Carl G. Jung and Carl Kerenyi, *Essays on a Science of Mythology,* trans. R. F. C. Hull, Bollingen Series, No. 22 (Princeton: Princeton Univ. Press, 1963), p. 126.

bib.   Jung, Carl G., and Carl Kerenyi. *Essays on a Science of Mythology.* Trans. R. F. C. Hull. Bollingen Series, No. 22. Princeton: Princeton Univ. Press, 1963.

Book, Group Authorship, Translator

note   [3]Zuni People, *The Zunis: Self-Portrayals,* trans. Alvina Quam (New York: New American Library, 1974), p. 83.

bib.   Zuni People. *The Zunis: Self-Portrayals.* Trans. Alvina Quam. New York: New American Library, 1974.

Book, Anonymous Author, Joint Editors and Translators

note   [4]*The Mwindo Epic*, trans. and ed. Daniel Biebuyck and Kahombo C. Mateene (Berkeley: Univ. of California Press, 1969), p. 59.

bib.   *The Mwindo Epic*. Trans. and ed. Daniel Biebuyck and Kahombo C. Mateene. Berkeley: Univ. of California Press, 1969.

Multivolume Work (separate titles for each volume, partly revised)

note   [5]Joseph Campbell, *Primitive Mythology*, Vol. I of *The Masks of God*, rev. ed. (New York: Penguin, 1969), p. 216.

bib.   Campbell, Joseph. *The Masks of God*. 4 vols. New York: Penguin, 1962–1969. Vol. I. *Primitive Mythology*, rev. ed., 1969; Vol. II. *Oriental Mythology*, 1962; Vol. III. *Occidental Mythology*, 1964; Vol. IV. *Creative Mythology*, 1968.

Multivolume Work (only one title)

note   [6]Theodore H. Gaster, *Myth, Legend, and Custom in the Old Testament* (New York: Harper & Row, 1969), II, 811.

bib.   Gaster, Theodore H. *Myth, Legend, and Custom in the Old Testament*. 2 vols. New York: Harper & Row, 1969.

The Bible and Other Sacred Scriptures

Cite chapter and verse instead of page location; indicate edition.

note   [7]Proverbs 3: 13–15 (King James Edition).
bib.   The Bible. King James Edition.

Unpublished Dissertation

note   [8]Herbert Paine Edmondsen, Jr., "Aspects of the Prometheus Myth in Ancient Greek Literature and Art," Diss. University of Texas at Austin 1977, p. 135.

bib.   Edmondsen, Herbert Paine, Jr. "Aspects of the Prometheus Myth in Ancient Greek Literature and Art." Diss. University of Texas at Austin 1977.

Pamphlet

note   [9]G. M. Kirkwood, *A Short Guide to Classical Mythology* (New York: Holt, Rinehart and Winston, 1959), p. 27.

bib.   Kirkwood, G. M. *A Short Guide to Classical Mythology.* New York: Holt, Rinehart and Winston, 1959.

Article in an Anthology

note   [10]Stanley Edgar Hyman, "The Ritual View of Myth and the Mythic," in *Myth: A Symposium,* ed. Thomas Sebeok (Bloomington: Indiana Univ. Press, 1955), p. 143.

bib.   Hyman, Stanley Edgar. "The Ritual View of Myth and the Mythic." In *Myth: A Symposium.* Ed. Thomas Sebeok. Bloomington: Indiana Univ. Press, 1955, pp. 136–153.

Article in an Encyclopedia

note   [11]Andrew Lang, "Mythology," *Encyclopaedia Britannica,* 1911 ed.

bib.   Lang, Andrew. "Mythology." *Encyclopaedia Britannica.* 1911 ed.

Article in a Scholarly Journal

note   [12]Dale F. Eickelman, "Form and Composition in Islamic Myths: Four Texts from Western Morocco," *Anthropos,* 72 (1977), p. 452.

bib.   Eickelman, Dale F. "Form and Composition in Islamic Myths: Four Texts from Western Morocco." *Anthropos,* 72 (1977), pp. 447–464.

Article in Popular Magazine

note   [13]Daniel Goleman, "Greek Myths in Pop Fiction: Jason and Medea's Love Story," *Psychology Today,* April 1976, p. 84.

bib.   Goleman, Daniel. "Greek Myths in Pop Fiction: Jason and Medea's Love Story." *Psychology Today,* April 1976, pp. 84–86.

Article in Newspaper (unsigned)

note   [14]"Origins of Walt Disney Cartoon Character Mickey Mouse in Mythology Noted," *New York Times,* 3 December 1977, p. 23.

bib.   "Origins of Walt Disney Cartoon Character Mickey Mouse in Mythology Noted." *New York Times,* 3 December 1977, p. 23.

Review in Magazine (unsigned, untitled)

note   [15]Rev. of *Zalmaxis, The Living God* by Mircea Eliade, *Choice,* 10 (June 1973), p. 604.

bib.   Rev. of *Zalmaxis, The Living God* by Mircea Eliade. *Choice,* 10 (June 1973), p. 604.

Congressional Record

note   [16]*Cong. Rec.,* 15 March 1980, p. 3751.

bib.   *Cong. Rec.* 15 March 1980, p. 3751.

Court Cases

note   [17]Clagett v. Daly, 87 S. Ct. 311 (U.S. Supreme Ct. 1966).

bib.   Clagett v. Daly. 87 S. Ct. 311. U.S. Supreme Ct. 1966. (*87 S. Ct. 311* refers to the volume, name, and page of the journal reporting the decision.)

Interview

note   [18]Personal interview with Romila Thapar, New Delhi, 9 June 1977.

bib.   Thapar, Romila. Personal interview. New Delhi, 9 June 1977.

Film

note   [19]Henrik Galeen and Paul Wegener, dir., *The Golem,* Germany, 1920.

bib.   Galeen, Henrik, and Paul Wegener, dir. *The Golem.* Germany, 1920.

Radio or Television Program

note   [20]"On the Road in Oscaloosa," narr. Charles Kuralt, CBS Evening News, 28 January 1980.

bib.   "On the Road in Oscaloosa." Narr. Charles Kuralt. CBS Evening News. 28 January 1980.

Recording

note   [21]Alfonso Cruz Jimenez, *Folk Songs of Mexico,* Folkways Record FW 8727, 1959.

bib.   Jimenez, Alfonso Cruz. *Folk Songs of Mexico.* Folkways Record FW 8727, 1959.

Written Assignments

1. For a research paper you have written or are currently working on, list the sources you refer to in the course of the paper. Explain (1) why you have included each reference, (2) what you hope to accomplish by the reference, (3) whether you have presented the reference through quotation, paraphrase, summary, or name only, and (4) why you have chosen each method listed in (3).

2. In the following excerpts from *A Study of Writing* by I. J. Gelb, identify where each reference is made to source material and the method used to present the reference. Then discuss the reason for each reference and the appropriateness of the reference method used.[11]

a. Simple ways of communicating feeling by the sense of touch are, for instance, the handclasp, the backslap, the lovestroke. A fully developed system of communication by handstroking is used among blind deaf-mutes, for which the best-known example is provided by the case of Helen Keller, the American writer and educator.

b. Objects are used as memory aids for recording proverbs and songs among the Ewe Negroes in a form quite similar to that which they achieved by means of written symbols. Carl Meinhof relates that a missionary found in a native hut a cord on which were strung many objects, such as a feather, a stone, etc. In answer to his query as to the meaning of the string with the objects the missionary was told that each piece was supposed to stand for a certain proverb. Another custom is related by Mary H. Kingsley from West Africa about native singers who carry around in a net all kinds of objects, such as pipes, feathers, skins, birdheads, bones, etc., each of which serves the purpose of recalling a certain song. The songs are recited with pantomimes. Persons in the audience choose a certain object and before the recital they bargain about the price to be paid to the singer. In a way, the net of the singer can be considered the repertoire of his songs.

c. A modern illustration of the use of objects for the purpose of communication is contained in the story from the Hungarian writer Jókai, according to which a man sent a package of coffee to another man to warn him about danger from police. The story can be understood on the basis of the phonetic principle by noting that the Hungarian word for coffee is *kávé* and that it resembles in sound the Latin word *cave,* "beware!".

A most interesting usage from the comparative point of view is reported from the same Yoruba country, where the cowrie mussels are used so frequently for communicating messages. During an attack of a king of Dahomey upon a city of the Yoruba one of the natives was taken captive and, anxious to inform his wife of his plight, sent her a stone, coal, pepper, corn, and a rag, conveying the following message: the stone indicated "health," meaning "as the stone is hard, so my body is hardy, strong"; the coal indicated "gloom," meaning "as the coal is black, so are my prospects dark and gloomy"; the pepper indicated "heat," meaning "as the pepper is hot, so is my mind heated, burning on account of the gloomy prospect"; the corn indicated "leanness," meaning "as the corn is dried up by parching, so my body is dried and become lean through the heat of my affliction and suffering"; and finally, the rag indicated "worn out," meaning "as the rag is, so is my cloth cover worn and torn to a rag." An exact parallel to this usage is reported in the fourth book, section 131 ff., of Herodotus. "The Scythian kings sent a herald bringing Darius the gift of a bird, a mouse, a frog, and five arrows. The Persians asked the bringer of these gifts what they might mean; but he said that no charge had been laid on him save to give the gifts and then depart with all speed; let the Persians (he said), if they were clever enough, discover the signification of the presents. The Persians hearing and taking counsel, Darius' judgment was that the Scythians were surrendering to him themselves and their earth and their water; for he reasoned that a mouse is a creature found in the earth and eating the same produce as men, and a frog is a creature of the water, and a bird most like to a horse; and the arrows (said he) signified that the Scythians surrendered their weapon of battle. This was the opinion declared by Darius; but the opinion of Gobryas, one of the seven who had slain the Magian, was contrary to it. He reasoned that the meaning of the gifts was: 'Unless you become birds, Persians, and fly up into the sky, or mice and hide you in the earth, or frogs and leap into the lakes, you will be shot by these arrows and never return home.' Thus the Persians reasoned concerning the gifts." Those modern cultural historians who may object to some of my reconstructions based on comparisons between ancient peoples and modern primitive societies cannot easily overlook the weight of such parallel usages from ancient and modern times.

3. In the library, find a scholarly journal from an academic or professional field that interests you. Describe in detail the documentation system and the format of notes and bibliography used in the journal. You may find a statement of documentation policy in the first few pages of each issue.

4. Using the format presented in this book, write both note and bibliography entries for each of the following items.

a. A quotation from page 137 from an article in the December 1979 issue of *Scientific American*, volume 241. The article is by David Regan and entitled "Electrical Responses Evoked from the Human Brain." The article extends from page 134 to page 146.

b. A summary from pages 10 and 11 of *Madame Bovary* by Gustave Flaubert in the translation by Francis Steegmuller, published in 1957 by Random House in New York City.

c. A paraphrase of an idea on page 123 of an article "Notes on a Conversational Practice: Formulating Place" by E. A. Schegloff. The article appears on pages 95 through 135 of *Language and Social Context*, an anthology first published in 1972 and reprinted in 1977, both times by Penguin Books of London. The editor of the anthology is Pier Paolo Giglioli.

d. A quotation from a book review of the novel *Darkness Visible* by William Golding. The review appears on page 108 of the November 5, 1979, issue of *Newsweek*, is entitled "The Inferno — Here and Now," and is by Peter S. Prescott.

Index